A PENNY A COPY

A PENNY A COPY

Readings from *The Catholic Worker*

**Edited by
Thomas C. Cornell, Robert Ellsberg,
and Jim Forest**

ORBIS BOOKS

Maryknoll, New York 10545

The Catholic Foreign Mission Society of America (Maryknoll) recruits and trains people for overseas missionary service. Through Orbis Books, Maryknoll aims to foster the international dialogue that is essential to mission. The books published, however, reflect the opinions of their authors and are not meant to represent the official position of the society.

Copyright © 1995 Orbis Books

Published by Orbis Books, Maryknoll, NY 10545-0308

This is a revised and expanded edition of *A Penny a Copy: Readings from* The Catholic Worker, Thomas C. Cornell and James H. Forest, eds. (New York: The Macmillan Company, 1968).

Grateful acknowledgment is made to the editors of *The Catholic Worker* for permission to reprint the contents of this book. Readers interested in subscribing to *The Catholic Worker* or seeking additional information may write to: The Catholic Worker, 36 East First St., New York, NY 10003.

Queries regarding rights and permissions should be addressed to: Orbis Books, P.O. Box 308, Maryknoll, NY 10545-0308.

Manufactured in the United States of America

Library of Congress Cataloging-in-Publication Data

A penny a copy : readings from the Catholic worker / edited by Thomas
   C. Cornell, Robert Ellsberg, and Jim Forest.
     p. cm.
   Includes index.
   ISBN 1-57075-012-2
    1. Catholic Church—Charities.   2. Church and social problems—
Catholic Church. I. Cornell, Thomas C. (Thomas Charles), 1934– .
II. Ellsberg, Robert, 1955– . III. Forest, James H.
IV. Catholic worker.
BX2347.P46 1995
261.8'08'822—dc20
                                    95-3417
                                    CIP

To Peter, to Dorothy
and to all those who came

❀ Contents

PART III • PEOPLE AND PROBLEMS 1946–1955

PART IV • RADICALS IN ACTION 1956–1965

PART V • WORKS OF PEACE 1966–1975

PART VI • SPIRIT OF LIFE 1976–1980

PART VII • THE JOURNEY CONTINUES 1981–

❀ Foreword

DAVID J. O'BRIEN

The Catholic Worker movement, with its always challenging and wonderfully inexpensive paper, occupies an important place in modern
history. When humanity finally attains the goal of peace, and then
rewrites its history, the center of the story, lighting the way across too
much darkness, will not lie so much in the centers of apparent power
but in the heroic experiments in truth and love. At least that is what
Christians believe. And this movement, whose voices speak in these
pages, has been such an experiment.

The Catholic Workers make large claims about the things that really
matter, and in that sense their message is truly catholic in the widest
sense. But it is the case that the Catholic Worker, movement and paper,
represents a very special *American Catholic* treasure. Though it has contained voices from across the globe, not all of them Catholic, it has also
been very American, speaking from within this American culture. Like
all Americans, these editors and writers cherish the gift of freedom;
more than most they acknowledge its accompanying responsibility to
tell the truth, simply and directly, in word and in deed. And in few
places in our history does one find richer expressions of our much
heralded, but hugely flawed, democracy.

Part of it is the living reminder of how many are left out, and of how
far we fall short of the ideal of equality. Dorothy Day and her disciples
even turned the marvelous doctrine of the Mystical Body of Christ in
democratic, almost populist directions. The *we* who constitute the one
body really includes everybody, all of us, whole and broken. Other
American, but rarely Catholic, voices have spoken of such democratic
solidarity; one thinks of Whitman. But few have spoken with the Worker's calm, unromantic acceptance of ordinary people, as they really
are. Anchored in voluntary poverty and the daily works of mercy and
hospitality, the Catholic Worker brings together radical Christian idealism, most simply the command to love one another, and personal
immersion in the realities of life as found in the centers of powerlessness.
Voluntary poverty is, as Dorothy claimed, a way to seeing the truth.

Truth-telling has its own dangers of pride and self-righteousness.
But the Worker, rooted in the sometimes painful sharing of life in
community, has largely avoided that trap. The authority that speaks

from the pages of this paper reflects the Catholic Workers' efforts to live the truths they tell, to narrow the gap we all experience between what we believe and what we feel compelled to do each day. When they tell us about their struggle to do that, we are always challenged and sometimes given a dose of hope. Maybe it is possible for all of us, if not in a soup kitchen on skid row or in a jail cell, to use our gifts and talents in service to our human family.

There is more to say about the Catholic Worker movement's place in our history. When we think of renewal of the church, the option for the poor, the recovery of a sense of Catholic identity through a mission of service to the human family, we are grateful for the Worker's witness and wisdom. When we American Catholics seek guidance in coming to grips with our church and our country in the latter days of a tragic century, our thinking and believing has been and remains enriched by Catholic Worker communities and by the reports and reflections in the Catholic Worker paper—still available at "a penny a copy." Thanks to the three editors and Orbis Books for making some of its best writing accessible to a new generation of seekers.

❁ Introduction

In a preface to one of her books, *Loaves and Fishes*, Dorothy Day addressed the question, "What is *The Catholic Worker?*"

> First of all, it is an eight-page monthly tabloid paper. The writing in it concerns work and men and the problems of poverty and destitution—and man's relationship to his brothers and to God. In trying to show our love for our brothers, we talk and write a great deal about works of mercy, as the most direct form of action. "Direct action" is a slogan of old-time radicals. In the thirties it meant bringing ideas to the man in the street via picketing and leaflets, storming employment offices, marching on Washington. Today, in the peace movement, direct action means boarding Polaris submarines, walking to Moscow, and sailing boats like *The Everyman* into areas where nuclear testing is going on.
>
> Peter Maurin, co-founder of *The Catholic Worker*, insisted that the works of mercy are the most direct form of action there is. "But the truth needs to be restated every twenty years," he said.

Those words were written in 1963 in the midst of the Cold War when *The Catholic Worker* was thirty years old. More than thirty years hence, much in the world has changed. The Cold War is over. Sensitivity regarding inclusive language would dictate some revision of Dorothy's style. But much remains the same. The division between rich and poor, the challenge of war and violence, continue unabated; and so do the imperatives of the Sermon on the Mount, the vision of God's Reign, and the ideal of Peter Maurin and the editors of *The Catholic Worker* to "create a society in which it will be easier to be good."

The Catholic Worker remains. And sixty years after its founding, fifteen years after the death of Dorothy Day, and almost thirty years after the first edition of this book, its message remains as fresh and relevant as ever. It deserves to be restated.

What is *The Catholic Worker?* Another way of answering the question is to say that it is the organ of the Catholic Worker movement. It reflects the vision, the actions, and the lives of those who have gathered around Peter Maurin and Dorothy Day, or their memories, over the past six decades, whether in houses of hospitality in skid-row sections of America's cities or in small farming communes on the land. It has sought to stimulate reflection on the social implications of the gospel, witnessing to the sacredness of life, the truth that we are each made in the image and likeness of God, and the real presence of Christ in the poor.

The means of the Catholic Worker are "clarification of thought" through study and dialogue, voluntary poverty, sharing in community with those whose poverty is imposed, direct action for the relief of the poor through the traditional works of mercy, both corporal (such as feeding the hungry, sheltering the homeless, and visiting the prisoner) and spiritual (instructing the ignorant, counseling the doubtful, forgiving injuries, and so forth). Sometimes these have been applied untraditionally. Instructing the ignorant might mean walking on a picket line or handing out leaflets. Visiting the prisoner has sometimes meant sharing a cell. All these actions are fueled with prayer and the sacraments, in conformity with the teaching of the church and a philosophy "so old it looks like new."

The paper came first, and the movement grew around it, both the offspring of an unlikely union. Dorothy Day was a Catholic convert, thirty-five years old, born of a thoroughly American family, the daughter of a conservative newspaperman. In her youth she was drawn to the radical cause and worked as a journalist on the major organs of the radical Left in New York City and Chicago. Her personal friends were Communists, socialists, anarchists, and the leading literary figures of the post-World War I period. In 1927 she surprised her progressive and Bohemian friends with the decision to enter the Roman Catholic church. The conversion was prompted in part by the birth of a daughter, Tamar, an experience of grace that awakened in her a dormant longing for transcendence. This conversion, as she described it in her autobiography, *The Long Loneliness*, was a painful process that left her alienated not only from her child's father but also, apparently, from the radical ideals to which she had committed her life. The church, after all, was renowned as a bastion of conservativism. And so she entered the wilderness, groping for a vocation, a way of reconciling her faith and her commitment to justice and the poor.

Peter Maurin, in contrast, twenty years her senior, was a peasant from southern France, an itinerant, illegal immigrant, a self-educated philosopher, a casual laborer, and a more casual dresser and bather whose deep accent forced people to strain to understand him. Peter was convinced that within the prophetic tradition of Israel, the Gospels, and the teachings of the Church Fathers, there lay hidden and hermetically sealed a dynamite that could explode the unjust social order of the day, and a technique of action capable of laying the foundation of a society worthy of the human person. Peter spent his days speaking to idle men and women on street corners and in Union Square, occasionally inviting himself to a Wall Street brokerage office, a newsroom, or editorial office to press his views upon unwilling listeners. Peter was looking for someone to respond and to put flesh on his ideas.

So it was that in December 1932 Dorothy Day found herself watching a "hunger march" parade past heavily armed police into the nation's capital. She was filled with frustration and grief that, however spiritually nourishing the church had become for her, it offered no adequate means to respond to injustice and the suffering of the poor. The march she was reporting for a Catholic journal had been inspired, organized, and led by Communists, not Christians. She ached with the realization that there were so many "comfortable church-goers" who gave so "little heed to the misery of the needy and the groaning of the poor."

Dorothy went from the march route to the crypt of the National Shrine of the Immaculate Conception. It was December 8, the Feast of the Immaculate Conception. "There I offered a special prayer, a prayer which came with tears and with anguish, that some way would open for me to use the talent I possessed for my fellow workers, for the poor." When Dorothy returned to the New York tenement apartment she shared with her brother and sister-in-law, she found Peter Maurin waiting for her. He had come because a red-haired Communist in Union Square and George Schuster, editor of *Commonweal* magazine, had told him they thought alike.

They did not think all that much alike, and never would. But they complemented one another—he the visionary, she the organizer; she at home in the city, he in the country. Her background was with strikes and labor agitation. He claimed, "Strikes don't strike me." Nevertheless, a partnership was formed.

Among other things, Peter proposed that they start a newspaper. "Nothing could have delighted me more, coming from a newspaper family as I do," Dorothy remembered. They worked in creative tension. He undertook to give Dorothy a Catholic education, a Catholic understanding of history. She came to catch his vision, and she revered him as her teacher and the real founder of the movement until his death in 1947 and hers in 1980. But Peter could still complain, "Man proposes, woman disposes." Right away there was disagreement about the name for the paper. Peter preferred "The Catholic Radical," since radical meant going to the roots. But Dorothy, perhaps thinking shrewdly of a counterpart to the Communist daily, had the final say. She called it "The Catholic Worker."

The first issue was distributed at a Communist rally in Union Square on May 1, 1933. The price was "a penny a copy"—as Dorothy put it, "so cheap that anyone could afford to buy it." The first articles, save for a few of Peter's verse-style "Easy Essays," were all written by Dorothy, dealing with labor, strikes, and unemployment—the stuff of Depression-era agitation. But there was a difference, indicated in Dorothy's memorable editorial for that first issue:

For those who are sitting on park benches in the warm spring sunlight.
For those who are huddling in shelters trying to escape the rain.

For those who think that there is no hope for the future, no recognition of their plight—this little paper is addressed.

It is printed to call their attention to the fact that the Catholic Church has a social program—to let them know that there are men of God who are working not only for their spiritual but for their material welfare.

Collaborators were quick to arrive—drawn from the reserve of unemployed Catholic students and workers. The Catholic Worker movement arose when homeless people came to the door and asked where to find these "houses of hospitality" they had read about in the paper. This gave rise to one of the cardinal features of *The Catholic Worker*: this was to be a newspaper in which the writers practiced what they preached. Soon there was a Catholic Worker house of hospitality where the hungry were fed and the homeless were welcomed. Then there was a farming commune, and before long new houses springing up around the country.

It was not all as simple as that, but few publishing ventures meet with such immediate success. Within six months the circulation had increased from 2,500 to 75,000 copies a month. Readers found a voice in *The Catholic Worker* that was unique among both religious and political journals. It expressed dissatisfaction with the social order and took the side of labor unions, but its vision of the ideal future challenged both urbanization and industrialism. It wasn't only radical but religious. The paper didn't merely complain but called on its readers to make personal responses. Avoiding a distant editorial tone, many articles were written as if they were letters between friends. Dorothy's own columns combined chatty accounts of her travels and activities with summaries of her reading and editorial reflections on the issues of the day. The paper was full of local smells, sounds, and events, but it wasn't just a neighborhood paper. In every issue an editorial balance was struck between theory and practice, the near and the distant. If the editors were attacking a social order in which people can be thrown away, they were also describing a life rooted in hospitality. In one column they were taking the side of labor unions and opposing fascist groups, in the adjacent column they were reporting experiments in forming rural communities.

Vitality, circulation of the paper, houses, soup kitchens, and farming communes have ebbed and flowed with the times. The articles included in this anthology reflect not only the vicissitudes of the Catholic Worker movement. Indirectly, they provide a kind of documentary of recent American history—as lived by a group of men and women who tried to respond to the challenges of their day in the light of conscience and the gospel.

The selections begin in the beginning—the heart of the Depression, when the paper was launched and the movement took shape. They continue with the advent of World War II, when the Worker's pacifist position caused the circulation to plummet, while houses across the country were closed. With the post-war decades the Worker maintained a prophetic and often quixotic witness against the arms race and the culture of militarism. With the 1960s the Worker held an honored place in the movement of resistance against the Vietnam war and the struggle for civil rights. In these years when so much was open to challenge, Dorothy struggled also to affirm her love and loyalty for the church— even when it seemed to be "the cross on which Christ was crucified." Contributions from the past fifteen years since Dorothy's death reflect the efforts of the editors to maintain this balance and tension between social radicalism and spiritual vision which was Dorothy's great gift to the American church, and which has ever been a distinctive hallmark of the Catholic Worker movement.

The first edition of this book was published by Macmillan in 1968, with the last entry written in 1966. Aside from bringing the story up to date, we have maintained the general flavor of the original volume. Rather than a textbook of "Catholic Worker positions," we have tried to assemble a book that reflects the best writing as well as the personalist style that is characteristic of *The Catholic Worker*. Thus, an article describing the practice of hospitality has been preferred over an article on the "idea" of hospitality. Readers new to *The Catholic Worker* will find illumination of many elements of the CW philosophy—nonviolence, the dignity of work, decentralist economics, and voluntary poverty. But these themes are generally discussed in the context of daily life. *The Catholic Worker*, above all, stands for ideas lived out in practice.

Otherwise, our main principle of selection has been to focus on writing that reflects the life and activities of Catholic Workers themselves. In this we depart from the paper, which has devoted extensive coverage over the years to other allied movements and organizations around the world, whether the United Farmworkers Union, the Community of the Ark in France, or the Gandhian Sarvodaya movement in India. Similarly we have passed over book reviews, news stories, articles reprinted from other journals, and the many marvelous profiles of the saints, writers, and intellectuals who have nourished the philosophy of the CW: Buber, Mounier, Eric Gill, Maritain, Gandhi, etc. It would be interesting to assemble another volume focusing exclusively on this "cloud of witnesses." But that project will await other hands. Unfortunately, our emphasis on the written word does not do justice to the physical appearance of the paper. The familiar illustrations of Ade Bethune, Fritz Eichenberg, and Rita Corbin often communicated the essential message of the Catholic Worker more effectively than any article.

As with the original edition, it is appropriate that Dorothy Day remains the most frequent contributor in these pages. Aside from her status as co-founder of the movement and arbiter of its editorial vision, her writing, with its combination of the everyday and the eternal, set a standard for other writers. There are represented in this volume a number of distinguished writers who, though not resident in the CW household, nevertheless identified with the spirit of the paper and lent their talents to the cause: Thomas Merton, Gordon Zahn, Daniel and Philip Berrigan, Henri Nouwen, Robert Coles, among others. But most of the contributors to *The Catholic Worker* have never aspired to be known as writers. They have been "journalists of the deed." The high quality of the writing points to the intensity and integrity of the lives lived in the community. This is a radical newspaper, but there is no bombast, no cant, no invidious swiping, and hardly a purple patch. There is, every so often, a burst of righteous wrath, but always tempered by a call to penance. House and farm columns show mild self-deprecation rather than pride of accomplishment. Few of these warrant republication because they are so topical, but those that are offered here are representative. Buried in many of them are nuggets of information that indicate the leading role the Catholic Worker played in sparking the nonviolent direct action campaigns to end the war against Vietnam, to dismantle racial segregation, and other social movements of our time.

When a movement centered around a charismatic personality survives its founder it usually either institutionalizes itself or it dissipates. The Catholic Worker, fifteen years after Dorothy's death, shows no sign of doing either. The movement has no constitution, no by-laws, no system of franchise. Anyone can start a house of hospitality, a communal farm or periodical and call it "Catholic Worker." There is no control from the "mother house" and there is no sign of withering away. On the contrary, there are now more houses and rural Catholic Worker centers than ever and more publications, regional Catholic Worker publications like the *Houston Catholic Worker, The Catholic Agitator* in Los Angeles, *Viva!* in Baltimore, *Via Pacis* in Des Moines. The New York paper and the New York community remain flagships, but a certain decentralism seems inevitable and desirable.

So very much has changed since the paper was first offered to the public. So much has changed since 1952 when Dorothy Day wrote, in the postscript to *The Long Loneliness,* that "it is still going on." Communism has gone, the Lower East Side of Manhattan is suffering gentrification. But wars and rumors of wars remain, and the poor and the homeless are with us in greater numbers than anytime since the Worker's beginnings. Those of us who have edited *The Catholic Worker* (including the three editors of this volume), know that there is no way of telling the whole truth about life in a Catholic Worker community. "So much heaven, so much hell," as Eileen Fantino once put it, "always the same." No one would believe it. There's only one way—to come and see. The next best thing: read the paper. It's still a penny a copy, twenty-five cents a year's subscription. It's still going on.

THOMAS C. CORNELL
ROBERT ELLSBERG
JIM FOREST

—

PART I

Depression Years

1933–1939

❧ To Our Readers

DOROTHY DAY

FOR THOSE who are sitting on park benches in the warm spring sunlight.

For those who are huddling in shelters trying to escape the rain.

For those who are walking the streets in the all but futile search for work.

For those who think that there is no hope for the future, no recognition of their plight—this little paper is addressed.

It is printed to call their attention to the fact that the Catholic Church has a social program—to let them know that there are men of God who are working not only for their spiritual, but for their material welfare.

FILLING A NEED

It's time there was a Catholic paper printed for the unemployed.

The fundamental aim of most radical sheets is the conversion of its readers to radicalism and atheism.

Is it not possible to be radical and not atheist?

Is it not possible to protest, to expose, to complain, to point out abuses and demand reforms without desiring the overthrow of religion?

In an attempt to popularize and make known the encyclicals of the Popes in regard to social justice and the program put forth by the Church for the "reconstruction of the social order," this news sheet, *The Catholic Worker*, is started.

It is not as yet known whether it will be a monthly, a fortnightly or a weekly. It all depends on the funds collected for the printing and distribution. Those who can subscribe, and those who can donate, are asked to do so.

This first number of *The Catholic Worker* was planned, written and edited in the kitchen of a tenement on Fifteenth Street, on subway platforms, on the "L," the ferry. There is no editorial office, no overhead in the way of telephone or electricity, no salaries paid.

The money for the printing of the first issue was raised by begging small contributions from friends. A colored priest in Newark sent us ten dollars and the prayers of his congregation. A colored sister in New Jersey, garbed also in holy poverty, sent us a dollar. Another kindly and generous friend sent twenty-five. The rest of it the editors squeezed out of their own earnings, and at that they were using money necessary to pay milk bills, gas bills, electric light bills.

By accepting delay the utilities did not know that they were furthering the cause of social justice. They were, for the time being, unwitting cooperators.

Next month someone may donate us an office. Who knows?

It is cheering to remember that Jesus Christ wandered this earth with no place to lay His head. *The foxes have holes and the birds of the air their nests, but the Son of Man has no place to lay His head.* And when we consider our fly-by-night existence, our uncertainty, we remember (with pride at sharing the honor), that the disciples supped by the seashore and wandered through corn fields picking the ears from the stalks wherewith to make their frugal meals.

MAY 1933

❈ Mary Is Fifteen

DOROTHY DAY

Children to take care of, meals to prepare, clothes to wash, boards over the bathtub to sleep on and two dollars a week—

—Mary's job.

IT IS NOT YET six-thirty in the morning and Mary is sleeping soundly, arms up, fists clenched gently like those of a baby. It is fortunate that Mary is still a little girl for the bed she is sleeping on is not very long. As a matter of fact, it is not a bed at all, but a bathtub, in the extra bathroom, and a rather short bathtub at that with table leaves stretched out over the top of it and blankets spread out on that. The Ferguson home was short on beds, but long on blankets. Of course it might have been possible to have bought another bed, but the apartment was small and what should have been the maid's room was already crowded with the children's cribs and there was no use messing up the living room by having a girl sleeping there.

So little Mary slept on the tub.

Mrs. Ferguson was a voluble woman and always had excuses for everything. Sleeping on hard boards was very good for the spine she used to say too. We do have to put up with so much in this time of depression.

For instance, she was putting up with Mary. What she would have liked, of course, would be a larger apartment with a spare room for a regular maid and she would have liked to have been able to pay a maid forty or fifty a month, the wages maids used to get. But she had to put up with little Mary and pay her two a week and sleep her on a board. It was the best she could do.

And of course, Mary had to put up with her. She was one of a family of six children. ("Why will poor people have so many children?" Mrs. Ferguson always frowned.) And by working out and being a mother's helper, Mary was supporting herself, and the two dollars she earned at least paid the milk bill at home.

Six o'clock. Mary didn't need an alarm clock. Young Junior acted the part perfectly well. Every morning he started his carolling, "Mary, Mary!" And Mary had to get up quick and take him and his little sister out to the kitchen before Mrs. Ferguson and her husband were awakened. They liked to sleep until eight. And even then their sleep was disturbed. It was impossible to keep the children quiet. They liked to make noise in the morning.

There was breakfast to prepare. Cereal, orange juice and milk and toast and a soft-boiled egg for each. It was good there was enough food always for breakfast. Usually there wasn't enough for lunch or for supper. Mrs. Ferguson cooked those meals and she watched the food carefully and complained bitterly over Mary's large appetite. "Really, people eat twice as much as they need to. And I do like to keep the food bills down."

By the time Mrs. Ferguson and her husband were up there was another breakfast to get, and then there were other little things to do for the children. And after breakfast dishes to wash, the floor to mop up—Mrs. Ferguson was a rigid housekeeper. And the tub of clothes. But if it were a nice day—"You can leave the clothes until you get back, Mary, and do them then. Take the children out now to the park."

Clothes changed, faces washed, and all the paraphernalia of a morning in the park. Leggings, rubbers, sweaters, coats, pull-down hats, shovels, pails, skates, bicycles—she was always laden down.

Her own coat was not very warm, and she used to think longingly of Mrs. Ferguson's second-best raccoon coat which she had once secretly tried on. "The nerve!" Mrs. Ferguson would have said had she known.

Two hours out in the wintry sun and then in to lunch, and the long task of making the children eat their lunch. "Now Bobby, don't put your plate on the top of your head!"

"Mary, you must be more careful! How many times have I told you? Don't keep saying don't to them. If you would read those books I gave you on the treatment of children you'd be learning something and fitting yourself for something better than just a mother's helper job. You might even be a kindergarten teacher some day."

After lunch, changing the children, washing them again, putting them away for their naps. Mary's eyes were pretty heavy too, just at this time of the day. Even the boards set up on the top of the bathtub beckoned invitingly. But there were too many things to do. Dishes again, and the floor around the children's table to be washed up, the table and even the little chairs themselves to be scrubbed. And then the clothes, neglected in the morning, to be washed.

Mrs. Ferguson always forgot that she had shooed Mary out with the children. "If only you had more system and got them done first thing in the morning! If you only moved a little faster!"

And so the day went. At three-thirty the children were up again. There were vegetables to be prepared for supper. Errands to be run. "And you might as well take Junior with you, he's such a nuisance around the house." Supper for the children, dishes, dinner for the grownups and sometimes company. Children to be put to bed, more dishes to be washed. And then sometimes interminable evenings when the children cried and fussed and Mary was kept running.

Oh, it was a long day, a hard day, and life with a succession of such days seemed too hard to be borne.

And this, unfortunately, is not a "story" but an account of facts. Of course, another sad little story could be written about the harassed mother who was used always to having help and what a difficult time she was having to adjust herself, and how she was put upon by the inefficient little girl she had taken in, and how the girl ruined more than she helped things, and how she neglected the children, and how she demanded afternoons off just when other plans had been made— and so on and so on—but somehow the condition of the mistress does not seem to us so moving as that of the little maid.

One could tell sad stories, too, of the bosses and how they are having to cut down on trips to Europe and doing with one car instead of three, and taking their kids out of expensive schools and putting them in public schools—and oh, the weight of responsibility on their shoulders! But that, too, does not seem so sad as the plight of the worker, who has had nothing in the past, nothing in the present, and to all intents and purposes, nothing to look forward to in the future of the present social system.

❋ Easy Essays

PETER MAURIN

WHAT THE CATHOLIC WORKER BELIEVES

The Catholic Worker believes
in the gentle personalism
of traditional Catholicism.
The Catholic Worker believes
in the personal obligation
of looking after
the needs of our brother.
The Catholic Worker believes
in the daily practice
of the Works of Mercy.
The Catholic Worker believes
in Houses of Hospitality
for the immediate relief
of those who are in need.
The Catholic Worker believes
in the establishment
of Farming Communes
where each one works
according to his ability
and gets
according to his need.
The Catholic Worker believes
in creating a new society
within the shell of the old
with the philosophy of the new,
which is not a new philosophy
but a very old philosophy,
a philosophy so old
that it looks like new.

NO PARTY LINE

The Catholic Worker
is a free-lance movement,

not a partisan movement.
Some of the Bishops
agree with our policies
and some don't.
We are criticized
by many Catholics
for some of our policies
and especially
our Spanish policy.
The Communist Party
has a party line.
The Catholic Worker
has no party line.
There is no party line
in the Catholic Church.

GOD AND MAMMON

Christ says:
"The dollar you have
is the dollar you give
to the poor
for My sake."
The banker says:
"The dollar you have
is the dollar
you lend me
for your sake."
Christ says:
"You cannot
serve two masters,
God and Mammon."
"You cannot,
and all our education
is to try to find out
how we can
serve two masters,
God and Mammon,"
says Robert Louis Stevenson.

IRISH CULTURE

After the fall
of the Roman Empire
the scholars

scattered all over
the Roman Empire,
looked for a refuge
and found a refuge
in Ireland,
where the Roman Empire
did not reach
and where the Teutonic barbarians
did not go.
In Ireland,
the scholars formulated
an intellectual synthesis
and a technique of action.
Having formulated
that intellectual synthesis
and that technique of action,
the scholars decided to lay
the foundations of medieval Europe.

In order to lay the foundations
of medieval Europe,
the Irish Scholars
established *Salons de Culture*
in all the cities of Europe,
as far as Constantinople,
where people could look for thought
so they could have light.
And it was
in the so-called Dark Ages
which were not so dark,
when the Irish
were the light.
But we are now living
in a real Dark Age,
and one of the reasons why
the modern age
is so dark,
is because
too few Irish
have the light.

The Irish Scholars established
free guest houses
all over Europe
to exemplify

Christian charity.
This made
pagan Teutonic rulers
tell pagan Teutonic people:
"The Irish are good people
busy doing good."
And when the Irish
were good people
busy doing good,
they did not bother
about empires.
That is why we never heard
about an Irish Empire.
We heard about
all kinds of empires,
including the British Empire,
but never about
an Irish Empire,
because the Irish
did not bother about empires
when they were busy
doing good.

The Irish Scholars established
agricultural centers
all over Europe
where they combined
cult—
that is to say liturgy,
with culture—
that is to say literature,
with cultivation—
that is to say agriculture.
And the word America
was for the first time
printed on a map
in a town in east France
called Saint-Die
where an Irish scholar
by the name of Deodad
founded an agricultural center.
What was done
by Irish missionaries
after the fall
of the Roman Empire

can be done today
during and after the fall
of modern empires.

FEEDING THE POOR

In the first centuries
of Christianity
the hungry were fed
at a personal sacrifice,
the naked were clothed
at a personal sacrifice,
the homeless were sheltered
at a personal sacrifice.
And because the poor
were fed, clothed and sheltered
at a personal sacrifice,
the pagans used to say
about the Christians
"See how they love each other."
In our own day
the poor are no longer
fed, clothed and sheltered
at a personal sacrifice
but at the expense
of the taxpayers.
And because the poor
are no longer
fed, clothed and sheltered
at a personal sacrifice
the pagans say about the
Christians
"See how they pass the buck."

BLOWING THE DYNAMITE

Writing about the Catholic Church,
a radical writer says:
"Rome will have to do more
than to play a waiting game;
she will have to use
some of the dynamite
inherent in her message."
To blow the dynamite
of a message

is the only way
to make the message dynamic.
If the Catholic Church
is not today
the dominant social dynamic force,
it is because Catholic scholars
have failed to blow the dynamite
of the Church.
Catholic scholars
have taken the dynamite
of the Church,
have wrapped it up
in nice phraseology,
placed it in an hermetic container
and sat on the lid.
It is about time
to blow the lid off
so the Catholic Church
may again become
the dominant social dynamic force.

OUT OF THE TEMPLE

Christ drove the money changers
out of the Temple.
But today nobody dares
to drive the money lenders
out of the Temple.
And nobody dares
to drive the money lenders
out of the Temple
because the money lenders
have taken a mortgage
on the Temple.
When church builders build churches
with money borrowed from money lenders
they increase the prestige
of the money lenders.
But increasing the prestige
of the money lenders
does not increase the prestige
of the Church.
Which makes Archbishop McNicholas say:
"We have been guilty
of encouraging tyranny

in the financial world
until it has become
a veritable octopus
strangling the life
of our people."

THE CASE FOR UTOPIA

The world would be better off
If people tried to become better.
And people would become better
if they stopped trying to become
better off.
For when everybody tries to
become better off,
nobody is better off.
But when everybody tries to
become better,
everybody is better off.
Everybody would be rich
if nobody tried to become richer.
And nobody would be poor
if everybody tried to be poorest.
And everybody would be
what he ought to be
if everybody tried to be
what he wants the other fellow to be.

WHY NOT BE A BEGGAR?

God wants us to be
our brother's keeper.
To feed the hungry,
to clothe the naked,
to shelter the homeless,
to instruct the ignorant,
at a personal sacrifice,
is what God
wants us to do.
What we give to the poor
for Christ's sake
is what we carry with us
when we die.
As Jean Jacques Rousseau
says:

"When man dies
he carries
in his clutched hands
only that
which he has given away."

People who are in need
and are not afraid to beg
give to people not in need
the occasion to do good
for goodness' sake.
Modern society
calls the beggar
bum and panhandler
and gives him the bum's rush.
The Greeks used to say
that people in need
are the ambassadors of the gods.
We read in the Gospel:
"As long as you did it
to one of the least
of my brothers,
you did it to me."
While modern society
calls the beggars
bums and panhandlers,
they are in fact
the Ambassadors of God.
To be God's Ambassador
is something
to be proud of.

NOVEMBER 1933

❈ Editorial—And Now a Note of Melancholy

LATE FALL IS HERE. A haze hangs over the city. Fogs rise from the river, and the melancholy note of the river boats is heard at night. The leaves are dropping from the fig tree in the back yard. There is the smell of chestnuts in the air, and if you buy the chestnuts, most of them are wormy. It is better to make popcorn over the fire at night. For we have fires now. The kettle sings on the range in the kitchen (the range cost eight dollars secondhand and doesn't burn much coal), and visitors to *The Catholic Worker* office are drinking much tea and coffee. The stove in the front office has burst in its exuberance and has to be mended with stove clay and a piece of tin.

And there is also the smell of grapes in the air—rich luscious Concord grapes. If this editorial has a melancholy note, it is not because chestnuts are wormy or because the stove has cracked, but because all our Italian neighbors are too poor this year to buy grapes and make wine. Grapes that used to be one dollar a box are now one dollar fifty. And the Italian fathers who love their wine and have it in lieu of fresh vegetables and fruits all during the long winter, are still out of jobs or on four-day-a-month work relief and this year there is no pleasant smell of fermenting grapes, no disorderly heaps of mash dumped in the gutters.

And Mr. Rubino and Mr. Scaratino and Mr. Liguori will not rent a wine press together this year, and the children will not hang over them with breathless interest in the mysterious basement while they manipulate the press rented for the house.

And, what is worse, Mr. Rubino will not be dropping into the office of *The Catholic Worker,* when he sees our light late at night, to console us for our long hours by the gift of a milk bottle of wine.

For the long hard winter is before us. Evictions are increasing, people come in to ask us to collect winter clothes and to help them find apartments where relief checks will be accepted.

We must work, and we must pray, and we meditate as we write this that it would be so much easier for all our Italian friends to work and pray, to have courage to fight and also to be patient, if they could make as usual their fragrant and cheering grape wine.

NOVEMBER 1933

❧ Day After Day

DOROTHY DAY

A DEER GETS TRAPPED on a hillside and every effort is brought to bear to rescue him from his predicament. The newspapers carry daily features.

Mrs. A., with her four children and unemployed husband living on $1.50 a week, is trapped by economic circumstance and everyone is so indifferent that it took three or four afternoons of Mike Gunn's time to see to it that the Home Relief came to the rescue. Though Mike has enough to do with his Labor Guild over in Brooklyn, he was doing his bit as part of the Fifteenth Street Neighborhood Council.

Three little pigs are crowded into a too-small cage, the case is brought into court, the judge's findings in the case being that pigs should not be crowded the way subway riders are. And a family of eight children, mother and father are crowded in three rooms and the consensus of opinion is that they're lucky to have that and why don't they practice birth control anyway.

One of the Home Relief workers came in the other day and was voicing just such sentiments. She was absolutely unacquainted with Catholic teaching on birth control and abortion, and we forced her to listen to a lecture on the subject which, though it may not have convinced her, at least served the purpose of toning down her propaganda among unemployed families, we hope.

A scavenger hunt is the latest game of "Society." An hilarious pastime, *The New York Times* society reporter calls it, and describes in two and one-half columns the asinine procedure of several hundred society and literary figures, guests at a party at the Waldorf Astoria, surging forth on a chase through the highways and byways of Manhattan Island. "The scavenger hunt of last night brought an enthusiastic response even from persons whose appetites for diversion are ordinarily jaded." The hunt was a search through the city streets for a "ridiculously heterogeneous list of articles."

Any morning before and after Mass and straight on through the day there is a "scavenger hunt" going on up and down Fifteenth Street outside the windows of *The Catholic Worker* and through all the streets of the city. People going through garbage and ash cans to see what they can find in the way of a heterogeneous list of articles. The *Times* does not state what these things were but probably the list was made up of something delightfully and quaintly absurd, such as old shoes, bits of string, cardboard packing boxes, wire, old furniture, clothing and food.

If the several hundred guests at the Waldorf had to scavenge night after night and morning after morning, the hunt would not have such an enthusiastic response.

Teresa, aged seven, member of the Fifteenth Street Neighborhood Council, took part in her first eviction the other day. She had a cold and was staying home from school in order to keep out in the air, it being a balmy day, so she had her chance to help.

The Friday before, a Home Relief worker from Twenty-second Street came to the office to get aid for a woman and child who were being evicted from a decrepit flat in one of the tenements of William Horn (on Union Square). There were five stalwart friends of *The Catholic Worker* in the office at the time.

Understanding that the eviction was at three in the afternoon, we sallied forth, but when we got there, the landlord's agent had called off his men, expecting us to do the job of putting the woman out, and thus saving him eighteen dollars.

We refused to move the woman's furniture until it had been brought down by the marshal. We explained to the agent that often a landlord who was unwilling to accept a Home Relief voucher offered to move the family himself, paying five dollars to a neighborhood truckman rather than eighteen to the marshal. This agent, standing sneering and scoffing by the door, refused to do anything.

"You have no sympathy for landlords, have you?" he wanted to know.

We assured him that our sympathy was rather with the weaker party. All right then, he would call the marshal! The eviction would be the following Monday then, at three o'clock.

It was hard to understand his unwillingness to have the poor woman moved. It was as though he delighted in the idea of heaping humiliation on her.

Monday came, and the relief worker hastened around to the office, to tell us that the marshal was about to arrive, though it was only one, not three in the afternoon. Only Harry Crimmins, Teresa, Dorothy Weston and I were in the office, so leaving Dorothy to mind the office, the three of us sallied out.

Several police and huskies were standing at the door of the tenement to greet what they thought was going to be a delegation of Communists, only to meet instead seven-year-old Teresa, Harry Crimmins and me. They dissolved into thin air. (It is a wonder they wouldn't stay and help us.)

Teresa carried toys, pieces of the baby's crib, parlor ornaments and dishes, and Harry Crimmins and I managed the rest. The Mission Helpers of the Sacred Heart, a community of nuns who run a day nursery and do visiting work in the neighborhood, promised to keep an eye on our evicted friend—she is a Protestant—taking charge of her two-year-old child while she works as a dishwasher for seven a week.

This is only one of the dozen eviction cases we have had in the last month. We have moved Jews, Protestants and Catholics. A German livery stable man lent us his horse and wagon to move a Jewish neighbor. Jews, Protestants and Catholics have helped us by contributing clothes, furniture and their services.

We call our readers' attention to the petition published in this issue against evictions which we urge you to clip out, attach to a sheet of paper and send back filled with the signatures of men, women and children who protest against this injustice.

❄ Editorial—Mid-Winter

IT IS A COLD NIGHT and we are writing in the kitchen where there are no drafts. Barbara, our cooperative apartment baby, sits on her mother's lap by the table and she, too, is writing an editorial though she is only five months old. In her zeal she tries first to eat the pencil her fond mother has given her, and then the paper.

On the wall there are three pictures which attract her attention. She calls out to them, trying to crow. There is a Polish Madonna, a Negro Madonna, and a picture of a Madonna and a worker by Ade Bethune. She likes that best of all.

Teresa is drawing pictures too, and when she shows them to the baby, Barbara laughs and makes bubbles. The black cat lies in restful abandon in front of the stove.

It is one of those rare evenings when there are no visitors, when the work of the day seems to be over, though it is only seven-thirty. It is a good time to sit and write editorials. An editorial, for instance, on charity. St. Saviour's High School and Cathedral High School sent down so many baskets of food, including hams and canned goods, potatoes and all the trimmings for Christmas dinners, that the office was piled high for at least three hours until they were all distributed.

It is true it did not take long to distribute them, there is such need around here.

There were toys too, dolls for the girls, and other toys for the boys, all beautifully wrapped and beribboned.

Bundles of clothes came in, including many overcoats, and they went out as fast as they came in. They came in response to the story of the man who had to accept a woman's woolen sweater in lieu of underwear or overcoat. I hope they keep on coming in.

I'd like to have everyone see the poor worn feet, clad in shoes that are falling apart, which find their way to *The Catholic Worker* office. A man came in this rainy morning and when he took off one dilapidated rag of footwear, his sock had huge holes in the heel and was soaking wet at that. We made him put on a dry sock before trying on the pair of shoes we found for him, and he changed diffidently, there under the eye of the Blessed Virgin on the bookcase, looking down from her shrine of Christmas greens. But his poor, red feet were clean. Most of the men and women who come in from the lodging houses and from the streets manage cleanliness, what with the public baths. I heard of one man who washed his underwear in the public baths, and sat there as long as he could in that steam-laden, enervating atmosphere until it was not quite too wet to put on. For the rest, it could dry on his skin. Not a pleasant thought in bitter weather.

Our prayer for the new year is that "the members might be mutually careful one for another. And if one member suffers anything, all the members suffer with it; or if one member glory, all the members rejoice with it."

It would seem, however, that the glory comes only through suffering this present day when we look upon the Mystical Body reviled and assaulted in Mexico, Spain, Russia, not to speak of the physical suffering of the poor all over the world.

The only immediate remedy is the practice of the corporal and spiritual works of mercy. When asked what is the program of *The Catholic Worker* by those who are interested in political action, legislation, lobbying, class war, we reply: It is the program set forth by Christ in the Gospels. The Catholic Manifesto is The Sermon on the Mount. And when we bring *The Catholic Worker* into the streets and public squares, and when we picket the Mexican consulate, it is to practice the spiritual works of mercy—to instruct the ignorant and to comfort the afflicted.

Unless the Lord build the house, they labor in vain that build it. There is no use looking for a revival in business, a return of prosperity, until the hearts and minds of men be changed. If we wish for a program, let us look into our own hearts. The beginning is there.

MARCH 1935

Christ and the Patriot

PAUL HANLY FURFEY

THE *"Patriot"*: I love peace as well as any man, but I am a realist. A strong system of national defense is our best assurance of peace. National defense is the patriotic duty of every American citizen. The R.O.T.C. affords the Catholic college student a fine opportunity to fulfill this patriotic duty.

Christ: All that take the sword shall perish by the sword.

The "Patriot": Yet we must be practical! There are, of course, some nations whom we can trust. Canada is a good neighbor. We shall never have a war with her. But unfortunately not all nations are like that. Japan and Russia are casting jealous eyes at us. Our basic policies conflict. We must arm to defend ourselves against such nations.

Christ: You have heard that it hath been said, Thou shalt love thy neighbor and hate thy enemy. But I say to you, love your enemies, do good to them that hate you; and pray for them that persecute and calumniate you.

The "Patriot": A noble doctrine! We must always keep before us the ideal of international good will. At the same time we must realize that it is merely common sense to be on our guard. We shall not start a war, but if some other nation starts one, then we must be in a position to defend our territory.

Christ: To him that striketh thee on the one cheek, offer also the other. Of him that taketh away thy goods, ask them not again.

The "Patriot": But national defense is not merely a question of defending our material rights. It is a question of life and death. Only a strong system of national defense will guarantee our personal security.

Christ: Be not afraid of them who kill the body, and after that have no more that they can do.

The "Patriot": But there is such a thing as a just war. Under certain circumstances a nation has a right to declare war. In the Old Testament war is approved under certain circumstances.

Christ: You have heard that it hath been said, an eye for an eye, and a tooth for a tooth. But I say to you not to resist evil.

Lord Jesus Christ, Lover of Peace, kindle in our poor hearts the flame of Thy heroic love, that we may see Thy beloved image in all men, our enemies as well as our friends, that we may rather suffer injury than protect our rights by violence, for Thy sweet sake Who died for all men. Amen.

JANUARY 1936

❋ Catholics Have No United Front with William R. Hearst

IN REGARDING YOUR RECENT congratulations to the Catholic press, and your editorial compliments to Catholics on their militant fight against

Communists, may we inform you that Catholics do not fight Communists, but Communism. Catholics do not fight Communism because they wish to support a vicious Capitalism or because Communism objects to the jingoistic Nationalism with which you fill your sorry sheets. Catholics do not subscribe to the class war which you are doing your best to advance. Nor do Catholics support the anti-peace movement you foster. In other words, Catholics are not working alongside you, so your compliments are lost. All these things are just as un-Catholic as is Communism itself. Which makes your papers and other media of propaganda un-Catholic, too.

The Catholic fight on Communism is one based on philosophies, not on economics. And by the same token your brand of Americanism, your bourgeois Capitalism, your class war, your militaristic attitude come in for the same condemnation as does the philosophy of Marx and Engels.

The difference is that the followers of Marx are honest enough to hold to a doctrine which they believe is right. You, like all Fascists, are a perfect pragmatist. Utility takes the place of morality for you. And unlike some pragmatists, the utility is not for the common good. It is utility for Hearst.

Please, Mr. Hearst, Catholics have a tough enough time trying to be understood. Do not complicate the issues more. Stay on your own side of the fence; do your own dirty work; work up the passions of one mob against the other; do your best to stir up world conflagrations; rant and rave about "my country, right or wrong"; support exploitation of labor; support everything that is evil in the world today, as you do; but please, please, do not try to convince the world that Catholics have any share in your sordid adventures.

MAY 1938

On the Coffee Line

ONE OF THE SERVERS

HAVING SPENT most of the night in heated discussion and neglecting the time, I was in no mood to crawl out at 5:30 this morning to do a turn on the breadline. But the quickest way to forget sleepiness is to roll out, wet my face and turn on the radio in the store—this I did.

It is hard to cut a mountain of bread and prepare it for serving. I say hard because it seems hours before the job is complete. The eyes of the men outside peering in keep saying—it's cold out here, or, he's about ready now. The bread is all set (this is about 6:15) and Scotty has the first of a hundred gallons of steaming coffee ready to serve as we open the door.

On a cold morning such as this I can imagine the stream of hope that flows through the long line right down Mott Street and around the corner on Canal. Cups are taken and the three-hour session of feeding our friends is under way. I can watch the faces and see thanks written between the lines denoting age and fatigue and worry.

Ade Bethune's drawings always arrest the attention of the men for a moment. No matter how anxious they are about reaching the coffeepot there is always time to cast eyes along the wall, and admiration for Christ the Worker momentarily makes them forget their hunger. Many are old faces who come every morning. One is called the "Cardinal" because of his purple knitted cap, so worn and shy of edges it looks like a skull cap. He always has a kindly word. As usual my Japanese friend comes early. He too always has a greeting.

Now today there are three youngsters with unkempt hair, wrinkled clothes and looking very tired. Knocking around the country with exposure to night air with no place to wash or get cleaned is new to them. In spite of their youth and strength the condition is more obvious. The oldsters are more used to it. Every morning there are several who carry shopping bags or bundles with their last few belongings. They place them under the table so as to better handle a hot cup and a huge chunk of bread.

One of the regular bundle-toters had a new coat this morning. All winter he has had a dirty trench coat heavy with the dirt of many nights' sleeping out and smoke from many a fire. His new coat must have belonged to some stylish young boy with extreme taste. In spite of this he looked better, the coat was warmer and he had a more confident air.

I am relieved now to go to Mass which means I must pass a whole block of hungry, waiting men. It seems a long walk some mornings, especially when it is cold or wet. I receive greetings from those who have come to know us. I wish many more would pass them during their long days to give them a chance to share and realize their troubles. The line is broken at the corner so to enable pedestrians to pass. The line running west on Canal Street extends for about two hundred feet. It is really impossible, then, to forget them at Mass.

On returning it is easy to recognize the familiar hats, coats, shoes and other misfitting clothing of the regular comers. Faces are mostly turned out facing the street. I know many of these men have no one for miles around here who knows them, yet every one of them feels that each passerby recognizes them. From the rear one can notice the long hair under the caps and hats of most men. All, after being out for hours in the cold, are hunched against the weather and have their hands in their pockets. Across the street three are at a fire made of cardboard boxes. The huge flames will soon die away. There is one Negro and two aged white men. None talk but just stare at the flames, absorbing the heat and probably seeing better days gone by.

I can recognize one of my regular friends. He is a midwesterner with an attractive drawl. He lives his nights in subway trains. The newspapers in his pockets he has picked up from trains, and generally he gives them to us. A small gift indeed, but a gift given out of real appreciation. He is tanned because of two warm days sitting in the park facing the new spring sun and catching up on much-needed sleep.

There is the usual complexity of disposition. Some are almost bitter. The hunger of some makes them a little too eager and they irritate those around them. Many are indifferent because they have accepted their condition as fate. Some even sing in keeping with the radio. Some whistle. Others engage in conversation. There are enough coming daily to understand there is no disciplinary measure used; kind treatment has effected a self-discipline. Some just stare and seem to be counting those in front of them.

Here comes the little Irishman who will ask for the softest kind of bread. He has no teeth and cannot chew the crusts of the rye bread. He appreciates our remembering this and he knows we will have some kind of soft bread ready.

They continue to come. When I am busy putting peanut butter on bread and can't see their faces, I can recognize the arms that reach for bread. One gets to know all the familiar marks of the garments. The hands of some tremble from age, sickness or drink. It is near closing time and the line thins out. They must go out now into a world seemingly full of people whose hearts are as hard and cold as the pavements they must walk all day in quest of their needs. Walk they must for if they sit in the park (when it is warm) on Chrystie Street, the police will shoo them off. Then there is the worry of the next meal or that night's sleeping arrangements. Here starts their long weary trek as to Calvary. They meet no Veronica on their way to relieve the tiredness nor is there a Simon of Cyrene to relieve the burden of the cross. It is awful to think this will start again tomorrow.

❋ Editorial—CW Stand on the Use of Force

DOROTHY DAY

DEAR FATHER:

You are one of many priests and laymen who have written to us of *The Catholic Worker* these past two years on the stand we have taken in the Spanish conflict. Many times we have been misquoted, or sentences from articles or public speeches have been taken from their context and distorted, and our friends have written us with pain that our attitude should seem to be at variance with that of Catholic leaders.

I am writing this letter to explain as best I can the points which we are trying to bring out in *The Catholic Worker*. I am writing it with prayer because it is so hard to write of things of the spirit—it is so hard to explain. If we had made ourselves clear before, we should not have to keep restating our position. But perhaps conflict is good in that it brings about clarification of thought.

We all know that there is a frightful persecution of religion in Spain. Churches have been destroyed and desecrated, priests and nuns have been tortured and murdered in great numbers.

In the light of this fact it is inconceivably difficult to write as we do. It is folly—it seems madness—to say as we do, "we are opposed to the use of force as a means of settling personal, national, or international disputes." As a newspaper trying to affect public opinion, we take this stand. We feel that if the press and the public throughout the world do not speak in terms of the counsels of perfection, who else will?

We pray those martyrs of Spain to help us, to pray for us, to guide us in the stand we take. We speak in their name. Their blood cries out against a spirit of hatred and savagery which aims toward a peace founded upon victory, at the price of resentment and hatred enduring for years to come. Do you suppose they died, saying grimly: "All right—we accept martyrdom—we will not lift the sword to defend ourselves but the lay troops will avenge us!" This would be martyrdom wasted. Blood spilled in vain. Or rather did they say with St. Stephen, "Father, forgive them," and pray with love for their conversion? And did they not rather pray, when the light of Christ burst upon them, that love would overcome hatred, that men *dying* for faith, rather than *killing* for their faith, would save the world?

Truly this is the folly of the cross! But when we say "Saviour of the World, save Russia," we do not expect a glittering army to overcome the heresy.

As long as men trust to the use of force—only a superior, a more savage and brutal force will overcome the enemy. We use his own weapons, and we must make sure our own force is more savage, more bestial than his own. As long as we are trusting to force—we are praying for a victory by force.

We are neglecting the one means—prayer and the sacraments—by which whole armies can be overcome. "The King is not saved by a great army," David said. "Proceed as sheep and not wolves," St. John Chrysostom said.

St. Peter drew the sword and our Lord rebuked him. They asked our Lord to prove His Divinity and come down from the cross. But He suffered the "failure" of the cross. His apostles kept asking for a temporal Kingdom. Even with Christ Himself to guide and enlighten them they did not see the primacy of the spiritual. Only when the Holy Ghost descended on them did they see.

Today the whole world has turned to the use of force.

While we take this stand we are not condemning those who have seized arms and engaged in war.

Who of us as individuals if he were in Spain today, could tell what he would do? Or in China? From the human natural standpoint men are doing good to defend their faith, their country. But from the standpoint of the Supernatural—there is the "better way"—the way of the Saints—the way of love.

Who of those who are combating *The Catholic Worker* stand would despise the Christian way—the way of Christ? Not one.

Yet again and again it is said that Christianity is not possible—that it cannot be practiced.

Today the whole world is in the midst of a revolution. We are living through it now—all of us. History will record this time as a time of world revolution. And frankly, we are calling for Saints. The Holy Father in his call for Catholic Action, for the lay apostolate, is calling for Saints. We must prepare now for martyrdom—otherwise we will not be ready. Who of us if he were attacked now would not react quickly and humanly against such attack? Would we love our brother who strikes us? Of all at *The Catholic Worker* how many would not instinctively defend himself with any forceful means in his power? We must prepare. We must prepare now. There must be a disarmament of the heart.

Yes, wars will go on. We are living in a world where even "Nature itself travaileth and groaneth" due to the Fall. But we cannot sit back and say "human nature being what it is, you cannot get a man to overcome his adversary by love."

We are afraid of the word love and yet love is stronger than death, stronger than hatred.

If we do not, as the press, emphasize the law of love, we betray our trust, our vocation. We must stand opposed to the use of force.

St. Paul, burning with zeal, persecuted the church. But he was converted.

Again and again in the history of the church, the conquered overcome the conquerors.

We are not talking of passive resistance. Love and prayer are not passive, but a most active glowing force.

And we ask with grief who are they amongst us who pray with faith and with love, and so powerfully that they can move the mountains of hatred that stand in our path. The soul needs exercise as well as the body and if we do not exercise our soul in prayer now, we will be puny and ineffectual in the trials that await us.

We are not praying for victory for Franco in Spain, a victory won with the aid of Mussolini's son who gets a thrill out of bombing; with the aid of Mussolini who is opposing the Holy Father in his pronouncements on "racism"; with the aid of Hitler who persecutes the church in Germany. Nor are we praying for victory for the loyalists whose Anarchist, Communist and anti-God leaders are trying to destroy religion.

We are praying for the Spanish people—all of them our brothers in Christ—all of them Temples of the Holy Ghost, all of them members or potential members of the Mystical Body of Christ.

And we add daily to this prayer for peace: "Lord, teach us to pray." "Lord, I believe; help Thou my unbelief." "Lord, take away my heart of stone and give me a heart of flesh."

This editorial is not intended to be a complete statement of *The Catholic Worker's* stand on the Spanish war. Neither does it purport to be anything dogmatic, merely an expression of the sincere convictions of *The Catholic Worker* staff.

———————————————————————————— OCTOBER 1939

❊ Editorial—To the Workers

An Appeal to Workers to Sacrifice for Peace

WE ADDRESS this appeal to the workers of America, you whose sweat and labor is the lifeblood of our country, you whose blood must flow if the United States engages in another imperialist war, you whose fellow workers are now dying for Capitalist gain and imperialist ambition in Europe.

Appeals are being made to your selfishness; you are told that prosperity will accompany a war boom, that if the United States shall sell to warring nations or other nations to be transferred to warring countries, the long-awaited lift from unemployment and depression is at hand. Those who tell you this speak the truth. They know how long you have suffered, they know the agonizing years have taken toll. And, depending on your despair, they would make you party to blood profits they hope to make in a war that is the result of their actions in the past.

Firmly believing in the essential integrity of the American worker, and his sense of brotherhood with the workers of the world, we address another appeal: an appeal to your idealism, to your desire for justice, to your Charity. No matter how the legislative tide turns, no matter what laws are passed abridging the neutrality of the United States, you hold it in your power to keep our country aloof from the European war. This is our appeal, then, that you use your power as workers to refuse to manufacture or transport articles of war that are intended for foreign nations, warring or neutral. That you serve notice on your employers, in organized fashion, that you will have no part of such blood money, and that you will strike if necessary to maintain your position.

Is this asking a tremendous sacrifice? We know it is. And yet, it is necessary sometimes for workers to make overwhelming sacrifices. You have made them in order that your right to organize, to strike, to picket, to get a fair share of the profits of industry be recognized. Hundreds of workers have suffered imprisonment, injury and death, at the hands of those very people who make war, in order that they and their work might be accorded the dignity that belongs to them. You do not think their sacrifices were in vain. You honor and revere the memory of labor's martyrs. Sacrifice has been labor's lot; it still is. Sacrifice is always the lot of the noble, and only sacrifice can keep noble what sacrifice has ennobled.

Have you the courage necessary? You, the steel workers, the seamen, the rubber workers, the cotton workers, the chemical workers? Can you, the steel workers, insist that the industry that is partly yours by virtue of your work engage only in peaceful pursuits, that the industry devote itself to the positive program of making only those materials calculated to build a better society, not wreck the one we have? You can if you have the capacity for sacrifice that we think you have.

Can you, the seamen, employ the same courage that carried you through the tumultuous years of organization, the strikes, the long hardships of picket lines in the dead of winter? You can, you can use the rights you have won through the suffering and deaths of your fellow seamen, to enforce a policy of real neutrality for the United States. You have the capacity for sacrifice, we have seen it; will you use it now in order that warmongers do not get the materials they need to kill your fellows in Europe? There's something greater than mere money bonuses to fight for. Don't let those who talk unctuously of neutrality by force of arms fool you into supplying guns and gas to kill and maim your fellow workers.

We address all workers in the same vein. It is yours to say whether the United States shall dip its hands in the blood of European workers. You can say NO! You can close the plants if necessary. You can proclaim to the world that at long last the workers are refusing to be the pawns of Capitalist and imperialist gain; that they have searched for truth and have found it; that you know now that workers' security lies in truth and justice, so truth and justice will be your aims. Actually, whether you know it or not, you, the workers, hold in your hands the power to tip the scales in favor of peace or crime. Are you afraid of your power? We are waiting for your answer.

PART II

A World at War

1940–1945

❀ Aims and Purposes

DOROTHY DAY

FOR THE SAKE of new readers, for the sake of men on our breadlines, for the sake of the employed and unemployed, the organized and unorganized workers, and also for the sake of ourselves, we must reiterate again and again what are our aims and purposes.

Together with the Works of Mercy, feeding, clothing and sheltering our brothers, we must indoctrinate. We must "give reason for the faith that is in us." Otherwise we are scattered members of the Body of Christ, we are not "all members one of another." Otherwise our religion is an opiate, for ourselves alone, for our comfort or for our individual safety or indifferent custom.

We cannot live alone. We cannot go to Heaven alone. Otherwise, as Péguy said, God will say to us, "Where are the others?" (This is in one sense only as, of course, we believe that we must be what we would have the other fellow be. We must look to ourselves, our own lives first.)

If we do not keep indoctrinating, we lose the vision. And if we lose the vision, we become merely philanthropists, doling out palliatives.

The vision is this. We are working for "a new heaven and a new *earth*, wherein justice dwelleth." We are trying to say with action, "Thy will be done on *earth* as it is in heaven." We are working for a Christian social order.

We believe in the brotherhood of man and the Fatherhood of God. This teaching, the doctrine of the Mystical Body of Christ, involves today the issue of unions (where men call each other brothers); it involves the racial question; it involves cooperatives, credit unions, crafts; it involves Houses of Hospitality and Farming Communes. It is with all these means that we can live as though we believed indeed that we are all members one of another, knowing that when "the health of one member suffers, the health of the whole body is lowered."

This work of ours toward a new heaven and a new earth shows a correlation between the material and the spiritual, and, of course, recognizes the primacy of the spiritual. Food for the body is not enough. There must be food for the soul. Hence the leaders of the work, and as many as we can induce to join us, must go daily to Mass, to receive food for the soul. And as our perceptions are quickened, and as we pray that our faith be increased, we will see Christ in each other, and we will not lose faith in those around us, no matter how stumbling their progress is. It is easier to have faith that God will support each House of Hospitality and Farming Commune and supply our needs in the way of food and money to pay bills, than it is to keep a strong, hearty, living faith in each individual around us—to see Christ in him. If we lose faith, if we stop the work of indoctrinating, we are in a way denying Christ again.

We must practice the presence of God. He said that when two or three are gathered together, there He is in the midst of them. He is with us in our kitchens, at our tables, on our breadlines, with our visitors, on our farms. When we pray for our material needs, it brings us close to His humanity. He, too, needed food and shelter. He, too, warmed His hands at a fire and lay down in a boat to sleep.

When we have spiritual reading at meals, when we have the rosary at night, when we have study groups, forums, when we go out to distribute literature at meetings, or sell it on the street corners, Christ is there with us. What we do is very little. But it is like the little boy with a few loaves and fishes. Christ took that little and increased it. He will do the rest. What we do is so little we may seem to be constantly failing. But so did He fail. He met with apparent failure on the Cross. But unless the seed fall into the earth and die, there is no harvest.

And why must we see results? Our work is to sow. Another generation will be reaping the harvest.

When we write in these terms, we are writing not only for our fellow workers in thirty other Houses, to other groups of Catholic Workers who are meeting for discussion, but to every reader of the paper. We hold with the motto of the National Maritime Union, that every member is an organizer. We are upholding the ideal of personal responsibility. You can work as you are bumming around the country on freights, if you are working in a factory or a field or a shipyard or a filling station. You do not depend on any organization which means only paper figures, which means only the labor of the few. We are not speaking of mass action, pressure groups (fearful potential for evil as well as good). We are addressing each individual reader of *The Catholic Worker*.

The work grows with each month, the circulation increases, letters come in from all over the world, articles are written about the movement in many countries.

Statesmen watch the work, scholars study it, workers feel its attraction, those who are in need flock to us and stay to participate. It is a new way of life. But though we grow in numbers and reach far-off corners of the earth, essentially the work depends on each one of us, on our way of life, the little works we do.

"Where are the others?" God will say. Let us not deny Him in those about us. Even here, right now, we can have that new earth, wherein justice dwelleth!

❁ A Baby Is Born

DOROTHY DAY

IT IS JANUARY 9, 1941, and *The New York Times* this morning is filled with news of total war and total defense. Every day four-column headlines of the costs of war: "1942 Budget $17,485,528,049. Funds for British to Be Sought Later."

Wonder what that $49 tacked on at the end of the $17,485,528,000 is for? Fifty dollars, we know, will pay for a baby, if you are poor, at any hospital in the city. A flat rate of fifty dollars, ward care, the ministrations of any doctor that happens to be on hand, and ten days' hospitalization.

At Bellevue Hospital, if you are poor, if you are a resident of the great City of the New York, it doesn't cost a cent.

William, our new baby down here at Mott Street, is hereby headlined on our front page, as the biggest news of the month, the gayest news, the most beautiful news, the most tragic news, and indeed more worthy of a place in a headline than the seventeen billion, four hundred and eighty-five million, five hundred and twenty-eight thousand and forty-nine dollars headlined in *The New York Times* this morning. William himself is worth more than that sum, more indeed than all the money in the world. He is indeed but dust, the Lord knoweth it, but he is also little less than the angels. He is a creature of body and soul, a son of God and (by his baptism down at Transfiguration Church last Sunday at 2 P.M.) a temple of the Holy Ghost. For his sake our Lord God came down from Heaven, was begotten by the Holy Ghost, born of the Virgin Mary, was made man, lived with us for thirty-three years, and suffered and laid down His life. For William's sake as well as for the sake of each one of us.

And this tiny creature who little realizes his dignity as a member of the Mystical Body of Christ lies upstairs from me now as I write, swaddled in a blanket and reposing in a laundry basket. He is rosy and calm and satisfied, a look of infinite peace and complacency upon that tiny countenance. He little knows what is in the world, what horrors beset us on every side.

We had awaited his arrival, the week before Christmas, breathlessly. Every night before we went to bed we asked the young mother, "How

33

do you feel?" and asked each other (us women on the two top floors of St. Joseph's House on Mott Street), "Is there taxi money?" in case it would be too late to call an ambulance.

And then, one morning at five, I heard rapid footsteps in the room above, the voice of the ambulance interne in the hall, "I'll be waiting downstairs." And I realized that the great moment had arrived.

It was still dark out, but it was indubitably morning. Lights were on in the kitchens of surrounding tenements. Fish peddlers, taxi drivers, truckmen, longshoremen, were up and on their way to work. The business of life was beginning. And I thought, "How cheerful to begin to have a baby at this time of the morning!" Not at 2 A.M., for instance, a dreary time of low vitality, when people sink beneath their woes and courage flags. Five o'clock is a cheerful hour.

Down in our little back yard (where we had the Christmas tree this year), down in that cavernous pit with tenements looming five and seven stories up around, we could hear them dragging out the ash cans, bringing in the coffee cans for the line.

Peter Clark and his crew were on hand, cutting pumpernickel (none of this already sliced, pasty, puffy white bread for us), getting out the cups, preparing the coffee for our eight hundred or so breakfast guests.

Out in front the line was forming already and two or three fires in the gutters brought out in sharp relief the haggard faces of the men, the tragedy of their rags. The bright flames, the blue-black sky, the grey buildings all about, everything sharp and clear, and this morning a white ambulance drawn up in front of the door.

This is not the story of the tragedy of the mother. We are not going into details about that. But I could not help thinking that while I was glad the morning was beginning, it was a miserable shame that the departure of the young woman for her ordeal should be witnessed by a long, silent waiting line of men. They surveyed her, a slight figure, bundled on that cruelly cold morning (and pain and fear make the blood run cold), come running down from the dark, silent house to get into the ambulance.

Not one man, not a dear husband, not a protector on whom she could lean for comfort and strength. There was no Joseph on this winter morning. But there were hundreds of men, silent, waiting and wondering perhaps as they watched the ambulance, whether it was life or death that had called it out.

"This is worse than war," one woman friend said a few days before, contemplating the situation. And we agreed, wondering if anything indeed could be more desperate and sad than a woman left to have her child alone.

There you have the tragedy of the refugee, there you have the misery of homelessness, the uncertainty as to food and clothing and shelter (and this woman had known hunger). And there, too, you have the pain and agony of the flesh. No soldier with his guts spilled out on the battlefield, lying for hours impaled upon barbed wire, suffers physically more than a woman in childbirth. Physically, I say, because does not the soldier in his horror and pain wonder what has brought him to this pass—what is being accomplished by the gigantic agony of war? With the woman the suffering brought forth life. In war, death. And despite shame and fear and uncertainty, as in this case, still there cannot but be joy over a child born into the world.

So it is with joy that we announce the newcomer to our House of Hospitality on Mott Street, knowing that our readers who have suffered with us in the past will be glad to rejoice with us now.

For us most truly this has been a season of happiness. "For unto us a son is born, unto us a child is given." Christ Himself came so truly to us this Christmas Day in this baby boy, just as in the persons of the hungry men. "For inasmuch as ye have done it unto one of the least of these my brethren, ye have done it unto me."

DECEMBER 1941

✤ Letter to Fellow Workers

BEN JOE LABRAY

DEAR FELLOW WORKERS:

We crept into the Soo in a ghostly fog at dawn today after a perfectly calm trip over Lake Superior. We are now nearly half-way over Lake Huron and it is calm and warm. Too warm for November 13, but it may wind up in rain and do nothing worse.

When the Union ships got their increase in July of this year, the phony Lake Carriers' Association, a ship owners' company union, broke out with the news that all who shipped before August 1 would be given a $25-a-month bonus if they finished the season and laid up the ship. Those who already had the first half of the season in would get theirs dating back to the spring fitout. It was a master stroke on the part of the ship owners. It held the crews on and greatly discouraged organization by the NMU, which was going forward very successfully.

Well, the boys stuck on and the company, the engineers and mates and stewards took full advantage of the situation. No one who had already sailed five months would want to get off now as he'd be throwing $125 away. So the abuse began. The fighting began and the trouble. The stewards began cutting down on the grub and competing with other cooks of the other ships of the line, knowing no one would dare squawk as they might get fired and lose their bonus. Fights of all kinds, and on this rust pot they all seem to hate each other's guts. Everyone afraid to talk to the other.

The other day Shorty, the deck watch on my watch, had a cup of coffee and when finished poured the remains in the sink. The steward growled and one word got louder than the next. A battle started and while they were wrestling near the door, the steward's wife walked up and slapped Shorty so hard he nearly went over the side.

Their nerves are all on edge and they all say they'll never fall for that bonus stuff again. I take advantage of each beef to talk on the glories of a free union where nobody worries, gets fired or hungry and the wages are always ahead of the Lake Carriers, etc. etc. Say I: "Let freedom ring"—down with the Lake Carriers' Association! Day before yesterday the steward on a steel trust ship hung himself in his stateroom. Another "bonus jittered" case, I suppose.

A clear, sunny, calm trip all the way here! Passing Detroit this P.M. it was like summer. We are now running along slow speed heading into Lorain, to anchor and await orders. It's warm out and the stars are blazing and the lighthouse blinks right ahead and the fog horn is howling its mournful, weird, eerie and blood-curdling moan as though to rebuke us for throwing off the lad into the seething maelstrom near here last trip.

The ship continues to be hungry and at six tonight when I came off watch I ran into a dish of half-cooked baked beans, etc. This guy is a prize belly robber. If we were living in a land without laws and without Christianity we'd all bump each other off in no time. Without restraint the race wouldn't last three generations. It's bad enough if one is a Christian or trying to be one.

I just had to cease writing awhile to put out a fire. I miscued with a cigarette butt and my partner's dungarees caught fire. He's sleeping blissfully right under me. He's a Hungarian and says I write more than anyone he ever saw. He's a patient soul—my orange fell off the nail this morning and bounced off his dome. He didn't say a word—just retrieved it, peeled it and ate it. If only all problems could be solved as easy as that. A little thing like that aboard ship could cause a murder.

I see by the papers that King, Ramsay and Connor have been paroled out on the west coast. Everyone of *The Catholic Worker* crowd that wrote in to the Governor and talked about the case to their friends and got them to write had something to do with getting them out. Visiting the prisoner is one of the works of mercy. When you start doing something for people it is like praying for them.

Work is prayer, St. Benedict says. Let's ask them to pray for Wallace, the fink that committed the murder for which the other three were framed. That'll get a laugh! And yet, that's what Christianity means. Forgiving your brother. Or let's scrap Christianity, forget about Christmas and join the Communist party. They've got more love in them than many a Christian. Love Hitler? Pray for Stalin? That's what Christianity means. No wonder Christians are persecuted.

Please excuse the sermon. It's Christmas and I feel I'll be off the lakes this month with plenty of money to last through the winter on, and I'll be walking the streets, looking in all the lighted windows and basking in the warmth of the holiday.

But come to think of it, there's that appeal of yours. Why should I think of the morrow. True, I'm not exactly a lily of the field but with the help of God I'll get by. So enclosed is a hundred and fifty, no more and no better than that dollar some young woman sent in from scrubbing floors with the thermometer up to a hundred.

Yours for the green revolution,

BEN JOE

JANUARY 1942

❀ **Our Country Passes from Undeclared War to Declared War; We Continue Our Christian Pacifist Stand**

DOROTHY DAY

In Addition to the Weapon of Starvation of Its Enemy, Our Country Is Now Using the Weapons of Army, Navy and Air Force—In a Month of Great Feasts, a Time of Joy in Christian Life, the World Plunges Itself Still Deeper into the Horror of War

DEAR FELLOW WORKERS IN CHRIST:

Lord God, merciful God, our Father, shall we keep silent, or shall we speak? And if we speak, what shall we say?

I am sitting here in the church on Mott Street writing this in your presence. Out on the streets it is quiet, but you are there too, in the

Chinese, in the Italians, these neighbors we love. We love them because they are our brothers, as Christ is our Brother and God our Father.

But we have forgotten so much. We have all forgotten. And how can we know unless you tell us. "For whoever calls upon the name of the Lord shall be saved." How then are they to call upon Him in whom they have not believed? But how are they to believe Him whom they have not heard? And how are they to hear, if no one preaches? And how are men to preach unless they be sent? As it is written, "How beautiful are the feet of those who preach the gospel of peace." (*Romans* X)

Seventy-five thousand *Catholic Workers* go out every month. What shall we print? We can print still what the Holy Father is saying, when he speaks of total war, of mitigating the horrors of war, when he speaks of cities of refuge, of feeding Europe. . . .

We will print the words of Christ who is with us always, even to the end of the world. "Love your enemies, do good to those who hate you, and pray for those who persecute and calumniate you, so that you may be children of your Father in heaven, who makes His sun to rise on the good and the evil, and sends rain on the just and unjust."

We are at war, a declared war, with Japan, Germany and Italy. But still we can repeat Christ's words, each day, holding them close in our hearts, each month printing them in the paper. In times past, Europe has been a battlefield. But let us remember St. Francis, who spoke of peace and we will remind our readers of him, too, so they will not forget.

In *The Catholic Worker* we will quote our Pope, our saints, our priests. We will go on printing the articles which remind us today that we are *all* "called to be saints," that we are other Christs, reminding us of the priesthood of the laity.

We are still pacifists. Our manifesto is the Sermon on the Mount, which means that we will try to be peacemakers. Speaking for many of our conscientious objectors, we will not participate in armed warfare or in making munitions, or by buying government bonds to prosecute the war, or in urging others to these efforts.

But neither will we be carping in our criticism. We love our country and we love our President. We have been the only country in the world where men of all nations have taken refuge from oppression. We recognize that while in the order of intention we have tried to stand for peace, for love of our brother, in the order of execution we have failed as Americans in living up to our principles.

We will try daily, hourly, to pray for an end to the war, such an end, to quote Father Orchard, "as would manifest to all the world, that it was brought about by divine action, rather than by military might or diplomatic negotiation, which men and nations would then only attribute to their power or sagacity."

"Despite all calls to prayer," Father Orchard concludes, "there is at present all too little indication anywhere that the tragedy of humanity and the desperate need of the world have moved the faithful, still less stirred the thoughtless masses, to turn to prayer as the only hope for mankind this dreadful hour.

"We shall never pray until we feel more deeply, and we shall never feel deeply enough until we envisage what is actually happening in the world, and understand what is possible in the will of God; and that means until sufficient numbers realize that we have brought things to a pass which is beyond human power to help or save.

"Those who do feel and see, however inadequately, should not hesitate to begin to pray, or fail to persevere, however dark the prospects remain.

"Let them urge others to do likewise; and then, first small groups, and then the Church as a whole, and at last the world, may turn and cry for forgiveness, mercy and deliverance for all.

"Then we may be sure God will answer, and effectually; for the Lord's hand is not shortened that it cannot save, nor His ear heavy that it cannot hear."

Let us add, that unless we combine this prayer with alms-giving, in giving to the least of God's children, and fasting in order that we may help feed the hungry, and penance in recognition of our share in the guilt, our prayer may become empty words.

Our works of mercy may take us into the midst of war. As editor of *The Catholic Worker*, I would urge our friends and associates to care for the sick and the wounded, to the growing of food for the hungry, to the continuance of all our works of mercy in our houses and on our farms. We understand, of course, that there is and that there will be great differences of opinion even among our own groups as to how much collaboration we can have with the government in times like these. There are differences more profound and there will be many continuing to work with us from necessity, or from choice, who do not agree with us as to our position on war, conscientious objection, etc. But we beg that there will be mutual charity and forbearance among us all.

This letter, sent to all our Houses of Hospitality and to all our farms, and being printed in the January issue of the paper, is to state our position in this most difficult time.

Because of our refusal to assist in the prosecution of war and our insistence that our collaboration be one for peace, we may find ourselves in difficulties. But we trust in the generosity and understanding of our government and our friends, to permit us to continue, to use our paper to "preach Christ crucified."

May the Blessed Mary, Mother of love, of faith, of knowledge and of hope, pray for us.

❉ Excerpt from Day After Day

DOROTHY DAY

HERE IS A STORY that began March 19, the feast of our patron, St. Joseph. Every now and then someone came in and said, "Did St. Joseph send you a present yet?" And then later in the day the telephone call came, from a lawyer, saying that someone had just died and left us around five hundred dollars in a will.

We were overjoyed. St. Joseph had behaved as we expected him to do on his feast day. We were broke and that five hundred dollars could have gone to the printer, to the coffee man, to the bread man or for an installment on the farm mortgage.

We went around beaming for days. Only twice before had we been willed anything. An auto worker in Hamtramck had willed us five dollars, and a Finn miner in Minnesota had told his mother when he was dying to send us five dollars. And here was another legacy!

And then this situation arose. We were unincorporated and we did not wish to be incorporated. Nor did we intend to be, either for five hundred or five thousand dollars. It is hard for our friends and readers to get the point of this. It is difficult to explain, too. It is one of those ephemeral things, felt rather than understood, even on our part.

The way we feel about it is this. No one asked us to do this work. The mayor of the city did not come along and ask us to run a bread line or a hospice to supplement the municipal lodging house. Nor did the Bishop or Cardinal ask that we help out the Catholic Charities in their endeavor to help the poor. No one asked us to start an agency or an institution of any kind. On our responsibility, because we are our brother's keeper, because of a sense of personal responsibility, we began to try to see Christ in each one that came to us. If a man was hungry, there was always something in the icebox. If he needed a bed—and we were crowded—there was always a quarter around to buy a bed on the Bowery. If he needed clothes, there were our friends to be appealed to, after we had taken the extra coat out of the closet first, of course. It might be someone else's coat but that was all right too.

Our Houses of Hospitality are scarcely the kind of houses that Peter Maurin has envisioned in his plan for a new social order. He recognizes

40

that himself, and thinks in terms of the future to accomplish true centers of Catholic Action and rural centers such as he speaks of in his column this month.

Our houses grew up around us. Our bread lines came about by accident, our round-table discussions are unplanned, spontaneous affairs. The smaller the house, the smaller the group, the better. If we could get it down to *Christian families,* we would be content. Ever to become smaller—that is the aim. And to talk about incorporating is somehow to miss the point of the whole movement.

So all right, St. Joseph, if you have brought about clarification of thought by your little joke on your feast day, all right, we are grateful to you. Meanwhile there is that printing bill of $1100 that needs to be paid. We are only hinting to you about this, because St. Francis de Sales is the special patron of writers and journalists. Maybe we had better ask him.

DECEMBER 1942

❈ A Letter to Christ's Poor

JOHN COGLEY

GOD WAS NO LESS a God because he came into the world destitute. Nor was he less a king.

Neither are you less a man because you have been stripped of respectability. Neither are you less a child of the king because you share his destitution. You are still made to the image and likeness of God though you are beaten and scarred. A man is a man for all that. The whole creation of God trembles before your dignity for all that.

We are keenly conscious of the injustices of the world. Religion does not soft-pedal injustice. We know that hopelessness and discouragement often overtake you and that the faith in your hearts can turn to ashes. A stupid, respectable world lets you eat its garbage and bed in its gutters; and a stupid, respectable world lets its God be born in a beast's hut. If you remember the birth of Christ, faith can brighten for you who are among the world's outcasts. Religion is a fire, a roaring flame, a thundering passion that can drive the lowliest of men to the very heights. Don't let it die within you.

It demands courage to cling to faith when all the world has crumbled around us. It calls for strength to cling to the old beliefs, to keep the old truths in mind. And yet religion is not for the coward or the weak. Religion is a mighty battle for the strong.

When a man has been knocked around, as some of you have, it calls for fortitude to throw back your head and sing a song to the sun, a paean of thanksgiving to God for your very being. That is for strong warriors of the spirit. Spiritual strength is the stuff of saints.

Religion is a warrior's battle, a mighty fortification to be seized, a city to be taken by storm. The Holy Ghost comes like a tempest of wind.

If on Christmas eve your home is the streets, your bed is a gutter, your clothes are rags—remember the stable. You are little kings, and an animal's hovel enthroned the King of kings.

If on Christmas day you receive your Lord in Holy Communion, you are host to the Lord of the world, and angels shall tremble before the temple that is your body. Though a world passes by, all heaven will stand still.

OCTOBER 1943

❈ No Clothes Today

DAVID MASON

IT IS EARLY Sunday morning. There is a penetrating October chill in the air. This is the kind of morning that makes you feel fine if you've had a good breakfast, or anticipate one, and are well dressed. But the man who hobbles into our courtyard hasn't had breakfast, good or bad, and he is far from well dressed. In fact, he is scarcely dressed at all. His left shoe is missing. So are his socks, shirt and coat. His torn undershirt and beltless trousers are filthy.

He mumbles his plea for help through chattering teeth and quivering blue lips. No need to ask how he got that way. It's an old story. He was drunk last night, and some wretch relieved him of the missing garments, or else he tossed them off in a drunken fit. Either way, it is an everyday occurrence. It is not hard to see in him the "man who fell among thieves," and he has come to us with faith that we will help him. Can we refuse because "it's his own fault"? Yes, if the Good Samaritan looked into that phase of the case before he "bound up his wounds."

Fortunately, we have some clothes that fit him, even a pair of shoes. There is a razor for him to shave with, but first he must have a cup of coffee to steady his shaking hands.

An extreme case, certainly, but there are more extreme cases than you might imagine. Yes, it may often be their own fault, but who are we to judge? So long as we have anything to give, it is our duty in Christian charity to give it.

So long as we have anything. There's the rub. Too frequently, these days, we have nothing, or next to nothing, in the way of old clothing that can be worn by men who come to us in dire need. Some days we have to put a little sign on the door which reads:

NO CLOTHES TODAY
I'M SORRY TO SAY

MAY 1945

Cologne: A Cross for the World

GORDON ZAHN

AT FIRST the story seemed too good to be true. The Cologne cathedral was "structurally intact" in spite of the thoroughgoing obliteration bombings that wiped most of the city off the face of the earth. Some of the papers we read went so far as to refer to its escape as miraculous. Miracle or not, we heaved a great sigh of relief and thanked God for the accuracy of our bombardiers and turned to the other news of that day—including the report that Dortmund had been added to the list of "dead" German cities in one powerful blow by Allied air power.

Relief and reverent gratitude were the first reactions. But, strangely, this was not to be all. This news item did not drop so easily from our interest. Instead it grew and took on new aspects, so that every now and then we found Cologne—or rather, the memory of Cologne—forcing itself into our thoughts. Maybe it was the poignant little report about the children who were terror-stricken whenever they heard the sound of a plane, or any sound resembling that of a plane. Perhaps it was the impact of a vision of hundreds of thousands of people spending most of their waking hours in rat holes under a shaking city. Sometimes we found ourselves asking, "Why?" Sometimes we felt a chilling realization of Cologne's future meaning to the world when our consciences struggled with persistently probing, challenging thoughts. God! How they must hate us.

But always we could comfort ourselves by recalling that picture of the cathedral, the prize of the ages, preserved. True, the historic Rathshaus, the quaint Gothic houses and shops lining countless ancient streets—these things that most of us will know only by description—were gone. Perhaps we caught ourselves questioning this, too. After all, these objectives were not too military in their individual importance (except in so far as they housed and served civilians engaged in the same "total war effort" we praise so highly in our own civilians), these objectives were not too strategic in their value (in fact, the destruction of the city meant merely another headache to its eventual reconstruction authority and served to add new and precious spirit to a dying and desperate nation). There must have been some reason for mercilessly saturating Cologne with exploding death; that much is evident upon looking at the honeycombs of ruin that once were homes. Reason would almost tempt us to doubt the assurances from on high that "terror bombing" is not, and has never been, an Allied policy. And anyway, we were told, the cathedral was saved—or, rather, remains "structurally intact"; that should be cause enough for joy.

I do not know how many decades have passed since the completion of that structure; nor could I tell you how many generations it took to build that structure. These facts could be easily obtained at any public library. But they would prove nothing except that the building was quite old and took quite a while to finish. The name of the master planner (if any one man were responsible for the magnificent architecture) is also immaterial, although it probably is available. Such things are always available in history books or encyclopedias. But they are not always important.

The important item in this case is the fact that men—generations of men—were sufficiently inspired to undertake, plan, dream and build, and *pray*, until they had created an edifice suitable to the honoring of their God, worthy of expressing a faith that enabled them to challenge a span of years beyond their individual lifetimes. To those of us who felt joy in hearing that their work still stands, it didn't matter too much (if it occurred to us at all to remember the fact) that these men who built were of the barbarian, war-creating strain of mankind, the Teutonic monster whose sole aim on earth (we are told by all the better minds of our day) is to crush the innocent and destroy the righteous. We probably forgot also that these very men whose lives were dedicated to the work our men so considerately spared lived in some of those very same dwellings, walked the very same streets that did not fare so well.

The importance of the cathedral lay not in the fact that it was built, but, rather, in *why* it was built. Just so, we must not place our emphasis on the fact that it stands; instead, we must consider *what it stands for.*

Whoever had the desire to undertake so great an effort must have had a mighty faith; and the men who struggled to achieve his goal shared that same faith. No tyrant could have driven men to create so enduring a monument to life. These men of faith were content to add their part to a work they would never see in its completed glory because they knew that what they were expressing could never die. And so they toiled and died, and their sons and their descendants followed the same pattern of life until finally the cathedral stood, not as a mound of stone honoring some departed hero but as a work of faith to house the presence of a living God—a God whose message was eternal love and who poured forth His love in agony, who in that agony suffered even this day when man would reject Him, when man would return ten Colognes for the evil of one Coventry in His Name.

For remember we must that their present-day descendants who also worshipped in the cathedral, lived in the ancient dwellings and walked the ancient streets—these "hateful barbarians," these "murdering, plundering" brothers in the Mystical Body of Christ to our gallant, crusading defenders who flew above their city and so artfully and accurately snuffed out its life, share with us the heritage of Calvary's sorrow and glory and carry the obligation to forgive us these trespasses as we might have forgiven them for trespassing against us.

The miracle of faith that built the cathedral marked the contribution of its builders to the ages. This generation has scarred its monuments into the face of the earth in an ever-increasing crescendo from blockbusters to townbusters—and eventually, we may suppose, to worldbusters. Where they left a miracle of construction, we have accomplished a miracle of destruction. The two have met at Cologne. The cathedral that towers over a sea of rubble and ruin is, as the papers say, structurally intact. It is for us now to determine whether it is still intact in the spirit that gave it substance—if the faith of the Christians of today is strong enough to overcome the fury of the prides and hatreds and vengeance they have created and bring all men to their knees in an international prayer for forgiveness.

If we fail in this, if we refuse to accept the cross of responsibility for a peace based on justice, forgiveness and love, we shall have lost our chance to bring about the kind of world toward which these men of ages past were building. And then, perhaps, it might have been just as well had some bombardier done by accident what we will have done by intentional neglect—reduce the Cologne cathedral structure to what it actually is, a pile of old stones.

❀ We Go On Record—

DOROTHY DAY

MR. TRUMAN was jubilant. President Truman. True man; what a strange name, come to think of it. We refer to Jesus Christ as true God and true Man. Truman is a true man of his time in that he was jubilant. He was not a son of God, brother of Christ, brother of the Japanese, jubilating as he did. He went from table to table on the cruiser which was bringing him home from the Big Three conference, telling the great news; "jubilant" the newspapers said. *Jubilate Deo.* We have killed 318,000 Japanese.

That is, we hope we have killed them, the Associated Press, on page one, column one of the *Herald Tribune,* says. The effect is hoped for, not known. It is to be hoped they are vaporized, our Japanese brothers, scattered, men, women and babies, to the four winds, over the seven seas. Perhaps we will breathe their dust into our nostrils, feel them in the fog of New York on our faces, feel them in the rain on the hills of Easton.

Jubilate Deo. President Truman was jubilant. We have created. We have created destruction. We have created a new element, called Pluto. Nature had nothing to do with it.

"A cavern below Columbia was the bomb's cradle," born not that men might live, but that men might be killed. Brought into being in a cavern, and then tried in a desert place, in the midst of tempest and lightning, tried out, and then again on the eve of the Feast of the Transfiguration of our Lord Jesus Christ, on a far off island in the eastern hemisphere, tried out again, this "new weapon which conceivably might wipe out mankind, and perhaps the planet itself."

"Dropped on a town, one bomb would be equivalent to a severe earthquake and would utterly destroy the place. A scientific brain trust has solved the problem of how to confine and release almost unlimited energy. It is impossible yet to measure its effects."

"We have spent two billion on the greatest scientific gamble in history and won," said President Truman jubilantly.

("UNRRA meets today facing a crisis on funds. It is close to scraping the bottom of its financial barrel, will open its third council session

46

tomorrow, hoping to get enough new funds to carry it through the winter.")

(Germany is told of Hard Winter by Eisenhower.)

(Pall of Apathy Shrouds Bitter, Hungry Vienna)

The papers list the scientists (the murderers) who are credited with perfecting this new weapon. One outstanding authority "who earlier had developed a powerful electrical bombardment machine called the cyclotron, was Professor O. E. Lawrence, a Nobel prize winner of the University of California. In the heat of the race to unlock the atom, he built the world's most powerful atom smashing gun, a machine whose electrical projectiles carried charges equivalent to 25,000,000 volts. But such machines were found in the end to be unnecessary. The atom of Uranium-235 was smashed with surprising ease. Science discovered that not sledgehammer blows, but subtle taps from slow traveling neutrons managed more on a tuning technique were all that were needed to disintegrate the Uranium-235 atom."

(Remember the tales we used to hear, that one note of a violin, if that note could be discovered, could collapse the Empire State Building. Remember too, that God's voice was heard not in the great and strong wind, not in the earthquake, not in the fire, but "in the whistling of a gentle air.")

Scientists, army officers, great universities (Notre Dame included), and captains of industry—all are given credit lines in the press for their work of preparing the bomb—and other bombs, the President assures us, are in production now.

Great Britain controls the supply of uranium ore, in Canada and Rhodesia. We are making the bombs. This new great force will be used for good, the scientists assured us. And then they wiped out a city of 318,000. This was good. The President was jubilant.

Today's paper with its columns of description of the new era, the atomic era, which this colossal slaughter of the innocents has ushered in, is filled with stories covering every conceivable phase of the new discovery. Pictures of the towns and the industrial plants where the parts are made are spread across the pages. In the forefront of the town of Oak Ridge, Tennessee, is a chapel, a large comfortable-looking chapel benignly settled beside the plant. And the scientists making the first tests in the desert prayed, one newspaper account said.

Yes, God is still in the picture. God is not mocked. Today, the day of this so great news, God made a madman dance and talk, who had not spoken for twenty years. God sent a typhoon to damage the carrier *Hornet.* God permitted a fog to obscure vision and a bomber crashed into the Empire State Building. God permits these things. We have to remember it. We are held in God's hands, all of us, and President Truman too, and these scientists who have created death, but will use it for good. He, God, holds our life and our happiness, our sanity and our health; our lives are in His hands.

He is our Creator. Creator.

. . . And I think, as I think on these things, that while here in the western hemisphere, we went in for precision bombing (what chance of *precision* bombing now?), while we went in for obliteration bombing, Russia was very careful not to bomb cities, to wipe out civilian populations. Perhaps she was thinking of the poor, of the workers, as brothers.

I remember, too, that many stories have come out of Russia of her pride in scientific discoveries and of how eagerly and pridefully they were trying to discover the secret of life—how to create life (not death).

Exalted pride, yes, but I wonder which will be easier to forgive?

And as I write, Pigsie, who works in Secaucus, New Jersey, feeding hogs, and cleaning out the excrement of hogs, who comes in once a month to find beauty and surcease and glamor and glory in the drink of the Bowery, trying to drive the hell and the smell out of his nostrils and his life, sleeps on our doorstep, in this best and most advanced and progressive of all possible worlds. And as I write, our cat, Rainbow, slinks by with a shrill rat in her jaws, out of the kitchen closet here at Mott Street. Here in this greatest of cities which covered the cavern where this stupendous discovery was made, which institutes an era of unbelievable richness and power and glory for man. . . .

Everyone says, "I wonder what the Pope thinks of it?" How everyone turns to the Vatican for judgment, even though they do not seem to listen to the voice there! But our Lord Himself has already pronounced judgment on the atomic bomb. When James and John (John the beloved) wished to call down fire from heaven on their enemies, Jesus said:

"You know not of what spirit you are. The Son of Man came not to destroy souls but to save." He said also, "What you do unto the least of these my brethren, you do unto me."

PART III

People and Problems

1946–1955

❀ Will They Go Again?

JACK ENGLISH

MANY FORMER GI's are today hesitant sheep wandering with both ears cocked for the clear, confident voice of their shepherds.

They are wondering about the justice of their varied activities in the past war, not that they have a "guilt complex" for they know that sin is not *ex post facto,* but because the promised era of peace and justice grows more improbable and because they believe that once again they will be called upon to make a decision and this will have to be made in the light of a whole mass of war experiences.

Many of us were interested in pacifism before World War II. *Interested* but not convinced. Our interest was not lost during the conflict but rather it deepened as the war seemed to conflict more and more with the qualifications necessary to wage it justly. Sometimes we consulted our chaplains on the subject, sometimes we wrote to friends but more often we just sweated the whole thing out in anguish by ourselves. Usually the whole question of a decision was pigeonholed for we were in the army and that was a *fait accompli.* When we got out of the service we would study and investigate. We would talk to our priest friends. This much we promised ourselves. There would be some definite word from the theologians on this subject for after all it was one in which millions of people were involved.

There would be answers for the flyers who were told at briefings that if the target was overcast to dump the bombs any place over the city. And there would be answers for the Ranger who made his way out of the prison camp near Berlin and walked to freedom in Paris. He had to leave a whole trail of dead men and women and children behind him to make his escape final. Should he have remained in the camp and sat out the war or should he obey orders and make the attempt to make his way back home when the opportunity presented itself? Then there was the question of the atom bomb, of guided missiles. With peace came the notion of the proportionate good and evil in the war, and wouldn't these proportions be accentuated in another conflict?

These are general notions and each GI had his personal problems, the old question of temptation and consenting to evil in his personal life. Various men reacted in various ways. I dare say that some exercised self-discipline. But what was the overall picture?

And what has been the tenor of the replies to our questions? "Yes, perhaps the pacifists have something." *Perhaps.* "The question will have to be investigated."

And yet no discussion comes up. "Look at the list of the soldier saints." "A man who dies in the defense of justice gains a martyr's crown." "The last Pope canonized ordered a crusade." But the soldier-saints, the martyrs, and that Pope didn't live in an age of unleashed atoms. Is it right to ask the mass of humanity to stand the test of martyrdom, of a life of heroic sanctity?

Most of us are not eccentrics. We don't want to be divorced from the common experiences of our fellows. That perhaps is the great temptation. We are sheep, not the shepherds. We are the laity, not the ordained preachers and theologians. We sheep are hesitant about following a lone voice here and there. We would like our shepherds to call to us and say in pretty much one voice, "Here is the path, this is the way," and not stand perplexed and unsure while the sky darkens and another storm gathers itself around us. Are we bleating in vain?

OCTOBER 1947

❊ House of Hospitality

JOHN COGLEY

TODAY THE CHICAGO PAPERS all carried headlines about the heat wave that for a week has been hanging over the city like a guilty conscience. "Heat wave breaks all records; no relief in sight" was the discouraging head in the evening papers, and tomorrow morning, according to the radio know-it-alls, there will be a repetition of the same grim prediction.

Everyone is talking about the weather. The still, hot air is clogged with platitudes about the heat, and the whimpered, wordless complaints of people too listless for more than a tired "Whew!"

There has been about the last week something of a movie twice seen. An incredible familiarity. The same dialogue, the same heavy movements, the same weary responses, the same inevitable sweating it out.

Older people go through their lines and their complaints with a knowing, querulous patience. They've all been through it before; it is as familiar as an ancient liturgy. Only babies and very young children voice their rebellion with any vigor, ignorant yet of the impotence they'll learn.

For the grown-up, the summer heat wave is familiar enough to recall a mood, to recapture an impression from the past, or to catch again some fleeting insight. Hearing the complaints, reading the headlines, exchanging the platitudes, it is something like hearing a snatch of some once-popular song. It brings back other times, other years.

I remember the summer of 1942, the first summer we were in the war, when the army's training camps, ubiquitous, were tightly crowded with fresh soldiers like cigarettes in a pack. Across the country that summer the air rang with the bellowing orders of drill masters and basic training instructors. All through the hot months, millions of men every sundown marched in elaborate formations for newly omnipotent colonels.

A handful were dying alone on Guadalcanal, but while the necessarily slow business of basic training held up the millions at home, the brass luxuriated in precision displays and the stylized devoirs that were their military due.

Oh, there were some parades in those days at the basic training camps, even bigger and better than those the seasoned veterans put on at the end of the war.

At a place like Jefferson Barracks, Missouri, tens of thousands of green GI's marched every late afternoon, eyes-right toward the colonel, haughty and proud in the reviewing stand, while the sun beat down and the ambulances stood waiting on the sidelines to carry away those who collapsed.

And when enough men had died of sunstroke that it was whispered around and four-letter curses called down on the parades, there was a notice on the bulletin board, brief and military, pointing out that the hot sun beat down on the Pacific islands, too, and on the deserts of Africa and the fields of India. This one, men, it said, is a global war. After all, the sooner the better . . .

Marching out to their parade grounds and passing in review, the millions were a mass of men, soldiers row on row like poppies on Flanders Field or the white crosses of Arlington: each man swallowed up in the whole, moving, marching, saluting, almost breathing as one impersonal mass.

And if a fly or a mosquito challenged the ideal of military uniformity, then that was a moment of agony, a petty pain of war, to be accepted as such. "Don't move for anything less than a mad dog," the non-com instructors said. "And then only if he's actually biting you."

The blasted inconvenience of having nerves when the colonel was standing proudly with his four-year-old grandson in the reviewing place of honor!

The idea was to put off manhood for an hour and to melt into the mass like a drop of water into a sea, then move in unified precision as a proud army before a proud colonel.

"Like one man; move like you was one man," the non-coms kept saying. And sometimes it came off beautifully, like the Rockettes on a good day, and there would be reports that the colonel had been pleased. But, oh, the damage those sand flies did, the affronts they offered to West Point dignity.

After the parade was over and the colonel and his grandson went back to their quarters, while the stretchers were carried into the station hospital, the GI's marched back in squadrons to their tents.

Away from the parade ground and out of the colonel's sight, the order for "Route Step" was given, and this meant that you could be yourself again, could walk any way you wanted to, and you could talk if you had a mind to. You usually did have a mind to, to call down curses on the army, the war, the parade grounds, tradition, the colonel, and the mosquitoes. And because there were thousands of you, there was always somebody to talk to and to share your curses with.

At the sound of the sergeant's order "Route Step," personality seeped back into the men returning to their quarters, almost like God ordering life into the primeval slime.

The proud army became a group of men, each one an individual person. By a toss of the head, a gesture of the hand, a tone of voice, by these things it was now possible to pick out a friend, to know one man from another.

Now there were all kinds: the soft drawls and the slow carriage of Texans, each drawl unmistakable, each carriage unique; the hearty cheerfulness and the horseplay of the guys from Brooklyn, each with his own brand of horseplay, each with his own style of cheerfulness. And maybe someone would draw out a *Reader's Digest* from his back pocket and read as he walked, while two more might converse seriously in low tones.

It was possible now to distinguish the guys who were really unhappy in the army, homesick perhaps, from those who could take it with a grin. Happy men, sad men, troubled men, carefree men, serious men, pinheads, roughnecks, scholars, gentlemen and bums; the sanguine, the melancholic, the phlegmatic, the choleric and a thousand variations of each: at the sergeant's bellow each man was himself; and it's a shame the colonel never saw them that way. It's always a shame when men are not seen as individual men but as part of a mass, whether they be soldiers or Displaced Persons, slain German Jews or Bowery drunks.

Bringing people back to life, the way the sergeants did, is never as easy as it was in the army. In the world outside the army, it can't be done with the mere shouting of a command.

Outside the army, it's a slow business; and the price of life returned is patience and charity, understanding and sympathy. The price is often hospitality. Four summers before that hot one at the basic training camp, I knew another army that was dehumanized and stood silent and still, motionless in the sun. This was the tragic depression army, the mass that used to be called glibly "the great army of the unemployed."

They stood in the sun, stretching in a long listless line down the alley in back of the Chicago House of Hospitality; standing in line, tormented not by the clean sand flies of an immaculate army post but by the hateful, degrading vermin of unwashed bodies, they waited for a bowl of soup.

There were hundreds of them, but they were a silent, still crowd, with the quiet distraction of men who are missing something precious, call it the spark of ambition, interest in life, or whatever you want to call it. Anyway, whatever it was, it was gone; and it was something essential.

On the weary walks back and forth to the House of Hospitality for meager meals, on the fruitless searchings for "another chance," a job, a place to sleep, a way to kill a day; during the lonely futility of their day wanderings and the threatening insecurity of their night passings, they left behind them a trail of spent life, dripping from them like blood from an open wound.

A listless group of men, these men in the line taken as a whole, discouraged, indifferent, even to each other, shamed, and beaten by life.

How they got that way, what happened, why: there are a thousand different stories. It would be nice maybe if the eager people who want general answers to these questions could be satisfied; but you just can't answer a silly question like: How do men get that way? or: What would you say is the cause of their present condition?

If you could answer, a flat "booze" (which is much more often an effect than it is a cause) or "laziness" or "bad home life" or "an unhappy marriage" or something resounding and satisfying, then the people who demand an easy explanation might be happy. But you can't account for a thousand human tragedies with a single phrase.

The point is that they were men. What was the cause, what happened, how do you explain, isn't it their own fault, don't you think if they had to do this or that or the other thing, etc.—all these things are beautifully beside the point.

When life is dripping away from men, it is not the time for speculation or self-satisfying theory-applications. This is the time to stop the flow, to heal the wounds, to bathe the sores.

A man is a man, a human person with intelligence and free will, living in a world of men, capable of heights and depths, of human tragedy and all the machinations of the world, the flesh, and the devil. Easy phrases and pet theories are no answer to human wreckage. God will mock us if we treat his great creature Man like a brute specimen in a laboratory.

And so, for whatever reason they found themselves there, the men in the breadline were a silent group; among them personality was as generally stifled as among any group of soldiers on a parade ground. The line was a sorry impersonal mass, and it moved as a single impersonal body; this one not proud but humbled and shamed.

There was room in the House of Hospitality for forty men. As an old man went off to a job or on to some other place, a man in the line took his bed in the House.

Then it was that life came back, slowly, painfully, almost shyly. Men we knew in the breadline for months as dour, wordless, dull people gradually took on a completely new (new to us, that is) character after they were established in the House of Hospitality for a while.

The security of the House, poor as it was, regular meals, a sure place to sleep, work to be done, the knowledge of being useful to others (such a little thing as slicing bread for the line or serving coffee was enough) and the casual but very real fellowship of the everchanging household of the place—these things were enough. It was often as if you could see a change taking place before your eyes, like something visible happening—color returning to a face after a faint.

Even the crudest kind of hospitality can work miracles. It is no wonder the wisdom of the Bible tells us to practice it in season and out of season and adds "without grumbling."

The slow miracle of restoring life to the joyless, of bringing back hope and a sense of belonging to the friendless, is more wonderful— much more wonderful—than the miracle the sergeant's short command brought about on the walks from the parade ground back to the tents.

But it can't be done with a word. What a man needs most is to feel like a man, to be treated like a man, to live in decency with other men.

What man can do for man! Man can raise other men from the dead, can rekindle hope, bring back the zest for living, inspire plans for the future, restore self-respect and pride in manhood—even mirror dimly the infinite charity of God.

This is the ideal of hospitality: being brother to brother, children of the same Father. Not scientific social work—hospitality. Not haughty superior dealing with "problem cases"—hospitality. Not condescending judge dealing with errant accused—hospitality. No, hospitality is derived from the Latin word for guest. It expresses a relationship between equal men: host and guest. It is bound by the rules of courtesy and human companionship, and ruled by the law of charity.

There are always men and women who need hospitality, for one reason or another. There are, in an imperfect world of imperfect men and women, always those who need a calling back to life, a restoration of personality. There are always those lonely people, in all times, in all places, who need the knowledge of being respected as men and women, of living with other men and women with dignity, of sharing their own burdens with others and bearing some of the burdens for others.

Hospitality reminds people that they are brothers, children of God, dependent on others and capable of being depended on by others.

It is not a specialized work, requiring scientific training. It is something for everyone to practice according to the measure he is able to do so.

The House of Hospitality is a striking, almost dramatized expression of hospitality. But hospitality can be practiced by everyone, in the home, in the parish, in the club, sodality, school. It has a thousand forms and can be practiced in a thousand different ways.

The charm of hospitality, because it is peculiarly human, appeals to all men. And "the soul is naturally Christian": it is not surprising that often God should use the hospitality men give each other as an instrument of His grace.

DECEMBER 1947

❊ The Unwashed

TOM SULLIVAN

A MIDDLE-AGED MAN just walked into the office in search of a clean pair of socks. Informed us that he had a pair of socks on his feet, however they were in need of a washing. He pointed to his blue shirt and said, "You people gave me this several days ago." As he attempted to smooth out his suit coat he remarked, "This came from a Bowery mission." We didn't have a pair of socks to help the man out with, and glancing down at our own socks we noticed that they too were in a sad condition. We couldn't help but wonder as to the whereabouts of those new socks that we had at the early part of the summer.

We remembered our own mother's horror whenever she noticed holes in our socks, which openings frequently revealed dirty feet. She would generally mention how appalling and shameful it would be if we had an accident and strangers would be able to view our great unwashed feet. Our middle-aged visitor seemed to have the same terror of the dark night of the feet, and he promised to return the next day in search of socks. Before he left the office he insisted on telling his story.

"Yeh, I got drunk on paynight and found myself down on the Bowery where I was beaten up and rolled [robbed]. They hauled me over to the city hospital where they tossed me into the psycho ward, didn't even bother to put stitches in my wounds. I was released in a couple of days since it was decided that I wasn't psycho. Personally I thought the patients were saner than the people who work there."

HOW LONG?

A priest called here the other day. He wanted to know if we were acquainted with a Mr. ——. We replied in the negative. "Well," he said, "this man says he is in need of carfare to get over to Jersey for a job. And he states that you people have been giving him money for his bed over at the Union Hotel on the Bowery." We told our caller that we frequently give bed money to people whom we can't put up for the night due to overcrowded conditions. The voice on the other end of the wire inquired, "You mean that you don't know the names of these people you help and you don't keep a record of them?" We confirmed that. "Well, aren't some of these men unworthy and using you?" And we replied that they probably were if there is such a person as an unworthy case. However we don't feel competent to decide who is unworthy and who is not. Another one of those things we prefer to leave up to God. We were concerned with the present need and taking care of that. After further conversation our priest friend asked if he could not come over and discuss this matter further and get acquainted with the people here in the house.

MARCH 1948

 # Pax

ROBERT LUDLOW

LOVE PROCEEDS from truth and Gandhi proceeded in love to the very end for he proceeded in truth—the truth as he saw it—he did not compromise; he was not a liberal or a relativist. His was devotion to an

Absolute. And he could proceed in love because he could proceed without violence—it was the limit of his responsibility that he proceed without violence, that he *willed* no violence. It was his adherence to truth that, in the nature of things, brought about a violence that he never ceased to regret. But as life pushes forward, as decisions must be made, as truth must be upheld, and as it is impossible to uphold truth without running into opposition, so, in the nature of things, it was impossible that the nonviolent revolution of Gandhi should not have produced violence. But that violence was met with nonviolence on Gandhi's part—to the end he forgave, reconciled, loved. He was consistently pacifist. He was the subject of wranglings and hatreds. His acts set the stage for turmoil—and yet he was consistently pacifist throughout, he proceeded in love. Love which is never an easy thing, which can be harsh, which does not compromise truth, which penetrates revolution with pity, which forbids violence, which is indeed the very substance and meaning of divinity.

There is also the joy of life and the joy of death. Of life that is psychological freedom, of death that realizes the end of freedom in the Beatific Vision. There is the joy of Gandhi's death, the fittingness of his end—the baptism of blood. The blood of Gandhi, the redness of his blood, the joy of the soaked earth, the mother earth which receives him, receives his blood and his ashes till the resurrection. Rests, rests awhile in peace in the cool earth, to enter her life, to fertilize her vegetation, to have calm—respite from animated flesh, from the tyranny of glands, the ennui of physiology. It is tomorrow that the body arises; today, let it rest awhile, let it taste the earth, let insects crawl in its decay and worms wiggle their funny little paths in the debris. Today let there be no tiredness but only rest in the close hug of the earth; let it explore the secrets of matter while its life explores the creator of matter. Let it wallow a bit in mud, live with the carnal—exult and stretch lazily in the body brown earth, reach, reach out and spread. Spread to feed animal and vegetable in recompense for having fed on them when walking upright and setting foot ahead of foot as is the way with man. Drink, drink back the blood of baptism, the martyred soakings, the blood-mud. The glory of the blood, and the warm trickle of its spread, the slow spread of the blood penetrating the earth like the slow spread of revolution as it penetrates man. It is tomorrow that the body arises; today it is the wind, the gentle play of the wind with the ashes of Gandhi, today it is the coolness of evening, the red-blood sunset and the wind, the wind to scatter the dust of Gandhi. It is the wind today; tomorrow it will be the resurrection. The resurrection tomorrow—but today, today let the body collapse and enter the earth, let the tired body of Gandhi rest lightly on the earth, give him to the wind today, to the elements, to the flesh and to the material that he may enter into the very bowels of nature that she may cling yet to his resurrected flesh, for tomorrow is the resurrection.

According to what norm did Gandhi operate? He operated on the level of the absurd; in relation to the prevailing ethos of communities his norm lies in the regions of psychoses, as the Christian norm must ever be in relation to the things of this world. He moved in the supernatural and could not but appear strange to those whose concepts do not embrace this sphere. Even as Our Lord he traveled the earth in nostalgia for heaven and yet with no indifference to the multitude; he was detached from the things of time and yet through it all he loved man and nature, and his asceticism was tempered with pity and human warmth. His relation to the Absolute was in no direct line, for it rebounded in his love for man; it encompassed a redeemed earth. I could not have much to say of the theory of mysticism to which he adhered, but there was in it enough truth and it bore fruit in the love of God and neighbor. As such it placed him in the soul of the Church. In a very real sense he was Christian and Catholic. I do not think that he can be classed with those mystics who, as Kierkegaard writes, become impatient of the revelations of God. For in that direction lies intellectual and spiritual pride and repugnance for the stench of the flesh, the sensual. Till finally there is conceived an impossibility of incarnation. So that one can no longer believe that God became man, that He stood on feet and saw through eyes and received nourishment. That He wept in sorrow over Jerusalem, sorrow that she was to go, for He loved her as one can love the strange beauty of cities, and the familiar streets and the noises of the streets. That He handled asceticism with indifference, as realizing its necessity and yet never pursuing it when higher claim was upon him. Claims of pity and hospitality, the call to souls that might lead through many channels and to strange places, so that oftentimes he ate and drank, but as a means to an end, as using things lightly, as keeping ever before Him the Divinity which He was. And the final criterion, the criterion on which He based judgment, was the love of God expressed visibly in the love of man. It seems to me that that was also the fruits of Gandhi, that he embraced a mysticism that went beyond preoccupation with self, even the self as related to God, and loved all men as an indispensable condition of perfection. It was for that he received the baptism of blood which brought him at once into the light of glory, the everlasting contemplation of God, having no further need of purgation.

We who walk the earth in sorrow! Who wear out the lonely watches of the night with our cries, who would all but despair if there were not in us the everlasting hope of resurrection, the absurd persistence of divinity, the unsatisfied longings for transcendance. And the strange beauty of night, the everlasting night of time, the cry of nature for liberation, the cry of those lost in the embrace of night, the sadness of night and the beauty of it. The beauty of Gandhi's death. Poor little one of God! Who is there left to wander the earth in your behalf, who to suffer for you, to join atonement in Christ? Have they buried their talents in the world, or are they hidden in convents and monasteries, or preoccupied with individual sanctity? Where are the Christians? Who among us to compare with this man of God, who to burst the black bowels of death, to pursue God down the night roads till the eternal dawn, to press revolution without violence, to give love for hate, to have joy in sorrow, hope in despair, victory in failure? Poor little ones of God! To whom shall we turn save only to Him who abides always in the heart of man, who in the days of time is lifted up as bread, who some time ago was lifted to the gaze of men at Golgotha. The eternal dripping of His blood fills the earth with divinity, makes holy the brown warm earth, redeems nature and man, takes to Himself the wasted body of His saint—for as He lives and as Gandhi lives, there will again be those who hear the whisper of His voice, the insistent call of the Absolute, the promptings of conscience. And once again there will be a pilgrim walking, walking the lonely stretches of the night.

APRIL 1948

❀ **Picking Cotton**

AMMON HENNACY

HAVING A FEW FREE DAYS after the winter lettuce season at the large vegetable ranch where I had worked, I left my shack situated between a cabbage field and a lettuce field on land of the Russian pacifist Molokons and went to Phoenix to visit an atheist friend and spend the night in order to get the cotton truck before daylight. (This friend had bought a *Catholic Worker* from me in front of the library in Milwaukee one Saturday in 1941. He later read an article of mine in the *Catholic C.O.* His admiration of the courageous pacifist spirit of these papers led him to deviate from his atheistic norms.)

The next morning two bonfires were already burning along the curb where Mexicans, Indians and Anglos, many of the latter being "winos," were waiting to select the truck in which they would go to work. Just now there were only cotton trucks, there being a lull in citrus picking. Cotton pickers carry their own eight-foot to ten-foot sacks fastened with a strap around the shoulders and dragging behind them like a giant worm. There were eight trucks and several pickups. Most of them were shaped like the traditional covered wagon with canvas. There were benches on either side and in the middle. I walked around searching for someone I might know, but my friends of the lettuce fields were wary of cotton picking, considering this the hardest job to be had and one to be taken only as a last resort.

"Last call! Take you there and bring you back. Three dollars a hundred. All aboard gentlemen!" shouted a good-natured Negro in a bright mackinaw. The truck to which he pointed was box-shaped, of good veneer, with a short ladder leading inside from the rear. I entered and found a seat between a colored woman and a colored man. After a few more calls the doors were shut, and we could see each other only as one would light a cigarette.

Later on the truck stopped and we were joined by a large group of laughing Negroes of all ages. There were three whites besides myself, and one Indian.

Our destination was nine miles beyond Buckeye, which is about thirty miles west of Phoenix. After several sharp turns, when all in the truck were thrown this way and that, we came to the field. The Indian and I did not have sacks, so we rented them from the boss for a quarter.

This was tall cotton, and harder to pick than the small variety. The field was a quarter of a mile long and a mile wide. A young white man worked in one row, then the Indian, and then myself. I had never picked cotton before. The Indian, a Navajo, said this was to be clean picking, he understood.

Where the cotton was fluffy it was easy to grab, but where the boll was only partly open it was difficult to extract and hurt your fingers. As we worked along the row from the far end of the field toward the weighing scales and truck, my Navajo friend said that he was learning a lesson which he sadly needed. Now he had just enough money from day to day. Before this he had spent money freely and never had to count his pennies. He paid a dollar a night for a cot in a cheap hotel in Phoenix. He had an older brother who had been quite wealthy before the depression and was a big shot among his people because of his holdings in cattle. He drank, bought fine cars. Now with the "plowing under" and rationing system of the government he was a poor Indian indeed.

In speaking of the Navajo he said that they had always been poor in these last years, but that the suffering was now no greater than last year. If left to themselves in sheep and cattle raising and in growing corn they would be able to get along. But the government restrictions as to grazing and its refusal to provide schools for the Navajo according to treaty had given them little to do in their spare time except to succumb to the temptations of liquor and the allurements of the cities. The recent provision of half a million dollars for food from Congress was coupled with three times that amount to "rehabilitate" the Navajo. This was another word for jobs for the white bureaucrats to feed on the misery of the Indian with boondoggling experiments.

Navajos do not eat fish, bear, pork; in fact any animal that does not eat grass is not "clean" to them. They will not kill a coyote for the bounty as do the whites.

We had worked three hours and took our cotton in to be weighed. I had thirty pounds and he had forty-two. The white man near us had eighty-five. In talking over this discrepancy we found that we had been picking only the clean white cotton, while the more experienced pickers picked the bolls along with the cotton and more than doubled the weight.

As we waited our turn for weighing our cotton, groups were shooting dice in the roadway. A Negro woman served coffee, chili, pie, weiners, etc., at reasonable prices. Some of the truck drivers sold food to their passengers.

Returning to the field we picked in more of an orthodox fashion, and in the total five and a half hours the Navajo picked eighty-two pounds and I picked sixty-two. Before we left I gave him *The Catholic Worker* to read with my letter about the Hopi refusing to go to war.

The next morning I met my Navajo friend beside the bonfire at Second and Madison. The truck of Negroes did not go out on Sunday. One truck took only those who had sacks. I got in a small pickup which headed westward about thirty miles to Litchfield Park. Several young girls kept us merry with songs. When we arrived at the field my Navajo friend came in on another truck. We happened to get sacks at different times, so did not work together.

An old man said that the rule here was "rough picking" which meant everything that had white in it, but no stems or leaves. When I emptied my sack, I had fifty-four pounds. The man next to me seemed to work rather expertly, and I asked him what time they quit on weekdays here. He replied that he only came on Sundays. "Make $1.25 an hour at my job in town, and time and a half overtime."

I commented that unless a person had a large family that was a good wage.

"I don't work here for the money," he continued. "I just come out here so I can keep sober. Was drunk from Christmas until yesterday—ten days. I can keep sober if I'm working, but I can't stand to be quiet or to loaf. And as I have eight kids, I need to keep working."

There was not much cotton left to pick in this field, and the word went around that we would quit about two P.M. At that time my second sack weighed thirty-one pounds, which, after paying for my sack, netted me $2.23. My Navajo friend had not done so well, picking only sixty-eight pounds. He said he had liked my reference to the Hopi in *The Catholic Worker*.

As we were going into town in the truck the man who picked cotton to keep sober was discussing the merits of different brands of liquor with another picker. This man was telling of going to a town upon receiving a paycheck as a "gandy dancer" on the railroad, going to the police and asking them how much the fine was for being "drunk and disorderly." They said it was $17.50 so he paid it at once, for he intended to get drunk and disorderly. I did not hear the rest of the story for the truck soon passed lateral 20, nearby where I lived, and I proceeded homeward with $3.93 for two part-days spent in the cotton fields.

Later in the day, sitting in my doorway, resting, I was asked by a man who drove up in a car to work for him for a week irrigating at $7.20 per day. Gladly I was willing to let this two part-days of cotton picking suffice. Good pickers can make from $8 to $12 a day, but I was not in that class.

MAY 1948

Revolution and Compassion

ROBERT LUDLOW

IT IS IN ISRAEL that God revealed himself under the aspect of a national deity and it belongs to the Old Dispensation that there was a mission in the national state. And yet even there it was a state under law, subject to the moral law. There was distinction then between Jew and Gentile; there was not then fully realized the universal brotherhood of men. And so there was war. And yet even then there was realization of the sinfulness of war, there was the pacifism of the prophets, the cry of those who perceived what was beyond the law, who had a foretaste of the spirit of Christ, who longed for the brotherhood of all men that was to be proclaimed in the New Dispensation.

With the consummation of Christ's sacrifice on Calvary there was an end to the Old Dispensation, an end to morally justified war, an end to national states as desirable entities. For there is then no distinction between Jew and Gentile: all men take on the heritage of Israel, all men are admitted by the Divine Jew to the mysteries of Israel, all men are brothers in Christ. Therefore it is that, as the ideals of Christianity are realized, as they become exteriorized in society, so will national states wither away as being impediments to the realization of human brotherhood. And so will war be outlawed as rendering asunder the mystical body of Christ. And nations and peoples who today lie bleeding along the wayside, bleeding in the murder of war, will not be passed by and left in agony by the orthodox who dispute about "just and unjust" war and seek to lay down rules for murder. It will be seen that orthodoxy involves pacifism as the visible expression in society of that love for all men which is a precept of Christ.

It has been a slow process, this matter of realizing the social implications of Christianity—and it has not as yet been realized in any great degree. Mostly it has come about by indirection. Ecclesiastics suddenly realizing, or being forced by circumstances to realize, that the adoption of a new order, the success of a revolution, has not threatened religion but in reality has purified and brought out unsuspected implications of the faith. So slavery (formal slavery) ended and there is no theologian to defend it today—it is seen to be incompatible with Christianity that a man should own a man. So it may be with war; it may be seen that it is incompatible with Christianity that man should kill man. So it may be with the national state; it may be seen that it is incompatible with Christianity that man should be separated from man by artificial and antagonistic barriers. And so will be swept aside a whole host of casuistry, a logic that tries vainly to fit the spirit of Christ into syllogisms, a legalistic Catholicism that is concerned with how close a man can get to hell without tumbling in. And this is what is meant by Christian anarchism which opposes freedom to slavery, nonviolence to war, decentralization to the national state. It is a revolution which invites the cooperation of all radicals, which stretches out the hand to all men of good will whose consciences have been tortured in the totalitarian regimes of the day.

To our Communist brethren, to Communists throughout the world, many of whom burn yet with a zeal for righteousness, a love for the oppressed, a desire to see justice achieved, we would ask once again that they pause to reconsider the events of the past, the history of violence, the mockery the state has made of any attempt at unity with all men. And to consider if their good and laudable aims in the economic field are not being obtained because the *method* of obtaining them has swallowed up the end and become the end. That the state does not wither away, it becomes stronger; that violence does not disappear, it becomes the ordinary instrument of governance. And that a new slavery replaces the old slavery of private capitalism. That there really was no dynamism in the stupid materialism and atheism of the bourgeois and that to retain it as part of the Communist ideology is the height of reaction. For the truth did not end with Karl Marx, for he did not rid his thought entirely of the false progressivism and scientism and materialism of the nineteenth-century bourgeois. Indeed, in one sense he glorified them, he made them the criterion of justice. People like those connected with the Social Democratic Federation who are fast becoming professional anti-Communists (to say nothing of the Catholic press) are going also along this same road of illusions: the illusion that another war will at last settle the totalitarian business, that Nazism is done with and now we must have done with Marxism. And again war is to be waged by national states, and again it will not determine the right and wrong of anything. It will fashion other totalitarianisms; it will make a world of conscript slaves; it will pulverize the world. For if we will *not* use the Christian means of nonviolence, if we will not accept the example of Gandhi, then we have no right to expect the end will be any different than the means we use warrant; it will rise no higher, and there will be no redemption from this choice.

Someone said to a friend of mine that it seemed to him more compatible with the faith to be a Communist than to be an industrial capitalist. I think he is right. I could conceive of a Communism devoid of materialism and atheism and being in harmony with Catholicism; I cannot conceive of industrial capitalism being such. I know there are those in the Church who say that to be a Communist you *must* be an atheist. But they are wrong. Wrong as far as acceptance of the purely economic theories of Communism go. For if one rejects the philosophical basis of Marxism and the means advocated to obtain the goal of Communism, there is nothing to object to from a moral standpoint. And by rejecting those things the way would be opened for a great union of radicalism with religion in a last desperate attempt to achieve that justice on earth which would be the visible expression of the love of Christ. It is along that road the Church will triumph, never will she do so by coercion and personal intolerance. It may be the road to which she will eventually be forced.

But it is not the road in which Catholic Action tends, at least as we know it in this country. And the peculiar value of *The Catholic Worker* seems to me to lie in these largely unexplored possibilities. It gives opportunity for what, in the long run, may prove very valuable service to the Church. So it would seem to be a mistake to channel this into what most Catholics would regard as the "safer" course. It is well that it proceed pretty much as it has, reaching always more and more people and influencing minds rather than concentrating on organization and pressure group technique. There must be room also in the Church for these different approaches and for different temperaments and for as much freedom as possible. A good priest once said to me that the more canon law there is, the less religion, and in a sense it is true. For organization and rules only too often gain efficiency at the expense of the spirit—they tend of their very nature to stratify, to provide a framework for the mechanical performance of duties. So that here also there is room within the Church for a Christian anarchism. Which, because it is Christian, is never synonymous with disregard for morality or for revealed truth. But which is unalterably opposed to any coercion of conscience. And that is the freedom of which St. Paul speaks well.

But we are weighed down with many things: the flesh, the world, and the world of the subconscious. And there must be compassion. Christ and Freud taught us there must be compassion. And a revolution without pity can end only in a reign of terror, in a new slavery. There must be no coercion of conscience. But if we bear the marks of original sin we bear also that of the redemption and we too often lose sight of the fact that the new life made possible in Christ holds the possibilities of greater achievement than any man has hitherto known. And yet we continue to talk as though man's nature was hopelessly corrupted by original sin. As though there was no use in doing anything, as though Christ never came. There is a dangerous tendency in all of us to hanker for the Old Dispensation, for natural ethics. To forget that there are unexplored depths that could be possible with that new life coming from Christ. That He would lead us beyond slavery and beyond war and beyond national states to a realization, even in this world, of the Brotherhood of man under the Fatherhood of God.

But it will be a revolution with pity or it will be no revolution at all. It will leave judgment to God; there will be no guillotine, no torture chambers. There will be no Inquisition, for it will be seen that the way of love is superior to all else and that as one grasps more and more of truth so does he love more. If these things cannot be then let us sit down and weep, for we are indeed lost and it is as well that we depart from the face of the earth.

❊ David

A Story of Love

WILLIAM GAUCHAT

DAVID CAME TO US last winter—to die. The doctor and his parents told us that almost casually. A week of life, perhaps a day, but not a month. Sometime that January, a spasm, a convulsion, a slight cry in his sleep, death would come like that.

He was six months old. The nurse who wrapped the last blanket about him told us, "He can't see—he is blind; can't hear—he is deaf; can't feel—atrophied; water pressure on the brain—hydrocephalous; lesion of the spine—*spina bifida*." (There was a lump larger than a baseball, full of fluid, soft as a balloon, ready to break.) Dorothy got violently sick when we got home. I cried bitterly, the first time since I can remember. . . . We thought of our three beautiful girls—and David . . . waiting for death.

The first evening he was with us I made the sign of the cross over him—his dull eyes followed the motion of my hand. "Dorothy, he can see!" Of course he could. The children verified that the very next morning, the way children will. . . . He chuckled at the antics of a torn teddy-bear. He loved it.

He grew into our hearts—instead of sobs and nausea, he was the Christ Child in the manger. He became beautiful.

After two weeks or so he wouldn't take his bottle. He sank into a coma, broken with little wails. His temperature, 105°. It lasted seven days. . . . We called his parents: "It is probably the end." We called the doctor who attended the birth. "Isn't he a mess?" And he said it so indifferently.

David pulled through that spell, and the next one, and so many more—but each time farther apart.

He could see, he could laugh, and he could love!

He was our boy.

June came and his parents took him. The house was empty. He had been the center of it for so long. . . . We never realized it until he was gone.

Remember, we'd say afterwards, how David used to laugh when Daddy came in from a trip to market and said, "How's my boy?" And so many other things like that.

And we used to remember when we'd question, "Why?" Why, but always unspoken—a broken, maimed boy child, in pain, doomed to die, why, God, why? The unspoken question in our eyes as we paced the rooms those nights his shrill voice protested. . . .

The sense of loss we experienced when he was gone gave us a clue to the answer. Six months later we saw him again and his parents. David had learned to talk a little—and his mother and father had learned to love him. That was the beautiful thing. . . .

There is no love without the cross, and no cross without a victim. And whether we be on the cross or beneath it weeping, there is Christ, and sorrow shall be turned to joy.

APRIL 1949

❈ Picket Lines and the Cardinal

JOHN McKEON

IT IS, OF COURSE, yesterday's news now. Eight weeks ago the workers in Calvary Cemetery, belonging to Local 293, which in turn was affiliated with the International Food, Tobacco and Agricultural Workers' Union, voted to go on strike for what they considered just demands against their employers, the trustees of St. Patrick's Cathedral. The demands were for a forty hour week for the same pay as the forty-eight hour week and time and a half for overtime. The trustees did not see these demands as justified, feeling, so they said, that they would put an unde-served burden on the public who owned graves in Calvary Cemetery.

That was the problem in essence. From there on in to the settlement of the dispute it became a classic lesson in how not to deal with a strike.

Eighty-five percent of the membership of the local and one hundred percent of the membership of the Calvary strikers were Catholic. Which is to say, all kinds, tapering down from the truly devout to occasional churchgoers. The peculiar slant this gave the strike became more appar-ent as the dispute went on.

The first day of the strike most metropolitan papers gave it minimum coverage and then left it strictly alone. To most of the non-Catholic population of New York, anything that is even remotely connected with St. Patrick's Cathedral is directly connected with His Eminence, Francis Cardinal Spellman, who is to them a figure of almost legendary proportions. No matter how rabidly anti-Catholic they may be, they still treat him with that odd mixture of vague distrust and respect that Americans usually reserve for visiting English royalty.

Because of his exalted position as a Prince of the Church, his being the most publicized figure in the American hierarchy and the best known the world over of all American cardinals, their patriotic, if not their spiritual, instinct led them to anticipate his wishes by treating the strike as if it did not exist. The fact was that in truth the Cardinal had nothing to do with the strike, until, weeks later when it had grown into an intolerable situation totally incapable of solution by the trustees, the trustees thrust it into his lap. Only then did the Cardinal enter the picture.

On the basis of some very strange information proffered him by an adviser, the Cardinal became convinced that the strike was Communist inspired and then that the strikers were using Communist tactics. Also that in some way the strikers had become guilty by association because the international union with which they were affiliated had been known to be organized originally by Communists—an issue that had not come up two years earlier when the trustees negotiated a contract with the local. When the strikers, bending over backward to please him, swore a solemn public oath that they were not Communist inspired, were not Communists, and abhorred Communist philosophy, the Cardinal was quoted by the papers as saying, "I am gratified, but they are getting repentant kind of late."

Each day in the last two weeks of the strike the papers credited the Cardinal with the strangest statements: "I am proud and happy to be a strikebreaker." "This is the most important thing that I have done in my ten years in New York," etc.

A sense of shock went through the Catholic population. News services grasped the statements avidly and flung them to the four corners of the earth through their wire services. Moscow took due note. The *Daily Worker* leaped gleefully into the fray, jeering, "Let Catholic working men and women note carefully the words of their Cardinal and realize that here, as in the case of Cardinal Mindzenty, the issue is not religion but the economic and political misuses it lends itself to."

We of *The Catholic Worker* came to know the strike and the strikers well. Early in the strike they started coming to us individually and in groups, having been cold-shouldered by all the other Catholic groups in New York, with the notable exception of the Association of Catholic Trade Unionists, who stuck by the strikers through thick and thin, giving unsparingly of their time, funds, and legal aid—convinced that the strikers' demands were just.

The Catholic Worker supplied pickets, direct relief, and encouragement whenever possible. We went among them, into their homes, attended their meetings, were on their strike relief committee, listened to their grievances, and formed our opinion: the strike was justified. We say it still.

It could have been headed off in the very beginning. The trustees could have shown the books to the workers if justice was on their side, proven in black and white that they were incapable of paying what the strikers asked. The strikers were not unreasonable or dishonest people. They were hard-working, simple people driven by what they considered intolerable conditions to strike. The dispute would have been settled there and then instead of becoming a fratricidal war.

It is all yesterday's news now: those strikers who had to drop their life insurance because they couldn't meet payments, the ones with savings dissipated, the rent owed, the vacation money laboriously put by and now swallowed up in the paying of bills owed to the butcher and the grocer. The striker whose only child was a boy of sixteen dying of a chronic kidney complaint, too ill to be moved to the hospital, and who needed money desperately for food, medicine, doctor bills, rent, who still stuck with his union and refused to scab. The striker with seven hungry children who said to us, "In the name of God, how can they keep saying that burying the dead is a work of mercy and we should be satisfied to take less and I've got seven kids to feed? Feeding my kids is work of mercy enough for me and it takes more than what they're giving me to do it on." And the shamefaced seminarians in buses, surrounded by heavy police guards, who drove through the picket line to help break the strike, past the signs in the hands of the strikers that read, "Is Calvary the Graveyard of Catholic Social Justice?"

Apart from all this a precedent of dubious worth has been set in the struggle of the laboring class for better conditions. Because of the Cardinal's refusal to deal with them so long as they were affiliated with the Food, Tobacco and Agriculture International, the strikers, on advice of legal counsel, voted to bolt their mother union, the CIO, and join the Building Service Employees International, affiliated with the AFL, headed by David Sullivan. Responsible labor leaders feel, and justly, that by forcing the strikers to do this the Cardinal has dealt a hard blow to the CIO in particular and labor in general. Hereafter whenever an employer comes to the conclusion that his workers' demands are unjust, he can use the Cardinal's action as a precedent to refuse to deal with their demands unless they give up their allegiance to what he can term a Communistic union. Today it is a local in the CIO but tomorrow it might be any labor organization at all.

It's old stuff now, except for those of us who went through it. And it will be a long time before we lose that nagging sense of shame and bewilderment that filled us when we first realized that there were eminent Catholic laymen surrounding Cardinal Spellman, advising him out of their own weakness, greed, and lack of diplomatic ability to follow a course that must inevitably lead him to loss of dignity and humiliation. And all because they, the lay trustees of St. Patrick's Cathedral, could not treat Catholic working men as human beings and brothers.

❖ Church in France

HENRI PERRIN, S. J.

I KNOW that a lot of your readers have been readers of my German diary and I would like to thank them by giving them some echoes of my actual life. For a year and a half I have been a workman in the district of Paris. I had sought work for a long time before finding it. Finally I was employed by a manufacturer of insulators and molded objects, a factory of plastic goods, plates, bowls, radio cabinets, etc.

First of all I worked as a molder on two steam presses; then they asked me to work as a turner. Interesting work, not too tiring, peaceful, too peaceful, because isolated. I was with a small crew of turners in a large factory of women.

In contrast to other factories, relations were slow to form; one talks little doing piece work, and salaries being small, the workmen concentrate on the job.

Only a few people knew that I was a priest. For various reasons I decided to try the experience of silence first of all for myself, to be more definitely one of them, to get in their rhythm, their thought, into their way of seeing things.

Later on, I believed that the moment had come to reveal that I was a priest; from each side they dissuaded me, saying how little we can imagine the distrust and the resentment at the heart of the people against priests and how little they are supposed to believe in our disinterestedness.

The reaction of my companions was at first some surprise, some curiosity, but there were no lively reactions or problems. Some believed that I must have been defrocked; others thought that I was forced to earn my bread; on the one side there was discreet reserve and distrust, on the other hand sympathy because of the companionship which had sprung up between us. It was only very slowly that my position was understood and confidence was given me, which was normal enough because this presupposes an occasion to explain myself and the occasion doesn't come up every day. Two kinds reacted more clearly on learning of my priesthood. The Christian sort, practicing Christians, C.F.T.C. etc., have received with joy and treated as a grace the presence of a priest in their midst. On the other hand, the Communists, except for a few militants among them who have all of a sudden become very sympathetic, have treated me for a long time with reserve and distrust—a reaction which I find very normal. They are awaiting my actions before forming any judgment. But with some of them, as with the others, a real friendship has been formed.

Then I left the factory in June and went to Paris in September. I could not find work until a month later. Then I worked for three weeks as a laborer in a sheet iron factory where I was fired by the owner as a bad worker, with a week's pay in advance. At this time I had a long and violent argument with the boss, who was on the point of striking me. I refused to take my discharge, which meant that I had to have a new interview with the inspector of work. Finally I gave in. I certainly was able to sense how the working man feels himself at the mercy of the employer and runs the risk of being from one day to the next deprived of his work.

Fortunately I found other work without much delay in an enterprise which in this district has four workshops and factories for manufacturing automobiles. I worked as a mechanic in a sheet iron gang which made fans for Ford trucks—work that was very new to me and which it took some adjusting to get used to. Because they cut off the current, we worked only four days a week, from Monday to Thursday, from nine in the morning until eight at night. Consequently on these days I could not say Mass in the evening because there is a meeting of the workers practically every night.

At this factory they don't know yet that I am a priest, except for the management and the union, but they suspect it, and I'm not going to wait much longer before I tell them. The union has given me an excellent welcome, which gives me confidence. When I was threatened with layoff because of lack of work (three workmen of our crew got their week's notice Monday), the union asked me to do everything possible to stay.

Once again I am amazed at the qualities that I find in my working companions, their faithfulness to their work. I don't say this is the way everywhere; I only say that here where I am I have again found real men, who to their professional pride, must often add the suffering and the greatness of a conscience in revolt.

Once again I have found the war between capital and labor, the acute feeling on the workman's side of his exploitation, and the misunderstanding on the employer's side of the workmen's problems. Of course, my experience of the working life is too recent to allow a complete understanding of the problem in its entirety.

Still, I must say that, after a month on this job, my factory life has been a slow and increasing revolt against the capitalist world, from the inhuman attitude of the bosses who inspect the workers as one inspects a room full of machines, to the questions of salaries and production, the work of women and the union struggle, by all this atmosphere of the factory where the workman feels himself wrung out and exploited. Apart from my own personal experience, there is that of my own foreman who has behind him forty years of working life. For me he is the finest type of qualified workman, the conscientious sort of man I like and admire as much as a scholar or statesman.

When it comes to a small thing like the workmen not having the right to break for nourishment between seven o'clock and noon, when it comes to the control of his time or the organization of production, the hired man is not a free man. He is alienated; he is not a *man* who works with an engineer and a foreman's power, but a *capacity* for production which one has hired and which must be exploited to the maximum; he is not a man responsible for his production, but a mechanic whose output alone is interesting. The tactic of increasing the output without increasing the salary is one of the strongest proofs. To which one adds the inflexibility, to say no more, of the employers in regard to trade unionism and the sabotage of the management committees when they entertain the worker delegates with problems of sanitation or of feeding nursing mothers, while obstinately refusing to frankly open up the question of their administration.

Far from being a community of men who work together, it isn't even being administered by a human sense of production, but by the most apparent scramble for profits and money. In short, everything contributes to create more than ever in the working man a justified spirit of revolt, and only the hardness of the times and the experience of distress can take away temporarily the hope and the material possibility of revolt. Capitalism distills more than ever in the conscientious workman the feeling of alienation and rebellion.

The second point which has been brought home to me a long time, as an experience hard won, is that of religious unbelief. This first plunge into the working world, or the world of youth, has brought me perception more and more acute of the profound gap between this world and the faith of which I am the carrier. The consciousness that the Christian message, as the people of the Church express it and put it to work, is so completely foreign to this world that it appears all the more as an object of curiosity or of fabrication, but surely not as a response to human anxiety which motivates our generation as the others.

The reasons for this rejection of Christianity are often enough expressed so that it should be easy to present some of them here. Men don't discuss the Gospel, for which, nevertheless, they maintain a longing, but they see in the Church only a temporal power, a political power, which has a past history of riches and domination and which appears always anxious to assure its influence. How many times have they not told me: "The Church is clever. She feels that she has lost her influence. She is using you to try to convert the left." The action of the Church appears to be purely tactical; its practical life, its ceremonies, present themselves to our contemporaries as enervated of all spiritual vigor.

All that and many other reasons besides make our Christianity appear to the unbelieving world as foreign as Buddhism. For five months with the Ajistes, workmen and others, I have never, so to speak, heard a question posed on the subject of religion.

I knew the external reasons that they give for this indifference, but it is on the internal reasons that it is most easy for us to act; the priests and the real Christians at present in the modern world are still too few in number and too unsaintly; there are too few saints among them for the demonstration of their faith and their hope, their poverty, and their love to be a sufficient witness.

In summary, I have the profound and confirmed conviction that it is normal and necessary for a priest to be in this factory as a simple working man. He must experience it to understand how much that is necessary as absolute evidence and for a good many reasons that I unfortunately do not have the time to explain here. Finally, I have the impression that I have entered, after others, a new world ignored by the Church, a new mission country, a world that I must slowly discover; it will take months, years. Why does the Christian laity tell us so little about how foreign this world is to us?

Nevertheless, it is clear even on the brink of its unbelief that the real world is waiting for this witness to the truth from the Christian. It is easy to call this world materialist; it is often because one hasn't known the faith and the hope which profoundly bear it up. One could cite marvelous daily demonstrations of the faith and the love which spring from the heart of the working world, in the tireless faith of the Communist, in the will to love and liberty of the anarchist, in the brotherhood of the taverns and the songs with which they express themselves. I will only cite, in closing, this strophe of a poem whose author, Marcel, a twenty-five-year-old docker, gave me as a goodbye gesture the day I left the factory:

One day peace will reign on the earth,
When all the people clasp hands.
  There will be no more war.

Then on this earth, where once
  so much blood flowed,
There will be the joy of living,
Of love and of spring.

From each nest
Will wing the blessed songs.

O people, my brothers,
Unite, give me your hand!
Do not make war any more.

I am afraid that the assembling of these impressions will seem pessimistic to you; I don't know enough English and I don't have enough time to acquaint myself by reading *The Catholic Worker* with how much our problems correspond to those facing the Christians of America. But I know that, here as over there, we cannot, we Christians, remain strangers to the sufferings of our people, whatever they are. I know that the love of God, in which we believe, has some practical demands that one cannot escape under pain of betraying the Gospel; I know that, with you as with us, one must pray ardently and humbly, so that slowly, across the history of our humanity, "the reign of God will arrive."

It is in this fraternal communion of prayer that I am happy to know you and to salute you and all your friends of *The Catholic Worker*.

JUNE 1949

❋ The Death of Peter Maurin

JOHN McKEON

WE WERE in a little, one-operator crossroads telephone exchange in the uplands of New Hampshire when we learned, in the course of a routine phone call to Maryfarm, that Peter had died the night before. Our mind registered the fact mechanically while we watched the girl beside us weaving the worries, the gossip, the hopes, the private lives of a whole county into an intricate pattern, as though the switchboard before her were an enchanted loom. No sorceress of old ever dreamt of such power at her fingertips, but it was exquisite boredom and a drag if the expression on the operator's face was valid. And yet she was living and young and apparently healthy.

When the call was over we thanked her and went out and started the long drive back, down out of the mountains. The mountains of New Hampshire are lovely in any weather and the weather of that day suited our mood, the mist shrouding the giant pines so heavily that the slopes seemed forested with ghosts, standing forever sentinel at the sides of the lonely, narrow, dirt roads.

On the way back I thought much about Peter. I had only known him briefly, in the past few months, when the walls of his mind had long since crumbled in ruin on his dream of a new society where "it would be possible for men to live and die as men, not as tortured animals." But even then, in his old age, uncaring, crippled in mind and body, he still had the power to attract, to seize the imagination. At Mass in the chapel at Maryfarm he would sit quietly in his seat by the window, seemingly oblivious, an old man, thickset, whose shoulders were still bowed with the heavy yoke of peasant muscle, but at the Sanctus he would rouse and force himself, unaided, to his knees. It was excruciating to watch, but an object lesson in spiritual discipline not easily forgotten. An old man, who all his life and now with his age on him and in great pain did not fail to render homage to his God.

An old man who all his life had sought to bring God and the vision of a Christian life into places that are usually left to themselves in our society: into flophouses and work camps and market places, among the foolish, the failures, the fanatics, those broken on the iron wheel of our time, the poor, the destitute, the homeless, the unwanted, the forgotten, the "weaker vessels." Those were Peter's apostolate and to the world that had formed them he addressed his mission.

Looking at him in the last few months, an old French peasant, sitting beneath the crabapple tree at Maryfarm, wrapped in a worn blanket and wearing a yellowed, ancient and donated panama, he might have been any old man sunning himself. There was nothing especially saintly about him, one sees hundreds such on park benches in big cities; the survivors—the ones who have outwitted their great enemy, winter, who sit warming themselves in the weak sunlight of a city spring. The ones who will, or will not, in the late afternoon go home to the meals cooked them by the wives of their sons, who will talk about their sons to you if you give them a chance, perhaps show you pictures of their grandchildren. The ones who will, or will not, be there next spring, and if they are not, the grave will be closed on them and they will be quickly forgotten.

But the old man underneath the tree at Maryfarm was different. He had no blood sons, no pictures of grandchildren to show, and the grave closed on him but he will not be quickly forgotten. He preached a mission clothed in language so simple that it appeared the speech of a fool or a child. Years ago, when I first read an essay of Peter's, I laughed and tossed it aside and the second time in impatience and the third time in anger. Did the man think he was talking to idiots? Did he actually believe anyone with the sense God gave a chimpanzee would spend his time reading such drivel, much less acting upon it? You would have to use better bait than that to fish for the minds of our time, minds that had slipped through the nets of prose cast by masters of the art, not once but many times, without effort. And yet, and yet . . .

He *was* speaking to fools, to minds weighted down by the dross of our time, the big ideas shouted from radio and forum, from newspaper and magazine, book and newsreel until the brain was dulled, surfeited, corrupted, unable to tell gold from glitter. The total of Peter's writing showed the same poverty that stamped his life; there is scarcely enough to fill a slender volume. Peter left as a legacy no weighty, hernia-creating tomes to be carried about by the future students of social action, no ponderous, inflexible terminology, merely a handful of ideas; but ideas of value, capable of buying many hours of reflective thought.

He was not an innovator, a prophet. The ideas and the ideals he preached were very old, the never-realized ideas, the ones that got lost in the shuffle centuries past and have been wandering in the wasteland ever since. The ideas of the Christian Revolution.

He was an agitator primarily, a very good one and fortunate. Fortunate because his star rose before him very early in life and all his life he followed it steadfastly and believed in it and never lost faith. Count on the fingers of one hand if you can those agitators of our time who followed into their old age the ideals of their youth without taint of either cynicism or opportunism. And the ideas of Peter's youth led him into some very strange places, with many opportunities for either.

He was poor by choice all of his life, eating by choice the poorest food, sleeping by choice in flophouses, on park benches, bus stations, content to wear any hand-me-down. And with all that keeping his humor and tolerance, his charity and understanding, the original force of his vision. Count on the fingertips of one hand the men who could do it and doing it could, incredibly, bind others to them, by force of personality, to do it also.

In the eyes of the world a man like Peter appears like a sorry joke. He wouldn't have fitted into a handsome office; his ideas didn't glitter; they didn't appear to have any drive; worst of all, they weren't practical. They left out too many buts and ifs and whereases and perhapses. The heads of corporations would have laughed at him if he had attempted to sell them his program; even ordinary people, those with a minimum stake in the system, often laughed. But Peter carried his ideas into the streets, explaining, exhorting, teaching, and there were those who listened. He had no car, no house, no speedboat, no stocks, no television set. He had nothing. And yet he had, in the end, what the heads of corporations do not have, people not of their families, not even acquainted with them, or who have ever seen their faces, who love them, for themselves and for their ideas and their lives.

There are tens of thousands living today who when they were hungry were fed because of Peter's efforts, and when they were naked were clothed because of Peter, and when they were homeless were harbored because of Peter.

He was an old man, dying alien and childless and a failure in the world's eyes, in a land not of his birth, and yet the spiritual seed of the poor French peasant, flung randomly on a hostile and uncaring world, bore fruit, and many were the sons of his spirit who wept at his coffin and who walked behind it to his grave.

There is no stone to mark his grave, but if there were, it could bear a memorable epitaph:

PETER MAURIN
BECAUSE OF WHOM THERE IS
A LAY APOSTOLATE

MAY 1951

 # Maurin House, Oakland

WILLIAM EVERSON

IN the ventless room,
Over the beds at the hour of rising,
Hangs now the stench and fetor of the crude flesh;
And at the grimed sink
We fill the basin of our mutual use,
Where our forty faces, rinsed daily,
Leaves each its common trace.

Is it then in this?
In this alone, then, that we find our oneness?
We never in cleanness, never in purity
Have ever truly met?

Oh my brothers! each brings our sin-deformed face to the
     greasy pan!
Is it not a terrible thing to come upon ourselves
Here in each other? In the inalienable commonality
Of our grosser selves? And found there
That sign and testimonial of our secret hearts!
Could it not have been other?
A true revealment of the soul's intent,
A freer gift, welcomed, and most dear?

Far off, in clefted rocks and dells, the springwater
Throbs out the faultless pulse of earth,
A lucent flow.

And God's sheer daylight pours through our shafted sky,
To proffer again the still occasion of His grace
Where we might meet each other.

JULY–OCTOBER 1951

Chrystie Street I

(Excerpts from the regular column)

TOM SULLIVAN

WE WERE VISITED a few days ago by a young man in an army uniform.
He said he had been reading the paper for some time and had several
questions he would like to ask. However now that he finally arrived at
our place he admitted that he couldn't remember them.

Nevertheless he did inquire as to what I thought of his wearing a
uniform in view of the number of articles on pacifism found in our
paper. I thought he looked quite sharp in his uniform and told him

so. I also told him that I was not a pacifist and was not likely to give the retort that he expected. He expressed his pleasure at finding such diversified points of view in our midst.

Then he wanted to know what Peter Maurin would have said regarding the uniform. As I seldom knew Peter to give a direct answer to a question I thought it was a late date to start in now for him and I sort of thought that Peter would have told the young man to read the life of the Curé d'Ars who deserted army and uniform during his life.

Recently we heard from a woman up in Woodstock, New York, who knew Peter Maurin before he began *The Catholic Worker*. She tells us that Peter was teaching French up there at the time. One incident in connection with Peter that she revealed to us made us glow all over. It seems that he inserted an ad in a local newspaper stating that he was starting a fund of money to which all readers were welcomed to contribute. Also those in need were just as welcome to borrow from this fund. There were to be no interest rates and no one was to be coerced to repay his loan at any specified date. The story ended as everyone but Peter would expect. The initial deposit by Peter disappeared rapidly through loans that were never repaid nor were there any other contributors besides Peter.

No one seemed to know where this woman came from. But she was standing in the office looking for the one in charge of the money. She demanded in a strident tone, "Who is in charge here? I want to pay this seventy-five cents for my supper. You see a priest uptown gave me two dollars and I insist on paying for my meal. I know what you people are up against."

Since two dollars was all she had in the world we firmly suggested that she eat with us and hold on to her money. She flatly refused to eat unless we accepted, which we finally did. During the meal this middle-aged woman's story fairly gushed out.

"Christ knows my heart is broke. The city placed my baby boy in a home. I am what is known as an incompetent mother. Just because I have no husband and make my living singing in local taverns.

"Tonight being Saturday I was thinking of going over to Newark and see if I couldn't make enough to pay for my room rent. Then again maybe I would be better off if I went to confession and to communion in the morning. It may help me to get my baby back."

The poor woman left us that night and we learned during the following week that she had been committed to a mental institution in the process of trying to effect the release of her child. However a priest friend is following the case.

Each month I spend some brief minutes trying to visualize the make-up and the printed material of the next issue of our paper. The same question always rears its beautiful head: How would the paper look without this column for the month?

The identical answer is right there beside the question. I find it easier to write the column than to answer people's queries as to why I didn't write this month.

This is all due to the fiction that I am reluctant to write, at least until the very last minute. Besides which, I dislike writing due to my lack of talent. It kills you to know you haven't got it.

This month I came very close to not writing this column because of the New York Giants' and Brooklyn Dodgers' baseball series play-off. I became emotionally involved as to a choice of a winner. You have to know who your team is. And I didn't. I wanted the Giants to win since they were bereft of the pennant for thirteen years, but I also pulled for Brooklyn simply because of their universal appeal. Besides, Brooklyn was the first major-league team to hire a colored player, thus breaking the racial discrimination practiced by all of the big-league teams.

What has all this to do with the Chrystie Street column? Well, that is what I was saying. You see, the lay apostles or reasonable facsimiles thereof as a rule are generally not interested in sports and usually peer at you very disapprovingly when you mention this indelicate subject.

So you can see that I am in no mood to be writing about the really important issues that we usually deal with. Such as the plight of the little people caught up in the terrible everyday predicament of life's injustices. Right now I feel cheated by having to meet a deadline with this tripe when I could be listening to the first game of the World Series.

A missionary priest who recently returned from his work in China spent a couple of hours with us the other day. He was probably the most informed person regarding the affairs of China that we have had the good fortune to come in contact with.

He sat in our office and spoke to us for almost two hours, commenting on one thing and another in China. Finally we asked him what political group in that country seemed to have the general welfare of the people at heart. This priest quickly replied that he thought that neither the former regime of Chiang Kai-shek nor the present rulers were the desirable directors of the people's welfare. He stated that the Chiang Kai-shek politicians were thoroughly corrupt from start to finish, at least from everything he saw and heard. He said that the present rulers aside from their persecution of religion were pestering the poor people to death with continuous indoctrination of their ideas from early morning till late at night. Although he did state that the present regime is breaking up the huge estates. This missionary priest saw only one group in the country that seemed to have the correct program for the country. They are a socialist group, small in number and lacking in any strong outside recognition or backing.

Before you dear readers begin to remind us, we do want to tell you that we are aware that the feast of the Little Flower is on the third of October. A couple of other careless proofreaders and I were responsible for permitting the mistake to slip by in our October appeal. If I had been properly impressed with the Little Flower's humility as described in the Office for that day I probably wouldn't have mentioned the other culprits nor I guess would I have mentioned the Office.

MARCH 1952

❊ A Friend of the Family

DOROTHY DAY

SOMEWHERE IN THE PSALMS it says that we can look forward to three score years and ten, if we are strong, but any more years are toil and trouble. Undoubtedly they are, but I suppose most people want to hang on to this life, life they know, as long as possible. Not that anyone will ever be ready for death in the sense that they feel prepared to face God and the judgment. Old Maurice O'Connell, who lived with us from 1936 to 1947 at Maryfarm, Easton, Pennsylvania lived to be eighty-four. After *The Catholic Worker* moved to Newburgh, Maurice remained behind. When the priest from St. Bernard's Church came to anoint him a few weeks before his death he announced jauntily that he would drop in to see him next time he was in Easton. His appearance there was not so casual. Yesterday, February 26, a requiem Mass was sung at ten o'clock and the body of Mr. O'Connell was laid in a grave in St. Bernard's cemetery, behind St. Joseph's Church, up on the Palisade over the Lehigh River. It was a clear, spring-like day, though the ground was hard under foot.

I thought, as the coffin was being lowered into the grave, a cheap grey coffin of proper shape but God knows what materials, the handles decorative rather than functional, that Mr. O'Connell had made a coffin for me back in 1940 or so, but that he had not made himself one. I should have brought him mine and let Hans Tunneson make me another. The coffin he made for me is of proper size and varnished with the bright yellow varnish that he had used on the altar, the sacristy closet, and the benches which he had made for our chapel at Easton,

Pennsylvania, when Father Palmer and Father Woods first came to vacation with us back in 1937.

Mr. O'Connell put in a lot of work on that chapel. The altar, vestment closet and benches are all now in use at Maryfarm, Newburgh, and will be for many a year to come.

In addition to my coffin, which my daughter now uses to store blankets and other bedding, and the chapel furnishings, Mr. O'Connell took an old tool shed and made himself a comfortable little house in which he lived for all the last years of his life, until this last year, when he went to the Smiths and Christophers and boarded there. He had an old-age pension and so preserved a strong feeling of independence. He enjoyed being with the children. He helped John Filiger remodel his chicken house and he constructed the Montague and Buley houses, all of them long rectangular affairs that could be divided into three or four rooms, small and narrow like the emergency barracks veterans are forced to live in now, utilitarian, with tar-paper-covered roofs and sides, neither beautiful nor imaginative.

We had to remind ourselves very often of how much Mr. O'Connell had done for us in the years that we lived at Easton because he possessed a violent temper. He was, in fact, something of a terror. He came from Ireland so many years ago that he remembered, he said, when Canal Street was not a street but a canal. He was one of twenty-one children, and his father was an athlete and a carpenter. Maurice pictured him as a jaunty lad with his children, excelling in feats of strength and looked upon with admiring indulgence by his wife, who, according to Maurice, nursed all her children herself, baked all her bread, spun and wove, did all her housekeeping and never failed in anything. It was, indeed, a picture of the valiant woman that Maurice used to draw for us when any of the women were not able to nurse their children (not to speak of other failures).

He was an old soldier and had worn many a uniform, in South Africa, in India, and in this country. He had no truck with pacifists. And as for community!

According to St. Benedict, there should be a benevolent old man at the gate to receive the visitors, welcome them as other-Christs, exemplify hospitality.

Maurice's little cabin was on the road at the very entrance of the farm, and he never missed a visitor. If they were shabby he shouted at them; if well dressed, he was more suave. He had many a tale to tell of his fellows in the community. He was not a subtle man. His thought was simple, not involved. "Thieves, drunkards and loafers, the lot of them," he would characterize those who make up what was intended to be a farming commune. And if anyone living on the farm had any skill, it was, "what jail did ye learn that in?" One man who became a Catholic after living with us for a year was greeted with taunts and jeers each time he passed the cabin door. "Turncoat! Ye'd change yer faith for a bowl of soup!"

He was ready with his fists too, and his age of course protected him. Once when he was infuriated by a woman guest who was trying to argue him into a more cooperative frame of mind, he beat his fist into a tree and broke all his knuckles. A violent and enraged man, if any one differed from him, was Mr. O'Connell.

By the ninth year of Mr. O'Connell's stay with us, he had all the tools of the farm locked up in his cabin and would guard them with a shotgun. That first winter when Peter and Father Roy and the men had a dormitory in the barn, Mr. O'Connell became ill and was persuaded to be nursed in the dormitory. He was kept warm and comfortable, meals were brought to him on a tray, and he soon recovered his vigor. He decided to stay for the cold months and ensconced himself by the side of the huge potbellied stove. One end of the barn was the sanctuary, and was separated with curtains from the center where the stove, benches, chairs and bookshelves were. Peter and Mr. O'Connell sat for hours in silence, the latter with his pipe and a book, Peter motionless, his chin sunk in a great sweater that all but engulfed him. Mr. O'Connell was a great reader of history, but it was hard to understand him when he was trying to make a dissertation, especially when his teeth were out, as they usually were.

It was a difficult few months, especially in the mornings. We sang the Mass every day, thanks to Father Roy, and Mr. O'Connell did not enjoy this at seven in the morning. He had been used to sleeping until ten or eleven. On occasion his very audible grumbling was supplemented by a banging on the floor of the dormitory with his shoe. Taken to task for this he would snarl, "I was just emptying the sand out of my shoe." It was a winter when we had to dig ourselves out to the outhouses.

When Lent came we were reading Newman's sermons during meals, and whether it was because Maurice did not like Newman as an Englishman, or a convert (he decidedly did not like converts), or whether it was because he thought the reading was directed at him, he used to stomp angrily away from the table and refuse to eat. Stanley had always gotten along well with him (he had never worked with him), but Stanley had a habit when he was reading pointed chapters from the *Imitation,* or Newman, of saying, "This is meant for Dorothy," or "This is meant for Hans." Mr. O'Connell decided the reading was meant for him, and would put up with it no longer. He moved back to his cabin, and his meals were brought to him on a tray. When spring came, he came up to the kitchen and fetched them himself.

The cooking was good that winter. Either Hans or Duncan managed the kitchen, and "we never had it so good." Especially since Father Roy used to go down to the A&P on a Saturday night and beg their leftovers. They were very generous, especially with cold-storage fish or turkeys that would not last, even in the icebox, until Monday. Part of our Sunday preparation was cleaning fish and fowl and seeing what we could do to preserve them. I shudder now when I think of the innards, so soft that all parts seemed to merge into one. However, we had good cooks. And most of the time we had simple foods that did not need to be disguised.

It was about that time, spring and summer, when many retreatants came, that Mr. O'Connell took to telling them all that we never gave him anything to eat, never anything to wear. The fact was that we respected his distaste for complicated dishes, and he had a regular order in at the grocer's for eggs, cheese, milk, bread and margarine and canned soups. Not to speak of the supplies on our kitchen shelves which Maurice (or anyone else) felt free to come and help himself to. Our cooks had good training in "if anyone asks for your coat, let him have your cloak too. To him that asks give and do not turn him away, and do not ask for a return of what is borrowed."

As Father Roy would say, "If you wish to grow in love, in supernatural love, then all natural love must be pruned, as the vine is pruned. It may not look as though love were there, but have faith."

We were being pruned, all right. Not only through Mr. O'Connell but on all sides. Putting it on the most natural plane, I used to think, "How sure people are of us that we believe in what we say, that all men are brothers, that we are a family, that we believe in love, not in use of force, that we would never put them out no matter how hard we are tried. If they act 'naturally' with no servility even to an extreme of showing bitterness and hatred, then one can only count that as a great victory. We believe in a *voluntary* cooperation. Our faith in these ideas must be tried as though by fire."

And then I would look upon Maurice with gratitude and with pity, that God should choose him to teach us such lessons. It was even as though he were a scapegoat, bearing the sins of ingratitude, hatred, venom, suspicion for all the rest of us, all of it gathered together in one hardy old man.

And, on the other hand, to go with these subtleties, what about this business of letting the other fellow get away with it? Isn't there something awfully smug about such piety—building up your own sanctification at the expense of the increased guilt of someone else? This turning of the other cheek, this inviting someone else to be a potential murderer, or thief, in order that we might grow in grace—how obnoxious! In that case I'd rather be the striker than the meek one struck. One would all but rather be a sinner than a saint at the expense of the sinner. In other words, we must be saved together.

And so I firmly believe, I have faith, that Maurice O'Connell, in addition to being a kind of friend who built the furniture of our chapel and some barracks for our families, who sat and fed the birds and talked ever kindly to the children on the sunny steps before his little house, was an instrument chosen by God to make us grow in wisdom and faith and love.

God rewarded him at the end. He received consciously the great sacrament of the Church, Extreme Unction, he was surrounded by little children to the end, and even at his grave he had the prayers of kind friends; he had all any Pope or King could receive at the hands of the Church, a Christian burial in consecrated ground. May he rest in peace.

MARCH 1952

❈ Chrystie Street II

TOM SULLIVAN

I SAT IN OUR LIBRARY this afternoon listening to Bishop Fulton Sheen broadcast his Sunday sermon. The Bishop was in his usual style, which hasn't changed in years. He always conveys the feeling to me that I am now getting my final instructions just before The Last Judgment. As the Bishop preached, Frank, our radiodial jockey, addressed several comments towards the receiving set. When the Bishop mentioned the woman at the well asking Christ for the Living Water, Frank snarled, "Everybody is always asking for something." As the Bishop made the point that the worst sinners against impurity stood a better chance for salvation than those who had sinned against pride, Frank broke in at the pause and said, "I wish you would come down here and tell that to this gang who are running *The Catholic Worker.*"

While Frank was indulging in this peculiar dialogue with the voice from the radio, a shivering stranger walked into the room in search of a coat. Someone found an extra coat for the stranger and he sat down to read a copy of *The Catholic Worker.* Shortly after he began to read the paper I noticed him study the Chrystie Street column. His eyes dilated and his cheeks puffed out as though he were going to spit on it. This, I couldn't watch any longer.

At the other end of the room an elderly woman sat waiting for the next meal; we had just finished lunch. Age had not proved any deterrent in her maintenance of a facial makeup, even to the penciled eyebrows.

She was engaged in a cross-examination of another visitor from the deep South. He wears a railroad engineer's cap and an army overcoat plus a pair of blue jeans. He supplies a considerable amount of the intellectual life around the house with his comic-strip books that he fishes out of local garbage cans and wastebaskets. The woman was asking him about this Southern hospitality that she had so often heard about. She wanted to know wherein it differed from the New York variety.

One morning last week an irritated handyman from the theater next door paid us an unpleasant visit. He sternly informed us that the owners of the theater had mailed a protest to the city authorities. It seems that their complaint is against the men who line up for our morning and afternoon coffee and soup. To keep themselves warm in the early hours of the morning while waiting for John Derry to start the serving of the coffee, the men are wont to build fires against the walls of the theater. The fires blacken and soften the bricks, so the handyman claims.

We agreed to speak to the men along the line regarding this matter. We did not consider this fire-building detrimental and hated the thought of having to tell the men that they would have to freeze and like it during these bitter mornings. Consequently, we decided to bring an equalizer into the conversation with this emissary from the theater. Human rights and values come first before property rights. So we proceeded to point out several complaints we had against the theater. In a kind but threatening voice we replied to the visitor that we could make things awfully difficult for the theater owners if we cared to go to the proper authorities. He went hard for that line and finally left our house stating that he was sure that we could all get along with one another.

St. Francis and His Revolution

ROBERT LUDLOW

THOSE who placed their hopes in political means during the recent elections and were disappointed, as they would have been eventually disillusioned if their candidate had won, might do well to pause in this busy world of ours and think somewhat on St. Francis and the method of St. Francis. "St. Francis," states Father Meyers, "effected his revolution on an entirely different field. To effect the change, he did not kill a single human being, he sequestered not a single man's property, closed up not one man's business, inaugurated no new banking policy, initiated not a single repressive measure, wrote not a single law into the codes of the day, indicted no political instrument." But, it will be objected, that is all very well and good. It is an area of life that was open to the technique of St. Francis, but we are concerned with the political, with economic systems, with day to day living, and what else is there but that we should go about those things in the only way we know how? We must elect our man and then you will see our ideas realized. Yet this is precisely the point—St. Francis, who eschewed violence and politics, was more instrumental in effecting the downfall of an undesirable social system than were any politicians of his day, or any committees, or any organized groups of dissidents. Says Father Meyers: "Francis struck at the iniquity of it—especially with two provisions of the rule of the Third Order. One was the provision that Tertiaries must not bear arms, the other was that Tertiaries must bind themselves with no oath, except where duly constituted authority rightfully required it." And it must be remembered that literally thousands of lay people joined the Third Order, so much so that the feudal lords were beside themselves with wrath and appealed to Rome to stop this madness. This madness which deprived them of serfs because the Third Order members refused to bear arms or to take oaths of fealty to the lords.

And it must be remembered that St. Francis regarded the rule of the Third Order to be a rule that was applicable to the ordinary Christian. It was no specific rule for the clergy; it was meant for all of the laity. And how popular is this pacifism of St. Francis today, how popular with the Franciscans? How popular with the members of the Third Order? How many of them know the sixteenth rule of the Third Order, "They are not to take up lethal weapons, or bear them about, against anybody"? Can we imagine the revolution it would cause should this rule be enforced among members of the Third Order so that they would all, as a matter of course, become conscientious objectors? But the same fate has befallen this idea of St. Francis as has happened with much else that he taught. Not only has this been true of St. Francis but of pretty much of all the pacifism in the Church. It has been made harmless by relegating it to the purely individual actions of clerics. St. John Chrysostom once wrote "We ought to be ashamed of ourselves, who act so differently when as wolves we rush upon our adversaries." (*Breviary*, June 11) And now, in the liturgy which bears the name of St. John Chrysostom (and which, of course, was not actually written by him) we are called on to pray, "For the honorable government of our country and its military forces . . . to aid it in battle and vanquish every enemy and adversary." So are the saints dishonored when we canonize them to make them harmless! So may the day come when we harken to their message and eliminate the vestiges of militarism and nationalism that have found their way into our very liturgy.

Of St. Francis, Father Meyers states: "Coercion, therefore, of another person against the latter's convictions was as repugnant to him as sin. Violence had no appeal to him, not even against Saracen or bandit. Similarly whatever amounted to compulsion, such as reducing his neighbor to a plight where self-preservation demanded his surrender to terms, was odious to him . . ." He was similarly opposed to repressive measures "because when you use violent repressive measures, you challenge secret resentment; what the victims cannot do publicly, they do in secret. Hence the tide of rebellious and satiric writings, mostly anonymous, characteristic of that day . . ." The attitude of St. Francis toward violence (he ignored the Crusades and went his own way unarmed to visit the Sultan), towards repression, is so much in advance of his time that many today look on him simply as a humanitarian born ahead of time. And, while there is a sense in which this is true, it must yet be remembered that, for St. Francis, it was merely a reiteration of what was contained in the message of Christ; it was no new teaching, and it was a teaching having supernatural sanction. It represented a development in natural law inasmuch as it applied to the social field the conclusions of revelation. It was superior to the logic of the philosophers who thought only in terms of a mechanical equality of justice; it went beyond that mischievous conception of ethics which, admitting the superiority of the Christian conception, yet felt called upon to accept an inferior brand suited to the condition of fallen man, hence, for all purposes, constructing a relativistic system in the name of Christianity. St. Francis did not so much oppose this as he ignored it and went about demonstrating the better way. He did not stop to argue theories about just and unjust wars, he simply stated that, should people (clerical or laity) wish to follow the path he laid down they simply did not bear arms; there was no argument about it, one accepted the position or one did not.

Wherein lay the strength of St. Francis? He traveled first the road of purgation. In Felix Timmerman's book, *The Perfect Joy of St. Francis,* we read of the days of sadness which burdened the soul of Francis as he wandered from place to place thinking of the flesh and feeling the pull of the flesh so that peace was a stranger to his mind; and we, who have not outlived this stage, feel kinship with him in his loneliness. But he emerged from the compulsive tyranny of the flesh, as those emerge who experience sex as liberation and joy. But for Francis, since he had chosen another path and was vowed to celibacy, his liberation came in a higher adjustment, in an awakening of consciousness, in the development of the super-conscious. "In the man whose thoughts dwell on the ranges of sense," we are taught in the Bhagavad-Gita, "arise attachments to them; from attachment is born love, from love springs wrath." And as St. Francis surmounted this, he realized that other saying of the Bhagavad-Gita: "He whose mind is undismayed in pain, who is freed from longings for pleasure, from whom passion, fear and wrath have fled, is called a man of abiding prudence, a saintly man." "My God and my all"—again and ever did Francis utter this phrase, for it was by participation in divinity that he became a free man, as light entered his whole being, as super-consciousness dominated, as he began to live outside of compulsive behavior, as much as it is given man to do so, then did he give forth in strength; as he lost himself in God, so did he resurrect a freedom undreamed of as long as it remains chained in potency by the ego.

St. Francis felt the redemption not only in himself, not only in all mankind, but in the earth itself and the birds and the beasts and the fishes of the waters. For St. Francis emerged from his purgation, not as a cold and austere ascetic, but loving and warm and tender. "Little brother rabbit," he cried, "come here to me. Why did you let yourself be trapped that way?" "Sister lark has a cowl like the religious have, and a humble bird she is. She is happy going along the road to find a few kernels for herself. Even if she must find them among dung she picks them out and eats them." "Notice that sheep there walking along so meek among those goats and their does: I tell you it was like that that our Lord Jesus Christ went about meek and lowly among the Pharisees and chief priests. I beg you therefore, son, to have pity on this poor little sheep with me for love of Him." "Be praised, my Lord, through Sister Water, for greatly useful, lowly, precious, chaste, is she." For Francis all things partook in some sense of divinity. And so we bear an affinity to all things; in and through all things the light of God shines, the divine syllable echoes, the earth closes in and we become all, so that to harm another is to harm ourself, to kill another is to commit suicide. This is no meaningless pantheism; this is the recognition of divine origin that vibrates through all creation redeemed in Christ.

If the revolutions of the right and of the left are shallow, if they are too narrow to satisfy, if they exercise each their own tyranny over man, if political means have demonstrated their uselessness, is it not perhaps that we have left unexplored whole areas of thought and being? If we have debased God to the point where what we call God is a chimera unworthy of the worship of free men, and if, because we know not what to worship, we worship the state or the race or our own compulsions, and if, in all these things, we have found no happiness, and if we then realize that Francis was divinely happy, may we not turn aside some day to learn of him and in doing so learn so much of ourselves that we could never turn back to the old ways or foster the old illusions or trust the old hopes but, in the eternal Francis, find the love and tenderness of God.

FEBRUARY 1953

❀ Five Years on the Land

JACK AND MARY THORNTON

WE READ DOROTHY'S ARTICLE in the December issue about the land movement and its hardships, and it inspired us to give a short report on our activities on the land.

It is now over five years since we have been married and have been gone from the CW, and, except for a brief stay in New York, and one year in Toronto, we have been on the land ever since. This is quite a while to spend at any activity, and one would suspect that we had learned quite a bit. We haven't learned very much. Having been born and reared in the city we did not know how to work, and this proved to be the cause of most of our troubles. Having had little capital, we never quite had enough tools and equipment. Spending quite a bit of time around the CW did not prepare us for the ways of the world of business, and we have been trusting where we should have been cautious, naive where we should have been wise. In short, we have been fools in the ways of the world, and, we hope, for Christ's sake. But in spite of all our trials and tribulations we are still on the land, though we haven't made much progress in farming it, and we still believe as Peter did, in Cult, Culture and Cultivation.

We have been on this farm since last May, and plan on staying here for some time to come. However, our record for sticking in one spot has not been enviable, for we seem to be only a little more stable than migratory workers. What this particular farm can use to great advantage is an experienced farmer and capital, neither of which we have. It needs an experienced farmer because the farm has been lying idle for fifteen years and there is not a decent blade of grass on it. It needs money because every building on the place is in need of repair, including the house. Only a few weeks ago we had to fell the ceiling in the living room as it was hanging precariously and we were afraid it would fall on someone. We have the new ceiling ready to put up and are waiting for someone to come along and help with it. Frank Coyle arrived the last time we had a ceiling problem.

The farm consists of eighty acres, a house, and several dilapidated outbuildings. There are no modern improvements in the house, such as running water, bath or toilet. We do have electricity though, and also propane gas. The water can be had by just stepping out the back door. Recently we purchased a tractor, on the installment plan, and expect to get something accomplished next spring. So far we have managed to plow up enough ground to put in an acre and a half of wheat. The whole process took well over a month. First we had to get the money for the seed and fertilizer, then we tried in vain to borrow a grain drill. People in this area do not like to lend their equipment. Finally we got a man to promise to come and plant it for us, but it rained before he could get around to it. It rained for about ten days and it was another two weeks before the ground was dry enough for planting. Finally, we hired a man to put it in and he came with a mammoth rig and did the job in about ten minutes. As one neighbor put it, it cost us more to put that wheat in than it would to go down to the feed mill and buy the same amount we might realize from the harvest. Next year it will be different though, at least with the wheat.

After we got the tractor we went to a sale to see if we could get a little equipment and some stock. We purchased a pair of small pigs, a side-delivery rake, a buzz saw and an old phonograph. The next day was Sunday, and after Mass and a leisurely breakfast, Mary shouted from the yard that the pigs were loose and headed for the highway. I bolted out the front door just in time to see them rounding the house onto the highway. I gave chase but they slowly widened the gap and never stopped running until they were clean out of sight. I chased them all over the countryside to no avail. We finally captured them after three or four hours, by hiding in the brush and diving on them as they came by. Things like that always happen on Sunday when you are in your good clothes. Several days later we decided to hook up the buzz saw and saw some wood. The wood was cutting fine, but the ashes were hitting me in the face, which seemed odd, and several times the log I was sawing cut loose and flew away. Finally one of the logs hit me on the wrist and I knew something was wrong. The trouble was that a John Deere tractor pulley runs backward and you have to put a hitch in the belt to get the saw to run right. These are some of the obstacles that you run into when you are trying to learn to farm by yourself.

We are partial to horses and would like to have gotten a team, but since we have no hay and no fencing they were out of the question. Besides, if you work off the farm, as we always have, it is difficult to get anything accomplished with horses. On the other hand, the fertilizer the horses provide is invaluable to the good life of the farm, and if there is one thing this farm needs above all others it's manure. I am employed as a janitor for the local grade and high school. It is a job that certainly is important to the community; there is a good deal of responsibility attached to it, and plenty of hard work. It is an ideal job in these respects. But like all jobs of this nature, it is low paying. In point of fact, only an old man who has raised his family or a single person could get by on the wages it pays, and most generally, those are the kind of people who are left with the responsibility of these jobs.

Are we discouraged? Well, somewhat. Who wouldn't be if we didn't seem to be able to do anything right? It is not encouraging to work the better part of a day on something without success, only to have someone come along and solve the problem in a matter of minutes. But we had little or no experience in any of these things and the mistakes are perfectly natural. However, this is the kind of situation that eventually breeds discouragement and finally abandonment. It is all too true of the land movement, in this country and in England, that many people were interested in it and liked to talk about it, but few took positive steps to prepare themselves for it. We are some of those many people. We would like others to avoid the same pitfalls. However, we still think that if you want to get settled on the land, the thing to do is to get on it and wrestle with it. But if you are young and not married it would be wise to learn something about farming.

Several years ago there was a series of articles or letters in *Commonweal* on the land movement. I recall that one gentleman remarked that it was a shame and a waste of talent that many young couples went onto the land, underwent almost unbelievable hardships, and returned to the city, sadly disillusioned and almost misanthropic, when otherwise they might have made a valuable contribution to society. This is always the risk that is run by people with idealistic tendencies. They seize upon an idea, and without stopping to consider the whys and wherefores jump into a situation, only to find that it is a spot where even angels fear to tread without preparation. But we think that the greater shame lies with those many who felt the call to the land, and for one reason or another put it off and are now engaged in other activities. There were many who saw the vision of the green revolution and liked what they saw. Many who dreamed a dream once, but never quite got around to doing anything about it. If all those who felt the call to the land had done something about it, their contribution to society would be great indeed. Some wag said that few people carry radicalism and idealism past thirty-five, intimating that by that time they learn something. This seems to be the awful truth. Sure it is tough on the land. The hardships and humiliating defeats are sometimes almost impossible to bear. But life is a struggle, and who wants to be afraid of life? Do not all spiritual writers tell us about the invaluableness of suffering? Yet most of us bend our every effort trying to avoid suffering, poverty, discomfort.

It is always a temptation to avoid suffering, but once you get on the land it quite naturally becomes a part of your life; you can hardly avoid it. It is not easy to rise in the pitch-black darkness on a cold winter morning, praying that there is a little bit of fire left in the stoves, and hoping you remembered to bring the kindling wood in the night before, to drive off to work long before most people are up. But it is a chance to suffer, a chance to put yourself in harmony with people all over the world who have few comforts, little to eat, no leisure. But we really have so much more than over two-thirds of the peoples on earth. We are indeed rich in earthly goods. While burning brush the other day, because it was in our way, we thought of the people in France, in the Middle East, and the boys on Chrystie Street waiting for the morning line to start. How much warmth they could have gotten from all that brush, and how they would like to have had it. Besides, what other alternative has one who wants to raise a large family, who wants to encourage them to accept responsibility, who wants to make an honest living, who is interested in catering to the whole man, who believes in poverty?

But to get back to our particular situation, our farm is like all other CW farms in that it has to be nurtured from without. We do not have the business acumen required to get the better end in a trade or even to break even; to recognize a bargain when we see one; to save for a rainy day; to give service for profit, etc. It seems to take all these things and more to be a successful farmer. Instead, we believe in mutual aid; in helping our neighbor even if he is better off than we are. It is unlike other CW farms in that we see few people, we get little opportunity to attend meetings, engage in discussions, make retreats, or a host of other things peculiar to CW farms. We do not mind receiving alms, in fact were it not for the help we have gotten up till now we would be poor indeed. Our children are all outfitted in cast-off clothes, as we are too; the furniture and household effects we have were given to us. In fact we seem to be getting without being able to give in return. We would much rather be engaged in a program of mutual aid, wherein we get according to our needs and give according to our means. It's true, as Dorothy points out, that the worst position people think they can get in is to be beholden to someone. This seems to be the cardinal sin of this decade. People have got to get even.

We would like to say that the future looks promising for us. Our two pigs are becoming fat, our goat is with kid and will freshen in the spring, our twelve chickens have quit laying but they are keeping the pot filled, and a reader of the CW from Texas is coming up to look for a farm in this neighborhood. And, though we are broke and it is cold out now and the snow is flying, it will not be long till spring when everything in nature will take a new lease on life, including us.

We would like to invite anyone who is interested in settling on the land to come visit with us, or work a little while with us, to become acclimated to some small extent to some of the problems of rural life. It would be an attempt at mutual aid. We would give a little and receive a little. If anyone is interested in purchasing a farm, we would like to say that farms are fairly reasonable in this part of the country and we would be glad to be of some assistance in locating places. We would like very much to give land to some families who would like to live in the country but not necessarily farm, as Lou Murphy did at the Detroit CW farm. However, we will not have title to the land for at least five years, and not a clear title for five more years.

JULY–AUGUST 1953

❧ Meditation on the Death of the Rosenbergs

DOROTHY DAY

AT EIGHT O'CLOCK on Friday, June 19, the Rosenbergs began to go to death. That June evening the air was fragrant with the smell of honey-suckle. Out under the hedge at Peter Maurin Farm, the black cat played with a grass snake, and the newly cut grass was fragrant in the evening air. At eight o'clock I put Nickie in the tub at my daughter's home, just as Lucille Smith was bathing her children at Peter Maurin Farm. My heart was heavy as I soaped Nickie's dirty little legs, knowing that Ethel Rosenberg must have been thinking with all the yearning of her heart of her own soon-to-be-orphaned children.

How does one pray when praying for "convicted spies" about to be electrocuted? One prays always of course for mercy. "My Jesus, mercy." "Lord Jesus Christ, Son of the living God, have mercy on them." But somehow, feeling close to their humanity, I prayed for fortitude for them both. "God let them be strong, take away all fear from them, let them be spared this suffering, at least, this suffering of fear and trembling."

I could not help but think of the story in Dostoievsky's *Idiot,* how Prince Myshkin described in detail the misery of the man about to be executed, whose sentence was commuted at the last moment. This had been the experience of Dostoievsky himself, and he had suffered those same fears, and had seen one of his comrades, convicted with him, led to the firing line, go mad with fear. Ethel and Julius Rosenberg, as their time approached and many appeals were made, must in hoping against hope, holding fast to hope up to the last, have compared their lot to that of Dostoievsky and those who had been convicted with him. What greater punishment can be inflicted on anyone than those two long years in a death house, watched without ceasing so that there is no chance of one taking one's life and so thwarting the vengeance of the state. They had already suffered the supreme penalty. What they were doing, in their own minds no doubt, was offering the supreme sacrifice, offering their lives for their brothers. Both Harold Urey and Albert Einstein, and many other eminent thinkers at home and abroad, avowed their belief in the innocence of these two. They wrote that they did not believe their guilt had been proved.

Leaving all that out of account, accepting the verdict of the court that they were guilty, accepting the verdict of the millions of Americans who believed them guilty, accepting the verdict of President Eisenhower and Cardinal Spellman who thought them guilty—even so, what should be the attitude of the Christian but one of love and great yearning for their salvation?

"Keep the two great commandments, love God and love your neighbor. Do this and thou shalt live." This is in the Gospel; these are the words of Jesus.

Whether or not they believed in Jesus, did the Rosenbergs love God? A rabbi who attended them to the last said that they had been his parishioners for two years. He followed them to the execution chamber reading from the Psalms, the Twenty-third, the Fifteenth, the Thirty-first. Those same psalms Cardinal Spellman reads every week as he reads his breviary, among those hundred and fifty psalms which make up not only the official prayer of the Church, but also the prayers which the Jews say. We used to see our Jewish grocer on the east side, vested for prayer, reciting the psalms every morning behind his counter when we went for our morning supplies. I have seen rabbis on all-night coaches, praying thus in the morning. Who can hear the word of God without loving the word? Who can work for what they conceive of as justice, as brotherhood, without loving God and brother? If they were spies for Russia, they were doing what we also do in other countries, playing a part in international politics and diplomacy, but they indeed were serving a philosophy, a religion, and how mixed up religion can become. What a confusion we have gotten into when Christian prelates sprinkle holy water on scrap metal, to be used for obliteration bombing, and name bombers for the Holy Innocents, for Our Lady of Mercy; who bless a man about to press a button which releases death on fifty thousand human beings, including little babies, children, the sick, the aged, the innocent as well as the guilty. "You know not of what spirit you are," Jesus said to his apostles when they wished to call down fire from heaven on the inhospitable Samaritans.

I finished bathing the children, who were so completely free from preoccupation with suffering. They laughed and frolicked in the tub when the switch was being pulled which electrocuted first Julius and then his wife. Their deaths were announced over the radio half an hour later, jazz music being interrupted to give the bulletin, and the program continuing immediately after.

The next day *The New York Times* gave details of the last hours, and the story was that both went to their deaths firmly, quietly, with no comment. At the last Ethel turned to one of the two police matrons who accompanied her and, clasping her by the hand, pulled her toward her and kissed her warmly. Her last gesture was a gesture of love.

NOVEMBER 1955

❀ Death of a Boy

EILEEN FANTINO DIAZ

RAIN FELL DULL AND LISTLESS on the roofs for the second day puddling on the black tar as a young boy high over the blurred street came to the edge and started down the fire escape. High in his hand was a flash of white and grey, bright against the darkly moving sky. It was a pigeon, one of the many that streaked over the tenements and soared away into the blue air on brighter days when sunlight shoots through the settling dust of afternoons.

He had caught a piece of flight in his arms and was bringing it down into his world, to his cavern of a street where the sky is unconquerable. And his heart was wild with rapture, the wings soft and wet; the eyes of the bird looked into his own as it shook to be free. With his hands full of stirrings, he dropped down like a puppet falls to the stage, dizzy and crazed, six flights down to the sleekly wet street, his head split open by his return.

One small boy came first to gaze at the body, the twisted looseness and the outpouring of anguish which was left of him. This spectator grabbed the pigeon out of the limp hand and beat it with all his strength against the moldy wall of the building until he had only strength for crying. Death again the sudden and cruel joke without sense or beauty or grace, shock breaking the steady humming beat of the rain.

The neighborhood came to express sympathy to the boy's parents and sit in a small room with the still body, strangers came and lived an image of the fire escape slippery with rain and the boy coming down holding a pigeon, and of the fall. Children talked about it, mothers shuddered. The complacency of life looking at death stilled the question, always that question.

The flight of birds is the bright streak of hope in a dark and fearful city. How many hushed wings had those eyes followed off the roofs and into the sky, like a vision of life not shadowed in the rooms of his life and the incessant coming of days. And there on that one dark day-in-his-hand all secrets, the meaning and striving and patience, his face wet with the world's tears falling from the abyss of the sky—this thing in his arms, the soft wings, the power of flight and life outside the prison of his confinement, this moment perhaps he touched God and died.

NOVEMBER 1955

Our Fall Appeal

DOROTHY DAY

Dear Friends of The Catholic Worker:

In the light of our present difficulties it is necessary to restate our position and tell our readers again just what it is we are trying to do—what it means to us to perform the works of mercy, spiritual and corporal. The most important thing in the world to us is to grow in the love of God, to try to do His will. Our Lord Jesus told us that what we do to the least we do to Him. St. Paul told us we are "members one of another, and that when the health of one member suffers, the health of the whole body is lowered."

We believe not only in St. Thomas' doctrine of the common good, but feel it can be affected only if each one of us, alone, realizes his personal responsibility to his brother, that his love for God must be shown in his love for his brother, and that love must be expressed in the works of mercy, practiced personally, at a personal sacrifice. So we live together, here at *The Catholic Worker,* pool resources of money and ability, and so are able to take care of far more than just ourselves.

People have so far lost that sense of personal responsibility that our country is becoming a country of institutions, and a gigantic part of our income goes to support them. State responsibility has come to take the place of personal responsibility. Doctors at mental hospitals and veteran's hospitals have said that a tremendous number of patients could be cared for at home if their families would take the responsibility. On the other hand houses and apartments become smaller and smaller so that there is "no room at the inn." We are able to have fifty in our own home here at Chrystie Street because it is two old houses thrown into one, built at a time when people wanted space. When people come to us we cannot say, "Go, be thou filled," and refer them to an agency. So we have come to be feeding and clothing a vast number of people who come in to us day after day, the lame, the halt and the blind.

But we are not organized as an institution of any kind and the city does not know how to classify us. We are not a multiple dwelling, a rest home, a convalescent home, a shelter or an asylum or a convent. We are a group of people living together under one roof, with one head, which is Charlie McCormack, now that Tom Sullivan has gone to the Trappists. Often I am considered the head, being older and the publisher of the paper. I get the summonses, the complaints. We are not registered as a charitable agency, it has been pointed out. But we hope our dear Lord recognizes us as charitable people. We try to keep the laws and regulations about housing, health and fire prevention, and take as good care of our family as we can. But we find we are always coming up against some ordinance, some infraction. We will always be in trouble with the city and the state because, though we also consider ourselves good citizens and lovers of our country as well as children of God and try to bear our share of the responsibility of brother for brother, the city and the state have come to feel that this is their field (since it has been left to them). A western Bishop said to me once that he did not believe in state ownership of the indigent. God wants man's free service, his freely bestowed love. So we protest and cry out against every infringement of that great gift of God, freedom, our greatest gift, after the gift of life.

That love of brother, that care for his freedom is what causes us to go into such controversial subjects as man and the state, war and peace. The implications of the Gospel, teaching of the works of mercy, lead us into conflict with the powers of this world. Our love of God is a consuming fire. It is a fearful thing to fall into the hands of the living God. It is a living God and a living faith that we are trying to express. We are called to be holy, that is, whole men, in this life of ours. We are trying to follow this call. It has led many of our workers into the priesthood, into Trappist monasteries, into convents. But we as a group, not having *this vocation*, are not classed as a *religious* group, not even as a *Catholic* group, and so do not have the protection of that classification. We are individual Catholics, not Catholic Action.

Many have left us to marry and raise a little community of their own, and endure all the sufferings of trying to lead this life in the factory, on the farm, enduring the frustrations of seeing their talents unused, their best energies of all their work days put into meaningless work in the cities, and not having the help we have of our community life and the assistance of our friends in our houses and farms.

We never intended to have breadlines, to care for so many, but it is always so hard to turn people away. Men out of hospitals, with no place but the public shelter housing other thousands, turned loose on the streets by day. We have had people come in to us from the streets who have died a few weeks after, from their long endured miseries. We still have people coming who sleep in doorways and spend their days with us and share our meals. It is so hard to limit oneself, and then too our Holy Father, Pius XII, told some Sisters once never to be afraid to run up bills for the poor. Of course it always comes back to the fact that we are not an accredited agency. We are not a charitable institution. And we are never going to turn into that because we are trying to make the point, by our lives, by our work, that personal responsibility comes first. We are born alone, we die alone, we must, each one of us, do what we can for God and our brother, not God and country, but God and our brother, as Christ stated it.

We are in difficulties now, not only with our bills, but with the state, with the city. We cannot print our usual fall appeal, without pointing this out. But we are begging you to help us keep going with these ideas of ours about mutual aid, voluntary poverty, and the works of mercy. If we were forced to cease, how great a burden which we are bearing now would fall upon the state or city—mental hospitals and convalescent homes, relief rolls and the breadlines of the Municipal Lodging House. And how many would be just wandering the streets, crouching in doorways. Oh God, look upon the face of Thy Christ in these poor, and help us to keep going.

So we are asking you, as our Lord Himself told us to ask, for your help once more. And may God and His Blessed Mother whose month this most specially is, bless you a hundredfold, heaped up and running over.

In His Love,
DOROTHY DAY

PART IV

Radicals in Action

1956–1965

❊ How Do You Like Our Jail?

DEANE MOWRER

WITH THE STIFF BEARING of authority, starchily efficient, you sit behind your desk which is at the very center of things, there in the main hall of the seventh floor, right next to the bulletin board and the elevators, between the dining room and the recreation room, looking toward either end of the hallway where the long corridors lead off like the arms of a cross down the rows of cells squatly frowning behind their ponderous barred gates. The morning hubbub has subsided. Most of the girls and women—they are preponderantly young, it seems—have taken the elevators to work assignments in laundry, kitchen, clinic, or prison offices. You can relax now; at least a little. And so it is I find you sitting, with your slightly sardonic eye and gleaming badge, as I pass somewhat awkwardly by with mop and pail toward my own particular cleanup operation in corridor A. This is my second day, the second of a five-day sentence. Yesterday you had said: "I remember you gals from last summer. You're not American. You're just impossibles." A woman prisoner at work nearby had caught up the derisive "impossibles" and sent the unflattering label tumbling down the corridors. To refuse to take shelter in an air-raid drill—no self-respecting criminal would be guilty of such. But then there had been that priest to see Dorothy—and Father McCoy he was, too—and all those telephone calls full of concern for her. You say no more about "impossibles." But as you see me coming, you can't resist hurling the question in your strident official voice: "How do you like our jail, Deane?" Again volatile guffaws of a prisoner proclaim this an official witticism, and the ensuing parrot-like cacophony covers my confusion as I falter a would-be non-committal, "It's interesting."

Now with the free unhurried view of retrospection, I recall your question and try to phrase a more specific reply.

How do I like "our jail"? You were right to say *our;* for ultimately each of us participates, I think, in the guilt of our time, is jailer as well as jailed. But to answer your question—suppose I said I liked it. Would you conclude that I am homesick for that narrow cell with the two uncomfortable cots, the cold toilet seat by the window, the slow-draining lavatory, the hard concrete floor, the dirty tiled walls, the cramped space where we could only sidle circumspectly? Yet there was a window cleverly contrived to open, pane by narrow pane; the good fresh air came in; and on a sunny day a large splash of sunlight fell across the little metal table where we could take turns sitting—toilet seat for chair—and write letters with a borrowed stub of pencil. And we could pray; even say our rosary, though our beads had been confiscated. Counting the *aves* on our fingers served with us as it has with many others; but then a fellow prisoner lent Dorothy a rosary which we shared to both pass and redeem the time.

How do I like our jail? Suppose I said I thought that it was holy. Would you think that I am referring to the chapel which we were not permitted to visit? Or to the religious literature and spiritual guidance which were so markedly not in evidence? Nor do I mean the touching little shrines which some of the longer term prisoners had been permitted to construct in their cells. Nor the many acts of kindness which we experienced and witnessed. Yet I found holiness there—great holiness. I saw Christ templed in suffering, in those imprisoned ones whom He commended to us so particularly: "I was in prison, and you came to me. . . . Amen I say to you, as long as you did it to one of these my least brethren, you did it to me." I heard His voice over the wailing love-hungry dissonance of Negro blues, the flamelike abandon of Spanish song, the defiant shriek of obscenity. I heard Him cry again: "Father, forgive them, for they know not what they do." And I knew that He was speaking not only of them but also of me, of you, of all of us who are imprisoned in this world, who wear the shackles of selfishness, who have participated actively or passively in man's inhumanity to man, who have forgotten or remember so seldom that we can love God only through loving our neighbor.

FEBRUARY 1957

❀ Life Behind Bars

DOROTHY DAY

WHEN I THINK of the long sentences served by so many others in so many miscarriages of justice, when I think of the accumulation of prisons, outmoded and futile, that dot the land of the free, I am not particularly interested in writing about my few days in jail last month. I am just glad that I served them, and am ready to serve again if there is another compulsory air-raid drill next summer. It is a gesture perhaps, but a necessary one. Silence means consent, and we cannot consent to the militarization of our country without protest. Since we believe that the air-raid drills are part of a calculated plan to inspire fear of the enemy instead of the love which Jesus Christ told us we should feel toward him, we must protest these drills. It is an opportunity to show we mean what we write when we repeat over and over that man is here on this earth to love God and His brother. We love our country and have no wish to give up citizenship. Peter Maurin felt himself to be not a Frenchman or an American, but first of all a Catholic, but just the same he loved both the country of his birth and his adopted country, where he had worked for forty years.

It was good to have the opportunity to "visit the prisoner" which is one of the works of mercy, even for so brief a visit, by being a prisoner oneself. One of the Little Sisters of Charles de Foucauld has had herself committed to a prison in France in order that she might live with her less fortunate sisters, and in her confinement live a life of work and prayer.

We have no complaint to make of the prison or of the attendants there. Our physical needs were supplied: blankets, sheets, towels, clothing. What if the clothing was a bit coarse, unbleached muslin and not cut to fit? What if the dress was a purple sack coming just below the knees? I would not say we were clothed with modesty, nor in Christian fashion, but we were clothed. Our food was coarse but adequate, a little too much rice and spaghetti of course. The cells were tiny and crowded but they were both warm and airy. One could open the window as wide as one liked, one or all of the five little panes. One pane of glass even was clear so that we could look out on Greenwich Avenue, on the swirling snow, the slushy streets, the people rushing to and fro, the brightly lit stores, the flower shop, food stores, all in the heart of Greenwich Village.

We were given thorough physical examinations, even to X-rays and Wasserman tests. There was a recreation room on the roof, a beauty parlor, a craftshop and in the few days we were there we were taught by a gentle teacher to make some brass enameled ashtrays. If there had been more time we would have worked in clay, leather, bound a book, dressed dolls.

The "ladies" as they called us worked in the laundry, kitchen, sewing rooms, cleaning and so on. We were given mop and pail to clean the corridors. But there was never enough work for the five hundred or so prisoners, so there were many idle. I saw one girl display with pride a dress she had made for herself, so there is a chance to learn a few useful things.

But the sadness of it all is that aside from talking day in and day out about freedom, and "how much time you got" and "when do you get out?" there are some there who are truly happy. Quite a few of the women who have lived with us at St. Joseph's House of Hospitality have spent short terms for disorderly conduct and drinking, and I remember one Jean especially. She was staying with us on Staten Island and as we all sat around the table one night sewing and talking (she was playing solitaire) she suddenly said, "I never was so happy as when I was in the clink." Born and bred on the Bowery, of a drunken father and mother, all her family scattered, she looked upon the jail as a place of comfort and security, a place where she could not get into much trouble, where there was warmth and companionship and movies on Saturday night and television every night until nine, and nobody expecting much of her, just taking her as she was. It is sad too that there is nothing much to come out to, not enough hospices, just the prospect of going back to the same old taverns to find your friends, to the same old work with its tensions and dirt and insecurity, and far more expected of you than you are able to give.

"I don't like to work," one little Puerto Rican said to me. She spent most of her time lying on her cot, singing melancholy songs. "What kind of work were you doing?" "Laundry work and I'm here for being a pickpocket," and she covered her face with her hands in mock shame and laughed at me.

Why are the jails so full, and why are the searches so rigid? And why are they all so young, these girls that fill the four corridors on the six or seven floors of the House of Correction which are used as cell blocks? It is mostly drugs, and the girls themselves say the problem is hopeless. "We will get out, and then we will be here again."

I remembered an article I had read in the magazine section of *The New York Times* on drug addiction, and the way it is handled in England and the way it is handled here. "Of course it is not a crime," one of the officers said to me. "But it is treated as a crime, and it certainly leads to more crime." The *Times* has also called the Women's Detention Prison a "black hole," because it is overcrowded, because girls are held there long before trial as well as after conviction. But physically speaking, it is not a black hole. The sad fact remains that it is more comfortable physically than many a slum tenement with its overcrowding, its vermin, its cold and dark and lack of hot water.

Our physical needs are cared for, but certainly not the spiritual. If you go in on Monday, you do not see a priest until the following Saturday, and if you ask for rosary or prayer book or Bible, you do not get it. And you wonder if there is any visitation, any preaching, any telling the stories of the lives of the saints, any glimpse for these prisoners of any other kind of life than the one they know of the flesh. Or is it only a half-hour Mass, one half-hour out of the one hundred and sixty-eight hours of the week, thirty minutes out of the ten thousand eighty minutes of the week?

APRIL–MAY 1959

❀ CW Staff Member Arrested by FBI

CHARLES BUTTERWORTH

"DON IS A DESERTER from the Army," said Agent McKeon and showed me Don's picture. He had found me alone in the office that day. "I don't want to get into this," I replied. "You will have to talk to Bob." Maybe Bob was somewhere around, so I left the office to look. Going back to the kitchen, I saw Don. It all happened so quickly. "There's a man in the office you don't want to see." "Who's that?" smiled Don. "A man from the government." There was a kind of a serious pause and then Don turned, got his jacket, and left.

About two weeks later agents McKeon and Stratton returned. They had learned that I had chosen to help Don instead of the FBI. It was suggested I go with them to talk to someone at the U.S. Court House, and I went voluntarily to clarify our general position. There was a wait and Agent McKeon asked with interest about my coming into the Church and all about the farm, the chapel, the crops and the animals.

The man I was to talk with didn't want to see me, and Agent Stratton arranged a complaint against me. He mentioned that my failure to cooperate would mean that much more money would have to be spent to find Don.

The complaint reads in part: "Butterworth, the defendant herein, knowing that an offense against the United States had been committed, did unlawfully, willfully and knowingly receive, relieve, comfort and assist the offender in order to hinder and prevent his apprehension, trial, and punishment in violation of 18 USC Sec. 3."

I was confused and felt fear that day and failed to tell them exactly what I had done. So the next day I handed in a written statement of how I'd warned Don and hadn't seen him since. It ended with the following statement of the reason for my action.

"I believe that modern atomic war is contrary to God's will and that God is calling many people to refuse military life. The best position a person can take is to openly refuse cooperation and accept the punishment due. It requires time and understanding to reach this position.

"Meanwhile it is not my duty to help the government force a person concerning a decision on military life. Instead I would try to help a person reach his own decision and would tell him if he was in danger of forceful return to the military."

Thanks to Ammon Hennacy and Bob Steed I'm out on $1500 bail. The trial should come in late May. I am not sorry, but grateful that I acted as I did. It gives me the chance to make a concrete choice for a nonviolent society as opposed to a military one. Therefore I shall plead guilty and accept the punishment due. I shall try not to back down on my choice to live now as we shall all live when God's peace comes.

JUNE 1959

❀ Grand Jury Indictment

CHARLES BUTTERWORTH

THE UNITED STATES case against me for refusing to give up Don to the FBI is still in process. The indictment had to be passed on by the Grand Jury and I went down to the Court House for that meeting.

There was a long wait so I told Agent McKeon how in the old days a fugitive could obtain sanctuary in a Catholic Church. He established his right of sanctuary by grasping a large ring or knocker on the church door. I said that a priest who refused sanctuary could be excommunicated. But maybe that's wrong. The *Catholic Encyclopedia* just says, "Violation of the protection of sanctuary was punishable by excommunication." Bob thinks this penalty probably applied to the person who tried to take the fugitive away, not the priest. But the position seems clear: No one can both "turn people in" and remain at *The Catholic Worker*.

Then I was called into the Grand Jury room. It was medium sized with a large table in the center and the jury of sixteen people on a raised platform nearby. I was seated at the table with Mr. Starkey, the prosecuting attorney, and several other officials. There is no judge; the district attorney instructs the jury on their duties. This arrangement helped to put me at ease; I was glad there was no raised witness chair.

The hearing lasted about a half-hour. The questioning was thorough and fair and a secretary wrote it down for the record. "Did you write this article?" Mr. Starkey showed me my article in the May *Catholic Worker*. Bob had sent a copy to the FBI. It was entered as evidence and then Mr. Starkey read it to the jury.

My statement was vigorous but not smooth. Several people got up and walked around, maybe to go to the washroom. Some paid good attention, but others showed by their wandering eyes they were waiting for the next case.

As near as I remember, this is what I said: "It is likely, it seems to me, that this law has been broken. If you find that to be the case, then it will be your duty to grant the indictment the government asks.

"But I want to draw your attention to something else. This law is part of the war system. It is part of the old way of trying to get peace—by arms, military service, and laws supporting them. Perhaps there is someone here who is beginning to lose faith in that way to peace. Now we at *The Catholic Worker* are pacifists; we reject the old way to peace. There is a new way which the world must learn that Gandhi used in freeing India. It is called pacifism or nonviolence. You can learn about it from *The Catholic Worker* or from the Quakers or you can learn it as I did from studying the life and teachings of Gandhi."

Then I spoke about an apparent contradiction. *Catholic Worker* policy is to encourage people to refuse military service but to refuse on moral grounds and openly by returning and accepting a possible jail term. In time a man can gain both his dignity and freedom this way. But I had told Don, "There's a man you don't want to see," and let him leave. My words don't deny our policy. They show that I thought Don wasn't ready yet for this open way.

In closing I told the jury that I was convinced, first, that the destruction of all life by war and atom bombs is not the future. A great era of peace lies in the future, and all present fears of total destruction are false. Second, that God is a living Person fully in control of events and the true leader of history. "Our God is a God of Peace."

That ended the statement, and Mr. Starkey, Agent McKeon and I waited outside for the decision of the jury. It wasn't long, and a "true bill" was granted.

The next step, ten days later, was the pleadings. This time Ammon went with me because he had to sign my bail papers again. Judge Dimock was very careful that I understood the meaning of pleading guilty to a felony, that I couldn't vote any more. He read the indictment, listened to what I'd done, and checked the law. After consideration he allowed me to proceed without a lawyer and agreed that a report on me should be made by the Probation Department.

In these hearings good men are seeking only to do their duty under law. That is as it should be. I am not fighting Mr. Starkey or Judge

Dimock, or the rule of law as such. I am fighting the war system which I see now as essentially immoral. But if law is used to support that system then such law becomes infected and loses all moral sanction. If such a war law touches me, I must react by non-cooperation to the limit of my strength.

The day at the Court House closed with a talk to my probation officer. He showed understanding and respect for our moral position. He had been assigned five conscientious objectors from Union Theological Seminary before the last war. The sentence will be given on June 10. Gandhi says do not exercise the imagination in such matters, expect the best and be ready for the worst.

My reading recently has been seeking a better understanding of the way of prayer of the Little Brothers and Sisters of Jesus. Their way is friendship, prayer, and sacrifice among the poor. This is the true way to peace: prayer and sacrifice. Jail is part of our sacrifice, penance for the social sin of war. And we have the certain promise of Christ through Mary at Fatima in 1917 that our efforts are not in vain. The problems of war, persecution and Russia will be solved and "a certain period of peace will be granted to the world."

DECEMBER 1959

❊ A Death in the Family

DOROTHY DAY

DURING THE FIRST WEEK of November, Beth Rogers called me from the farm and said that the body of a man had been found in the woods about a half-mile from the Peter Maurin Farm. It had been lying there for so long that it was just bones. The police had called the farm because we had reported George Clements as missing last March. Beth and Charles identified the clothes on the body, and it was taken to the morgue at the Farm Colony, in the center of the island, before the coroner had a chance to examine it to find whether the body was of a hunchbacked man, as George was. But it was George, as we knew from the clothes, even from the special shirt that Tommy Hughes had given him because he himself had outgrown it. If it had just been a matter of the clothes which came into our clothes room and which to a large extent outfit us all, we could not be sure. But Tommy knew his shirt. In the absence of any known relatives, the body was turned over to us, and George was buried, with Father Campbell, our pastor, offering Mass. He was buried in St. Joseph's cemetery on a little hill in back of the Church.

George Clements had become interested in *The Catholic Worker* when he lived on Skid Row in San Francisco on welfare and attended a meeting at which I spoke at St. Boniface Church, his parish. He was so fascinated by the work that he wandered around among his friends, among whom were priests, and collected enough money to take the bus to New York. We were surprised, of course, to see him arrive, but not at all surprised when he found the CW not at all the Utopia he had expected. He stayed for some months, and was able to make enough friends and write to enough friends in California to get the bus fare back again to San Francisco. But nostalgia for Mott Street drew him back, and in another six months he was back again, bag and baggage, this time to remain. I cannot remember whether it was fifteen or twenty years he was with us, getting older, quieter, more bent than ever. Probably his most animated moment was when Kieran Duggan chose him to act Santa Claus in the Christmas play he put on two years ago, called "The Trial of Aaron Heresy." Many in the house acted in the gay little skit, which drew people together in hours of practice down in the basement of Chrystie Street. Kieran's verses were sung to the popular tunes of a current Broadway musical and everyone enjoyed the frivolity.

Last January, when we were evicted from Chrystie Street, Slim and Molly and California George, as they called him, were moved down to the farm. They all settled down nicely and neither Slim nor George seemed to be disturbed by the move. Except that George kept writing to friends in San Francisco, asking for money to go back. So many years had passed that most of the letters were returned to him as *not found* or *deceased.* Once in a while he took a walk in the woods, but he was last seen, according to report, in front of the post office in Pleasant Plains.

When the police could find no trace of him through the Missing Persons Bureau, we began to think that, by some miracle, some friends of George had gotten the money together to send him back to California. He was always secretive. People who are forced to live in community often take pains to have a private life of their own outside of it.

It was a grave shock to us all to find that George had wandered off like a sick animal to die, covered over with leaves, hidden from the road, merging with the earth, overlooked by the mushroom hunters who scour the woods spring and fall, and finally found by a schoolboy playing in the woods on Sunday afternoon.

❊ This Money Is Not Ours

DOROTHY DAY

> *The Catholic Worker*
> *39 Spring Street*
> *New York 12, N.Y.*
> *July, 1960*

Treasurer
City of New York
DEAR SIR:

We are returning to you a check for $3,579.39 which represents interest on the $68,700 which we were awarded by the city as payment for the property at 223 Chrystie Street which we owned and lived in for almost ten years, and used as a community for the poor. We did not voluntarily give up the property—it was taken from us by right of eminent domain for the extension of the subway which the city deemed necessary. We had to wait almost a year and a half for the money owed us, although the city permitted us to receive two-thirds of the assessed valuation of the property in advance so that we could relocate. Property owning having been made impossible for us by city regulations, we are now renting and continuing our work.

We are returning the interest on the money we have recently received because we do not believe in "money lending" at interest. As Catholics we are acquainted with the early teaching of the Church. All the early councils forbade it, declaring it reprehensible to make money by lending it out at interest. Canon law of the middle ages forbade it and in various decrees ordered that profit so obtained was to be restored. In the Christian emphasis on the duty of charity, we are commanded to lend gratuitously, to give freely, even in the case of confiscation, as in our own case—not to resist but to accept cheerfully.

We do not believe in the profit system, and so we cannot take profit or interest on our money. People who take a materialistic view of human service wish to make a profit but we are trying to do our duty by our service without wages to our brothers as Jesus commanded in the Gospel (Matt. 25). Loaning money at interest is deemed by one Franciscan as the principal scourge of civilization. Eric Gill, the English artist and writer, calls usury and war the two great problems of our time.

Since we have dealt with these problems in every issue of *The Catholic Worker* since 1933—man's freedom, war and peace, man and the state, man and his work—and since Scripture says that the love of money is the root of all evil, we are taking this opportunity to live in practice of this belief, and make a gesture of overcoming that love of money by returning to you the interest.

Insofar as our money paid for services for the common good, and aid to the poor, we should be very happy to allow you to use not only our money without interest, but also our work, the works of mercy which we all perform here at the headquarters of *The Catholic Worker* without other salary or recompense than our daily food and lodging, clothes, and incidental expenses.

Insofar as the use of our money paid for the time being for salaries for judges who have condemned us and others to jail, and for the politicians who appointed them, and for prisons, and the execution chamber at Sing Sing, and for the executioner's salary we can only protest the use of our money and turn with utter horror from taking interest on it.

Please also be assured that we are not judging individuals, but are trying to make a judgment on *the system* under which we live and with which we admit that we ourselves compromise daily in many small ways, but which we try and wish to withdraw from as much as possible.

Sincerely yours,
DOROTHY DAY, Editor

FEBRUARY 1962

❈ Letter from Thomas Merton

DEAR JIM [FOREST],

It is really quite providential that the peace article I wrote for the *Commonweal* Christmas issue was held up by the censors and is now appearing this week, in conjunction with the General Strike for Peace. I do hope it helps even a little bit. Anyway, my heart goes with it, and I am with you all in spirit. I am glad that in that article I explicitly mentioned the point that all people, the ordinary people, the ones who don't want war, the ones who get it in the neck, the ones who really want to build a decent new world in which there will not be war and starvation, these should know the power of their witness against war, and the effect they can have by protest and refusal of cooperation in immoral war efforts.

Of course the tragedy is that the vast majority of people do not understand the meaning of this kind of witness. In their pitiful, blind craving for undisturbed security, they feel that agitation for peace is somehow threatening to them. They do not feel at all threatened by the bomb, for some reason, but they feel terribly threatened by some little girl student carrying a placard, or by some poor working man striking in protest. Somehow they feel that it is after all possible for people to change their minds and revise their whole attitude toward a setup that has its enormous disadvantages but—at least it is "what we are used to, and please God don't ask us to get used to something else." Unfortunately, the bomb is going to impose a terrible adjustment on those who may be left around to adjust. And it is with this that people want to defend themselves. We have to have deep patient compassion for the fears of men, for the fears and irrational mania of those who hate us or condemn us.

My Mass on February first, the Feast of St. Ignatius Martyr of Antioch, will be for all of the strikers everywhere in the world and for all who yearn for a true peace, all who are willing to shoulder the great burden of patiently working, praying and sacrificing themselves for peace. We will never see the results in our time, even if we manage to get through the next five years without being incinerated. Really we have to pray for a total and profound change in the mentality of the whole world. What we have known in the past as Christian penance is not a deep enough concept if it does not comprehend the special problems and dangers of the present age. Hairshirts will not do the trick, though there is no harm in mortifying the flesh. But vastly more important is the complete change of heart and the totally new outlook on the world of man. We have to see our duty to mankind as a whole. We must not fail in this duty which God is imposing on us with His own Hand.

The great problem is this inner change, and we must not be so obsessed with details of policy that we block the deeper development in other people and in ourselves. The strike is to be regarded, I think, as an application of spiritual force and not the use of merely political pressure. We all have the great duty to realize the deep need for purity of soul, that is to say the deep need to possess in us the Holy Spirit, to be possessed by Him. This takes precedence over everything else. If He lives and works in us, then our activity will be true and our witness will generate love of the truth, even though we may be persecuted and beaten down in apparent incomprehension.

Thanks for the issues of last month's CW. Did I thank you for the Christmas letter? The singing outside the Ladies' Jail warmed my heart. I wish I had been there with you. Small things like that have very great Christian meaning, so much more than a lot of more formal and pompous gestures.

I got a beautiful letter from a nun in Haiti, talking about the people there. Maybe they are among the very poorest on the face of the earth. One feels that Christ is almost visible among them, in them, in their poverty, in their abandonment, their destitution: why does not one look to see the face of Christ and to come to Him with help? But meanwhile His Heart has assumed all their sorrow, all the injustice done to them, and while He will comfort them, He will also do what He does, in mystery, to restore the balance, the violated order.

God was seemingly never more absent from the world and yet His Christ, the Word, is walking about all around us all over the face of the earth, and in a terrible hour.

With all affection to Dorothy and to all of you. Thank her for her good letter which I will answer. I am praying for all those intentions, tell her please.

God's love and blessing to all Christ's poor and all who yearn with Him for peace.

MARCH 1962

❀ What Is To Be Done?

KARL MEYER

I CAME HOME from work this evening firmly determined to excommunicate from St. Stephen's House of Hospitality (to cut off from all communication with) one of those men who was among the first to come to us, an alcoholic, who has been with us on and off, mostly on, for over three years. Not to cut him off because it is the Christian thing to do, or the Catholic thing, or the redemptive thing, or the kind thing, but because it is a thing that must be done. It must be done because he hasn't gotten any better over the years with us. He has in fact gotten much worse. He used to be amiable and pleasant, now he is bitter and often belligerent. He used to have some physical resilience; now he is groggy and confused. He was never sober enough to know the meaning of consideration for others, but he used to listen when you asked him to do a considerate thing. He used to have more control over the bladder when he slept on other people's beds without asking them, and sometimes he even took off his shoes.

It must be done because I haven't gotten any better over the years with him. In fact, I've gotten worse. I used to be gentle, sort of sentimental; now I've gotten hard-nosed. I used to be patient (my friends will laugh), but I haven't much patience any more. And then, I used to sleep in the back room where I couldn't hear him knocking on the front door at three A.M. which he always did, and the other people had to get up and let him in, or curse him and argue with him until he agreed to go away, which he used to do sometimes.

No, it must be done because he'll never go away and stay away until he knows that he doesn't have a chance here. Give him an inch, and he'll take a mile or two, and I don't have it to give any more. Give him a cup of water and he'll take the kitchen sink, and the rest of us have to wash our hands there, and our shirts and our dishes, because it's the only sink we've got.

So I came home from work this evening, and there was a letter from Jim Forest, asking me to write about Houses of Hospitality and why there should be more of them and what they should be like and how you start one. So I have to take time away from other things and people and write quickly what I know.

In his book, *What Is To Be Done?*, Leo Tolstoy tells of taking the census of a slum district in Moscow, and of the comprehensive institutions and plans he envisioned for eliminating destitution in the city. While he was planning, his old friend Sutaief came to his house for a visit:

> He sat immovable, dressed in his black-tanned sheepskin coat, which he, like other peasants, wore indoors as well as out. It seemed that he was not listening to us, but was thinking about something else. His small eyes gave no responding gleam, but seemed to be turned inward. Having spoken out to my satisfaction, I turned to him and asked him what he thought about it.
>
> "The whole thing is superficial," he replied.
>
> "Why?"
>
> "The plan is an empty one and no good will come of it," he repeated with conviction.
>
> "How is it that nothing will come of it? Why is it a useless business, if we help thousands, or even hundreds, of unhappy ones? Is it a bad thing, according to the gospel, to clothe the naked, or to feed the hungry?"
>
> "I know, I know; but what you are doing is not that: Is it possible to help thus? You are walking in the street; somebody asks you for a few kopeks; you give it to him. Is that charity? Do him some spiritual good: teach him—What you gave him merely says, 'Leave me alone.' "
>
> "No; but that is not what we were speaking of: we wish to become acquainted with the wants, and then help by money and deeds. We will try to find for the poor people some work to do."
>
> "That would be no way of helping them."

"How then? Must they be left to die of starvation and cold?"

"Why left to die? How many are there of them?"

"How many?" said I, thinking that he took the matter so lightly from not knowing the great number of these men. "You are not aware, I dare say, that there are in Moscow about twenty thousand cold and hungry. And then think of those in St. Petersburg and other towns!"

He smiled. "Twenty thousand! And how many families are there in Russia alone? Would they amount to a million?"

"What of that?" said he, with animation, and his eyes sparkled. "Let us unite them with ourselves; I am not rich myself, but will at once take two of them. You take a young fellow into your kitchen; I invite him into my family. If there were ten times as many, we should take them all into our families. You one, I another. We shall work together; those I take to live with me will see how I work; I will teach them to reap, and we shall eat out of one bowl, at one table; and they will hear a good word from me, and from you also. This is charity; but all this plan of yours is no good."

These plain words made an impression on me. I could not help recognizing that this was true; but it seemed to me then, that, notwithstanding the justice of what he said, my proposed plan might, perhaps, also be useful.

But the longer I was occupied with this affair, and the closer my intercourse with the poor, the oftener I recollected these words, and the greater meaning I found in them.

I indeed go in an expensive fur coat, or drive in my own carriage, to a man who is in want of boots: he sees my house which costs two hundred rubles a month, or he notices that I give away, without thinking, five rubles, only because such is my fancy; he is then aware that, if I give away rubles in such a manner, it is because I have accumulated so many of them that I have a lot to spare, which I not only am never in the habit of giving to any one, but which I have, without compunction, taken away from others. What can he see in me but one of those persons who have become possessed of what should belong to him?

I have my own Sutaief in Lemont who has been with me longer even than the alcoholic whom I mentioned above. I would not have you believe that all who come to a House of Hospitality are a burden. Quite as many are a source of joy and strength. There are good men and kind men and gentle, poets and wise men, scholars and philosophers.

Lemont has long hair and a long beard and wears his black coat and gloves in the house and washes less than most, so that the respectable suppose that he is very strange and alien. But he is more kind and wise and scholarly than all the bourgeois I know. He loves that passage from Tolstoy, and he always counsels me not to try to do too much for too many, because just as we must all bear one another's burdens, so too any one of us can only bear the burdens of a few. But there are so few of us here and the needs of the poor press in upon us overwhelmingly, so that "never to be safe again is all our lives."

It isn't that the man I must excommunicate could not be helped, but that behind him stand ten thousand more, and I can not take them all, starting with him. If you open the door they will come in by hundreds; I have seen them with my own eyes. At one time we fed eighty men a night in a kitchen ten feet by ten feet. The first thing is to survive, the first year and the second and the third. If you don't survive yourself, you can't do anything for anyone. There have been Houses of Hospitality where the householders drove themselves to insanity. Lesson Number One: Do not burden yourself beyond the limit of grace, humanity and survival.

We need more Houses of Hospitality where the strong will share the burdens of the weak. The more houses the better, because the more there are, the lighter will be the burdens in each house, and the lighter the burdens, the more the weak will be strengthened to walk. I am not saying that you should take alcoholics and psychotics into your house, because few can bear it or know what to do, but I am speaking of the sick and old and unemployed and orphans (so many of the alcoholics and psychotics were raised in orphanages).

I mentioned that I come home from work in the evening. Why am I not home all day? I come home from work in the evening because I work all day to earn a living for my household. Dorothy and my good priest often tell me I should quit work and beg for our living, so that I could do more for the poor. But if I did more for the poor by begging money from people, the people would do less for the poor by paying me to do a bad job for them. You can have a real estate broker and an insurance broker, but you can't have a broker for your charity. If people gave me money they would not be able to take the poor into their own homes, nor would they be able to ask their boss for a reduction in salary so that the low-paid workers in their hospital or restaurant or business could be paid more, nor would they be able to go into a high-class restaurant and offer to pay double the check so that the fifty-cents-an-hour dishwasher could be paid a decent wage, nor would they be able to cut their pay in half so that the unemployed could be hired to share the piled-up work that puts such pressures on the employed and often breaks up homes and ruins lives. I have to fight with my employer to keep from doing overtime and getting home even later in the evening. I tell him, "There are thousands unemployed. Go out and hire them to do overtime."

Yes, if people were to give me money, we would have one big House of Hospitality in every major city, and one hundred would be inside and ten thousand would be outside, and the people would say "We have a House of Hospitality in our city. Let the poor get themselves over there before it closes at eight P.M."

Now I hope no one will say, "Well, I was going to send you a dime, but I see you don't want my money so I'll go out and get an ice cream cone instead." In that case I'll take the dime; but it isn't the better way.

So that is why we need Houses of Hospitality, and why I work and have a small House of Hospitality.

Now, when and how do you start a House of Hospitality and what is it like?

I started my first *Catholic Worker* house in Washington, D.C., when I was nineteen years old and not even a Catholic. I was working as a messenger for Dean Acheson's law firm, one of the biggest, and most of our work was defending giant corporations in anti-trust suits. Not every anarchist starts out by being perfectly consistent.

I rented a store on the roughest street in the roughest neighborhood in town, on O St. between Sixth and Seventh, though I didn't know about it at the time. It was just where I happened to get a store. There were more murders around there than in any other precinct. I was the only white man in the block, and when I came home from meetings late at night the police used to stop me and warn me to get out of the neighborhood. My father wasn't in Congress yet; my parents were home in Vermont and my mother never really knew.

The store had a middle-sized front room with a show window, a very small kitchen with a sink, and in the back, a larger room with no windows and a small alcove with a toilet. The floor was of concrete, and water used to come in and stand around in various spots in the back room. For this I paid fifty dollars a month, cash on the barrelhead, and I had not a grain of trouble renting it in spite of my age, its location and the strange purposes I proposed for it. I bought a stove, refrigerator and a gas heater in successive months. Instead of getting beds and chairs.

I got fifty dollars worth of lumber and constructed six benches to do double duty service for sleeping in the back room and meetings in the front room. The neighbors, and also some cops, came in to see what all the hammering was about, and they wanted to know what kind of racket I was setting up, but I didn't say much. Some of them wanted to buy the benches then and there. I should have sold them. I had everything set up and was ready to receive my guests. But I sat there and sat there and nobody came. I started in June and for several months nobody came. Summer passed. In early autumn I was walking along the street and I saw a man lying on the steps of a Protestant church. I wakened him with difficulty; he was loaded. I loaded him into a cab and brought him home. I was exultant.

In *The Catholic Worker* of January 1962, I wrote of my exultation after my first venture in alley picking. It could not have compared with my joy in my first action of hospitality. But within three days my joy was to turn to desperation. My new guest was stone drunk, and if I had known anything about it I would have observed that he was absolutely punchy from years of drunkenness. But I immediately determined upon his redemption from wine. I put him to bed, or rather to bench. For the next two days I tried to sober him up, but what was my despair to discover that in the morning he was as drunk as the night before.

Somehow he managed to elude me and to oil himself up frequently. I didn't get much sleep because he didn't seem to keep regular hours. All he could eat was sugar with coffee. By the morning of the third day I was exhausted and desperate.

I called my friend Jim Guinan of Friendship House (who was to become my godfather at my baptism a few months later) and he told me to bring him over. As soon as the poor man was delivered into Jim's old hands, I went upstairs, lay down on a couch and cried for half an hour. After that I was all right. I had learned a lesson—Lesson Number Two: Don't demand prompt success from anyone else, or from yourself. After five months of operations and one three-day guest, I closed my first House of Hospitality. I would only mention that Jack Biddle drove me home once with Ammon Hennacy from a meeting where Ammon spoke, and they stopped and had a look at my place when they dropped me off. That was before Ammon knew me at all, but perhaps he remembers that house.

After all this I went to New York and, the following June, joined the people of *The Catholic Worker* in their Civil Defense protest, and served my first thirty days in jail.

A year later, Ed Morin and I started St. Stephen's House (I got the store and he got the people), which has met with some success in its almost four years. I have written all of this preface so that you might say, "If such a fool as this can do it, perhaps I can too."

As my Washington experience illustrates, setting up house is easy: it's the hospitality that brings problems.

St. Stephen's House is located with a view to the major relevant factors. I am poor and I am taking the poor into my house, so we are going to be even poorer. Therefore we are set on the edge of a small slum pocket, a back pocket just three blocks away from Chicago's glittering Gold Coast. We are in a poor neighborhood because slum landlords are tolerant of poverty, slum tenants are tolerant of poverty, and police and building department officials are tolerant of poverty, in poor neighborhoods; we get along well with our neighbors. It is no crime to be poor here. Some houses have had to move time and again because they kept moving into places where it was a crime to be poor.

Furnishings and food we get from the Gold Coast alleys. Fortunately, it evidently is not a crime to salvage the criminal wastes of these rich neighbors. They think us quaint, seeing us going about at late hours poking our heads in garbage pails or dragging bed springs through back streets.

We live in a store on account of the marginal nature of small business in the slums; storefront properties offer more space for less rent than regular housing units. We have five rooms with steam heat for seventy dollars a month. The steam comes once a day, if it comes at all, but the kitchen oven warms the whole house. There are four floors of tenement flats above, and at least once a month the plumbing breaks down above us and water pours from floor to floor on its way to the sea, but I haven't met a pipe I couldn't plug. In between the floods we are warm and dry and life is pleasant here.

In ten months of 1960 (I was in jail for two months) my expenses for the house and personal concerns totaled $2,102.56. Monthly expenses ranged from $131.28 up to $347.97. The basic monthly costs were approximately as follows:

Rent........................	$ 70
Gas..........................	10
Electricity..............	10
Phone....................	8
Laundry.................	12
Food	40
	$150

Miscellaneous costs include the following:

Raincoats for an American Friends Service Committee peace vigil	$18.48
Payment of a fine and costs to spring Ed Bodin from the city jail	29.00
Leaflets for the protest in behalf of Eroseanna Robinson	15.00
Travel to and from peace conferences and meetings	49.74

There were ten beds in the house, always taken, and occasionally extra people would sleep on the floor for several days, or even several weeks.

Around six or eight men came from outside each night for supper.

We had clothing for those who needed it, and bread for some of the families in our building.

Three of the men in the house lived here through the entire year, and I was able to claim them as dependents for non-tax purposes.

The meals were cooked and the house was kept by Joe Patrofsky, who worked seven days a week, because he was a working man "too old to work" and the work was there and who else did it, and all he got for it was sixty minutes an hour, as Richard says when he mops the floor. I realize now that we exploited him by not giving him more help, and my only excuse is that I worked as hard myself, though I took a day off whenever I pleased.

Well, what of these people to whom we offer hospitality? They are of every shape and sort, and every state of poverty and destitution. Three may be old or sick and "unemployable"; two may have mental illness or psychosis; one may be an alcoholic, or a wandering man of God, an indigent student or an unpaid peace worker, or simply an unemployed worker. We have had here a journalist, of the Jewish faith he always made clear, who was unemployed because the FBI kept going around and telling his employers that he had twice refused to testify before the House Un-American Activities Committee about his activities in behalf of integration in the South. We have had here a poor rich young man who was doing alternative service as an orderly in a Catholic hospital and trying to meet the payments on a small sports car. We have had here a generous, kindly, handsome, strong, hardworking young gentleman, who happened to be a Negro, and who didn't just happen to be employed except for occasional work as a porter in a cheap drugstore, and who happened to wind up in a penitentiary for attempting armed postal robbery. We have had connected with us Mr. Cable, a madman whose behavior was shocking by his own account. We have had here an inferior decorator, of checks that is; he didn't make a good living by it. There are only two of us who don't eat meat, but we managed at one time to keep two butchers unemployed. One of them has died now, but the other is still unemployed.

There are workers and scholars and non-workers and non-scholars. If a house is small and the people are different and individual, the strength of one gives help for the weakness of another. The house is a center of thought and action. It is a microcosm of the world. Many visitors come and take away more than they bring. The workers and the non-workers and the non-scholars hear the discussions among the scholars about peace and love and politics and sociology, and they become informed and aware by diffusion. The non-workers and the scholars see the workers at work, but I can't see that it does them much good.

I believe that a dying man is more alive here, and a living man is more alive still. We have here a community of need, where the first man who comes in need is received, and a community of diversity, where all are welcome. We have a communion between the living and the dying in the natural order, and are often dying unto ourselves in order to live unto others in the supernatural order, but I believe that we become more alive ourselves.

I have walked across the world from Chicago to Moscow, and the scene bored me much of the time. But I am not bored here. We don't walk past the world and its problems. The world comes in with its problems and sits down for a cup of coffee and a word of consolation.

❊ This Night I Carry the Banner

KARL MEYER

Holy Thursday
164 W. Oak St.
Chicago, Ill.

AT FIVE O'CLOCK we went to Mass at St. Dominic's Church, and as on Palm Sunday, the people were called to join the procession, for which we were grateful.

After Mass we held a Paschal supper at St. Stephen's House. Eleven residents and guests sat down to feast on lamb sent us by Father Damian, and a twelfth sat down to vegetables, having some concern for the poor lamb.

After the supper we had a reading of St. John's story of the Last Supper.

At nine-thirty, seven of us set out for St. Dominic's for an hour of vigil and prayer, a part of the actions of the Week for Peace in Chicago. Seven of us—four Romans, two Jews and one Anglican—set out for a vigil of prayer before the Eucharist for the intentions of the Pope for world peace. Is it strange that two Jews and an Anglican should go out with four Romans to such an event? Each man has his own Christ, though we seem in this movement to have a power to draw the estranged together. We had plotted together, and had it in mind to bear him away and make him a king over a pacifist kingdom, to bring the people into subjection to his universal law of joy. "Each of us," said Mauriac, "makes Christ a prisoner of his own limited way of thinking and feeling." But somehow he always resisted.

Down on skid row they are "carrying the banner"—a euphemism of the destitute meaning to walk the street through the night with nowhere to sleep, taking only a temporary refuge from cold or rain in all-night coffee houses, movie houses or taverns, hoping to be spared cops, night court and jails. This is the night when Christ "carried the banner." To commemorate his night of prayer and his arrest, I walk the chill streets without sleep, taking my refuge for a few hours before the Eucharist.

I walked down North Clark and over on Madison. The street was empty. Everyone was seen through dingy windows slumped at bars. I began to say to myself, here is a man seeking to emulate Christ in his presence to the destitute, and yet he has never stood at the bar with them to drink a glass of beer. How shall he know them? How shall he be present to them? So I began to ask myself, will I dare to go into one of these places and ask for a glass of beer? And if I dare, how shall I ask? Will I know what brand of beer to name? Will I be conspicuous to them in all the newness of this experience? Will the bartender question my age, who have no draft card to prove it?

So discussing with myself, an hour passed quickly and I found myself beyond Madison and Morgan. I turned back toward some likely bar I had passed.

I had gone a few feet, when, looking down just to my left, I saw a small white pigeon standing against the wall. I bent to touch it and it backed away, then flew off weakly, almost settling in the middle of the street, and then, reaching the far side, stopped against the opposite wall. I crossed the street and now took the bird in my hands and sheltered it under my coat and brought it home to rest safely.

What is the meaning of this omen on such a night, the night of these words: I am going away—but I will ask my Father to send you another—peace I leave with you; it is my own peace that I give you; I do not give peace as the world gives it.

Tomorrow, we will carry the banner of protest in the Easter March for Peace. Yes, let us go on doing that. But if we really would go in search of peace, we must carry the banner of poverty, of cold and sleepless nights, walking the pavement among the poor in spirit. Down there on Skid Row (not Park Row), down there on Madison Street (not Madison Avenue) we will find the love of peace, weak and unsheltered in the darkness of the shabby night.

The hour going down, passed in meditation, moved quickly and carefree; but the hour returning was very long and I was impatient, weighted down under the burden of a small pigeon carried under my coat. When I had brought the bird home and placed it in my room, I went back to the church. A Methodist came too in the small hours.

Later on I went out onto the streets again and made the Gold Coast rounds, digging up a couple of cleft potatoes and some fruit in a small basket. When I had brought that home, I set out for the church again. Along the way I heard boxes rustling in an alley and being interested in such things, I stopped to look, and behold, there was Brother Rat trying to make a go of it too.

❀ Peter Maurin Farm

(From the regular column)

DEANE MOWRER

THE DAY of the great Staten Island fire—the worst in the history of New York—was Agnes' birthday, a day that she and we are not likely to forget. The winds were blowing with such impetuous ferociousness that morning that I felt apprehensive and worried, knowing how tinder-dry the woods, fields, and buildings were, and how April, that "cruelest month," has brought us not much-needed, seed-nourishing rain, but wild, windy weather that might have come right out of the March lion's mouth. As a consequence, a rash of brush fires had kept the fire engines clanging up and down our roads almost every day. I suggested to Charles as we drove to Mass that we say a litany novena for rain and he agreed. Shortly after our return from church I heard the first fire engine go by, and someone said the fire did not seem to be too near. The winds swirled and screeched like demons at play so that the flames leapt from place to place with no perceptible pattern. More fire engines went clanging by. Finally I braved the winds to go to the chapel and pray. After a bit Charles came in and said he thought we should start the litany now. We said a litany of Our Lady. Then Charles went out to help the other men take what measures they could against the fiery enemy.

When the dinner bell rang, I walked out into winds that were even more angrily berserk. The air had filled with the acrid smell of smoke. Most of us did not feel much like eating; Agnes did not eat at all. Stanley tried to relieve tensions with a few jokes, but they sounded more like whistling in the dark. I wondered why so many firemen with so much equipment had not been able to stem the fires that were now threatening to encircle us. Then Charles told me there was no water. Not one drop in the taps in our house. Not one drop in the hydrants in our vicinity. Charles said that Agnes and I should stay downstairs and be ready to go at any moment. Neither of us wanted to go, but we knew we could be of little use in fire-fighting. Agnes is old and I am blind. As I walked out of the house toward the car in the driveway I felt the full demonic fury of the wind, blowing with such scorching impact that I had an immediate visual impression of that hot, heavy, spark-filled smoke mass, like an amorphous dragon spewing fiery deluge on all in its path.

Charles drove to Pleasant Plains and left us sitting in the car in front of Levinson's fruit and vegetable store. The talk from passers-by floated in to us, talk that became more excited, more filled with facts and rumors of disaster as the afternoon wore on. We learned that there were fires in other areas of Staten Island. Someone said that all of Tottenville was ablaze. Another that there were big fires in Huguenot and Annadale. I began to worry about Marge Hughes and her family and our houses on the Annadale beach. Someone said that Mount Loretto Orphanage was in danger; another that they were evacuating everyone from the hill. The hill would include Peter Maurin Farm. I wondered where the others were being taken. We sat in the car and waited. I said another prayer while the talk about me seemed louder and louder, like headlines of a disaster.

Meanwhile at the farm, as I learned later, the men kept struggling valiantly to beat out the flames springing up in nearby brush and grasses. Buckets of water were carried from our little pond and the roofs of the men's cottages moistened; tubfuls of water were placed at strategic points, and all the fire extinguishers placed in readiness. Charles offered the water from our pond to the firemen, but they said their engines could never get down to the pond and went clanging dolefully away, leaving our neighbors' houses blazing in the April afternoon without a fireman's nozzle lifted in protest. The police evacuated the others from the farm, some to St. Louis Academy, others to Red Cross and Salvation Army stations.

There is no doubt that the special Providence of God was with us that day, but I think He made use of the strange caprice of those tempestuous winds which blew where they listed, and of the unflagging vigilance and efforts of all those men, the men, not the firemen, but the men of Peter Maurin Farm who battled the flames that fiery Saturday of Easter Week.

By the time Charles finally came for us I felt I had learned a little of what it is like to be a refugee. We had to return by back roads. Charles and the others exclaimed about house after house that had burned completely down leaving only charred debris or a chimney standing alone amid the ashen ruins of a home. Around about us were scorched fields and fire-ruined woodlands. I felt as though I were passing through a war-devastated area. I was deeply grieved for those who had suffered such losses, and indignation rose in me at the thought of the criminal negligence of those responsible for the lack of water pressure in this area, that precious water that might have saved some of these homes. I wondered too why chemical fire-fighting equipment had not been used. But there was no salve for my indignation, only the harsh acrid smoke that rasped in my throat and nostrils.

Larry Doyle managed to prepare supper. Afterward Charles and Lucille put candles on a birthday cake, which Lucille had baked the night before, and there was a small procession to Agnes' room and a happy birthday song. Whatever Agnes may have thought of this particular birthday, her eighty-second, there is no doubt that it was for us all unforgettable.

The thing that struck me the most next morning was the absence of birdsong. I heard a lone robin singing, with a kind of cheerless bewilderment, his familiar cheer-up cadences. When I went downstairs to Mass, Andy told me that just before dawn he had heard a whippoorwill, lonely, with sad song grieving over the desolate embers of his woodland home.

In contrast to this fiery Saturday, the day of the funeral of Tom Cain and Molly Powers was like one stolen from a pastoral idyll. It was Thursday of Easter week, only a few days after the fire, a day softly warm and beautiful, fragrant with cherry blossoms, sweet with birdsong, just such a day as Tom and Molly would have loved. As we stood there beside the graves of the Catholic Worker plot in St. Joseph's cemetery I could hear birds singing not far away. I thought that, though we did not have a high Mass, these were the very choristers that Tom and Molly would have chosen to sing them into Paradise.

I had often heard Molly tell of how she first came to the Catholic Worker. It was a cold day and she was cold and hungry. She walked into the Mott Street house, walked up to the stove and asked if she could warm herself. Tom Sullivan, who was then in charge, welcomed her with his accustomed warmth and love. Since that day Molly was very much part of the CW family. She had many ailments and was in consequence sometimes irritable and quick of temper. She was deeply affectionate by nature, loved life, good food, laughter, Irish melodies, young people, and children. She was a woman who had suffered much but had worked hard all her life. As long as she was able she always tried to do her share of the work at the farm. She died on Holy Saturday night, ready to share in the Easter Resurrection of Our Lord.

Tom Cain was a scholarly man, with much learning in many fields. He was a naturalist and knew the flora and fauna of our region intimately, and kept me informed about any interesting developments. He was also an amateur astronomer, and many of our visitors enjoyed looking through Tom's telescope and hearing him talk about the stars. He was first of all a fervent Catholic, and when he was young attended a minor seminary. He acted as our sacristan and usually served Mass in our chapel. He also worked in the parish, attending Holy Name Society meetings and helping with the choir at St. Joseph's as long as he was able. He was a man of strong and resolute will, and although tubercular resisted to the end any suggestion of hospitalization or medical treatment. Moreover, though he favored the strictest observance in matters liturgical, he cared little for conventional usage in matters of personal hygiene and cleanliness, and preferred to live in a room that was a shambles. But he was faithful to rosary and compline even in his last illness. He died early Tuesday morning, where he would have preferred to die, in his own room, above the chapel, at the beginning of Easter week, the week of Resurrection.

❀ From Rome

DOROTHY DAY

MONDAY, JUNE THIRD, I landed from the *Vulcania,* an Italian Line ship at Forty-fifth Street in New York, at eight o'clock in the morning. Pope John was still alive. (On board ship we had been getting only the most meager reports as to the Pope's health. Each morning at Mass the chaplain had asked our prayers for the Holy Father, and each afternoon at Benediction we had repeated those prayers.)

At three o'clock that afternoon we were still sitting at our lunch with people coming and going in the little apartment on Kenmare Street when someone came in with news of the Pope's death. It had been a long agony and daily I had prayed the Eastern Rite prayer for "a death without pain" for this most beloved Father to all the world. But I am afraid he left us with the suffering which is an inevitable part of love, and he left us with fear, too, if the reports of his last words are correct, fear that his children, as he called all of us in the world, were not listening to his cries for *pacem in terris.* He was offering his sufferings, he had said before his death, for the continuing Council in September, and for peace in the world. But he had said, almost cheerfully, that his bags were packed, that he was ready to go, and that after all death was the beginning of a new life. "Life is changed, not taken away," as the Preface in the Mass for the dead has it. And just as Thérèse of Lisieux said that she would spend her heaven doing good upon earth, so in his love, John XXIII will be watching over us.

It was on the day before I sailed for New York, May 22, Wednesday, that I had the tremendous privilege of being present at his last public appearance. He stood in his window looking out over the crowd in front of St. Peter's. An audience had been scheduled as usual for that Wednesday at ten-thirty, and the great Basilica was crowded to the doors when the announcement was made that the Pope had been too ill the night before to make an appearance that day but that he would come to the window and bless the crowd, as he was accustomed to do each Sunday noon.

I had had an appointment that morning for ten-thirty at the office of Cardinal Bea, to see his secretary, Father Stransky, the Paulist, about a meeting I was to have with the Cardinal that night and was leaving the Number 64 bus at the colonnade to the left of St. Peter's. I noticed that the people leaving the bus were hastening to the square. Word gets around Rome quickly and when I inquired I was told that the Holy Father would be at the window in a moment. I hastened to a good position in the square and was there in time to see the curtains stir and the Pope appear. I had not realized how tremendous that square was until I saw how tiny the Pope's figure seemed, up at that window of the apartment under the roof. Those rooms used to be servants' quarters and had been occupied by the Popes since Pius X.

The voice of the Holy Father came through a loudspeaker, of course, and seemed strong. He said the Angelus (which we say before meals at the Peter Maurin Farm) then the prayers to the guardian angels and ended with a requiem prayer for the dead.

It was the last time the public saw his face. (Many of the crowd had opera glasses, so one can use that expression.) Questioning those at the little convent where I had been staying in Rome the last week, I learned the subject of the Pope's last talk, at his last Wednesday audience. He had urged all to read and study his last encyclicals, the call to the Council, *Mater et Magistra* and *Pacem in Terris*. He had said all he had to say; this was the message he left to the world:

> There is an immense task incumbent on all men of good will, namely the task of restoring the relations of the human family in truth, in justice, in love and in freedom; the relations between individual human beings; between citizens and their respective communities; between political communities themselves; between individuals, families, intermediate associations and political communities on the one hand and the world community on the other. This is a most exalted task, for it is the task of bringing about true peace in the order established by God.
>
> Admittedly, those who are endeavoring to restore the relations of social life according to the criteria mentioned above, are not many; to them We express Our paternal appreciation, and We earnestly invite them to persevere in this work with greater zeal. And We are comforted by the hope that their number will increase especially among those who believe. For it is an imperative of duty, it is a requirement of Love.

Yes, we will meditate on his words to us all, because he said he was addressing *all men of good will,* and we will know too, as we have known in the past, how difficult it is to apply these words to individual situations. We need all the gifts of the Holy Spirit for our work; we need all the help of our guardian angels; and to make our non-Catholic and non-believing readers know what these words mean, we are printing together with this usual column of pilgrimage, definitions of the gifts of the Holy Spirit, as well as what the guardian angels mean to us who believe. And not to know these things, for those of us who do believe, means not to know the treasure we have, the resources we have to draw upon.

To report further about the trip to Rome: it came about because a group of women, mostly of other faiths, and including those who did not believe, had called for this attempt to reach the Holy Father with a plea for a condemnation of nuclear war, and a development of the ideas of nonviolent resistance. This very attempt brought out clearly how difficult are these attempts at unity and coexistence.

It is no easier to receive a hearing with Princes of the Church than it is to receive one from the princes of this world. There is protocol; there is hierarchy and blocs of one kind or another; there is diplomacy in what we generally consider to be the realm of the spirit.

The day of the audience arrived and the big buses came to the door, and it did not seem that we were being treated as of any more importance than the bus loads of school children who were coming from all over Europe during their Easter holiday to see Rome and attend the large general audience which took place each Wednesday at St. Peter's.

We waited, as everyone else waited, outside in the square, two of our members in wheelchairs. We passed through the gates showing our unprivileged tickets, and back past the bureau of excavations and through one of the side doors and around into a section already packed with people.

It was long to wait. Probably people were standing two hours, and it was not until twelve-twenty that finally there was a surge in that vast mob and a sudden silence followed by almost a roar of greeting. Borne aloft on his chair (and how could any have seen him if he were not conducted in this way), the procession proceeded around the columns and then the Pope, blessing all, was conducted up to his throne where he sat while a list of all the groups of pilgrims was read aloud. As the names of the villages of Italy, and the schools on the Continent, and of England and the United States were read out, applause came from various parts of this vast group. And our pilgrimage was not mentioned!

But then the Pope began to speak and the words that fell from his lips seemed to be directed to us, to our group, speaking as he did about the "Pilgrims for Peace" who came to him, and his gratitude for their gratitude and encouragement. The young woman who had helped us find our places was translating his words as fast as he spoke them and writing them down while two of us read over her shoulder. She kept beaming at us, and all those around us, seeing our buttons, large almost as saucers, bright blue and bearing the legend "Mothers for Peace" in Italian; she also smiled and indicating the Holy Father and us in turn, seemed to be letting us know that he was speaking to us especially.

It seemed too good to be true and if all those around us had not kept assuring us he was speaking to us, I would have considered it but a coincidence. Our messages had reached him we felt, impossible though it had seemed they would.

JULY–AUGUST 1964

❊ The Case of Cardinal McIntyre

DOROTHY DAY

OF ALL HOSTILITIES, one of the saddest is the war between clergy and laity. We have written and spoken many times of all the aspects of war, the beginnings in our own hearts, the hostilities in the family between husband and wife, parents and children, children and parents—the entire conflict of authority and freedom. *The Catholic Worker,* pacifist and anarchist in philosophy, has had to discuss and write about all these things.

The works of mercy are works of love. The works of war are works of the devil: "You do not know of what spirit you are," Jesus said to his disciples when they would call down fire from heaven on the inhospitable Samaritans. This is to look at things in the large context of modern war. But as for the hostilities in our midst, the note of violence and conflict in all our dealings with others—everyone seems to contribute to it. There is no room for righteous wrath today. In the entire struggle over civil rights, the war which is going on in which one side is nonviolent and suffering martyrdoms, every movement of wrath in the heart over petty hostilities must be struggled with in order to hold up the strength of the participants.

"Let us but raise the level of religion in our hearts, and it will rise in the world," Newman wrote. "He who attempts to set up God's kingdom in his heart, furthers it in the world." We cannot all go on Freedom Rides. But we can sustain them by our contributions, money, prayers, and by works in our local area along these lines.

This is what seminarians and the Catholic interracial group have been doing in Los Angeles, not only this year but for many years, only to meet with prohibitions from the hierarchy, prohibitions of meetings, of setting up interracial councils, and so on. This silence and noncooperation on the part of the priest and bishop and cardinal, this more than silence—this censure, this prohibition—has increased the separation of clergy and laity, and has built up *a wall of bitterness.*

Last month a young priest in the Los Angeles diocese wrote a letter to the Holy Father, asking for the removal of Cardinal McIntyre from the work of the diocese. His letter was given to the press all over the country and was reprinted by both secular and Catholic press. I had not intended to write at length about this Los Angeles incident since it has received such ample coverage. But I recalled letters I had received in the last year, asking my advice as to what to do—and when I recalled too my long acquaintance with Cardinal McIntyre (shall I say friendship?) I decided I would write at length, and personally. What I say about him, I could say also in one way or another about Cardinal Spellman and Cardinal Cushing.

I first met Cardinal McIntyre back in the late twenties when I was filled with the longing to be a Catholic and could not because of marriage difficulties. One goes to a priest in the chancery office to straighten out these difficulties and Cardinal McIntyre, who was then a monsignor, was the one assigned to me to take care of my inquiries. His office was not a private one. His was one of a long row of desks on either side of the room, far enough apart so that one could talk privately. There was always a long line of people waiting in the outer office and, one by one, we were ushered in. There was never any haste about these interviews. He always gave me most courteous and sympathetic attention and I remember times when I was there at noon and he had a sandwich and a glass of milk brought to his desk. He said the Angelus when the clock struck twelve. I remember thinking how hard these young priests had to work, the tales they had to listen to. They had to be lawyers, psychologists, priests, all in one. Between him and Father Hyland, another young priest at Tottenville, Staten Island, I was helped along the way, over a period of several years, and was baptized.

When five years later I started *The Catholic Worker* at the instigation of Peter Maurin, I did not ask permission—I did not discuss it with the chancery office. I had been writing articles for *The Sign*, for *America*, the Jesuit paper, and doing clerical work for Fr. Joseph McSorley, the Paulist, and when I spoke to them of my venture, all three editors advised me to launch out, but not to ask permission. It would not be given, was implied. But I understood why. Why make the hierarchy responsible for such an unproved venture?

At any rate the first issues of the paper came out and it was greeted with enthusiasm by clergy and laity alike. The circulation soared, enough contributions came in so that hospitality could be provided for the down and outs that made up our first staff. Workers and scholars alike were down and out in the Depression, and we have always been the lame, the halt, and the blind, the off-scouring of all, to use St. Paul's phrase, all through the years. "The gold is ejected and the dross remains," one of our friends said of us. We were greeted by those who did not know us as a pack of saints, and the legend continued to grow, such a term giving an easy way out to those who felt themselves to be happily more publicans than pharisees. Our standards were too high, could not possibly be lived up to, but it was good to be reminded of them. Such principles would not work, they showed pride and presumption in a way, but they evidenced the longing in every human heart for the lost Eden of the past and the Paradise we all hoped for in the future. In other words, we were Utopians.

Well, we have hung on to our personalist communitarian philosophy over the years. But through all the years, there was never any criticism from the chancery office in New York about our philosophy, even when it led us to jail.

The Baltimore House of Hospitality was closed as a public nuisance. It was interracial when it was against the law to have both black and white under the same roof in a hostel. Civil disobedience began for us then.

Irene Mary Naughton was arrested for picketing in an interracial demonstration at Palisades Amusement Park. This was in the forties and was just the beginning of CW involvement. But still the chancery offices never interfered. They never committed themselves either.

We were called to the chancery office occasionally. At first I saw only Monsignor McIntyre, and later it was Monsignor Gaffney. It was always over some trivial matter. After a few years, I felt that I understood the technique. I would get a letter reading, "Dear Dorothy, if you happen to be in the neighborhood, would you please drop in." I very seldom was in the neighborhood of Fiftieth Street, all our work being on the East Side, but I took care to go at once. Monsignor McIntyre would greet me in most friendly fashion, and then press a button for a stenographer. She would bring in a file, and he would open to a letter, one of a long pile of letters, and holding his hand over the signature, he would say, "We have received a complaint about something in the last issue of the CW," and he would read out some line like, "Would you have your daughter go to the marriage bed with a Negro?" (I remember that line well. This was from a satirical article by Robert Ludlow. Quite often the sentiments objected to were from his writings.)

There was never any comment, but a few friendly inquiries about the work. I do not recall how many times I had these meetings with Monsignor McIntyre. But he tried to help us. Before we got our Peter Maurin Farm in Staten Island, I found a place on the beach down near Tottenville that I wanted very much to buy and Bishop McIntyre, sympathizing with our money problems, offered to back or sponsor a bank loan for us for fifteen thousand dollars. The deal fell through because of the usual housing, health, and fire department restrictions on our work.

No comment was ever made by the by-then bishop or archbishop about political views. When we started to run articles like "War and Conscription at the Bar of Christian Morals," by Monsignor Barry O'Toole of the Catholic University, and "The Crime of Conscription" and "Catholics Can Be Conscientious Objectors," by Fr. John Hugo of Pittsburgh, Bishop McIntyre merely commented, during one of these aforesaid visits, "We never studied these things much in the seminary." He shook his head, adding doubtfully, "There is the necessity of course to inform one's conscience." And I assured him that this was what we were trying to do.

A recent paperback called *The Essential Newman* carries part of Cardinal Newman's correspondence with Gladstone in which he discusses *conscience,* and he is reported to have said that if he were called up to propose a toast to such a subject, which was unlikely, he would propose, "To conscience first, and to the Pope second." This was at a time when there was great discussion of the new dogma, the infallibility of the Pope.

Bishop O'Hara of Kansas City once said to Peter Maurin, "You lead the way—we will follow." Meaning that it was up to the laity to plough ahead, to be the vanguard, to be the shock troops, to fight these battles without fear or favor. And to make the mistakes. And that has always been my understanding. This business of "asking Father" what to do about something has never occurred to us. The way I have felt about Los Angeles is that the lay people had to go ahead and form their groups, "Catholics for interracial justice," form their picket lines, as they are only now doing, and make their complaints directly, to priest and cardinal, demanding the leadership, the moral example they are entitled to. How can any priest be prevented from preaching the gospel of social justice in the labor field and in the interracial field? One can read with loud agreement those messages from the encyclicals, which are so pertinent to the struggles which are being carried on. One can tell the gospel stories in the light of what is happening today. Do the poor have the gospel preached to them today? Do we hear that resounding cry, "Woe to the rich!" Do we hear the story of the rich man sitting at his table feasting while the poor sat at the gate with neither food nor medicare?

It is voluntary poverty which needs to be preached to the comfortable congregations, so that a man will not be afraid of losing his job if he speaks out on these issues. So that pastors or congregations will not be afraid of losing the support of rich benefactors. A readiness for poverty, a disposition to accept it, is enough to begin with. We will always get what we need: "Take no thought for what you shall eat or drink—the Lord knows you have need of these things."

If more seminarians spoke out, even if the seminaries were emptied! If more young priests spoke out while they continued to work hard and continued to "be what they wished the other fellow to be," as Peter Maurin put it—what happy results might not be brought about.

But often the critical spirit results in desertions, from church and priesthood and seminary, and I suppose that is what the hierarchy fears. We have plenty of experience of the critical spirit and have seen the ravages that can be wrought in family and community. We have had many a good worker leave because he could not stand the frustrations, because "those in charge" did not throw out troublemakers, or *force* people to do better. The critical spirit can be the complaining spirit too, and the murmurer and complainer does more harm than good.

If we could strive for the spirit of a St. Francis, and it would be good to read his life and struggles, we would be taking a first step. But it is only God Himself who can make a saint, can send the grace necessary to enable him to suffer the consequences of following his conscience and to do it in such a way as not to seem to be passing judgment on another, but rather win him to another point of view, with love and with respect.

When a man, black or white, reaches the point where he recognizes the worth of his soul (what does it profit a man if he gain the whole world and suffer the loss of his soul?), when he begins to realize what it means to be a child of God, the sense of his own dignity is so great that no indignity can touch him or discourage him from working for the common good.

It is for this that our shepherds are to be reproached, that they have not fed their sheep these strong meats, this doctrine of men divinized by the sacraments, capable of overcoming all obstacles in their advance to that kind of society where it is easier to be good.

Let Catholics form their associations, hold their meetings in their own homes, or in a hired hall, or any place else. No thought should stop them. Let the controversy come out into the open in this way.

But one must always follow one's conscience, preach the gospel in season, out of season, and that gospel is "all men are brothers."

❊ Red Roses for Her

(In Memoriam: Elizabeth Gurley Flynn)

DOROTHY DAY

I DREAMED of Gurley Flynn last night, and woke up thinking of how on Christmas Eve in 1957, Ammon Hennacy and I had gone to her apartment just off Second Avenue, which she shared with her sister. Not long before, she had been released from the Women's Federal Reformatory, at Alderson, West Virginia. Ammon and I had just come from the Women's House of Detention, over in Greenwich Village, outside of which we had been singing Christmas carols with a group of about fifty young people, a custom we had started the year before after the first of four brief sentences a number of us served for breaking the State Civil Defense Law by refusing to take shelter during the air-raid drills.

I had served a sentence of thirty days. But Gurley Flynn had spent twenty-eight months in a jail (I hate to call them "reformatories") far away from home and friends. Her sister had faithfully visited her each month. Ammon had brought a red rose for each of them, but it was really to Elizabeth Gurley Flynn that he was paying tribute. First of all, because she had valiantly endured jail many times; she had laid down her life for her brothers in this way. Certainly going to jail is dying to oneself, and living according to the great commandment of Jesus, who went beyond the Old Testament when he said: "A new commandment I give you." (Not only loving your neighbor as yourself, but loving him enough to lay down your life for him.)

In my dream I was there again with Ammon and Gurley Flynn, experiencing again her warmth, her equanimity, her humor, and above all, the *purpose* of her life. Her aim to help bring about the kind of society where each would work according to his ability and receive according to his needs, truly one of the noblest possible aims in life.

I had first met her when I was eighteen and she was lecturing at some workers' hall in Brooklyn. I was a reporter on the New York *Call*, which boasted a staff of socialist, anarchist, and Wobbly reporters, in addition to trade-unionists who divided their allegiance between the American Federation of Labor and the Amalgamated Clothing Workers, who had stayed outside the Federation. She was a member of the I.W.W. (Industrial Workers of the World), that truly indigenous form of unionism and radicalism. There had been no revolution in Russia as yet, and the I.W.W. was fought as bitterly as the Communists are today. In fact, it seems to me that anything that threatens money or property, anything that aims at a more equitable distribution of this world's goods, has always been called Communism. I like the word myself; it makes me think of the Communism of the religious orders. In fact, the success and prosperity of religious orders shows how beneficial Communism could be if it were practiced for all, rather than for only those professed religious who give up family, marriage and personal belongings to devote themselves to the problems of poverty. But, as the Ecumenical Council has stressed, this is the age of the laity, and the laity comprises all those who are not monks, priests, or nuns, but just ordinary brothers and sisters, in the widest sense of the word. Gurley Flynn was of the laity, and she was also my sister in this deep sense of the word. She always did what the laity is nowadays urged to do. She felt a responsibility to do all in her power in defense of the poor, to protect them against injustice and destitution.

On that night I first met her, she was speaking in behalf of the Mesabi iron miners of Minnesota, who were on strike at the time, and her words moved the large audience to tears. She charmed us out of our meager money; people emptied their pockets when the collection was taken for the strikers. I forsook all prudence and emptied my purse, not even leaving myself carfare to get back to the office. (My salary at the time was not more than ten dollars a week.) In this way she aided countless workers—miners throughout the far west, workers in wheat, lumber, textiles, all have benefited from her early work. If there had not been an I.W.W., there would have been no CIO.

You must forgive me if my emphasis is religious. Whenever Jesus spoke about the attitude man ought to have towards his brother, He always emphasized the problems of wealth and poverty. He told the story of the rich man who burned in hell while the poor man who had sat at his gate, sick and unemployed, was taken up into Abraham's bosom. (How loving a phrase that is!) He told the story of how the men who came to work at the end of the day got paid as much as those who had worked since early morning. How different from the attitude of the associated farmers of California, who consider themselves Christians! And when people asked Jesus, "When did we see you hungry or homeless, or in jail or sick, and did not visit you?" He answered them: "In so far as you did not do it to the least of these my brothers, you did not do it to me."

The great English writer George Orwell once said that one of the greatest tragedies of our age has been the loss of a sense of personal immortality. It may sound exaggerated to say that Gurley Flynn's *name* will be immortal in the labor and radical movements, but it brings out the point I wish to make. Orwell spoke of *personal* immortality, and that is the kind people who have a religious faith believe in, because it is clearly taught in the New Testament. "If we did not believe this, how vain our faith would be," St. Paul wrote. It is the core of our faith.

I don't think anyone really wants to die. Unless, of course, he is in such pain that he seeks death as a relief. But not a person as vital as Gurley Flynn, who enjoyed life so much, found so much to do, lived so keen an intellectual life (not in a philosophical sense, but rather in a "sociological" sense), who loved so ardently—no, I do not think that she wished to die, to go into oblivion, personally, she herself.

She has long been in my prayers, and I really believe that one's prayer is always answered. "Ask, and you shall receive," Jesus said, and He also said that God wills that *all* men be saved. I was once told by a good priest, and have often read it since, that there is no *time* with God. That is a difficult concept, philosophically and theologically. But it means that in this particular case all the prayers I have said, and will say in the future, will have meant that Gurley Flynn held out her arms to God (and the word God itself means Good, Truth, Love, all that is most beautiful) at the moment of her death, and was received by Him. And she will be judged by the love that is in her heart.

ED. NOTE: *Elizabeth Gurley Flynn, Secretary of the Communist Party of the United States, died in Moscow on September 5, 1964, at the age of seventy-two. Dorothy Day, invited to speak at the memorial meeting held for her in Community Church, New York City, in October, was in Vermont and unable to attend. However, she sent a message to the meeting, which was read aloud by Associate Editor Tom Cornell. Above is the substance of her remarks.*

OCTOBER 1965

❃ Chrystie Street

NICOLE D'ENTREMONT

EVERY DAY a little brown packet comes in the mail to 175 Chrystie Street. Inside there is usually a carefully wrapped sliver of soap or a half-roll of toilet paper or an envelope of sugar like the ones you find in restaurants. No one is quite sure who sends them. Bob Stewart tells me he remembers them coming when the CW was at Spring Street, a good five years ago. In any event the little packets continue to come and Walter files them in a basket on his desk. In moments of whimsy I often transplant the whole scene downtown to Merrill Lynch, Pierce, Fenner and Smith. I see visions of a three-buttoned, angular executive snapping the command, "Fisby, would you place these little packets in my basket?" The incongruity of the scene always amuses me. In fact, if a definition were ever attempted of our house on Chrystie Street I think it would have to symbolically include these little packets, since one of the facts of our community is that each person contributes what he can, with no thought as to whether the gift contributes to material gain. I wonder if Merrill Lynch, Pierce, Fenner and Smith could ever run that way.

There is a difference, of course, between profit and subsistence, and it looks as if we're in for a lean year of subsistence on Chrystie Street. The car is now running on two cylinders out of six and although Chris Kearns is a good mechanic, he's not a magician. A working car is a necessity for our house, since we have to pick up vegetables twice a week and run errands around the city. As it is, it's only a wish and a prayer and an expert kick from Chris that gets it going when we need it. Rents keep piling up, both on the Chrystie Street house and the apartments, and with winter on our heels the gas bills will soon rival the rent. Even Charlie's soup bones cost money, and lately these have been dwindling. Dorothy says that it's expensive to be poor and the truth of that statement is continually confirmed in any tenement community.

Even though the wolf's at the door, there is a lot of activity in the house with people working to mail out both the appeal and this issue of the paper. Quite a few new people have arrived since the summer. Terry Sullivan, fresh from Ammon Hennacy's house in Salt Lake City and enthused by the Peacemaker conference in Tivoli, has set up a program of traveling peace teams to go around and visit Catholic high schools and colleges, speaking on Vietnam, alternatives to the draft, and Christian pacifism. Three weeks ago we visited LaSalle College in Philadelphia, showed a film on Franz Jagerstatter, the Austrian peasant who refused Hitler's draft and was beheaded, set up a table in the Student Union with literature, and tried to talk with the students on a personal basis. It's hard to talk with students who have, for the most part, been systematically conditioned by both Church and state to reject pacifism. Almost every student I spoke to said that we must stop Communism now, and most, when pressed to suggest how, unhesitatingly answered that we should bomb China. Usually when speaking with students about the war in Vietnam you have several options. You can speak the language of logistics, suggesting that land war in Southeast Asia is doomed to a fruitless stalemate; you can speak historically, pointing out the United States prevented free elections in accord with the

Geneva Agreement; or you can speak of the witness of Christ. We found that the third option is irrelevant to most Catholic students, who have yet to realize that religion is a way of life and not only a cult of worship. Jim Wilson, a young draft refuser now at *The Catholic Worker,* has recently written a pamphlet on a Christian approach to peace in which he speaks unequivocally on war, the Church and Communism. In it he says:

> Most of us feel that we must fight or kill in order to defend something; a way of life, freedom, religion or Christ Himself. Many ask what would become of Christendom if Communism were allowed to spread. We cannot use Christ as an excuse for killing. We don't have to defend Christ or the Catholic Church by taking up arms. This was Peter's reason for raising his sword, to defend Christ from the mob that had come to crucify Him, and he was told by Christ Himself to put up his sword. We are being told today to put up our bombs, and not to defend Christ with violence but with love. This is not a defeatist attitude of "better red than dead." You must be ready to die if you are going to make a commitment to Christ. Anyone who states that he will not be able to remain a Christian under the Communist way of life, cannot really believe that he is a Christian now.

Terry, Paul Mann, Jim Wilson, Cathy Swann, Dave Miller and myself plan to leave tomorrow for New Hampshire to speak at St. Anselm's College, and then go on to Connecticut to speak at Albertus Magnus and St. Joseph's College. We are not so naive as to think we will convert people to pacifism because of a one-day or two-day stay on campus; what we hope to do is to challenge concepts of war and peace that need drastic rethinking in the twentieth century.

Paul, Jim and Dave are what is known in the unprejudiced argot of the press as "draft dodgers." Dave, now working for *The Catholic Worker* and a recent graduate of Le Moyne College, is one of the sanest and most temperate individuals I've ever known. Yesterday, at the Whitehall Street Induction Center in New York, he publicly burned his draft card while Federal agents and the press looked on. Such symbolic disobedience is not the action of a man out to dodge the draft but the action of a man who wishes to confront the system he opposes. The young men working at *The Catholic Worker* are conscientiously opposed to war. Perhaps after having seen the victims of the class war here in this country sleeping forgotten on the Bowery, running up and down the steps of crumbling tenements, or staring wide-eyed and alone in state mental hospitals, they do not want to fight for a materialistic system that cripples so many of its citizens. These are young men committed to the nonviolent revolution of our time. They are not the doctrinaire Marxists whom many of our right-wing friends oddly resemble, with their belief in the inevitability of a bloody conflict between East and

CHRYSTIE STREET • 143

West. These are young men who have learned well one historical fact, and that is that you can never win over an ideology by killing the men who have the idea. The job of the twentieth-century Christian is that of a peacemaker performing the works of mercy, not the works of war. Are such young men dodging or are they confronting reality?

PART V

Works of Peace

1966–1975

✢ Random Reflections on Poverty and Selling *Catholic Workers*

THOMAS P. MURRAY

THE CUSTOM of selling *The Catholic Worker* on the street began with Volume One, Number One, when Dorothy Day and Peter Maurin distributed the paper at the May Day celebration of 1933 at Union Square. Since then, many people have gone out to sell papers on the streets of New York. Ammon Hennacy has a regular schedule for paper sales in various locations, and sometimes I looked up his schedule in his book, *The Book of Ammon.* I would try to follow his schedule because the locations and times were well tested and productive, and many of his old friends still came by these places.

Several months ago, money being especially hard to come by, I began to sell papers in order to get carfare to get around the city. I would leave my place on Avenue A and 14th Street and walk over to Broadway and 14th Street, where I would sell papers until I had fifteen cents for a subway token. On my way back from wherever I had gone, I would sell fifteen cents' worth of papers to get back.

One day I decided to walk through the cars of the subway train and sell papers. I had always enjoyed selling papers on the street, with people whizzing by. I would watch all of their reactions—ignoring my outstretched copy of the paper, pausing and deciding if they wanted it, telling me they already had it at home, asking me what the paper had to say to Jewish workers, telling me in no uncertain terms that the paper wasn't Catholic and that if I was a worker I'd be out working instead of standing on a street corner doing nothing.

The subway was different. I am not sure I can explain completely how, but it was. On the streets people are in too much of a hurry to let a "newsboy" attract any more of their attention than is comfortable for them. On the subway they are trapped—they have to notice you. On the street I am reminded of the self-sufficient CW "salesmen" like Ammon and Jim Forest, but in the subway I am constantly aware that the looks I get from people are the same ones I notice when a blind or halt beggar moves through the car.

Perhaps that is the essential difference. On the subway I am a beggar. There is no getting around it, no losing sight of it. Sure, I am giving people something worth much more than the penny it costs. I am still begging. I am taking nickels, dimes and quarters because I need them. I am thrown upon these people. I am reduced to asking them to give— not in the impersonal exchange of a business transaction, or the friendly banter of the street, but in the bare reality of my need and my imposition of that need on largely unwilling and captive eyes and ears. Before I could analyze it or understand the dynamic of it I found myself, for a time, unable emotionally to bring myself to that first "*Catholic Worker*— only a penny—the Catholic anti-war paper—only a penny." I would stand mutely as station after station went by, trying to bring myself to speak up and at the same time trying to define whatever it was that was keeping me silent. I am only now beginning to realize what my feelings were and what their genesis was.

Voluntary poverty is hard to come by, and most often we really don't work as hard as we should to understand and practice it. Living in community helps somewhat, because you learn to accept the disappearance of your personal property into the community to meet the needs of others; but even this can happen without that stripping of self which poverty demands ever taking place. Voluntary poverty has to be a sharing in the lot of the poor. A great part of that poverty is the realization that *you* are poor, that is, you are dependent upon the giving of others. If you are poor, *you* become the beggar—not in enjoying the fruits of others' begging, but in the humiliating stares of people on the subway. What the subways had that frightened me was the stark confrontation with the fact that I was a beggar—not for others who were in need but for myself. The people sitting there didn't see a soup line or a clothing room, they saw *me*, were forced by my imposing chant to see *my* need. One of the things which brought me to see the personal nature of my fear was an encounter with a young college girl. We were standing on the BMT platform at Times Square, and I was churning inside at the prospect of selling papers on the train. As it pulled into the station this girl saw my papers and asked if I was selling the current issue. When she bought the paper I wasn't as clearly—in my own mind—the blind beggar, but the bearer of good news once again, and this gave me strength to sell papers after we got on the train.

Now I like to sell papers on the subway. It is still hard, but now I understand it and it helps to remind me of who I am and what my poverty is. It helps me to gain more understanding of my relationship both to those upon whom I am imposing my need and to those others who are brought to impose their need. I have got to let this teach me the necessity of letting others see my need and of letting them give. It is so easy to hide our need, to disguise it—to ourselves as well as to others.

This concept of letting other people give is also a "hard saying." It is really a part of our poverty. One night, during a snowstorm, my wife Jan and I decided to take a cab home from downtown. It was a bitter cold night, the snow was deep on the ground and heavy in the air. It was late, with no bus in sight. Our driver was a man with a full black beard, and he had a Bible on the dashboard. I assumed that he was an orthodox Jew, but he told us he was a Jehovah's Witness. As the cab came along the Bowery to Houston Street we saw a man lying across the traffic island in the middle of the street. He was struggling to get up but each time was thwarted by the snowy slush and his own inebriation. I asked the cab driver to pull over and went over to help the man across the street to the sidewalk. He was very drunk and had no home. He said that he had been staying at a flophouse nearby but had no money to stay there that night. I helped him upstairs and paid him in for the night. The night clerk knew him and gave him the room he had had the night before.

After the man was registered I went back to the cab. The driver asked if I knew him. I told him that I didn't but that the group I belonged to regularly paid men into the hotels on the Bowery when they had no place to go. When we got to the end of our trip, and I paid the driver, he asked me how much the flop had cost and offered me fifty-five cents, to pay half the cost. I started to refuse it, explaining that the *Worker* had a fund for this purpose and that I would be reimbursed, but he insisted that I had to let him share in my giving to the man on the Bowery. He was right. I had been all set to deny this man the joy of giving, the satisfaction of being a part of this act. Why? Because of the same image of self-sufficiency which made selling papers in the subway so hard. I didn't need his help to give. I could do it by myself—I could give without needing to take in this very personal way. I could not admit that I was as dependent upon the cab driver as the man on the Bowery was upon me—in fact, we were all equally dependent upon each other.

Jan tells another story which brings this home. During the subway strike, while she was walking uptown, she was approached by an elderly lady who asked if Jan would take her arm for the remaining two blocks. The woman only lived a block out of the way Jan was going, so Jan took her to her destination—a cheap hotel. While they walked Jan mentioned that she was on the way to buy a link for her bicycle chain. When they reached the hotel the woman reached into her handbag and took out some change. She offered it to Jan to buy the link—two quarters, a nickel and a penny. Jan could tell that the woman didn't have much, she was not richly dressed and the hotel she was living in was not an expensive one, and she didn't want to take the money. Then she realized that she had to take something. Even though the woman didn't have much, Jan couldn't refuse or just take a nickel as a token gesture. She had to take enough for the bicycle link—one of the quarters—because she couldn't refuse the woman the dignity and joy of giving. Even though the woman couldn't afford the quarter, she could even less afford to lose the opportunity to give.

This is a real truth about our voluntary poverty. We must constantly allow ourselves to see that we are beggars, that our poverty is a calling to allow others to give, not to take pride in our own giving. We all must be humble takers so that our giving will be real instead of self-serving. There is a Shaker hymn that Ed McCurdy sings:

'Tis a gift to be simple, 'tis a gift to be free,
'Tis a gift to come down where we ought to be,
And when we find ourselves in the place just right,
It will be in the valley of love and delight.

When true simplicity is gained,
To bow and to bend, we will not be ashamed,
To turn and to turn will be our delight,
'Till by turning, turning we come round right.

I guess the subway was part of the turning which leads to true simplicity. Once it is gained, I guess I won't be ashamed to be the bowing beggar. I guess that is part of what our voluntary poverty is for.

———————————————————————————————— DECEMBER 1966

❀ **Albert Camus and the Church**

THOMAS MERTON

"Why do you call me 'Sir'?" said the prison chaplain, "why don't you call me Father?"
"You are not my Father," said the condemned prisoner, "you are with the others."

AT THE END of Albert Camus' novel *The Stranger,* there is a long dialogue between priest and condemned prisoner. The chaplain, an average, sincere, zealous and not overbright priest is trying to grapple with the stolid unbelief of a man whom he considers the worst possible type of hardened criminal. He finally drives the man to complete desperation which explodes at last into a curious blend of Zen-Satori and existentialist revolt: the unexpected result of priestly zeal! The prisoner is a single-minded Algerian clerk, Meursault, who in a moment of thoughtlessness shot a man. He felt himself to have been partly irresponsible but failed to realize the importance of defending himself in terms that his society was willing to understand and accept. As a result he got the death penalty when, in fact, there were enough extenuating circumstances to warrant a much lighter sentence.

One of the themes of the novel is the ambiguity and "absurdity" of a justice which, though logical and right in its own terms, is seen to be an elaborate tissue of fictions—a complicated and dishonest social game in which there is no real concern for persons or values. Meursault is condemned, in fact, for not playing that game, as is made abundantly clear when the prosecution proves to the jury's outraged satisfaction that the accused did not weep at his mother's funeral. In the trial the sentimental exploitation of this fact curiously assumes a greater importance than the murder itself. The whole prosecution is sensational, pharisaical and indeed irrelevant to the actual case. All through the trial the accused, though not particularly smart, gradually realizes that society is interested not in what he really did, but only in completely reconstructing his personality and his actions to make him fit its own capricious requirements—its need for the complete evildoer.

And now the prison chaplain, having taken for granted all that has been decided in the courtroom, proceeds to work the prisoner over in the interests of other requirements: the need for a complete penitent. Since to repent one must first believe, the chaplain simply tries to convince Meursault that in his heart of hearts he "really believes" but does not know that he believes. Meursault replies that though he cannot be quite sure what interests him, he is quite certain of what does not interest him; and this includes the whole question of religion. Meursault is right to feel offended by the priest's self-assurance, which simply adds to the affront that the court has visited upon his dignity as a person.

All through the imprisonment and the trial, the prisoner has in fact been treated as if he were not there, as if he were so complete a nonentity that he was not able to think or even experience anything validly for himself. "I am with you," says the chaplain with smug assurance based on perfect moral superiority, "but you cannot realize this since you have a blinded heart." In the end the prisoner reacts with violent indignation against this cumulative refusal of lawyers (his own included), judges, jury, the press, the Church and society at large to accept him as a person. There is considerable bite in the sentence: "I answered that he was not my Father, he was with the others." After all what is a Father whose relation with his "son" is no more than his relation with a chair or a table—and a chair that is about to be thrown out with the rubbish?

Another ironic sentence shows up what Camus thought of the Church, as exemplified at least by this priest: "According to him the justice of men was nothing and the justice of God everything. I remarked that it was the former that had condemned me." The chaplain appears to make a distinction between the justice of man and the justice of God, but in actual fact he has assumed that the justice of man *is* the justice of God and that the truth of the verdict is the truth of God. When *bourgeois* society speaks, God speaks. This is taken so much for granted by him that he does not even think of questioning it.

Another priest, more subtly portrayed by Camus, is the Jesuit Paneloux in *The Plague*. In this novel Camus created a great modern myth in which he described man's condition in this life on earth. It refers more especially to French society. We know that *The Plague* is also about the German occupation of France, and Paneloux represents in some sense the French clergy under the Nazis. But he also represents the Church as she confronts man in his moral and metaphysical estrangement—his "lostness" in an absurd world. What will she offer him? Can she give him anything more than a predigested answer and a consoling rite? Does she ask of him anything more than conformity and resignation? At the outbreak of the plague Paneloux delivers a hell-fire sermon on the Justice of God and the punishment of iniquity, the need for penance and for a return to decent churchgoing lives. In other words the plague is a punishment. But for what, precisely? Sin! Later he learns, by working with the doctors in the "resistance," that things are not quite so simple as all that and that such a black-and-white interpretation of social or moral crises no longer convinces anyone. He proceeds to a new position which is, however, still unconvincing because no one can make out quite what it is. He now, in fact, demands a wager of blind faith that sounds like fatalism. In the end he lays down his life, but his sacrifice is ambiguous because, for obscure motives of his own, he has refused medical help.

There is in *The Plague* a decisive dialogue between Rieux the doctor and Paneloux the priest after they have witnessed the sufferings and death of a child. Paneloux no longer has any glib explanation, but only suggests that we must love what we cannot understand. Rieux replies, "I have a different conception of love. And I shall refuse to the bitter end to love this scheme of things in which children are tortured." This is a caricature of the theology of evil. Does Christianity demand that one "love a system, an explanation, a scheme of things," which for its coherence demands that people be tortured? Is that what the Gospel and the Cross mean? To some Christians, unfortunately, yes. And it is they who present Camus with an absurdity against which he must revolt. This is not a question of ill-will or culpable scandal—only a tragic misunderstanding. Camus' evaluation of the Church is not unusual and not totally unsympathetic, but it is especially worth attending to, since Camus has retained a kind of moral eminence (which he himself often repudiated) as the conscience of a new generation. By reason of his personal integrity, his genius, his eloquence and his own record in protest and resistance, Camus still speaks to our world with resounding authority. His judgments carry much more conviction than those of Sartre, for example, who has thrown in his lot with Marxist power politics, or those of Marcel and Mounier, who, though respected outside the Church, have exercised their influence mostly inside it.

If we as Catholics wish to get some idea of what the secular world thinks of us and expects of us, we can still with profit turn to Camus and question him on the subject. As a matter of fact, shortly after the end of the War the *avant-garde* Dominicans at the publishing house of Le Cerf invited Camus to come and answer this important question. Notes on the talk were preserved. They were very instructive and have lost none of their vitality today.

Camus opened his remarks to the Paris Dominicans with some interesting observations on dialogue. We are by now familiar enough with the fact that dialogue requires openness and honesty, and this supposes first of all that on both sides there is a complete willingness to accept the other as he is. This also presupposes a willingness to be oneself and not pretend to be someone else. On the part of the nonbeliever (Camus courteously begins with the nonbeliever), it is essential to avoid a kind of secular pharisaism *(pharisaisme laique)* which in the name of Christianity demands more of the Christian than the secularist demands of himself. "I certainly believe that the Christian has plenty of obligations," Camus admits, "but the man who himself rejects these obligations has no right to point them out to one who has recognized their existence." This is charitable of him, indeed. Pharisaism works two ways: on one hand the man who thinks that it is enough to *recognize* an obligation by a purely formal and punctilious fulfillment is a pharisee. On the other the man who detects the failure and points to it, without fulfilling an equivalent obligation himself, is also a pharisee. Camus had an exquisite eye for this kind of a thing, as his novels show. (See especially the perfect pharisaism of Clamence in *The Fall.*) According to him, pharisaism is one of the worst plagues of our time. In *The Stranger* the whole trial is an exhibition of the pure pharisaism of French *bourgeois* culture. Camus is no less aware of the pharisaism of Marxists, as we see in the long section devoted to them in *The Rebel.*

If it is not the business of the nonbeliever to judge the Christian's behavior, it is nevertheless essential that the Christian be a Christian if he is going to engage, as Christian, in dialogue with somebody else. Already in those days Camus had run into Catholics who, in their eagerness to be "open," were willing to throw their Catholicism out the window. True, the example he cites is not convincingly scandalous. In a discussion with Marxists at the Sorbonne, a Catholic priest had stood up and exclaimed, "I too am anti-clerical." There are a lot of us who know exactly what he meant and would, by now, be willing to join him in his declaration, if by "anti-clericalism" is meant weariness and exasperation with the seminary veneer of self-assurance, intolerance, expert knowledge of inscrutable sciences, and total moral superiority to the laity. Nevertheless, if one is a priest, one cannot allow oneself the rather indecent luxury of repudiating one's fellow priests *en bloc* in order to indulge one's own vanity or wounded feelings. It is quite true, and we must admit it, that life as a priest in these times of questioning and renewal is neither simple nor easy. One has to live with things that do not seem to be authentic or honest, let alone agreeable. One is likely to be impatient for reforms that are not only long in coming but may never come at all. And one may at the same time be the target of criticism which, though ambiguous, has enough ground in fact to be irritating. A cleric might well be tempted to free himself of these distressing conditions by joining some radical minority and taking up a position from which he can righteously attack his fellow clergy. If what he seeks by this is comfort for his own ego and recognition by an in-group of his own choice, Camus warns him that he is deluding himself.

Nevertheless, we must not take Camus' dislike of "anti-clerical priests" too absolutely. He did not mean to silence all public opinion and self-questioning within the Church. On the contrary, he called for such self-criticism and self-examination and he approved of it when he met it, for example, in his friend the Dominican Père Bruckberger ("Bruck"). Camus' notebooks abound in spiritual nosegays like these, culled from the garden of Bruck's conversation:

"G. has the look of a priest, a sort of episcopal unction. And I can hardly bear it in Bishops."

"Those Christian Democrats give me a pain in the neck."

Camus naively said to Bruck: "As a young man I thought all priests were happy." Bruck replied: "Fear of losing their faith makes them limit their sensitivity. It becomes merely a negative vocation. They don't face up to life." And Camus added: "His dream, a great conquering clergy, but magnificent in its poverty and audacity." Poverty and audacity were two qualities that appealed more and more to Camus. He looked for them, as we shall see, in the Catholic Church but did not always find them.

It would unduly complicate this article to go into Camus' difficulties with the Augustinian theology of sin and grace, and the reasons why he took scandal at a certain pessimistic religious approach to the problem of evil. But we recall that at the University of Algiers, Camus wrote the equivalent of an M.A. thesis on "Plotinus and St. Augustine." It is not enough to say, as one recent writer has said, that if Camus had read Teilhard de Chardin instead of Augustine he would have been more likely to become a Christian. Maybe so, maybe not. But he remained more or less impaled on the same dilemma as Ivan Karamazov:

if there are evil and suffering in the world, and if God is omnipotent, then the fact that He permits the evil must mean that He is responsible for it. And if the evil has to exist in order somehow to justify the divine omnipotence, then Camus will return his ticket to paradise, he doesn't want to go there if it means admitting that this is "right."

Stated in the terms in which he states it, the problem becomes an esthetic one which cannot really be solved by logic or metaphysics, a question of structure that is unsatisfactory because it lacks harmony and unity—it is in fact to him esthetically and morally absurd. He cannot accept it because it repels his imagination. It is like a play that falls apart in the third act. To demand that one simply accept this with resignation and to say it is "right" (in the sense of satisfactory to man's deepest sense of fittingness and order) is simply an affront to man, thinks Camus. And a lot of other people go along with him. We need not argue the theoretical point here.

What is crucially important in our world is not evil as an abstract scenario but evil as an existential fact. It is here that Camus speaks most clearly to the Church. The unbeliever and the Christian both live in a world in which they confront evil and the absurd. They have different ways of understanding these facts, but this does not make too much difference provided they offer authentic protest and resistance. Camus then raises the question that recently has been hotly debated as a result of Hochhuth's *The Deputy*. Why did not Rome speak out more clearly and forcefully against the crimes and barbarities of Nazism?

Why shall I not say this here? For a long time I waited during those terrible years, for a strong voice to be lifted up in Rome. I an unbeliever? Exactly. For I knew that spirit would be lost if it did not raise the cry of condemnation in the presence of force. It appears that this voice was raised. But I swear to you that millions of men, myself included, never heard it; and that there was in the hearts of believers and unbelievers a solitude which did not cease to grow as the days went by and the executioners multiplied. It was later explained to me that the condemnation had indeed been uttered, but in the language of encyclicals, which is not clear. The condemnation had been pronounced but it had not been understood. Who cannot see in this where the real condemnation lies? Who does not see that this example contains within it one of the elements of the answer, perhaps the whole answer to the question you have asked me? What the world expects of Christians is that Christians speak out and utter their condemnation in such a way that never a doubt, never a single doubt can arise in the heart of even the simplest man. *That Christians get out of their abstractions and stand face to face with the bloody mess that is our history today. The gathering we need today is the gathering together of men who are resolved to speak out clearly and pay with their own person. When a Spanish bishop blesses political executions he is no longer a bishop or a Christian or even a man. . . . We expect and I expect that all those will gather together who*

do not want to be dogs and who are determined to pay the price that has to be
paid if man is to be something more than a dog.

This is strong meat and it has lost nothing of its strength since 1948. It can be repeated today and perhaps with greater effect than before, since the Vatican Council has so obviously and explicitly told all Catholics to listen to what the world has to say to them. This is it!

Camus' challenge is nothing new. We can say the same thing to ourselves and we do when we are in the mood. And yet there remains always that fatal ambiguity, that confusion, the muddle, the fuss, the hesitation, the withdrawal into obscurity, and finally the negation of what we just said. We give it out with one hand and take it all back with the other. We promise everything and then cancel it all out by promising the opposite to someone else. In a word we have to please everybody. So we are uncertain, dubious, obscure. And finally we just give up and keep our mouths shut.

Fully to understand the implications of Camus' stark demand we have to see it against the background of his thought and not against the background of what has been standard practice in Christian society for centuries. We can accept with great good will Camus' declaration of the necessity to protest against injustice and evil. But when we look a little closer at society the picture is not so simple. It is on the contrary very intricate, and threads work within threads in a complex social tapestry in which, everywhere, are the faces of bishops, of priests and of our fellow Catholics. We are involved everywhere in everything and we have to go easy. . . . Perhaps that is why it is so simple to blast off against Communism. There are no bishops of ours in Russia and we have nothing invested there except hopes. Communism has made it easy for us; by its single-minded hostility to the Church it has become the one force we can always condemn without compromise at any moment—until perhaps we start making deals with Communism too. Then there will be nobody left!

Where we see unavoidable, distressing and yet "normal" complications, Camus sees the "absurd." What we accept and come to terms with, he denounces and resists. The "absurd" of Camus is not the metaphysical absurd and *neant* of Sartre, and his "revolt" is not the Sartrian nausea. The absurd of Camus is the gap between the actual shape of life and intelligent truth. Absurdity is compounded by the ambiguous and false explanations, interpretations, conventions, justifications, legalizations, evasions which infect our struggling civilization with the "plague" and which often bring us most dangerously close to perfect nihilism when they offer a security based on a seemingly rational use of absolute power.

It is here we are forced to confront the presence of "the absurd" in the painful, humiliating contradictions and ambiguities which are constantly and everywhere evident in our behavior as Christians in the world. To mention only one: the scandal of men who claim to believe in a religion of love, mercy, forgiveness and peace, dedicating themselves wholeheartedly and single-mindedly to secular ideologies of hate, cruelty, revenge and war and lending to those ideologies the support of a Christian moral casuistry. And when the Church officially examines her conscience before the world and repudiates this contradiction, many Catholics still find ways of ignoring and evading the consequences of what the Church has said. "The arms race is an utterly treacherous trap for humanity and one which injures the poor to an intolerable degree.... Divine Providence urgently demands of us that we free ourselves from the age-old slavery of war. But if we refuse to make this effort..." (Vatican Council II, *Gaudium et Spes*, 81.) Who is making a really serious effort? A few of us are perhaps thinking it over! Certainly the Church has spoken without ambiguity though still in official language: but if Christians themselves do not pay attention, or simply shrug the whole thing off, the ambiguity persists, and it is perhaps more disconcerting than it was before. The prisoner in *The Stranger* did not even hope that the chaplain would be any less absurd than the lawyers and the judges. He knew in advance he was "with all the others"!

To really understand what Camus asked of Christians that evening at the Dominican house of Latour-Maubourg, we would have to understand his difficult analysis of two centuries of cultural and political history in *The Rebel*. This book is, admittedly, a failure. But its insights remain nevertheless extremely precious, and they enable us still to see through the specious claims of the power politician (so often accepted without question by Christians both of the right and of the left) and to detect beneath the superficial arguments the absurd void of nihilism and mass murder. At this point we might quote a Catholic thinker, Claude Tresmontant, who restates in purely Catholic terms exactly what Camus means by being a "Rebel" against the "absurd."

> But the child is going to inherit also, and especially by the education he is going to receive from his environment, a set of ready-made ideas, a system of judgments, a scale of values which, as often as not, he will not be able to question or criticize. This system of values, in the aggregate of nations, in large part is criminal. It is the reflection of a criminal world in which man oppresses, massacres, tortures, humiliates and exploits his brother. The child enters into an organized world, on the political, economic, mental, mythological, psychological and other planes. And the structure of this world is penetrated and informed by sin. The child is not born in Paradise. It is born in a criminal humanity. In order to have access to justice, to sanctity, the child, as it grows up, will have to make a personal act of judgment, of refusal, of choice. It will have to make a personal act of opposition to the values of its tribe, of its caste, of its nation or of its race, and of its social class, in order to attain justice.

To a certain extent it will have to leave its tribe, its nation, its care, its class, its race, as Abraham, the father of the faithful did, who left Ur of the Chaldees to go into a country that he did not know. Holiness begins with a breach. Nothing can dispense this child from breaking with "the world." In order to enter into Christianity, the child will have to choose between the values of the world, the values of the tribe, its nation or its social class, and the values of the Gospel. It must renew its scale of values. It must, as it were, be born anew from the spiritual point of view: it must become a new creature. Tertullian said one is not born a Christian. One becomes a Christian. The access to Christianity represents a new birth. One can then legitimately distinguish between the state which precedes this new birth and the state which follows it. The state which precedes this new birth is the state which the Church calls "original sin."

(Christian Metaphysics)

But does the Catholic Church clearly and always define the relation of the Christian to secular society in these terms? Does it not, in fact, like the chaplain in *The Stranger,* identify itself at times with this society?

For Camus it is clear that a certain type of thinking and talking, a certain type of mental attitude, even though it may be vested in the most edifying clichés, betrays a firm commitment to economic and political interests which are incompatible in the long run with the message of the Gospel, the true teaching of the Church and the Christian mission in the world. It is the commitment that speaks louder than any words. It manifests itself in the peculiar absurdity of official double-talk, the language of bureaucratic evasion, which, while nodding politely to Christian principles, effectively comes out in full support of wealth, injustice and brute power. For Camus it is axiomatic that any ideology, any program, whether of the right or the left, which leads to mass murder and concentration camps as a direct consequence is to be revolted against, no matter how "reasonable" and "right" it is made to appear.

Speaking in an interview in São Paulo, Brazil in 1949, Camus said: "Only the friends of dictatorships, the people who set up concentration camps, can be in favor of war. It is the duty of writers to sound the alarm and to fight against every form of slavery. That is our job."

The Camusian "Rebel" fulfills the role of the prophet in modern society, and it is to the writer and the artist that Camus looks above all to carry out this essential task. Nowhere in his work do we find him expressing any real hope of this prophetic voice being in the pulpit or in the documents of the Church, though as we have seen, he still says it is the Church's job to speak out also. He no longer looks to her for guidance—but he does at least hope for a little support. If she cannot lead, she can at least follow!

In the same interview, speaking of the poet René Char, "the biggest event in French poetry since Rimbaud," he says he expects far more from poets than from moralists: "When you say 'poetry' you are close to love, that great force which one cannot replace with money, which is vile, nor with that pitiable thing they call *'La Morale'.*" (Note that in French primary schools there is—or was—a weekly class in *"La Morale"* in which the children memorize the most appalling platitudes. One wonders if our catechism is much better.)

It was said above that *The Rebel* is not a fully successful thesis on revolt. In spite of some acute and detailed analysis and diagnosis nothing is very positively prescribed. But there remains a basic ambiguity in the book. In his study of modern revolutionary violence and his analysis of its inevitable trend toward tyranny and mass murder, Camus attributes this to the godlessness of modern revolutionaries. At the same time he admits that without God there can be no rational philosophy and practice of non-violence. Yet he still cannot make the Pascalian wager of faith (by which he seems at times to be tempted). If there is to be a choice between faith and the absurd, his stoic conscience will, in the end, dictate the choice of the absurd. And the "absurd man" of Camus remains strangely isolated, even though, if he is consistently faithful to his steady view of the absurd, he should proceed to a revolt that joins him in solidarity with other men of his own kind. But this solidarity lacks human validity unless it is in the service of life and humanity. In other words, revolt is legitimate only if it refuses all complicity with mass murder and totalitarianism of whatever kind, whether of the right or of the left.

"There is one problem only today," said Camus in a statement of 1946, "and that is the problem of murder. All our disputes are vain. One thing alone matters, and that is peace."

However, Camus was never an out-and-out pacifist. He always admitted the possibility of a strictly limited use of force. He had various reasons for this, besides the rather complex one of his rejection of faith in God, which at the same time implied the impossibility, for him, of consistent nonviolence and pacifism. Since many can attain only an "approximation of justice" then it is futile for him to hope to avoid all use of force, but he must restrain himself and exercise full, indeed heroic responsibility in keeping the use of force down to the minimum, where it is always provisional and limited and never in favor of a cause that consecrates and codifies violence as a permanent factor in its policies.

The peculiar isolation of Camus' position comes from his inability to cope with the idea of God and of faith to which his sense of justice and his instinctive nonviolence nevertheless enticed him. In the same way, he was led up to the "silence of God" by his interest in the studies on phenomenology of language written by his friend, Brice Parain, an existentialist who became a Catholic in the late forties, when he was closely associated with Camus. In fact we cannot do full justice to Camus' relations with the Church without taking into consideration his interest in the ideas of Parain. It is here that Camus' dialogue with Catholicism developed on the most intimate and profound level.

In an age of highly academic linguistic analysis, Camus appreciated the courage of Parain, who sees the problem of language as ultimately a *metaphysical* problem. The questioning of meaning raises the whole question of reality itself and in the end Parain is asking one thing above all: can language make sense if there is no God? In other words, what is the point of talking about truth and falsity if there is no God? Is not man, in that case, reduced to putting together a series of more or less arbitrary noises in the solitude of a mute world? Are these noises anything more than the signals of animals and birds? True, our noises exist in a very complex on-going context of development and are richly associated with one another and with other cultural phenomena: but can they be true? And does this matter? Or are they merely incidents in a developing adventure that will one day end in some kind of meaning but which, for the time being, has none?

Parain rejects this post-Hegelian position and returns to the classical ideas of language as able to provide grounds for at least elementary certitude. If language has no meaning then nothing has any meaning. Language has enough meaning, at least, to reassure us that we are not floating in a pure void. In other words, communication becomes possible, and with it community, once it is admitted that our words are capable of being true or false and that the decision is largely up to us. "To name a thing wrong is to add to the miseries of the world." We are thus called to take care of our language, and use it clearly. "The great task of man is not to serve the lie." These words of Parain might have been uttered—and have been uttered equivalently, many times—by Camus. And so Camus says in a review-article of Parain's books: "It is not altogether certain that our epoch has lacked gods: it seems on the contrary that what we need is a dictionary."

It is certainly true that the twentieth century has been distinguished for its single-minded adoration of political and cultural idols rather than for the clarity and honesty of its official speech. The sheer quantity of printed and broadcasted double-talk overwhelms the lucid utterances of a few men like Camus.

But once again, Camus remains sober and un-idealistic. Our task is not suddenly to burst out into the dazzle of utter unadulterated truth but laboriously to reshape an accurate and honest language that will permit communication between men on all social and intellectual levels, instead of multiplying a Babel of esoteric and technical tongues which isolate men in their specialties.

What characterizes our century is not so much that we have to rebuild our world as that we have to rethink it. This amounts to saying that we have to give it back its language. . . . The vocabularies that are proposed to us are of no use to us . . . and there is no point in a Byzantine exercise upon themes of grammar. We need a profound questioning which will not separate us from the sufferings of men. . . .

It is unfortunately true that the "Byzantine exercises" not only of logical positivism (which nevertheless has a certain limited value) but of all kinds of technical and specialized thinking, tend to remove us from the world in which others, and we ourselves, are plunged in the dangers and the sufferings of an increasingly absurd and unmanageable social situation. As Camus and Parain have seen, we have to *rethink* that whole situation and we no longer possess the language with which to do it.

Such a language will necessarily confine itself at first to formulating what is accessible to all men. But it will not talk down to them or cajole them. It will enable them to lift themselves up. Yet if the artist, the peasant, the scientist and the workman are all going to communicate together, their language will have to have a certain simplicity and austerity in order to be clear to them all without degrading thought. This means not the attainment of a pure classic prose (though Camus admits he thinks of a "new Classicism") but rather of a kind of "superior banality" which will consist in "returning to the words of everybody, but bringing to them the honesty that *is required for them to be purified of lies and hatred.*"

It is at this point that we can see what Camus is asking not only of intellectuals but also of the Church: this *purification and restitution of language so that the truth may become once again unambiguous and fully accessible to all men, especially when they need to know what to do.*

I think that everybody will readily admit that the language of the Church is distinguished by a "superior banality," but this is not the kind that Camus was talking about. We can certainly say that the Church speaks without hatred and that she does not lie. On the other hand, as we saw, it is quite possible for her to speak in such complex, unclear, evasive and bureaucratic language that her message is simply inaccessible even to a reader of some education and average patience. With a few outstanding exceptions, the clergy, Catholic thinkers, teachers, writers, too often speak so confusedly, so timidly, so obscurely, that even when they are telling the truth they manage to keep it out of circulation. In fact one sometimes wonders if some of the writers of official documents have not trained themselves to tell the truth in such a way that it will have no visible effect. Then one can say indeed that one has "told the truth" but nobody will have gotten excited or done anything about it!

After all, it was not Camus who said to the Church: "Go, teach all nations." And the teaching of the nations is not to be accomplished by the triumphant utterance of totally obscure generalities. It is not enough for us to be at once meticulously correct and absolutely uninteresting and unclear. Nor, when we have clarified our speech and livened it up a bit, can we be content that we have merely *declared* the truth, made it public, announced it to the world. Are we concerned merely to get others to *hear* us? We have a hearing. But how many of those that hear us, and understand what we are saying, are convinced? Perhaps we are satisfied with proving to them (and thereby to ourselves) that we are convinced. But the kind of rethinking that Camus—and the world—calls for demands not only the publication of official statements but the *common effort to arrive at new aspects of the truth,* in other words dialogue, community, not only among believers but between believers and unbelievers as well.

The whole truth of Albert Camus is centered upon the idea of *telling the truth.* The relation of words to the inscrutable presence of what he called the power of words to identify the absurd as such. The function of words in establishing community among men engaged in resisting and overcoming the absurd. The power of words to lead revolt in a creative and life-affirming direction. The power of words against murder, violence, tyranny, injustice, death. The novels, stories and essays of Camus explore this question from many angles, and everywhere they reach the conclusion: we live in a world of lies, which is therefore a world of violence and murder. We need to rebuild a world of peace. We cannot do this unless we can recover the language and think of peace.

The tragedy that is latent behind the fair and true declarations of the Church on peace, justice, renewal and all the rest is that these words of truth and hope are being devoured and swallowed up in the massive confusion and indifference of a *world that does not know how to think in terms of peace and justice because in practice the word peace means nothing but war and the word justice means nothing but trickery, bribery and oppression.*

Anything the Church may say to such a world is immediately translated into its opposite—if indeed the Churchmen themselves are not already beguiled by the same doubletalk as the world in which they live. To all of us, Camus is saying: "Not lying is more than just not dissimulating one's acts and intentions. *It is carrying them out and speaking them out in truth.*"

❈ "In Peace Is My Bitterness Most Bitter"

DOROTHY DAY

IT IS NOT JUST Vietnam. It is South Africa, it is Nigeria, the Congo, Indonesia, all of Latin America. It is not just the pictures of all the women and children who have been burnt alive in Vietnam, or the men who have been tortured, and died. It is not just the headless victims of the war in Colombia. It is not just the words of Cardinal Spellman and Archbishop Hannan. It is the fact that whether we like it or not, we are Americans. It is indeed our country, right or wrong, as the Cardinal said in another context. We are warm and fed and secure (aside from occasional muggings and murders amongst us). We are among nations the most powerful, the most armed, and we are supplying arms and money to the rest of the world where we are not ourselves fighting. We are eating while there is famine in the world.

Scripture tells us that the picture of judgment presented to us by Jesus is of Dives sitting and feasting with his friends while Lazarus sat hungry at the gate, the dogs, the scavengers of the East, licking his sores. We are Dives. Woe to the rich! We are the rich. The Works of Mercy are the opposite of the works of war, feeding the hungry, sheltering the homeless, nursing the sick, visiting the prisoner. But we are destroying the crops, setting fire to entire villages and to the people in them. We are not performing the Works of Mercy but the works of war. We cannot repeat this enough.

When the apostles wanted to call down fire from heaven on the inhospitable Samaritans, the "enemies" of the Jews, Jesus said to them, "You know not of what Spirit you are." When Peter told our Lord not to accept the way of the Cross and His own death, He said, "Get behind me, Satan. For you are not on the side of God but of men." But He also had said, "Thou art Peter and upon this rock I will build my church." Peter denied Jesus three times at that time in history, but after the death on the Cross, and the Resurrection and the Descent of the Holy Spirit, Peter faced up to Church and State alike and said, "We must obey God rather than men." Deliver us, O Lord, from the fear of our enemies, which makes cowards of us all.

I can sit in the presence of the Blessed Sacrament and wrestle for that peace in the bitterness of my soul, a bitterness which many Catholics throughout the world feel, and I can find many things in Scripture to console me, to change my heart from hatred to love of enemy. "Our worst enemies are those of our own household," Jesus said. Picking up the Scriptures at random (as St. Francis used to do) I read about Peter, James, and John who went up on the Mount of Transfiguration and saw Jesus talking with Moses and Elias, transfigured before their eyes. (A hint of the life to come, Maritain said.) Jesus transfigured! He who was the despised of men, no beauty in Him, spat upon, beaten, dragged to His cruel death on the way to the cross! A man so much like other men that it took the kiss of a Judas to single Him out from the others when the soldiers, so closely allied to the priests, came to take Him. Reading this story of the Transfiguration, the words stood out, words foolishly babbled, about the first building project of the Church, proposed by Peter. "Lord, shall we make here three shelters, one for you, one for Moses and one for Elias?" And the account continues, "for he did not know what to say, he was so terrified."

Maybe they are terrified, these Princes of the Church, as we are often terrified at the sight of violence, which is present every now and then in our houses of hospitality, and which is always a threat in the streets of the slums. I have often thought it is a brave thing to do, these Christmas visits of Cardinal Spellman to the American troops all over the world, Europe, Korea, Vietnam. But oh, God, what are all these Americans, so-called Christians doing all over the world so far from our own shores?

But what words are those he spoke—going against even the Pope, calling for victory, total victory? Words are as strong and powerful as bombs, as napalm. How much the government counts on those words, pays for those words to exalt our own way of life, to build up fear of the enemy. Deliver us, Lord, from the fear of the enemy. That is one of the lines in the Psalms, and we are not asking God to deliver us from enemies but from the fear of them. Love casts out fear, but we have to get over the fear in order to get close enough to love them.

There is plenty to do, for each one of us, working on our own hearts, changing our own attitudes, in our own neighborhoods. If the just man falls seven times daily, we each one of us fall more than that in thought, word, and deed. Prayer and fasting, taking up our own cross daily and following Him, doing penance, these are the hard words of the Gospel.

As to the Church, where else shall we go, except to the Bride of Christ, one flesh with Christ? Though she is a harlot at times, she is our Mother. We should read the book of Hosea, which is a picture of God's steadfast love not only for the Jews, His chosen people, but for His Church, of which we are every one of us members or potential members. Since there is no time with God, we are all one, all one body, Chinese, Russians, Vietnamese, and He has *commanded us to love another.*

"A new commandment I give, that you love others *as I have loved you*," not to the defending of your life, but to the laying down of your life. A hard saying.

"Love is indeed a harsh and dreadful thing" to ask of us, of each one of us, but it is the only answer.

❀ Spring Appeal

St. Joseph's House of Hospitality
175 Chrystie Street
New York, NY 10002

DEAR FELLOW WORKERS IN CHRIST,

We reach those we can, which means those who come to our door. Holy Mother the City and Holy Mother the State are doing much to relieve the want of the unemployable and the displaced. But there is plenty of room for the non-governmental agencies, and for the individual who believes with Eric Gill that Jesus Christ came to make the rich poor, and the poor holy.

I think most of us wish to be poor, to simplify our lives, to throw out the trash and make more room for the good—to put off the old man and put on the new—to be new creatures, as St. Paul said. It's the essence of Spring that it makes all things new, though there is not much suggestion of Spring on this March snowy day that I write. But none of us wishes to be destitute. And it is the destitute who come to us day after day for help. "Deal your bread to the hungry and take those without shelter into your house," we are told at the beginning of Lent. That has meant that we have grown into a community of sorts, and somehow or other the Lord has blessed us and sent us what we needed over the years. But He told us to ask, "Ask and you shall receive, seek and you shall find, knock and it shall be opened to you." I love those words and recommend them to all. Pascal even elaborated on the second part and put the words into the mouth of our Lord, "You would not seek me if you had not already found me," thinking, I suppose, that there is no time with God. The seeking is the finding. So I write with confidence in regard to the rest of the Lord's words and I am asking again, and knocking again at your doors, as we have done for many years, twice a year, and you have kept answering. But it is like the manna—there is enough for the day, and we never have anything left over. Someone said once, "You are certainly a success in your voluntary poverty. You have managed to maintain it for these many years." But again I repeat, it is not destitution, but a sharing which the Lord Jesus enables us to do because He continues to multiply the Loaves and Fishes for us, day after day. What need of foundation funds or government funds to do the work we do? St. Hilary commented once, "The less we have of Caesar's the less we will have to render to Caesar." And Jesus Himself said, "Your heavenly Father knows you have need of these things," food and shelter, and the means to keep on doing the work He has given us to do, the corporal and spiritual Works of Mercy.

It is the month of St. Joseph, traditionally speaking, and being a woman I appeal in the name of St. Joseph, as the head of our house, and he in turn appeals to the foster Son he cared for. I am appealing to him, not only to send us the money, through your generous hands, to pay our bills, but also to help us obtain the house we are trying to buy to take the place of the scattered apartments we are now living in. (The roof is in danger of falling in on the house we occupy during the day for office, meeting room, and bread lines.) We must move—but how, when the housing code calls for such changes in the repair of a house before we can move in and which four contractors estimate will cost us $50,000? An enormous sum, which we shudder to think of, let alone ask St. Joseph to concern himself with. And yet, the city estimate of the cost of a new house to provide shelter for homeless women is $700,000, according to a news story, whereas the house we have in view costs $35,000 plus the repairs of $50,000. As I speak of these sums it is almost as though I were playing a game of Monopoly with my grandchildren and not talking about Catholic Worker needs.

But to count the way city agencies count—we have provided 8,700 nights' lodging for women (not counting the men) in the last year, and at Chrystie Street alone we have served meals to 109,500 guests, men and women, those who work with us as volunteers and those who come to get help, because we sit down to the same table, "knowing Christ and each other in the breaking of bread."

So, hoping against hope, as St. Paul said, I appeal to you again, our dear readers and fellow workers.

Gratefully in Christ,
DOROTHY DAY

❀ Fear in Our Time

DOROTHY DAY

PEOPLE PROBABLY DO NOT realize with what fear and trembling I speak or write about the Catholic Worker, our ideas, and our point of view. It is an extreme point of view, and yet it is tested and proved over and over again; it is almost as if God says to us, "Do you really mean what you say?" and then gives us a chance to prove it. We have to live with the positions we take, and at the same time we are bound to be beset with all kinds of human doubts: who are we, who have so seldom been tried and have not suffered as others have in war, to take such a position? I know what human fear is and how often it keeps us from following our conscience. We find so many ways of rationalizing our positions. There are all kinds of fear: fear of losing our bodily goods, fear of poverty, fear of losing our job, our reputation, and not least of all there is the strange business of bodily fear. Gandhi's son once described the humiliation he felt at seeing his father beaten up in a railway station in South Africa. Nothing is worse than that sense of utter humiliation we feel when pain is inflicted on us. We are reduced to an animal status; we are lesser men for having taken a blow or endured pain.

One of the situations when I was most afraid was in my visit some years ago to Koinonia, an interracial community in Americus, Georgia. A very wonderful Baptist minister named Clarence Jordan and a few of his companions from a theological seminary in the South had decided to tackle the problems of poverty, interracial conflict, and agriculture by taking over two thousand acres of land and starting a community based on diversified farming. They had cattle and cultivated fruit, nuts, cotton, and all kinds of vegetables. This truly interracial community thrived and prospered until they came to public attention when they endorsed some young Negro men who were trying to get into a white college. This precipitated a real reign of terror.

The elaborate roadside stand with a refrigeration system that the community used to market its smoked ham, bacon, and other meats, was dynamited and completely destroyed in the middle of the night. Community members were shot at, some of the houses were burnt down, marauders cut the wire that fenced in the cattle, and threw torches into the hay barn, setting fire to the hay. They were boycotted, couldn't buy oil for their tractors or cars, couldn't buy seed or fertilizer, couldn't get insurance on their cars or houses.

When Clarence Jordan came up to New York City and spoke in Community Church, many people volunteered to go down there and help out. Four of us from the Catholic Worker went down and stayed for two weeks each, during the spring, when they were planting. One day I went out with some of the community members in a truck to try to buy seeds. When we entered a store we were called "nigger-lovers," and I was called a "northern Communist whore." And similar expressions of hate and contempt and venom were flung at us in every store we went into. We drove from town to town trying to buy seed, and were, of course, unsuccessful. But we did learn something of what mob hatred is like. And I must say that it makes your blood run cold. Not many of us ever experienced this kind of venomous hatred. Even though we know what has happened, what unbelievable atrocities have been committed in the South over the years: Negroes dragged behind cars and killed and cut into pieces for souvenirs, unbelievable hatred and murder and torture going on over the years. It has been lessening, of course, year by year. When a year passes without a single lynching, everybody congratulates themselves.

The men were so busy with the spring planting that the women volunteered to watch at night. We signed up for two or three hours of watching at a public road that ran between two pieces of Koinonia property. We were supposed to sit in the station wagon and if we saw a car coming down the road, get out with lanterns and walk up and down to let them know people were there. If any injury was offered, we were to try and get the license number of the car.

About two o'clock in the morning, while I was engaged in conversation about voluntary communities with the woman who was sharing the watch with me, a car with no lights on came down the road and suddenly the car we were in was peppered with shots. The car was there and gone before we could realize what had happened. It is strange how the fear always comes afterward, your bones turn to water, and your whole body seems to melt away with fear.

A few years ago I went down to Danville, Virginia, at the invitation of a white nun. There again I had an opportunity to experience this sense of fear, to realize how strong and persistent it is. The nun, Mother Teresa, had taken part in a protest on the steps of City Hall, along with a group of Negroes. Three ministers who had helped organize the demonstration had been herded into an alley, where fire hoses had been turned on them. They were then beaten unmercifully and thrown into prison.

After Mother Teresa spoke on the local radio station about the protest, the priest of her district told her that she would be put under interdict if she continued these activities and that he was going to ask the bishop to see to it that her work was stopped. She was an elderly woman and her work, which she had been building up for the past twenty years, was very dear to her. It is a small order, the Order of Christ the King, which serves both Negroes and whites. So she telephoned me and asked if I would come down and take her place at a Negro meeting where she had promised to speak. The meeting was held in a large church which was filled with people. They sang hymns, prayed together, and listened to speakers who had just been released from prison. I spoke about nonviolence. It is very hard to speak on such occasions and I haven't the slightest idea now what I said.

When you're with a group, when there's a whole night of singing, in the churches, on the streets, in the prisons, the very act of singing produces a tremendous courage and all fear evaporates. You can walk on the picket line and though you are conscious of the terrible hostility around you and there is a wrecked building across the way and a whole vacant lot is filled with bricks, handy for a battle, you have this sense of courage. Why? Because you have prayed for it; and because you are with others. The women on the picket line with me had never been on a picket line or taken part in any kind of demonstration, although one of them was carrying a sign which said, "I forgive the chief of police the beating he gave me." She had been kicked and trampled on and had her face smashed. The same brutality that was inflicted upon the men had been inflicted on the women and children. It is something that can scarcely be understood or described. I think that we should acknowledge this fear and recognize that it is something valid, but also something that we have to fight against.

It seems to me that we must begin to equal a little bit the courage of the Communists. One of the ways my Communist friends taunt me is by saying, in effect, "People who are religious believe in everlasting life, and yet look how cowardly they are. And we who believe only in this life, see how hard we work and how much we sacrifice. We are not trying to enjoy all this and heaven too. We are willing to give up our life in order to save it."

There is really no answer to this kind of taunt. When I was in Cuba in September 1962, I witnessed what a Franciscan priest, Herve Chaigne, has called an "exemplary" revolution. I felt that it was an example to us in zeal, in idealism, and in self-sacrifice and that unless we began to approach in our profession of Christianity some of this zeal of the Communists, we weren't going to get anywhere. But we have to go ahead and think in terms of a third way, not just those two alternatives, capitalism or communism, or my country or the fellowship of all men. We have to begin to see what Christianity really is, that "our God is a living fire; though He slay me yet will I trust him." We have to think in terms of the Beatitudes and the Sermon on the Mount and have this readiness to suffer. "We have not yet resisted unto blood." We have not yet loved our neighbor with the kind of love that is a precept to the extent of laying down our life for him. And our life very often means our money, money that we have sweated for; it means our bread, our daily living, our rent, our clothes. We haven't shown ourselves ready to lay down our life. This is a new precept, it is a new way, it is the new man we are supposed to become. I always comfort myself by saying that Christianity is only two days old (a thousand years are as one day in the sight of God) and so it is only a couple of days that are past and now it is about time we began to take these things literally, to begin tomorrow morning and say, "now I have begun."

Everyone used to laugh at Ammon Hennacy who boasted about how many times he had been in prison and would always ask people, "Have you been in jail?" If you hadn't been in jail you were scarcely of the fraternity. Well, you go to jail, and you think that here maybe you will have a chance to be really poor. We talk about poverty and being poor in spirit. But meanwhile we have to admit that we have comfortable backgrounds, we have had an education, we have all kinds of enjoyments, like reading and listening to music. We have our luxuries even while we talk about voluntary poverty. And we realize that all the time.

When you go to jail you finally feel that you are being stripped of whatever you have. You look on as the police empty your handbag. You start right out being humiliated by having so much in your handbag. I remember when we first demonstrated against taking shelter in an air-raid drill, in 1955. There were twenty-eight of us and we had to be photographed, finger printed, stripped, showered, and examined. It went on until 4:00 in the morning. We were put in tiny cells that were anything but clean; the mattresses were stained and dirty. You look at the equipment of a city prison in the great city of New York in the richest country of the world and you think how unbelievable it is that they cannot afford anything better than this for their prisoners.

There's a little element of fear there too because one of the things that has been done when people are in prison for conscience is to instigate, to build up resentment, especially in wartime, among the other prisoners, by saying that pacifists are spies, Communists, etc.; people have been maltreated and abused in prison because of this. There is also the hostility between Negroes and whites that is quite apt to break out, so that there is an element of fear in your imagination that conjures up these things.

But in general, there is a feeling of relief when you are in prison. Here you are now, stripped of everything, no responsibility of any kind, no telephones, no mail; you are there, and Holy Mother the State is taking care of you. The food in the city prison was good, just as good as Catholic Worker food, and there was a great abundance of it. As a matter of fact, we saw so much being thrown out after every meal, as it is in the army, and thought, what a horrible waste.

The cells were small, we were confined and got little air; there were tiny little windows and we almost stifled in summer time. So we had our discomforts. But there was a commissary and I was able to buy some instant coffee and take my missal and lie down on my cot free of all responsibility. So there was luxury even there.

I have often thought of the youths in the fiery furnace who sang the Psalms and the fire was just like a gentle wind and they were conscious of another person with them. In Shackleton's account of his exploration in the Arctic he tells how he and two companions were going over a horrible glacier, a journey that involved much danger and suffering. And all of them said afterwards that they had been conscious of another person along with them. The youths of Uganda, Protestant and Catholic, who were buried alive in the 1880s also went to their doom singing hymns. Since then we have the example of Buddhist monks and American war protesters submitting themselves to the flames. It is hard to believe and we cringe in fear at the very thought. And we don't believe that we'll ever have the strength to take the way of nonviolence which may result in physical martyrdom. We don't believe in God's mercy, and we can only say, "Help thou mine unbelief. Take away my heart of stone and give me a heart of flesh. In thee have I hoped, let me never be confounded." These are the acts of faith, hope, and charity.

Before World War II one of our friends used to drive a truck around to factories in Baltimore, selling coffee, sandwiches, and doughnuts, and began to drop off the leftovers at our House of Hospitality in that city. Pretty soon he came to feel that this was not doing enough for the poor, so he joined the group and donated his truck. He stayed with us for a long time. He was the kind of person who went to great extremes. He slept on a bundle of clothes in the clothing room and was abused by the poor who came. When he didn't have anything for them, they would accuse him of being a drunken bum who had sold the clothes for a bottle. He put up with this kind of contempt and abuse and lived a life of complete sacrifice. Later he joined the Trappists and was put to work baking bread. One day the spiritual reading at table described a soldier who used to utter ejaculatory prayers, while machine-gunning the enemy. Poor Smitty suddenly began to weep and cry in the most uncontrollable fashion. He rushed up to the Father Abbot and fell on his knees by him, weeping and sobbing and asking how the Mystical Body of Christ could thus rend itself.

It is not worthwhile writing or speaking unless you say what is in your heart and say it as you see things. This is the way. This is what converts expect when they find it in the lives of the saints who accept the idea of death in whatever form it takes. We say all these things in our prayers and don't mean them. And God takes us at our word, fortunately, and so we are saved in spite of ourselves; we are just dragged in by the hair of the head. But this is the message that we try to give at the Catholic Worker. It is painful to speak of and that is one of the reasons we rejoice in tribulation; we rejoice in suffering and so we can speak in those terms.

We have been called necrophiliacs, we have been accused of taking a morbid delight in the gutter and worshipping ash cans. The fact of the matter is that God transforms it all, so that out of this junk heap comes beauty. We have poetry and painting and sculpture and music and all of these things for the delight of the senses that are given to us right in the midst of filth and degradation and mire so that I often feel we know whereof we speak. God certainly comes to the rescue over and over again and enables us to do what seems utterly impossible. Many a person comes into the Church under utterly impossible circumstances; it as though they were taking their own life, as though they were dying, in order to do this. I have seen people unhinged by it. We have quite a few with us who are disturbed, who have suffered extremely, have cut themselves off from their families and backgrounds. It is a terrible thing to fall into the hands of the living God. It is not anything that we can take except with the utmost seriousness and yet it is, of course, the greatest joy in the world.

JULY–AUGUST 1968

"To Stand Where One Must Stand . . ."

BOB GILLIAM

EDS. NOTE: *The following reflections were selected from the letters of Bob Gilliam, a Catholic Worker sentenced on August 14, 1967 to two years in Sandstone Federal Correctional Institution for refusing induction into the armed forces.*

August 26, 1967 (County Jail, Minneapolis): I am almost looking forward to the time at Sandstone. It will give me a valuable perspective on society, time to study, and a chance for the first time in my life to get a good solid grounding in news and current events. I got a visit tonight from the American Civil Liberties Union. The guy wants to make a test case out of my noncooperation. The argument would be that my religious freedom is being limited. He admits the chances of winning are small but feels a test case should be argued. He was sympathetic and persuasive. It would mean changing the plea and dragging through the courts, being free for a year or two, and then doing the two years. I am going to say no, but I am upset. I cannot give him any clear, intelligent, theoretical answer (though the personal dislocation of our life and plans is enough). I feel it. I hear David Miller saying, when being tried for refusing induction, legal arguments are as "a clanging brass or a tinkling cymbal." Though I would like to see it done, I feel clearly that it's not for me to do. I know that I could not put my heart into such a fight.

September 9, 1967 (Sandstone F.C.I.): My impressions of Sandstone are very mixed. Physically it is quite comfortable. There is a pleasant yard in the middle. At any rate, the prison surrounds a nice "compound" of grass and flowers. The library is small but has some happy surprises—I have read Fromm's *Sane Society* and Frankl's *Man's Search for Meaning,* and *Huckleberry Finn* so far, and have some Paul Goodman and Kierkegaard checked out. There are movies every week—which aren't too good, but take up some time. The food is not bad at all. This is not a prison but a "correctional institution," you see. Its aim is to develop a goal-oriented program suited to the needs of each inmate in order that he may be rehabilitated. I have not been able to determine what this means in my case. I think eventually they would admit I am not being rehabilitated—all fall down and worship—but detained, imprisoned, punished. The facade of liberality here takes the edge off rebellion, confuses the issue. I felt in a way more comfortable in the county jail because relationships were clear there. There could be no doubts when the doors clanged shut on the ugly cell. No matter how you dress it up, prison is slavery. I had, a few days ago, some serious thoughts about not cooperating—to force clarity. It certainly is a clear and honorable position. When one first realizes how they "bribe" you with all these "privileges" (especially mail and visits) the gut response, mine anyway, is rebellion. But I don't think it will come to that. Not sure I have the resources; I hope the time here can be in some way meaningful, there are friends to be made here, and because I feel it can be borne without much of a price. I hope anyway that I will only have rarely to be here, that I can live with thoughts, books, in your letters, with all our holy and beautiful friends. The state only imprisons the body—can only imprison the body.

September 14, 1967: I have been a little depressed lately, more than usual, about the war. It is such a pervasive cancer. Danny O'Laughlin (a cousin) dead and Mike [Bob's stepbrother] on his way over there. How many innocents, Vietnamese and Americans, will they sacrifice on the altar of this madness? The whole thing is almost beyond discussion, it seems. If people can't see that the war is vile and rotten, how can anyone tell them? Opinion seems so permanently, hopelessly polarized. The hawks hawking, the liberals liberalling, and the radicals crying, shouting, giving up, and some burning themselves. Still, to be a person you have to visibly and clearly oppose it.

I amuse the two other noncooperators that I have gotten to know. They say they just want to see me in four months to see if any of my insanity, cheer, and happy sarcasm are left. They both say prison has pretty much sucked out their vitals. One guy said the toughest thing of all is to adjust yourself to the fact that you just have to chalk the time up as a total loss. He feels that nothing really can be salvaged and that all his energy goes into just keeping himself together. I still hope. I have more resources—not of myself, but I have you, the Catholic Worker, the family, the "community," and the exciting prospects of the future. Despite all this I still have my twinges of irrepressible joy!

The "thing" here seems so permanent, so impenetrable. Criminals are not romantic. They mirror the society—sick, mentally deficient, greedy, violent—often anyway. Conversation is consistently low or at best trivial. My grossness is of a different kind entirely. There are, don't get me wrong, some really fine people here. Thoreau's line about "quiet desperation" comes to mind. So many who grew up and live in a loveless world ... things bad on so many fronts simultaneously—social, economic, political, educational, moral—and yet a man can only address himself to a few on one front. Perhaps community is relevant here. We as a community with different gifts, different vocations, could be so much more effective. One last thought that has been plaguing me lately. This is not morbid but serious. I wonder how ready I am to accept death. It is essential to nonviolence. The satyagrahi must believe that to die for the truth bears fruit. Gandhi knew, or had good reason to suspect, that he was going to be killed, and still he refused bodyguards and held his regular prayer meeting. I know that I value my life excessively. One cannot take his own life too seriously and still be really a satyagrahi.

October 2, 1967: I made a long visit to chapel the other day in an attempt to pray. Something came. An old, deep, primarily, I think, aesthetic response. The room was dark with one light on simple tabernacle, lamp, and Book, soft light filtered through the rich green stained glass at my feet. Quiet and really gut-level peaceful. It's too dark to read the Bible, though, alas.

October 11, 1967: I endure this small—and really it is small compared to the sacrifices of the men in Vietnam—sacrifice in the hope of drawing people's attention to the war, to the question of war and our complicity in it, to the innocent people who are dying and to the simple unmistakable words of Jesus, whom we all claim to dig so much. I am grateful for people worrying about me and the violation of my conscience but I am more concerned that according to their own lights and position people do something about stopping this stinking war—that they vote, write, speak, read, march, vigil, and break the law if necessary (and it is).

October 17, 1967: I remember when I used to fear "losing my faith"; I was afraid of the doubt, darkness, and of the terrible task to decide from scratch what you believe. Realize now this simple fact—when you strip away all the learned doctrines you "believe" and look at yourself naked and ask what can't be taken away, what is part of me, what truths do I live by (believe) then you know what your faith is. Then you can begin to reinterpret the religious myths and metaphors, to make them your own in a new and more meaningful way. I think I am at the beginning of all this.

October 24, 1967: Can I send you the fruit of some recent reflection? I have been thinking about "something" that the people I most admire seem to have in common—a prophetic quality, a sense of vocation, seriousness. (Remember what Peguy described as *un homme serieux*). They are people who have grasped—or more rightly been grasped by—two or three essential truths with a kind of lightning clarity. They become in a sense almost fanatical. They do not see other truths with any unusual clarity and tend instead to see other truths in relation to their personal vision. They have a kind of unscholarly and outwardly unjustifiable certainty of their own rightness. They do not blindly refuse to consider the intelligent arguments against them but they are beyond these arguments. For them, their truth is so clear and certain that it demands not only verbal proclamation but possesses them with an urgency to give it living form in action, in their own lives. They are compelled to witness and strive to discover a form of life that embodies clearly, even starkly, and speaks to even the simplest man, the truth they have seen.

December 26, 1967: You might like this line of Dan Berrigan's on Jesus' parable-speaking: "The purpose of His speech: to create imaginative men, capable of imagining the real world." He also says "to stand where one must stand, to plant the landmarks by which the unborn will be enabled to walk."

January 10, 1968: A small reflection: Part of the suffering and anguish of embracing nonviolence is the result of the fact that nonviolence is in its infancy as a tool for social change; that is, as an alternative to violence it remains largely unexplored. I refuse to believe that pacifism is simplistic and foolish, because ultimately the question of war must be reduced to its personal moral limits: will I kill?

The perception of the futility of violence and the fact that it cannot be a means to the transformation of the world, along with the refusal to kill, are the foundations of pacifism. To be a pacifist means 1) to be a center of new values to demonstrate and incarnate (or perhaps more modestly to point to), to be a sign of that spirit (or as George Fox says, "that life and power that take away the occasion of all wars"; 2) to serve and build, to be a constructive and reconciling force; 3) to develop, explore, and experiment with nonviolence as a technique (as well as the above suggests a way of life). One aspect of the fantastic wisdom of the Catholic Worker is the balance that it offers in this regard.

January 19, 1968: One of the terrible problems about the future is that you can't do everything. Choosing means eliminating. This becomes especially difficult now when I am removed, inactive. Involved in action, the question doesn't really arise, there is the sense of a great deal to do, of things undone, and yet the demands and satisfactions of what you are doing seem sufficient. To decide one must first know oneself— where am I strong, where weak, what can I do best? Know the times— every season has its work—and be aware of the possibilities, the variety of historical responses, what others are doing today.

January 30, 1968: I'll start cold. The parole board denied me. I got word in the mail yesterday. It was hardly unexpected and I had thought I had completely set myself to accept it. Still there was some disappointment. As many reasons as there are for not wanting parole it is impossible not to want to get out a few months earlier. If I get extra good days—I am applying for them—I will get out in February 1969; otherwise it will be March. Thirteen or fourteen months to go.

February 3, 1968: Sandstone is such a violent world. The earth is so incredibly violent. Did you hear about the Maryknollers in Guatemala? Again the question of violence. It is a question weighing so heavily on so many dear people today. Me, too. I go through it a million times and the answer in my heart, my head, and my bones is always the same—nonviolence. I have been reading the *Liberation* double issue on A.J. Muste. All of me says yes. Still there is the frightening failure of words. The suffering of the people seems so unbearable, so interminable sometimes. When will the earth be born? Scalding tears frequently fill my eyes just reading the news. I worry—am I a fanatic? A purist? Do I set my "conscience" above liberation? No, I don't. I believe this way is right. Still there is a danger. I must be more flexible, more genuinely tolerant. Other good men have different lights. It is a sign of my lack of maturity that I feel defensive with and alienated from those who have chosen a different way.

February 8, 1968: I got a copy of the *Worker* yesterday. What a light in the darkness! I have only read the Chrystie Street column so far but that was beautiful. The Worker is many things, but the foundation, the beginning, the roots, are Chrystie Street. There is a phrase of Peter's that has been on my mind much lately. It throws light on many things. Peter talks about "the gentle personalism of traditional Christianity." To hope to see things rightly I know that I must stand firmly in that ground. That is why poverty and the works of mercy are so essential and any movement that is cut off from them is constantly subject to the cancer of ideological self-righteousness and gives way to ranting.

June 9, 1968: About Catonsville. [Nine Catholics, including the Fathers Berrigan, napalm Selective Service files as an act of protest in Catonsville, Maryland.] I remember something Staughton Lynd said at a Fellowship of Reconciliation meeting. He said we should have faith in those acts which are commensurate with our deepest anguish over the war, our sense of sin, a faith that those acts will be redemptive and powerful. The act does speak to me, it is immensely powerful—for me. I don't know how it can be seen as "an offensive sort of prank" (*National Catholic Reporter* editorial). The editorial faults them wrongly, attributing to them a "conscious malevolence" to the American ruling class. Obviously, this is irrelevant, because once you admit things are as they say, it is really not too important how conscious the criminals are or what their motives are. I suspect the nine people know or are learning the limits of their action. Perhaps we do not know too much about suffering. We reel at a prison term for friends but barely flinch over the incredible suffering the Vietnamese bear. The act points at this, I think, as well as much else. This act may be later seen as an early light in a continuum. The actors are willing to take a little chance. The Spirit breaks in clumsily, but it breaks in.

DECEMBER 1968

❈ Dear Employer

STANLEY VISHNEWSKI

DEAR PROSPECTIVE EMPLOYER:

It has come to our attention that your firm is seeking to employ one of our Catholic Workers. We have on hand your request for a confidential report on the honesty and integrity of said Worker. However, before we can recommend our brother to your firm there are several questions that we would like to have you answer. Please print carefully and in triplicate answers to the following questions:

1. Why do you want our Fellow Worker to work for you? Please state the reasons in detail. Take as much time as you need in filling out the questionnaire.

2. What is the nature of the work performed by your firm? a) Military b) Civilian.

3. Please state if your firm is engaged in the production of essential needs: i.e., food, clothing, housing—or is it engaged in the production of non-essentials: i.e., advertising, television, luxury items?

4. Do you feel that your firm is engaged primarily in making things, or performing social services for a profit and for the benefit of its stockholders? If so, state why in 100 words or less.

5. Our Fellow Worker is conscientious and is interested in doing work that will benefit humanity. Do you feel that your firm will be able to measure up to his expectations? If not—please state the reasons in detail.

6. Are all profits plowed back into the company in the form of higher wages, better working conditions, free education, and lower prices to the consumer? If not, state the reason. Be accurate and state facts.

7. Are the workers in your company reasonably happy; do they feel that the work they are doing is important? Please state if there are any exceptions to the above.

8. Have any of the managers of your concern spent time in prison for any of the following reasons: embezzlement, forgery, defrauding the poor, cheating on income taxes, violation of Federal antitrust laws? Please state other reasons.

Circle number of years spent in prison: 1 year/5 years/10 years/life.

9. Please send us in triplicate references from ten of your former employees and the reasons they gave for leaving your employ.

10. Please send us ten pictures (glossy print) of your plant. These must show actual working conditions. It is important, for our files, that we have a group picture of your executives.

11. Please send us a 1,000-word essay describing the nature of the work that will be performed by our Fellow Worker and the reasons why you would like to have him work for you. (See question No. 1)

NOTE: *Failure to answer any of the questions will automatically disqualify your firm from receiving the services of our Fellow Worker.*

Yours in Christ the Worker,
STANLEY VISHNEWSKI

❄ On Pilgrimage

DOROTHY DAY

I WAS TALKING TO Mike Gold, my old Communist friend, when he returned from France with his wife and two sons years ago. Our Christian-Marxist dialogue went like this:

"My sons are named Karl and Nicholas," he reminded me as we spoke of his children and my grandchildren.

"My second grandson is called Nicholas, too."

"But mine is named after a different person than yours. Mine is named after Lenin."

"Mine after the saint by that name and the Nicholases in Russia are, too, though they may not know it."

So I stopped the argument, having had the last word, by inviting him over, and he brought me a present, a picture of St. Anne, from Brittany, carefully rolled in a newspaper, so that it was flat for framing. While we stood in the Catholic Worker kitchen and talked the dialogue continued:

I said: "How hard it is to have faith in men when we see their racist attitudes, their fears of each other fed by the daily press. There is a lot of racism around the Catholic Worker movement, made up as it is of men from the Bowery and skid rows, as well as from the colleges. Class war and race war go on daily and we are a school for nonviolence." His eyes alight with faith, Mike said, "But it is the poor and the wretched, the insulted and the injured, who bring about the change in the world, the great changes that are taking place."

I could not help but think that just as we cannot love God whom we do not see unless we love our brother whom we do see, it followed that our faith in man (as he could be) should increase our faith in God and His ever-present aid. "I can do all things in Him who strengthens me." "Without Him I can do nothing." And this very small conversation made me pray the more.

But how can we show our love by war, by the extermination of our enemies? If we are followers of Christ, there is no room for speaking of the "just war." We have to remember that God loves all men, that God wills all men to be saved, that, indeed, all men are brothers. We must love the jailer as well as the one in prison. We must do that seemingly utterly impossible thing: love our enemy.

This last month I spoke to fifty members of the Association of Urban Sisters, working in Roxbury, Massachusetts. The meeting was held on Ash Wednesday, and I spoke of penance. I said that I could understand a Kateri Tekakwitha taking on the severest of penances to atone for the cruelty of her people to the Europeans and for the white cruelty to the Indians. (One must judge oneself first.) Or the penances of a St. Rose of Lima, in a time when the Indians were systematically being killed off, and African slave labor was being imported to supply the labor which the Indians could not endure.

Penance seems to be ruled out today. One hears the Mass described as Sacrament, not as Sacrifice. But how are we to keep our courage unless the Cross, that mighty failure, is kept in view? Is the follower greater than his masters? What attracts one in a Che Guevara and Ho Chi Minh is the hardships and the suffering they endured in living their lives of faith and hope. It is not the violence, the killing of one's enemies. A man is a man, and to hear him crying out in pain and anguish, whether he is friend or enemy, is to have one's heart torn in unutterable sorrow. The impulse to stand out against the State and go to jail rather than serve is an instinct for penance to take on some of the suffering of the world, to share in it.

Father Anthony Mullaney, O.S.B., who is one of the "Milwaukee Fourteen" priests and laymen who burned draft records with napalm— "burning property, not people"—told me, when I met him in Boston the other day, that over a hundred of the students of St. Anselm's in Manchester, New Hampshire, signed a petition to the court, which they are going to send when the Milwaukee 14 are sentenced, offering to divide up the months or years the fourteen have to serve, and take on the sentences for them. He will be speaking next month at Town Hall, and we will learn more about this. What is this but an offer to do penance, another example of trying to follow in the steps of Christ, who took on himself our sins and in so doing overcame both sin and death?

This is, in effect, what Chuck Matthei, Chicago draft refuser, is doing in not cooperating with the prison authorities when they seized him most brutally and literally dragged him handcuffed, to West St. Federal prison in New York, where he is now fasting from food, and sometimes water, too.

Just to read about these things or hear of them is not enough. One must meet Chuck and see the brightness of his face, feel the gentle and joyous and truly loving spirit, to get a glimpse of an understanding of what he is doing.

The thing is to recognize that not all are called, not all have the vocation, to demonstrate in this way, to fast, to endure the pain and long drawn-out nerve-racking suffering of prison life. We do what we can, and the whole field of all the Works of Mercy is open to us. There is a saying, "Do what you are doing." If you are a student, study, prepare, in order to give to others, and keep alive in yourself the vision of a new social order. All work, whether building, increasing food production, running credit unions, working in factories which produce for true human needs, working in the smallest of industries, the handcrafts—all these things can come under the heading of the works of mercy, which are the opposite of the works of war.

It is a penance to work, to give oneself to others, to endure the pinpricks of community living. One would certainly say on many occasions, "give me a good, thorough, frank outgoing war, rather than the sneak attacks, stabs in the back, sparring, detracting, defaming, hand-to-hand jockeying for position that goes on in offices and 'good works' of all kinds, another and miserably petty kind of war." St. Paul said that "he died daily." This, too, is penance, to be taken cheerfully, joyfully, with the hope that our own faith and joy in believing will strengthen Chuck and all the others in jail.

So let us rejoice in our own petty sufferings and thank God we have a little penance to offer, in this holy season. "An injury to one is an injury to all," the Industrial Workers of the World proclaimed. So an act of love, a voluntary taking on oneself of some of the pain of the world, increases the courage and love and hope of all.

FEBRUARY 1970

❈ Ammon Hennacy—A Christian Anarchist

DOROTHY DAY

EDS. NOTE: *Ammon Hennacy was one of the most disciplined individuals ever to come to the Catholic Worker. A tireless propagandist and an ardent peace worker, Ammon inspired the Worker in those years to a new level of public witness. He called himself a Christian Anarchist. An anarchist, by his definition, is "someone who doesn't need a cop to tell him what to do." For many years he was an associate editor of* The Catholic Worker. *When he grew tired of the city, he moved out west to Salt Lake City, where he died in January 1970.*

ONE OF THE GREAT things that Ammon did for the Catholic Worker back in the thirties (we began publishing in 1933) was to increase our ecumenical spirit. There was not much talk of ecumenism in those days in the Holy Roman Catholic Church. His association with us began in the city of Milwaukee where he was living at that time and where we had a house of hospitality. Communists, socialists, anarchists, and an assortment of unbelievers and Protestants, of who knew what denomination, used to come to our Friday night meetings. The discussions were lively. It was not long after the Spanish Civil War and some of our friends had served in the Abraham Lincoln Brigade. The discussions were mostly on social questions. The group in New York and other centers where we had houses were going in strong for the liturgy then, and lauds and compline were recited in many of our houses. A cardinal once asked me some years later, "What do they think they are, that Catholic Worker crowd—a bunch of nuns and priests?" The separation between the clergy and the laity was pretty distinct. It was considered remarkable that we lay people were living what is called dedicated lives of voluntary poverty, working without salary and serving our brother Christ in the poor, "inasmuch as you have done it unto one of the least of my brothers, you have done it unto me."

In New York there were complaints among the staff that they never knew whether I was quoting the Douay version of the scriptures, or the King James version. (Now there are a half dozen English translations.) When we started to publish Ammon Hennacy's articles, "Life at Hard Labor" in *The Catholic Worker,* and he made slighting remarks about Holy Mother Church, there were adverse comments among the staff and also more severe criticism from some of our readers. It was in vain that we pointed him out as the most ascetic, the most hard-working, the most devoted to the poor and the oppressed of any we had met, and that his life and his articles put us on the spot. He was an inspiration and a reproach.

Before he came to New York to join us on the staff of the Catholic Worker, while he was still working at farm labor, he introduced us to the Molokans, the Doukhobors, the Hutterites, and many another sect which had come to this country to escape war and conscription in their own countries. When he came to live with us he began to attend the meetings of the War Resisters League, meetings at Community Church, at Methodist churches, and with Jewish, Episcopalian, and other war resisters. He was interested, in fact, in all religious points of view if they resulted in a real effort to conform one's life to one's profession of faith. He still spoke contemptuously of Jesus-shouters and religious demagogues who blessed the state of war, and he stated unequivocally that he did not like St. Paul, and that St. Peter had betrayed Christ again when he said, "Servants, obey your masters." He didn't see the point of St. Paul sending Onesimus back to his master, in the hopes that the master would be converted so that there would be "neither slave nor free."

Obedience, of course, was a bad word. Authority was a bad word. In vain I pointed out to him that when the retired army major for whom he worked in Arizona told him to do a particular job, he did it, and he did it as he was told to. He admired the army officer because he knew farming. And he cooperated with Ammon in paying him by the day and thus evading the federal income tax which the tax man was trying to collect from Ammon.

I pointed out that he accepted the authority of those who were authorities, and knew what they were doing, and how to do it. He admired the courage of the major who subdued a bull which was wild with the pain of a snake bite, and had the courage to handle him with confidence and without fear. But he continued to balk, Ammon did, at the words authority and obedience.

On his coming to New York in the late forties, he attended a "retreat" at Maryfarm at Newburgh on the Hudson which Fr. Marion Casey of Minnesota gave. During the Mass each morning he knelt on the hard floor next to a Greenwich Villager by the name of Kenneth Little. He died some years ago and I always remember him with gratitude (not only for the gardening he did with us but for those retreat days with Ammon). Kenneth knelt next to him and kept pointing out to him all the words in the Mass that had to do with peace.

"Mercifully give PEACE in our days. The PEACE of the Lord be always with you. Lamb of God who takes away the sins of the world, grant us PEACE. Lord Jesus Christ, who said to your apostles: PEACE I leave with you, my PEACE I give to you, be pleased to grant to your Church PEACE and unity according to your will."

Poor Kenneth, he did so want to assure Ammon that the Church, indeed, did desire peace, but I am afraid that neither Ammon nor I could forget how the scrap iron and metal was heaped in the church yards during the Second World War and blessed by the priests, and war stamps sold to the children, and bombers named after the Blessed Mother, and so on. It was still all too much like rival armies in Mexico carrying banners with representations of the Blessed Virgin of different localities to bless their wars.

Ammon knew much labor history but very little about Church history. He could get no encouragement from the fact that in ages past there had been far greater scandals of wealth and warfare than even today. Or, were there? One priest said, of Ammon's anticlericalism, that, perhaps, he saw the sins of the Church as a human institution far more clearly than we did. Another priest said of Ammon that he had received so great a light during that first jail sentence of his in Atlanta Penitentiary, that it had blinded him. He had read through the Bible nine times and all but memorized the Sermon on the Mount. When he came out he had become a Bible Christian, not in the sense of a sect, but of one who accepted the WORD. He read the Tolstoi who wrote *Anna*

Karenina, and his faith deepened. In that great novel Levin struggled and fought for a faith. He went through such agony that he was on the verge of suicide (like the Maritains before their conversion) because he felt he could not believe as his wife Kitty and as the serfs around him did. There is a triumphant note of joy in the end of Levin's struggle which warms the heart. It was not the bitter, later Tolstoi, who derided religion in the novel *Resurrection,* who could not separate the wheat from the chaff.

For a time Ammon was a Catholic. It was before the aggiornamento, and though he had been christened a Baptist, a valid baptism, he was conditionally baptized again by Fr. Marion Casey in Minnesota. His instruction had been slight in spite of retreats and conferences which we were in the habit of having at the Newburgh farm. He assented to what he agreed with, had no mind for philosophy or theology, and he no longer read the Scriptures. "I read them nine times in jail," he said on a number of occasions. And once, flippantly, "If I had only a telephone book I would have read that nine times." Just as he said later on, "If Dorothy had been a Methodist, I would have become a Methodist." These were wounding words. I could never understand them.

He was with us—how many years? Long enough to make an impression on that great pagan city of New York.

He had already, while living on the outskirts of Phoenix, Arizona, made an impression on that city with his picketing, as well as on the few local Communists who lived there. I taunted him. "You'll not make the impression on New York that you did in Phoenix. Those Republicans like to show how liberal they are in having a pet anarchist confronting them on their streets every Sunday and legal holiday."

But he did make an impression, and when I travelled on my own pilgrimage around the country I met hundreds (of course, there were thousands), who had encountered him when they, themselves, had visited New York.

Which brings me again to Ammon's life of hard work and voluntary poverty. In those two aspects he outshone everyone. There were a few hall bedrooms in the old Chrystie Street house and Ammon had one of them most of the time, though he never hesitated to give up the room to guests. That was one of the reasons he had it, because he could be trusted to relinquish it immediately. He claimed nothing as his own, nothing but the clothes on his back, and when he gave up his bed, he slept on the floor in the big living room where we had our meetings. He slept side by side with all the Bowery men whom Roger O'Neil brought in on cold winter nights.

He went to Mass early every morning and kept a list of all who had asked his prayers in the front of his missal which he read over after Communion. After Mass he went to the post office for mail, opened it, entered any donations in a big cash book, answered every note or letter in a short and almost illegible script, sent out papers, and by noon was ready to take his stand on the streets to sell the *CW*. He had a regular route. I cannot remember without consulting old papers exactly how it went, but this will give an idea of it. Mondays, Wall Street; Tuesdays, Lexington Avenue and 43rd Street; Wednesdays, Fordham University gates; Thursdays, New York University, and so on.

Evenings it was the same: Cooper Union on the nights they had lectures, the New School, and any radical meetings which were taking place around the city. He was there rain or snow, with anyone who would accompany him, selling the paper. Often conversations would last into the night at some coffee shop. He sold the papers and so always had a pocket-full of pennies or silver to buy extra food or an occasional book, to feed others, or go to some movie with social significance. He used to say that Wall Street clientele gave pennies, and charitable ladies in the shopping centers gave dimes and quarters.

Peter Maurin quoted Cardinal Newman: "If you wish to reach the man in the street, go to the man in the street." The War Resisters have a motto, "Wars will cease when men refuse to fight." Ammon went directly to people and persevered in friendship with them though he soon realized that they were not going to go very far in building up a new society. In spite of his critical attitude he had a great warmth and loved to be with people and made them feel his closeness to them. I would not say he ever despaired or felt hopeless. He could not have gone on if he did. Part of his love for people came from his great inner loneliness—there were so few to work for the nonviolent revolution, so few ready to sacrifice all for it.

Of course, Ammon was a romantic Irishman, basically, and never lost that sense of drama, that love of life, tragic though its outcome so often was. He literally would have liked to give his life for the obliteration of wars and all injustice from the face of the earth. He would have welcomed being shot as Joe Hill was, that labor martyr after whom he named his House of Hospitality in Salt Lake City. But Ammon's death was a triumph just the same. His first heart attack came to him on the picket line on his way to the Federal Court building in Salt Lake City. He died suddenly a week later, when his friends thought that he was on the way to recovery.

He died in protesting the execution of two of the least of God's children who had been justly sentenced, as the Mormons thought (believing as they did in the shedding of blood to atone for the shedding of blood).

I have said that Ammon was a romantic and once he said to me, "I do not remember the time that I was not in love with some woman." Believing as I do that being "in love" is a reflection of the love God has for each and every one of us, I am glad that this kind of love illumined the last seven years of Ammon's life.

Ammon had long ceased attending Mass, though on his travels, as his wife states, he went to Mass with her and even received Communion. But, "in peace was his bitterness most bitter." He rejected the "institutional church," even while he received the Sacrament. The monks at the Holy Trinity monastery with whom he was friends never questioned him, nor would I. Who can understand another, who can read another's heart?

I do not think that Ammon expected to die, since all felt he was on the way to recovery, so there was no question of his preparing for death in the way of confession or asking for the last rites, or the sacrament of the sick, as this sacrament is now called. In fact, I am not sure if Ammon knew what the sacraments were, or what they were all about, that they were channels of grace. If they had been explained I am sure he would have considered that grace had already been poured out upon him abundantly in the sufferings he had endured in jail. God's ways are not our ways.

One of Ammon's favorite quotations from Scripture was, "Let him who is without sin cast the first stone." And he used it in relation to judges who sat as Judge Julius Hoffman has been sitting all these long months in the Chicago 7 trial.

But I must admit that Ammon was a great one to judge when it came to priests and bishops, and his words were coarse on many an occasion, so that it was hurtful to me to hear him, loving the Church as I do. But there's that love-hate business in all of us, and Ammon wanted so much to see priests and bishops and popes stand out strong and courageous against the sin and the horrors and the cruelty of the powers of this world. But we cannot judge him, knowing so well his own strong and courageous will to fight the corruption of the world around him.

MAY 1971

❋ The Church as Accomplice

GORDON ZAHN

IT IS NOT AN easy charge to make. But the facts are there for all to see. They have been there for quite some time, however few may be disposed even now to acknowledge them, and they lend themselves to a sad conclusion: that the Christian churches of America—and this applies with special force to my own Roman Catholic communion—have permitted themselves to become fully responsible accomplices to war crimes and atrocities that have been committed by our nation and her allies in Vietnam.

Past ignorance and timidity masquerading as prudence may explain but can no longer justify a posture of Olympian detachment. The awful facts are now a matter of public record. Murder has been done, murder of a kind and on a scale that cries for retribution. We have reached the point where silence for whatever reason is completely indefensible.

It is generally acknowledged that one who observes a crime in progress and persists in silence which permits the criminal to go unchallenged and unpunished takes upon himself a share of the guilt. Neither fear of the inconvenience or hazards that might result from speaking out, nor a personal relationship with the wrongdoer, can free him from his responsibility or the burden of his contributory guilt. The same rule, I would insist, must apply to the religious community, "the Church," and its responsible leaders.

Years before the massacre at My Lai, a German writer made what seemed to be an outrageously extravagant accusation: Lidice and Oradour, he said, are today villages in Vietnam. We know now that he was right. In fact, we have known since 1966, when *Ramparts* first published Donald Duncan's account of his war experiences and Frank Harvey's report of our murderous air war appeared in the pages of *Flying* magazine. In 1968, *In the Name of America* presented a well-documented survey comparing the record of U.S. military behavior with the laws of war and revealing the extent to which atrocities and war crimes had become a recurring pattern and not, as we are still so easily persuaded, rare and certainly unplanned excesses. Finally, the initial My Lai revelations forced a moment of shocked awareness and even brought into being the 1970 Congressional Conference on War and National Responsibility. It was a brief and passing moment, however, and the prevailing mood soon became one of "understanding" rationalization and, let us be honest enough to admit it, something actually approaching justification of that atrocity.

Now the brutal facts have been spelled out for us again in shocking detail in the testimony given at the various court-martials convened to try the men involved. There is no longer basis for doubt that this event occurred, and men have formally admitted taking part in the killings. Still, one after the other of the men on trial have been acquitted or heard the charges against them dismissed. There is every reason to assume that this pattern, too, will be unbroken: if by any chance some defendant is found guilty, chances are that he will be spared any serious penalty for the crime.

None of us, I suppose, should be entirely satisfied with an outcome which finds incontrovertible evidence of the brutal slaughter of non-combatant old men, women, and children going unpunished. At the very least, justice should demand that the individuals involved be given a dishonorable discharge for their willing cooperation in an act that will remain a permanent blot on the nation's record. Having said this, we should also be prepared to acknowledge that it would be unjust to put the full burden of the blame upon the immediate perpetrators of the crime and to exact the more severe penalties of prison or death sentences. In a very real sense, and we must never forget it, the men who held the guns in their hands at My Lai must be counted among the victims, too. I, for one, give credence to the statements of former neighbors and friends that Lt. Calley was a quiet, well-behaved high school boy. What happened in between is the responsibility of the nation which took that high school boy, trained him, and—to apply the harsh but unanswerable indictment voiced by the anguished mother of another of these men—sent him back a murderer. It might be sooth-ing to the national ego to "throw the book" at Calley and the others; but to do so would let the real culprits, the complacent and compliant Americans who sent them there to "do the job" and paid the bills, off the hook.

This, of course, is where the Church comes in. Sunday after Sunday they are there, the murderers of My Lai, and never once are they likely to hear a troubling word from the man in the pulpit. Massive organizational superstructures testify to the presence of Christianity on the American scene; yet, even though more than a year has passed since the My Lai disclosures burst upon the national consciousness, no official spokesperson of any of our major denominations has seen fit to take public notice of the atrocity in the name of the Church, no resolution has been passed by episcopal conferences to give voice to the outraged conscience of humanity. Individuals, yes, but the usual, the "unofficial" individuals, the "troublemakers" who have made it their practice (at the cost of no little embarrassment to their respective communions) to "arrogate" to themselves the task of giving witness to the Christian mission of peace. Needless to add, their efforts have had no support or encouragement from the duly designated leaders of the Christian establishment.

This illustrates the extent to which the official spokesmen of the Church (and, let me insist again, this applies to all the major Christian churches) have abandoned their responsibility to speak the prophetic word when dealing with issues of war and peace. This is nothing new, of course. In past researches and writings I have documented the scan-dalous failures of the Catholic Church in Nazi Germany to give witness against the immorality of the Hitler regime and the injustice of its wars. The same scandal, the same failure is now ours. If we have now been forced to confess the parallel between My Lai and Lidice, we must also confess that it has its match in the refusal of our American bishops to protest the former, just as their German counterparts turned eyes away from the latter. Actually, if we are honest, the American hierarchy suffers by comparison on two counts. First, at Lidice only males were "executed," whereas at My Lai the killing was indiscriminate so that even infants in their mothers' arms were not spared. Second, the German bishops knew that they and their flocks would face certain Gestapo retaliation had they chosen to protest; our American bishops cannot claim even that much "justification" for their silence.

Where, one must ask, were the chaplains assigned to Charley Company, and why have they not been heard from in the almost three years that have passed since the dreadful slaughter took place? I put the question though I think I know the answer. Based on research interviews conducted with R.A.F. chaplains in England some time ago, the following would probably hold true: The chaplains of Task Force Barker and Charley Company either accepted what happened as a tragic "military necessity" or, even more likely, avoided involving themselves in what they would regard as an intrusion into the commander's sphere of authority by even raising the question. A chaplain exceptionally sensitive about such things as murder might have gone further and voiced a personal protest, but it would have been a cautious protest and kept "within channels." Only the rarest of chaplains would even consider bringing the matter to public attention—a conclusion fully supported by the fact that it remained for a discharged serviceman to expose what was a topic of general conversation among the men in Vietnam!

An even more appropriate question: How has Cardinal Cooke, Roman Catholic Bishop to the Armed Forces, defined his role in all of this? The answer here, too, is obvious enough. Like his fellow bishops, and despite the additional and specific responsibilities imposed by that office, he has been silent. Twice now since the facts first came to light he has made his ritual, morale-boosting Christmas excursions to Vietnam. It would have been a simple enough matter to visit the scene of the atrocity and offer his own Mass for the victims as an act of penance and reparation for the evil committed there by men in his spiritual charge. Instead, silence.

To charge the churches with complicity in this atrocity carries implications that extend far beyond the criminal acts that took place at this particular time and place. We must recognize that a failure of this dimension brings into question the credibility of their religious teachings as well as their professed commitment to the moral and spiritual values they proclaim. Many Christians today are concerned, and with good reason, about what appears to be an accelerating "leakage" of young people, especially those young people who have demonstrated their acute moral sensitivity and concern for social problems. Those who have "fallen away" from the institutional churches have made it clear enough. They are leaving because what passes for the Christian church in their experience has given ample evidence that it has little or nothing to say to them about such things as war, racism, and the extremes of affluence and poverty, both at home and in the world at large.

The loss of credibility for the churches in the eyes of the young may not be the most immediate threat we must consider. Those who occupy the seats of temporal power are also well aware of the gap between stated principle and effective follow-through, and this could lead to even more destructive consequences. For many years now, moralists and magistrates have carried on a probing dialogue in which they have sought to establish guidelines and relationships between national security imperatives and ethics. The spokesmen for religion, sometimes official and other times not, have always assumed, as did their partners in the dialogue, that the churches were represented there because they were, in a sense, the keepers of the nation's conscience. This assumption, so logical in statement, is almost entirely without substance in fact. The failure of the churches to give voice to that conscience in the face of unassailable evidence of actual war crimes and morally questionable military policy has made it clear that the magistrates and their strategic experts have nothing to fear from that quarter; they are free to revise sharply downward whatever they may have given to organized religion as a possible source of opposition and restraint.

Even Vatican II's condemnation of area-bombing has not been translated into official denunciation of napalm blankets covering 50-square-miles of territory or designation of "free-fire" zones open to indiscriminate aerial strafings and similar forms of wanton destruction. Nor has the established policy of spraying agricultural areas with chemical defoliants reminded ecclesiastical spokesmen of those old moral theology teachings which included "starvation blockades" among the immoral acts of war. And now we have My Lai, tying it all together in one bloody bundle, with its frighteningly simple lesson and its even more frightening implications for the future: A church which can be a silent accomplice to these crimes committed today is almost certain to find itself accomplice to crimes infinitely worse tomorrow.

❈ A Return to Life

JIM CHAPMAN

I AM A Bowery bum. You have seen me (and many, many others) lying in doorways, in the middle of sidewalks, or sprawled in alleys, or on a discarded mattress among the trash cans and the garbage bags.

I am not sleeping. I am comatose—rendered that way by two or three or four bottles of cheap, chemically hopped-up wine.

Even if you overcome your nausea and revulsion and try to rouse me with an idea which includes food, hospitals, with sympathetic, empathetic doctors and nurses, medications to make withdrawal painless, and massive doses of B complex, to be turned over to a very hip, sophisticated social worker (also symp. and emp.), even if you can arrange all this—forget it. I've had that kind of therapy before, not once, but three or four times. (I'm a little vague on matters involving time, place, and people.) What I'm telling you, friend, is that your TLC approach to my problem just didn't work. I spent the money you gave me (meant to sustain me until I found a job or got my next welfare check) on two bottles of wine. The rest of the money—lost or stolen. I just noticed my shoes are gone, and my wallet, so I guess I was hit by head hunters—groups of two or three who prowl the Bowery area looking for easy marks: the old, the weak, and the handicapped—and drunks like me who have drunk themselves into a state of deep unconsciousness.

So here I am. They threw me out of the room that the agency rented for me. In short, I'm broke, trembling with imminent withdrawal symptoms, weak from lack of food for several days—and shoeless. I haven't washed or shaved since I bought the first bottle—and I stink. So bad I might tip the very delicate air pollution balance from acceptable to undesirable, or even unbearable.

Well, now do you understand? It is useless to try and help me. I've been helped more times than I can remember, and here I am, back where I started, and I'm not interested in any salvation-type project— what I want now and need and have to have is a bottle of wine. To get it I have to walk to a corner without shoes and bum 55¢. I will get it, but, of course, it will take time. I will be rejected, insulted, maybe assaulted, and the withdrawal symptoms will become very bad. I may go into D.T.s or have a convulsion—the severity and frequency of both having accelerated over the last few months.

So you see I am a derelict and I do not respond to any therapeutic type of help. What you can do is give me a cigarette. Thanks. Look, can you let me have 55¢ so I can get me a jug? No? A quarter then? Well, thanks anyway, thank you and God bless you. . . .

Listen, dear reader, I have been putting you on a little bit—for a good reason. I was telling it not like it is, but like it was—so you will understand and believe that a small miracle has happened to me.

What happened is that about two months ago, wild-eyed and terrified, I came running into the Catholic Worker, exhausted and more than a little insane. I could walk only a short distance when, without warning, I would fall down, hard, bone-jarring falls that left me helpless to get up without help. I could squirm and wiggle, but I could not get up. I kept trying and with enormous effort I could get to my knees, only to fall over on my back again. All through this a cop and one of the desk clerks at the flop house where I was living were following me, keeping pace with me, when I walked and stumbled along, stopping when I fell—and just watching me struggling to get up on legs that had turned to jelly. They would watch and wait while people walked by, glanced at me, and walked away—fast. Then when somebody helped me up (how kind some strangers were to me that day) the squad car would start up and stay with me till I fell again. Finally they got tired of the game, shoved me into the back seat of the squad car, and took me back to the hotel.

I woke up the next day, weak, sick, tremulous, and in a complete state of paranoia. The television was blaring, people were talking, and I could clearly hear them making plans to force me to run naked through a gauntlet (everybody invited) of men with sticks and stones, clubs and iron pipes.

After a long time, while the terror increased, I became desperate enough to risk the ordeal I was sure was waiting for me outside my room. I opened the door, and walked slowly and carefully to the locked cage-type door and waited until the clerk pushed a button under his desk enabling me to open the door. Nobody was waiting for me, nobody gave me a second glance, and for a moment sanity returned—I saw how my sick imagination had, beginning with the clerk and his cop friend playing a game with me (truth), moved to an intricate plot involving great numbers of people who were planning first to take away the last vestige of my integrity, then destroy me (all paranoid delusions).

My sanity lasted until I hit the sidewalk. Then I realized that the enemy was waiting on every street corner, in alleys and door ways. I watched them signal to one another (hand signals, or piercing whistles, or yells). They were working on me in relays—when one stopped, another took over. I was never out of their sight. It was then that I began to run, stumbling and sobbing with blind, unreasoning terror. I do not remember whether I decided on the Worker as a sanctuary or just lucked into the only people who were able to help.

Despite my appearance—filthy, sweating, and so fouled up I could no longer separate reality from phantasy, so exhausted I could barely talk—they didn't turn me away. They suggested I sit down and rest, and brought me a bowl of soup, and bread. Also they listened, they paid attention. This hadn't happened to me for nearly a year. And they told me to come back any time. And for the first time in a year I had a place to go where there was sanity, and help of a kind I still don't quite understand. It began with the concrete fact that every morning I (and many, many others) could get a bowl of good hot soup, tea, and all the bread we wanted. But it went a long way beyond that. There were people there, most of them young, who called you "Sir," and just the way they said it made me—habituated now to being cursed, yelled at, put down, treated with contempt—feel a little flicker of life inside me. Gradually I began to realize that even now, when time was running out on me, I might yet become a human being.

Since then, very slowly and without any real conviction or motivation, I struggled through to the time (just a few weeks ago) when I discovered that a change was taking place within me. I came nearly every day to the Worker—and began to have friends, and with their help, or rather by their examples, I began to have a kind of faith I had never known. For several years I had believed in God, but I could not and would not trust Him. Now I began to trust Him to help me through the hard, painful time when it seemed useless to keep on trying.

Friends, my tale is nearly told. I still live on the Bowery, but I am not a bum any more. I shower and shave every day, my clothes are clean, and most important, I am able to make small efforts to contribute (not money) to the difficult, and at times nearly impossible job of trying to help the destitute—the ones who seem as hopeless as I was.

One last thing. This change in me is very new and fragile. I could very easily find myself back among the garbage cans. I don't want that to happen, and I don't think it will.

But it could, and I will tell you how you can help. Pray for me. Pray that my life will continue to have meaning and purpose. That when I die it will not be in some flophouse among strangers, but with dignity and with friends, and in a state of grace.

And pray for all the ones who are apparently beyond redemption. Pray for a miracle for them, because that is what happened to me.

❄ Therese

CHRIS MONTESANO

AFTER TEN MONTHS of joyous anticipation for the birth of our child, Joan and I were not only confronted with the mystery of life but with the mystery of death as well. Our daughter Therese was born with a severe congenital brain defect, and at the moment of birth, the doctor said she was dead. Joan requested a priest to baptize her. There being none available, I baptized her with the nearest water, a cup of melted ice chips. As I poured the water on her head and said the words of baptism, she gave a start and began breathing! I picked her up and shouted with joy, "She's alive!"

Her body was normal except that her head was small and her brain openly exposed. The doctor assured us that she would die shortly and mourned her loss. Amidst our tears, Joan and I told him that Therese's birth was part of the mystery of God, and *that* we could accept.

When I left Joan to go home, I couldn't leave the hospital without first checking on Therese. I feared that because of her severe deformity she might be shoved in some corner to die. I asked to see the pediatrician, and he assured me that as long as Therese was alive she would be properly cared for.

The next day Therese was alive. Joan and I decided to visit her and to hold and feed her. It seemed so natural that if her life was to be so short and there was nothing that could be done for her medically that we should give her all the love we could. This created a difficulty at the hospital. First, they were not accustomed to caring for malformed children (they sent them to another hospital usually); and secondly, they were not accustomed to parents who wished to see and love such a child. Often such children are shunned by their parents and perhaps signed over to a research hospital to be studied. We felt the unspoken pressures to do the same, and to relinquish our rights and desires as parents. I am sure that there are other parents who have been in our situation who have been intimidated by the hospital (perhaps not intentionally), and who were discouraged from following their natural inclinations.

When it became apparent that Therese would live for a longer time than they had estimated, we had to transfer her to another hospital.

We decided to transfer her to the University Hospital. There we were free to visit her when we could and to help take care of her. Since they were more accustomed to severely ill children, they were much more capable of dealing with the situation. After a week and a half when Joan was much better, we began to talk of taking Therese home. The staff was reluctant. We felt that since she did not require much more care than a normal infant, there was no reason why we should not take her home. As we talked it became clear that the reason why the hospital kept her was to spare us the pain of having to deal with a child like Therese. We explained that our lives are about the mystery of Faith and Love, that pain is a part of that mystery, and that we were willing to risk that pain to carry out our love of Therese. After much discussion the doctors agreed.

Early in the morning of the day we were to bring Therese home, one of the doctors called and told us that Therese had gotten worse and that we probably would not be able to take her home. Joan and I rushed to the hospital and spent the rest of the day with her. Late in the afternoon she died in our arms. We cried, prayed, and rejoiced. It was one of the most powerful and beautiful experiences of our lives—the giving over of our child to her Father.

Joan and I decided that we would take care of the burial ourselves. A friend allowed us to have Therese buried in a family plot of hers at Holy Cross Cemetery. All that was required was to obtain a permit from the Department of Public Health. After receiving her body, we brought her home. We dressed her and placed her in a coffin that Ken, my brother-in-law, and I had made.

Since Therese was the first child to be born into the Martin de Porres community, she was long awaited with joy and anticipation by the rest of the community. All shared in our pain of not being able to be with her. Since she was now finally home, the community had prepared a short and beautiful service to be said with her before we took her away to be buried. The next evening our families, friends, and community were present at a Mass of the Resurrection and celebrated the presence of our first Saint to be with our Father.

There are some lessons and insights into life that Joan and I have learned from this experience. There are so many people dying and suffering not only from natural causes but from the hatred and violence in our societies. The gift of human life is a rich and precious gift. It demands that our way of living and of being make that preciousness a reality for all and most especially for those who are considered the least. Some felt that Therese had no right to love and life because she was so much the least. That way of thinking and acting needs to be radically changed in all of our lives.

There is great wisdom in living one day at a time. Joan and I came prepared to face the mystery of birth and in such a short time birth was mixed with death at the very instant of birth; and then with the waters of Baptism, we were faced again with life. Just when we were prepared to bring Therese home, she died. At each point where we planned one thing, another was required. There is a liberation that occurs when we free ourselves from our expectations and fears so that it is fully possible to live in the present. "Do not worry about tomorrow. Set your heart on His kingdom and righteousness and all these other things will be given you as well."

The most special insight Therese taught us is the meaning of Christ's words when he said, "Unless you change and become like a little child you will not enter the kingdom of heaven." What a child draws forth from others is love. To us it seemed so natural to love Therese. What changing and becoming like a little child means is to change ourselves so that we become a source of drawing forth love from others. What a child does is to affirm the love that is in others so that it spontaneously comes forth. Our lives in all of their aspects must become as simple and defenseless as that of an infant so that we can allow even the heart of the exploiter to be moved and can be witnesses to affirming the dignity of those whose lives are lived in inhuman conditions. Our attitude should be like that of Christ, "What you do to the least of these my brothers and sisters, you do to me."

_____ MAY 1974

❦ Of Holy Poverty

MICHAEL DE GREGORY

"BLESSED ARE THE POOR in spirit, for theirs is the kingdom of heaven." In the Gospel according to Matthew these words begin Christ's first sermon to the world. This teaching is central to a Christian life, and marks Christianity as the religion of poverty. Aware of this, the Catholic Worker, since its inception, has embraced voluntary poverty as a way of life. Yet of every aspect of the Catholic Worker, voluntary poverty is probably the least understood. In our age, especially, voluntary poverty needs to be not only understood, but experienced in our daily lives.

To understand voluntary poverty as a way of life, it is necessary first to look at our world in which humanity is tragically divided into a rich minority and a poor majority. In the United States, the richest nation in the world, there are areas devastated by poverty and hunger. In urban ghettoes and on skid rows, among rural sharecroppers and migrant farm workers, material poverty is a fact of life. And among the other nations of the world, the economic division between the developed West and the developing Third World is more distinct. In the starkest statistical terms, the privileged 20 percent of the world's population control 80 percent of the world's resources. The United States alone, containing only 5% of the world's population, consumes 50 percent of the world's disposable resources and possesses 40 percent of the world's income. Such statistics on world poverty and hunger abound, but their significance is easily lost in their magnitude. The cold statistic that two-thirds of all deaths recorded each year in the world are due to hunger or problems arising from hunger is perhaps more comprehensible in all its human tragedy. This distribution of the world's goods does not abate, for whether it is within nations or between nations, the clearest economic trend in the world today is this: the rich get richer, and the poor get poorer.

To speak of voluntary poverty in this setting, to call poverty "holy" as St. Hilary does, is to invite confusion and misunderstanding. Yet as Dorothy Day wrote in the forties, "We can only talk about voluntary poverty because we believe Christians must be fools for Christ. We can only embrace voluntary poverty in the light of faith." For it is a paradox, like the Folly of the Cross, that it is only as we voluntarily embrace poverty that we can overcome poverty.

However, the poverty that the Catholic Worker embraces is not the poverty that the world knows. The poverty that Jesus Christ calls "blessed" is not the destitution experienced by the mass of humanity. Voluntary poverty is not material destitution, a want for the necessary food, clothing, and shelter so essential to make a human life worthy of the name. Rather it is a realization of what is actually needed, accompanied by a desire to amass no more. Voluntary poverty is an understanding of the truth that the less we take ourselves, the more others can have. It is to listen to the counsel of St. Paul to "Let our abundance supply their want."

Voluntary poverty is simply a means. It is not an end in itself. We must avoid the danger of making poverty a Christian ideal in itself. Human beings, made in the image of God, were not made to starve. Destitution is not the poverty we seek. St. Thomas Aquinas wrote that voluntary poverty "is good only because it is useful to remove the obstacles which stand in the way of spiritual perfection." Even though it is unattainable, we are all called to be perfect, so we are called to poverty. For voluntary poverty is not primarily a religious vow for the few, but a responsibility for all Christians. Dorothy further writes: "Once we begin not to worry about what kind of house we are living in, what kind of clothes we are wearing, once we give up the stupid recreation of the world, we have time—which is priceless—to remember that we are our brother's keepers and that we must not only care for his needs as far as we are immediately able, but we must try to build a better world."

At its deepest level voluntary poverty is a way of seeing the world and the things of the world. This vision is a liberation from the concerns of the world in order to serve, with charity and justice, both God and our neighbor.

In the Beatitudes according to Luke, the "poor in spirit" are given flesh, are made real human persons. Luke writes very simply: "Blessed are you poor, for yours is the Kingdom of God. Blessed are you that hunger now for you shall be satisfied." But to the wealthy, he warns: "Woe to you that are rich for you have received your consolation. Woe to you that are full now for you shall hunger."

Luke is not writing here to canonize or condemn any social class. He simply expresses a truth of Christianity: it is no accident that Christ came a poor man among men.

Although it is possible for a rich man to be detached from his goods, and a poor man greedy, voluntary poverty is surely not a comfort to the wealthy and powerful. The Gospels are quite clear: the rich man is told to sell all he has and give to the poor, for it is easier for a camel to pass through the eye of a needle than for a rich man to enter heaven. And we are clearly instructed that "you can not serve God and Mammon." Voluntary poverty is similar to the relationship of faith and good works in the Epistle of St. James. For its essence to be truly spiritual, voluntary poverty must be manifested in a visible way of life.

Some of the ambiguities about voluntary poverty are rooted in human uniqueness. Voluntary poverty cannot be regimented; in this it is clearly of the spirit. An individual's needs vary with culture and personality, often extending beyond basic food, clothing, and shelter. It is the degree of concern about these essentials that distinguishes the poor man in the biblical sense. (Surely the man who suffers hunger as a way of life is understandably concerned about his next meal.) However, Christians who are called to poverty and who are well fed and clothed should not worry about these needs. Gibran writes, "Is not the dread of thirst when the well is full the thirst which is unquenchable?" The poverty we seek to embrace is an absence of such "dread." We must believe that we are of more value than the "birds of the air" and the "lilies of the field." And we must be assured that as God cares for them He will care for us.

The poor man is the person who prays simply in faith, "Our Father . . . give us this day our daily bread," and who trusts that he will receive all that is required. He takes to heart the words of Christ, "Do not be anxious about your life, what you shall eat or what you shall drink, nor about your body, what you shall put on. . . . Your heavenly Father knows that you need them all. But seek first His Kingdom and His righteousness, and all these things shall be yours as well."

It is in seeking this kingdom that voluntary poverty is so important. For the vision of voluntary poverty is a vision of a new world, a world of justice and peace. The psalmist announces this coming kingdom in which "Kindness and truth shall meet; justice and peace shall kiss." Voluntary poverty provides not only the vision but also the way of life to "build a better world."

The poor man is the man of justice. Eric Gill understood this and wrote clearly, "The poor man, in the Gospel sense, in the sense of Jesus, is not he who has been robbed but he who has not robbed others." The Old Testament prophets shared this understanding, and the early Church Fathers taught it. The prophets vigorously condemned the causes of material poverty as exploitation and injustice. And the Mosaic Law offered legal safeguards for the welfare of the needy—in the year of the Jubilee, for example. This spirit of justice expresses a simple truth: what we have beyond what we need is stolen from the poor. We try to ignore this fact, to modify it; yet seldom do we face it and try to live it, though it remains the truth. The Church Fathers understood it and were faithful to its teaching. St. John Chrysostom wrote unequivocally, "No one is able to become rich without injustice." And Pope Paul remembered this truth in his encyclical "On the Development of Peoples," quoting St. Ambrose: "You are not making a gift of your possessions to the poor man. You are handing over to him what is his. For what has been given in common for the use of all, you have arrogated to yourself. The world is given to all, and not only to the rich." On this point the encyclical adds, "No one is justified in keeping for his exclusive use what he does not need, when others lack necessities."

To give necessities to the needy is an act of justice, not an act of mercy. Voluntary poverty provides a powerful means of preserving justice without which love is impossible. And as Gustavo Gutiérrez writes in A Theology of Liberation, "If the ultimate cause of man's exploitation and alienation is selfishness, the deepest reason for voluntary poverty is love of neighbor." In this spirit the early Christian church at Jerusalem held everything in common, not for any ideal of poverty, but for a true love of the poor; so that "there was not a needy person among them" (Acts 4:34).

The poor man is the man of peace. To seek nonviolence as a way of life is to embrace voluntary poverty as a way of living. They are two sides of the same coin. The more we have, the more we become attached to material things—to jobs, to status, to security—the more we will fear their loss, the more tenaciously we will fight to hold on to them. As Lyndon Johnson said to American troops in 1968: "Don't forget. There are two hundred million of us in a world of three billion. They want what we've got, and we're not going to give it to them."

War is, indeed, the health of the State. With modern economics so deeply involved in the military-industrial complex, voluntary poverty is no longer a choice, but an imperative for the person of peace. Nonviolence includes noncooperation with the works of war. Voluntary poverty is a call to the works of mercy, which are the works of peace. So we must embrace voluntary poverty and refuse to participate in the workings of war, the defense industries, stocks and bonds, corporate power. We cannot accept the comforts of a society which are manufactured by the exploitation and even the blood of others. And as our taxes pay for war and the weapons of war, we can only lead simple lives in poverty and refuse to pay these war taxes. The eighteenth-century Quaker John Woolman urged his fellow Christians to "try whether the seeds of war have nourishment in our possessions." In the search for peace, we must embrace poverty as a way.

The poor man is the man of vision. This was most certainly true of Peter Maurin. Like St. Francis, Peter embraced "Lady Poverty." Chesterton writes that Francis was a Tumbler for Our Lady, and would often see the world standing on his head. He concludes that this perspective was the most accurate worldview. As Francis would think, were it not for the grace of God the grandest buildings, the largest institutions, the greatest designs of men would only fall into the sky. Francis thus realized his utter dependence on God for his very sustenance. Renouncing all, he expected nothing, and was happy with everything.

Peter Maurin also realized the passing nature of the wealth of the world. To the modern world his vision seems as topsy-turvy as the vision of St. Francis. The wisdom of his slogan, "work, not wages," still escapes most unionists and clock-punchers. On riches Peter understood that it was not that "you can't take it with you," but rather, "when we die we carry in our clutched hand only what we have given away." Peter taught that it was the poor, the "ambassadors of God," who provided a service to the rich by giving them the "opportunity to do good," thus freeing them from "the shackles of wealth." He was not overlooking the misery of the poor, but simply understood that true revolution liberates the oppressor as well as the oppressed.

In embracing voluntary poverty, Peter was truly a free man. He was free to think, to work, to serve, to envision a new society. In such a society, voluntary poverty would be as natural as the law of gravity. Peter offered a wisdom which very few modern economists could dare imagine: "Everybody would be rich if nobody tried to become richer. And nobody would be poor if everybody tried to be poorest." Gandhi believed that true progress was found in the renunciation, not the accumulation of wealth. This notion, shared by Peter Maurin, is the opposite of the materialist worldviews, whether capitalist or communist. Gandhi preached a higher standard of spiritual well-being and insisted that a lower standard of material living was an essential prerequisite.

He once remarked that for the poor of the world, God can only come in the form of bread. And it follows that we who embrace voluntary poverty can only see God in the lack of bread. God can only come to us as we empty ourselves. Only in stripping away our possessions can we meet Christ in the service of others. We must become nothing so as to be filled with God who is everything.

As we embrace voluntary poverty, we begin "to create a new society within the shell of the old." Voluntary poverty is a witness to this world and a vision of a new world. It is a call to share with the poor, to share both their suffering and the earth's fullness. It is a call to share in justice and to protest the injustice which divides humanity into rich and poor. As we live to love both God and neighbor, we might recall the words of John, the beloved disciple, "If anyone has the world's goods and sees his brother in need, yet closes his heart against him, how does God's love abide in him? Let us not love in word or speech but in deed and in truth" (1 John 3:17–18).

MAY 1974

❧ Of Holy Work

PAT JORDAN

A POSTER HANGS on the office door of the Catholic Worker here in New York which proclaims, "Work is love made visible." This sentiment of the great Dominican Gerald Vann has been a guiding principle for generations of Catholic Workers, and it is central to a Catholic Worker philosophy of work. The very name of the movement indicates this.

Lewis Mumford writes: "There is no substitute for work except other serious work" (*The Pentagon of Power*). Peter Maurin would have agreed. A worker and student all his life, he insisted that all work be done well. He came from a family rooted in work, French farmers who knew what Charles Péguy has called the "honor of work." In the various houses of hospitality and farming communes which the Catholic Worker created during his lifetime, Peter taught the young volunteers who came what was in his blood for generations. "Work for them [the peasants] was joy itself and the deep root of their being, the reason of their being. There was an incredible honor in work, the most beautiful of all honors, the most Christian, perhaps the only one which stands of itself. And today everyone is bourgeois" (Péguy, *Basic Verities*). The last sentence indicates Péguy's disdain of those who live by the sweat of other men and women's brows, and Peter Maurin shared this disdain.

Peter Maurin saw in work a necessity and a gift, the fulfillment of one of the human person's highest urges, creativity. He rejected the modern concept that work is a commodity.

> The Catholic Worker
> does not credit
> bourgeois capitalism
> with an historical mission.
> It condemns it
> on the general principle
> that labor is a gift,
> not a commodity.

In conjunction with this he wrote in another of his *Easy Essays,*

> Labor is not a commodity
> to be bought and sold.
> Labor is a means of self-expression,
> the worker's gift to the common good.

Peter wished to create a new society, what he called a "functional society rather than an acquisitive society." In an interview he stated, "A functional society is a society in which each member strives to foster the common good, a society of go-givers instead of go-getters, a society of idealists rather than materialists." He saw the means of creating such a society in the responsible and daily work of all society's members.

Of the three levels on which each person functions (the personal, the social, and the spiritual), Peter Maurin saw the starting point for any development of the whole human being to be the personal. A person's work, as Mumford indicates, has bearing on one's whole nature and (as Peter learned from Eric Gill) on one's whole life.

We commonly identify creativity with the artistic process. But Peter extended this application to the work of all men and women: the baker, the farmer, the stonemason. Such creativity enhances and is the fruit of true individuation, the means of self-fulfillment and self-expression, a form of service to the whole community. This basic need for a sense of personal worth must be met. Sharon Atkins, a receptionist interviewed by Studs Terkel, put it this way: "I don't know what I'd like to do. That's what hurts the most. That's why I can't quit the job. I really don't think I'd mind going back and learning something, taking a piece of furniture and refinishing it. The type of thing where you know what you're doing and you can create and you can fix something to make it function" (Studs Terkel, *Working*). Work without some sense of creativity, of intrinsic worth, of dignity, is slavery. It hardly inspires love.

Peter Maurin saw that among the flaws of modern productionism is that, in its haste, modern productivity has taken the largesse out of time. Time is now money, and on the assembly lines and in the mechanized agricultural fields, the tempo of production has been increasingly accelerated. It can be seen even affecting our prayers. (A recent picture in the Catholic press shows a priest distributing communion on a train to commuters during Holy Week, his chasuble bearing the symbols of the Rail Road!) Lewis Mumford has wonderfully illuminated this matter of time. It was the widespread use of clocks in the thirteenth century, he contends, that more than anything else marked the end of the medieval period and the beginning of the modern, secular era. Of present day business, he concludes, "The modern industrial regime could do without coal and iron and steam easier than it could do without the clock" (*Technics and Civilization*).

This use of the clock as keeper of time, as the policeman which dictates all our moves for the sake of efficiency, has brought us to the brink of social neurosis. Terkel quotes another worker in conjunction with this slavery to the clock, and how such bondage mitigates against the creation of community amongst workers. Grace Clements, a factory worker: "We work eight straight hours, with two ten-minute coffee breaks and one twenty-minute break for lunch. If you want to use the washroom, you have to do that in that time. By the time you leave your tank [she dips felt in a tank before adhering it to the luggage the factory produces], you go to the washroom, freshen up a bit, go into the recreation room; it makes it very difficult to finish a small lunch and be back in the tank in twenty minutes. So you don't really have too much time for conversation."

Mrs. Clements goes through the same set of motions every forty seconds on the luggage factory assembly line. Each complete motion includes her taking about ten steps, and she accomplishes this about eight hundred times a day! Peter Kropotkin, who had a lasting effect on Peter Maurin, had this to say of such work: "Overwork is repulsive to human nature, not work. Overwork for supplying the few with luxury, not work for the well-being of all. Work, labor, is a physiological necessity, a necessity of spending accumulated bodily energy, a necessity which is health and life itself" (Essay on "Anarchist Communism").

Peter Maurin wished people to work four hours at manual labor a day and four hours at study. The rest of the waking hours could be spent at craft work, roundtable discussions, and the building of community. Peter also noted the importance of singing at work, for singing fosters the tempo, leisure, and beauty of human activity. The songs of the workshop, the chantey of the sailors, the singing of psalms in the fields by medieval peasants, all these gave an industrial value which is lost in the noise of modern-day factories. Song is also important because, as Peter pointed out concerning the medieval peasants, "That is how they related all things to God."

Finally, Peter noted that individuals have lost the value of their work because they have confused trading with making, have confused commerce for the task which is well done and rewarding in itself. "He [the worker] must see to it that the things he makes are fit to use rather than to sell. He must take pride in work well done, and must realize that labor is related to thought and thought is a spiritual faculty, not a commodity."

The second realm of the human endeavor is the communal or social. As if the personal level is not complicated enough, the social is even more so. And Peter used to say that the spiritual is the most difficult of all.

The social is complex because it compounds the complexities of all the individuals involved, giving to the social process something of the character of geometric multiplication, or perhaps atomic fission. As certain philosophers point out, one is not a person unless one is in relationship with others. And even the hermit's vocation is seen by the Church as a vocation in and for the whole Church.

Work has always been a means of inclusion among peoples. The Catholic Worker is a "community of work," the community resulting and growing from the shared tasks which are undertaken. The desire for sharing in great tasks which require great deals of human ingenuity and energy is almost metaphysical to man. This is one of the reasons so often men have been drawn into making wars. Modern war is an all-out effort on the part of a whole nation or society to achieve a particular victory. Our task remains to channel such productive energy into creative (not destructive) activities, into nonviolent campaigns for social revolution.

The social nature of the person has been severely hampered in its goal of "creating a society in which it will be easier to be good" (Maurin) by modern class structures and the inherent competition and inequality they spawn. A friend recently wrote of his work in a Chicago factory: "I was reading *The Diary of a Country Priest,* and it just happened to mention *Rerum Novarum,* and the fact that labor is not a commodity. Well, I was thinking about that while working in the factory, and I became quite class conscious. I began noticing the different levels that people were on. First of all there were the day labor workers, the regular employees, the foremen, the section bosses, the plant managers, and the executives. You do progressively less work as you move up the ladder, and you are paid more for it, too."

That such a status quo is desirable to many, even the well-intentioned, we should have no doubts. Every privileged group seeks to safeguard its status by various educational and/or licensing restrictions (profes-sionalism).

Julius Nyerere, the President of Tanzania, has stated that the purpose of Tanzanian socialism is man. In an effort to replace the old residual class structure of colonialism in Tanzania with the sense of service for the people, Nyerere has gone into the villages and worked with pick and shovel himself. He has encouraged government officials and students to do the same. Of course, he has met with no small degree of resistance. Status divests itself with little haste and cheerfulness. Yet there has been some progress, particularly in the villages. Nyerere equates indepen-dence and self-reliance, and sees freedom for people in their ability "to stand on their own two feet."

Thus, the societal problem we face has to do with responsibility. Mechanization, largeness, the bureaucratic cloud which engulfs our paper culture, these have made of us a puppet population which has lost all sense of responsibility for the work it does. Worse, says Eric Gill, we no longer desire to regain such responsibility! (Cf. *Beauty Looks After Herself*.)

Peter Maurin called for such a reclamation of responsibility. He said that the best kind of government is self-government. He encouraged this, and wrote further: " 'Fire the boss / and be your own boss' is a good slogan / for the worker."

To build a society based on cooperation rather than conflict, on just distribution of goods rather than greed, a functional society rather than an acquisitive society, this is what Peter proposed. Such a society is not based on the interests of usury, expediency, or manufacture, but on the protection and betterment of the standard of life of each worker.

While the sort of mammoth mechanization which has turned human work into a wasteland and polluted the earth must be checked (even reversed), doing away with all machinery is both impossible and undesir-able. E.F. Schumacher has called for the creation of intermediate forms of technology. He says that for every activity there is an appropriate scale (cf. his *Small Is Beautiful*), and gives examples of factories which are trying to get away from the assembly line by creating small workshops within big factories.

The most formidable effort of work remains to be exerted on the third realm of human nature, the spiritual. This is the deepest and most complex level of our existence, the natural resource we have least developed, the circle most often neglected.

That work applies to the spirit and the spirit to work can be seen in two of the classic religious Rules which influenced Peter Maurin's thinking, those of St. Benedict and St. Francis. Both speak of the right relationships of prayer to work (St. Benedict's "Ora et Labora"), and the necessity of daily labor. Francis dedicated the fifth chapter of his

Rule to work, and, we are told, dismissed one of the lazy friars as "Brother Fly."

In the classic sense of these Rules, the discipline of work is seen as a prerequisite in creating the order and openness necessary for growth in the spiritual life. Such discipline is needed in human relations as well, for often friendship and close proximity call for disciplined forbearance. Cesar Chavez has said that walking the picket line as an exercise, hour after hour, day to week to month after month, is the greatest teacher of nonviolence. This relates to the discipline, the silence, the coordinated effort, the meditation such a protracted experience entails, and suggests the spiritual power of nonviolence as well.

That the spiritual realm is related to the social is suggested by the words of Fr. Zossima in *The Brothers Karamazov:* that the work of each person contributes to the salvation of the whole world. That is why the "little way" of St. Therese has borne such a harvest for countless men and women, and for the Church as a whole. St. Therese was aware that "the one inexhaustible school of mortification is work. Every ordinary task of the day must be done precisely, as conscientiously, as composedly and faultlessly, as the strength of body and soul permits: without haste, without hesitation, without carelessness, without negligence. Anyone who has tried to do this knows well that such punctiliousness can be true penance" (Ida F. Gorres, *The Hidden Face*). It was through her work, seemingly inconspicuous to all who lived with her, that she rose to the heights of great sanctity, and in so doing, uplifted the level of the whole Church.

"The future will be different if the present is different," Peter Maurin was fond of repeating. I have found much excitement recently in reading similar thoughts in the work of Lewis Mumford.

Mumford should give great encouragement to those who seek to reconcile their work and the human purpose. He emphasizes, as did Peter Maurin, the necessity of each person cultivating various interests and activities simply to maintain one's psychological and ecological balance. He has a love of freedom associated with anarchists, and encourages workers to debunk their vocational pigeon-holes. Mumford says these should become increasingly meaningless as the "Vocation of Man" becomes the focus of our activity. He suggests that people develop multiple occupations, as have a number of people at the Catholic Worker. One woman not only assists at one of our houses of hospitality, she works and goes to school as well. Others give freely of their time by settling to work fewer hours at their own jobs.

All this changing of roles has a good purpose, says Mumford, for it leads to a diversification of human development, a deepening of the reservoir of experience, and an intensification of life. All this clarifies his dictum quoted before: "There is no substitute for work except other serious work."

What is this work for, and how can it be accomplished in a society which seeks to make its members conform more totally with each passing moon to its own dehumanizing purposes? Once again, Mumford has some suggestions akin to Peter Maurin's. Let me end with these as they are indeed hopeful, and shed light on the prophetic nature of Peter Maurin and his work:

> But for those of us who have thrown off the myth of the machine, the next move is ours.
>
> Each one of us, as long as our life stirs in him, may play a part in extricating himself from the power system by asserting his primacy as a person in quiet acts of mental or physical withdrawal. Though no immediate and complete escape from the ongoing power system is possible, least of all through mass violence, the changes that will restore autonomy and initiative to the human person all lie within the province of each individual soul, once it is aroused.
>
> The changes that have so far been effective, and that give promise to further successes, are those that have been initiated by animated individual minds, small groups, and local communities nibbling at the edges of the power structure by breaking routines and defying regulations. Such an attack seeks, not to capture the citadel of power, but to withdraw from it and quietly paralyze it. Once such initiatives become widespread, as they at last show signs of becoming, it will restore power and confident authority to its proper source: the human personality and the small face-to-face community. (*The Pentagon of Power*)

DECEMBER 1974

❀ Bread for the Road: A Poor Man's Journey

LARRY ROSEBAUGH

EDS. NOTE: *These notes from the diary of Fr. Rosebaugh are a "poor man's journey," describing his life with the destitute of our cities. "The Holy Spirit was calling me," he writes, "to the experience of being the poor man to whom the soup was ladled out." Fr. Rosebaugh is an Oblate priest. He spent twenty months in prison, ten of them in solitary, for his part in the "Milwaukee 14" raid on a Selective Service office in protest of the Vietnam War.*

Milwaukee, November 11. A year or two ago, when I was making a retreat, a woman prayed over me and discerned my direction. As I recall it, it had to do with my becoming a vagabond, a wanderer, one on the road.

The priest upstairs talks of Harlem, of the conditions there, his experience in the subways, and how we identify with this condition; that's precisely where the challenge exists. How prone I am to surround myself with this world's comforts until they overshadow my true calling!

The need to go deeper into myself and to the Spirit who speaks there has been vital. This summer I changed my living quarters from a shared apartment to an empty garage space, walking out on close friends to follow an inner drive. Then I built a tiny shack and lived there in the experience of silence. The need for prayer, for quiet is a gift; and that gift has been a further revelation into the reality of the Gospel as it is meant to be carried out by me. The last two and a half years here in Milwaukee have brought me to the point where, after testing myself in a whole realm of lived-out experiences of street conditions, the need to move on as a priest, an Oblate, overwhelms me. I have seen a certain level of human tragedy lived out by men and women in the State Street area of Milwaukee; the despair of drugs and confusion of people's minds as they go in and out of our city's mental wards. My inner drive is to see more of the reality encountered by men and women of our city streets. The people who show up for free meals at Salvation Army Shelters and missions are a portion of those who know destitution, but it is among these that I feel presently affiliated and with whom I am being called to identify. Hitting the road by way of thumb, and boarding down in the Skid Row facilities of our cities draw a whole new dimension from the gut: fear.

November 15 and 16. How does one recount what was in effect a prayer unfolding, a step into the dark, truly a faith excursion?

It was good going through the experience here in Milwaukee, a registering and going through the formal indoctrination that precedes admission into the Rescue Mission (a very cold, calculated speech given by one of the staff ministers of Jesus' love and forgiveness along with a series of quite personal questions about myself). But the Mission was clean, served good food, and promoted a pleasant atmosphere. From the beginning I sensed a rapport and generosity among the men of a depth I've found no place else. When a person gets down to the level of total dependence on others, he learns the lesson of brother and sisterly love—a love genuinely grateful for a drink given, a bed to sleep in, some food.

The clothes one gets accustomed to are important, the food one eats and how much of it is important; how much money one earns and on what he becomes dependent is important. As I hit the road I realize that I have never really known what it is to be totally without. There is a faith dependency about which I do not know much at this point, but if two or three persons were called to such a life of poverty correctly understood, of prayer, and of quiet: WOW! Back to the road.

November 17. Chicago library. Until the Church herself tastes poverty, the Church will not identify in any true sense with the poor.

Evely said, as I read his *Credo* this morning, that when the poor have nothing else left they can allow that union between the Son, Jesus, and themselves to make that bond between themselves in the name of Jesus a living reality.

My first ride came from a man who appeared to be from India. He drove a very expensive car, and asked multitudes of questions about my living status. Why was I so poor? He offered to give me a place to sleep for the night, get me a meal. And only as we came to the corner where he was to let me off did he suggest that the first thing I should do was visit a church and ask the Lord for help with trust in Him; then he took from his pocket a wad of bills, peeling off fifty dollars which he insisted I take. "Get a good meal," he repeated in parting, "a place to sleep, and remember to stop into a church." It struck me clearly that this was a sign of the Lord's care, a confirmation that I was following out his will. I got on the "L" for Chicago, and made for the bowery.

Just where am I, Lord? The reality of where the Spirit draws me is not easy: is it really You who calls me here, all alone, on Madison Street, Chicago? And for what? Without all my clothes, without my hang ups, without possessions. Jesus did have a message; He didn't just go and be poor; He knew the lay of the land and He spoke for the forsaken whilst being forsaken. Is that the call each of us has facing us? Can't I compromise whilst reading the Gospel? Be a little less than poor so I can accomplish my end?

I'm not sure what the meaning of all this is, but I trust the best I can. Amen.

November 17. Last night was a tough one for it spelled facing some of the fears and realities that bowery life has in store.

My entry in the rain and cold was a slow and prayerful one, a calming down within, a realization as to Who was calling me along this path. Finally, I came to the area lived in by persons who have hit the bottom. Places that the Salvation Army or Missions provide were closed, and only two hotels with rooms for $1.80 were open. A man with billy club in hand opened the door for me, about 11:30 p.m. Though I had a long weathered coat and worn clothes, they obviously knew from my face that I was new to the streets. They asked for my Social Security card; in the course of the night it would be checked in case I was wanted by the law.

This building, plus the other "hotels" commonly called flophouses, appeared to be gutted factory buildings, with five and six floors sectioned off floor by floor into hundreds of six by ten-foot cubicles, with wire mesh for a false ceiling (and the factory ceiling ten or fifteen feet above). What a shock as I opened the door to my "room;" whiskey bottles lined the floor, a spoiled container of cottage cheese sat on the chair, old clothing hung inside the locker. "Keep clothes inside locker at all times," read a sign on the inside of the door to the room. Later I understood why when the tossing of nearly empty wine bottles onto the wire mesh might bring dripping wine anyplace into one's quarters. The greatest shock came when I looked at the sheet which covered my bed: the dirt didn't upset me as much as the small jumping insects all over the bed along with many crawling roaches. Under the sheet was better than resting on top because insects were dropping down from the ceiling. All that plus the heat of the building and the bumping lockers unnerved me, not to mention the searching of police officers with the coughing and hacking of men throughout the night. All that is part and parcel of the lot of persons leading a street existence—day after day, year after year. Such a one knows nothing but scraping the barrel to survive; to have the roof over one's head is better than no roof at all; to have a cigarette butt or two is better than none at all; to have a few pennies toward a bottle gives a little more security than "shaking" the day through.

November 18. I stayed on another night in Chicago at the same hotel, primarily because I felt fear with an urge to get out of there. The same attendant at the desk, wearing dark glasses, who had threatened—as part of this spaced-out performance—to beat out my brains unless I conformed to "hotel" regulations the night before, granted me the same privilege this night. He also said his boss had raised the price fifty cents since the preceding night. That plus the manner in which he anxiously assigned me a room, a few steps from the elevator, made me realize I was being set up for something. But, because other places were closed, I didn't want to be stranded outside in the rain; I went along with it.

About 2:30 a.m., I supposed, an elevator came to our floor, stopped, and three men got off. Hearing mumbling, I realized they were stopping outside my door. As I peered through the six-inch opening at the bottom of my door, I saw three pairs of shoes. A key went into my door while I heard one whisper, "I'll get him first, you second," and another said, "I'm third." (Something one reads about in the morning paper, perhaps, but new to me.) Spontaneously I leaped up, jammed my cot against the door, and let out every bloody threat I could think of. Although they reciprocated with a few threats of their own, slowly they took off to disturb or upset someone else. I didn't dare sleep that night, to learn in the morning that three or four rooms had been broken into.

Frightened enough to question my ideas about getting a feeling for the other side of the soup line, I was approached by an older man, who walked with me around the corner to a Mission where we heard an early morning Scripture greeting and words of encouragement; plus sweet rolls and steaming hot coffee. About two hundred men stood around the high tables, sharing the meal. The climate was friendly, and the men told me of other places where food could be gotten and free lodging for the night provided. Tales were shared and there, like no place else, I saw the face of Him who has called us, speaking to me again.

How do I continue my journey in writing? What is pertinent and what is not? It's hard to know, for everything on this trip seems essential: essential that I use my time well, and in the spirit of faithful prayer. That is what the trip is all about from the beginning.

I carried a knapsack full of books and articles planning to catch up on my reading in libraries along the way.

One afternoon I stopped for a visit in a large church in downtown Chicago. I pulled out this notebook to write down some reflections while also reading from a book. An usher, decked in a blue uniform, approached to inform me that such carrying on was not proper in church. Not wanting to upset him, I put away my papers until he got busy about other things. But soon he was back, ordering me to leave the church, threatening to have me arrested if I didn't comply: "You're just one of those dirty bums from Madison Street here to give us trouble." I should have left, but instead I responded defensively: "What if I told you I'm a priest?" He said, "Show me your credentials, or I'll call the police." I left then, regretting that I had replied in favor of myself, but just the same, I did not feel like going back to that church. Can't poor men visit peacefully in our churches? Must we be properly dressed to do so? This was a good experience for me.

It became noticeable as I continued my travels that persons tend to stare when one dresses for existence on the streets: three or four coats, long johns, heavy pants are part of it. Appearances are not important when the possibility of being stranded outside for the night in the cold and rain is always present. I felt annoyed when, without pretense, people turned to look at me, and continued to look: a different creature. Though there are no words to express those glares, I was made aware of the fact that when one doesn't meet certain acceptable standards of dress and appearance, he becomes less than human in many eyes. How does the man or woman who has only a few tattered, not too clean, clothes feel in our cities? Out of place in churches, restaurants.

November 20. The frustration of dire poverty doesn't really impress until we become utterly impoverished. The pains of hunger become real to us only when they are ours. In the meantime, we can only try to put ourselves in the place of such victims, and attempt to alleviate some frustration and pain.

I reflect on what Jim Douglass is saying in his book, *Resistance and Contemplation:* we keep going down into the pit of nothingness, sacrifice at the experience of the whole, and there in the nothingness we'll be given light and bread to sustain us.

November 21. The road: getting from one city to the next; being stranded on rainy, cold nights, sometimes all night; never knowing whether it would be two, three, or four hours before the next ride comes along; alone. The cities, the streets. Two different aspects of poverty, but they blend into a powerful experience: when one has nothing else to turn to the Spirit speaks many things about people, about life, and about an all-encompassing love.

November 22. Arrived in Rochester, N.Y. The phone directory gave the name of a Mission which, after walking across town, I discovered did not exist. As it began getting dark, I came upon two men sharing a pint of wine, and asked where a place to sleep was available. They replied that this city had no such place, but that I could get a meal at St. Joe's church—which turned out to be a Catholic Worker house of hospitality. After walking in the cold for hours in a strange city, not knowing where to go, it is meaningful to have two friendly poor men direct one to a place to stay. I went through the soup line at the Catholic Worker. Although my experience has turned me against Day Labor Agencies, I wanted to get a sense of how many persons file into such places, so at 6:00 a.m. I went to one. A day at factory cleaning and sweeping made me appreciate physical work, despite the fact that it was at the hands of those who make money off those desperate for a day's pay. On the road again for New York.

Cold, rainy dark highways greeted me. Thoughts of turning back; doubts of hitching in this kind of weather, came tumbling in. These kinds of thoughts would be a common thing: doubting thoughts, a prayer, a call on the Father—and then, usually, but not always, a ride, a resurrection, hope and life arising from the grave. Such a warm feeling comes to me when people pick me up, and immediately relate as if we'd known each other for years.

November 23. Yesterday was Thanksgiving. All works together: the speaking of the Spirit is all around. We must be discerners, and pray that slowly all is seen as a movement toward the God of Abraham.

November 26. Cold again. Very few cars on the road, and miles from anywhere, and again the need to put myself at the disposal of the Father's way. Soon a pickup, driven by a young man, stopped. He was not going far, but I was welcome to stay with him for the night.

December 1. New York City without a dime in my pocket. I gave my last dollar to a needy person, becoming needy myself. I pick my way down new streets, having to ask for a dime to call the Catholic Worker house. It's late, not much room there, but come anyway. One a.m. before I find my way to the bowery, a weird experience walking the streets asking for a dime to ride the subway, humiliating. Now it's cold and damp, and the Catholic Worker is closed tight. I begin to walk by park benches, alleyways, door fronts. A taste of poverty: to walk all night with nowhere to go, knowing that the Salvation Army has good food but wants 25 cents a meal, and I don't have 25 cents. Men standing out in the cold, here and there. Finally, feeling exhausted, I saw a woman with a coat over her head sitting by a wire basket, trying to keep warm from the tiny fire she had made within it. Another man and I approached together, and these two began to talk about survival on the city streets, where one could go to get warm, how the subways are closed and don't allow men and women to sleep there anymore at night and certain apartment buildings leave entrances purposely open for persons to get in out of the cold, how to build a fire that would last the night using only one piece of wood at a time.

Hundreds of men this morning in the social center, many sleeping on the floors with sores, wounds, glad to have the bare floor as their blanket, bed, pillow all combined. This I needed to see: to leave Milwaukee, and go places where I had never been, and leave myself open to injury, fear, the crazed minds of the despairing, the misery of the night. Now I am getting that for which I prayed: an understanding of some of the pain of the Third World. I did pray to know better what this existence of the street is about, and it's been given to me: mean, cruel, everyday routine. There didn't seem to be much Christlike this month on the bowery.

December 3. Definite types of work, practical and needed, seem to be emerging from this trip: a free, floating brotherhood of the streets, helping where one can and as best as one can, being present among those with nowhere to go. Perhaps the depression must set in most completely, and maybe flares and rockets fly over our cities, before a brotherhood and sisterhood occurs that is real, meaningful, to the hundreds of human persons on the streets. We must not remain sterile, but open and prayerful, full of hope given us in silence.

FEBRUARY 1975

Freedom to Serve

JAN ADAMS

THE FALL OF 1974 at Martin de Porres House will be remembered as the months the San Francisco Health Department stole from our lives and work. For nearly thirty days, the several hundred people who depend on our free meals had to find other resources. While every newspaper spread the news of growing hunger, we were forced to spend thousands of dollars, which might have gone for food, on equipment and fixtures. Installing these fancy gee-gaws was physically exhausting, but worse was the demoralization which accompanied this waste of energy.

It is tempting to view the episode as a kind of natural calamity: as those who build on geological fault-lines must expect earthquakes, those who deal with food must expect Health Department hassles. I think this is too easy, that it is a way to avoid the painful experience of thinking the miserable business through. Instead, I see the episode as a political defeat. Its only possible compensation is the occasion offered to reflect on how, in a more humane society, people might have some control over the safety and quality of meals served in a public eating place.

Why do I think we suffered a political defeat? To understand this you have to know how Martin de Porres House is at odds with our society. Politically you could call us an anarchist collective. A group of us do this work because we want to, without organizational charts, without leaders, arriving at functional harmony (not efficiency) through the rhythm of the work and shared goals. In prevailing economics we make no sense at all—no one owns the enterprise; we aim at neither profits nor wages, but carry on the work through the generous help of our friends. For ourselves, we are content to work at outside jobs a few days a month to earn a simple living. We are generalists, not experts. You will find us trying our hands at such diverse tasks as cooking meals, fixing plumbing, hauling garbage, writing articles and washing dishes. Instead of owning expensive equipment, we count on this willingness to work at anything and muddle through. Even the aim of much that we do is anomalous in this society; rather than attempting the "rehabilitation" of "clients," we simply try to make ourselves available to our neighbors' needs, to be with folks in a spirit of love.

Enter the health inspector. He is a "neutral" outside observer, an expert. That is, he has never eaten our meals, never even helped serve a meal, but he knows a lot about restaurant equipment. He looks at our equipment, finds it primitive, deduces the operation is unhealthy, and orders us to buy the approved equipment. He has the power to stop our meals if we do not comply. We recognize that some of our equipment is poor in quality, but we don't like his demanding attitude. We weigh our outrage against our neighbors' needs and cave in before his power—a betrayal of all we stand for as outlined above.

What does the health inspector stand for? He is supposed to embody the principle of "objectivity." That is, since he knows nothing about our operation, he is more qualified to judge it than if he did. This claim of "objectivity" is such nonsense, yet so pervasive, that it is valuable to try to fathom its hold on people. I think that when we succumb to it we are confused by a false analogy to physical science. Experiments with matter will only yield true results if the scientist can exclude extrinsic variables. But what is extrinsic in trying to observe something people are doing? Certainly experience in how it actually works is not. Yet by false analogy, this experience comes to be thought of as "prejudicial." "Objectivity" comes to be equated with "fairness." Even at a linguistic level this is absurd: "objectivity" is a property of rational thought, while "fairness" is an attribute of a person.

Further, we should realize that even if "objective" standards are applied by a person attempting supreme fairness, those standards are still unfit to measure almost anything of importance. The aim of such standards is to separate a situation into its elements so that these elements can be compared in different contexts.

Another curious consequence of dependence on "objective" standards for equipment is that restaurant inspection has little to do with food. One department official actually told us that he had no worries about our meals causing sickness. Nonetheless, we just could not operate without the approved fixtures. I noticed another indicator of the unimportance of food during our dealings with the bureaucrats. I have been calling the health inspectors "he" not generically but literally. The only woman we heard of in a non-secretarial position in the department was the city nutritionist—perhaps an indication of how low food stands among department priorities.

In addition to being "objective," the health inspector also claims to be an "expert." In our capitalist society—one definition of which is that everyone must have something to sell in the market in order to live—to be an expert is to claim exclusive property in some knowledge which has a market value. This knowledge has to be guarded closely (for example, by credentials and "professional standards"), otherwise non-experts might flood the market and put the expert out of a job. Hence, mere ability to run a restaurant means nothing about our ability to keep the operation healthy. In fact, it can reflect negatively on our qualifications, since running a restaurant may require knowing a little of this and a little of that. Now everyone knows that "generalist" is only a polite euphemism for "unskilled," and everyone knows that to be unskilled is to be next to worthless in the market.

One of the ways the expert defends his or her corner in his or her specialty is by displaying proper deference toward the specialties of other experts. Thus, a visiting health inspector calls down a whole gamut of other inspectors—building inspectors and fire inspectors in our case, plus the threat of a multitude of what-have-you experts, whom we fortunately avoided. All of these, of course, insist that their objections be met by our hiring the services of the appropriate building trades experts, various contractors such as plumbing, electrical, sheet metal, etc. The health experts have even demanded that we buy the services of the garbage experts to dispose of our waste, instead of letting us haul it three blocks to approved bins. For the actual repairs we were fortunate enough to avoid the system to some extent. Thanks to our friends, with and without the appropriate credentials, we were able to do most of the work ourselves.

In justice to the various practitioners of the expert racket whom we met, I should say that some of them did come out of their roles and respond to us and our work as people. We met several who offered quite practical suggestions. We noticed especially that the fire inspectors, perhaps as a consequence of being in a department which confronts real risks, took a realistic view of what should be done. Yet, I wish that I had found the words to tell those inspectors who were sympathetic that, much as I might appreciate their personal concern, I could not absolve them for participating in what I can only see as a systematic racket.

If health inspection is a racket, what would we put in its place? Angry as we became at the absurdity of it all, we never denied that by running a public eating place we must be accountable to people for health standards. It seems clear to me that the competent persons are those who eat the meals or perhaps those who live in the neighborhood. These are the only people with any actual, as opposed to professional, interest. And what would be their concern? Clearly it would be food, not equipment. In fact, they might see a premium in operating with the minimum necessary fixtures since it would reduce costs. This is to say nothing of the increase in human wholeness which results from the struggle to do adequately a great variety of things instead of being a helpless dependant of a specialized technology.

It might be objected that an assorted group of consumers or neighbors would have no power to enforce compliance with their demands. Suppose the folks running a public eating place would not take notice of them? The consumers could probably go elsewhere, but what of the neighbors who had to live with an erring restaurant's garbage? Isn't it worth risking the growth of the sort of racket I've described by creating an agency with powers of inspection in order to protect these people?

I contend that this sort of thinking is a disguised effort to evade responsibility and freedom, a cop-out which ultimately places us at the mercy of arbitrary authorities. If we are ever to have a better society, we are going to have to learn to carry on these struggles ourselves, not to look to someone else, a leader or an agency, whom we invest with the sanction of force. We are going to have to experiment with and develop ways to solve disputes with our neighbors which do without hierarchical violence. In this instance, offended consumers and neighbors must learn to persuade, boycott, picket and ostracize offending restaurateurs—to think and act as competent and potent persons.

Some readers will have noticed that these comments on health controls in a better society do not apply very well to Martin de Porres House. Our "consumers" have no choice of going elsewhere or bringing other pressures on us—those who eat our free meals are the powerless indigent. In a better society there would be no powerless indigent, and hence, no Martin de Porres House. The extent to which our existence is an accepted, even comforting, fact to many people is a shame on the existent society. For those of us here, the satisfaction we get out of feeling needed by brothers and sisters more desperate than we is a grave spiritual danger. It is our business and the business of our friends to strive to put us out of business. If thinking out the implications of this fall's ghastly encounter reminds us of that, the Health Department may have done us a good turn, all unknowingly.

PART VI

Spirit of Life
1976–1980

❊ Woman and the Peace Message of Jesus

EILEEN EGAN

"WOMEN OF THE ENTIRE universe . . . you to whom life is entrusted at this grave moment in history, it is for you to save the peace of the world."

This was the concluding sentence of a message to women, one of the closing messages of the Second Vatican Council, spoken on December 8, 1965. Just the day before, on December 7, a crucial document, "The Church in the Modern World," had been accepted by little more than the required two-thirds vote. The peace message of the Council was contained in this document, including an assertion of the right of conscientious objection to war, the consonance of nonviolence with Gospel teaching and the condemnation of indiscriminate warfare as "a crime against God and man." This condemnation constituted the one ban of the entire Council, a contrast to earlier Church councils which were heavily concerned with bans and anathemas.

Women had not been permitted to speak at the Council, even on the subject of saving the peace of the world. Laymen, however, were allowed for the first time to speak to the assembled Fathers of the Church.

There had been a peace lobby at the Council, a lobby which was intensified at the last of the four sessions when the issue of war and peace was debated and voted upon. The women who took part in this lobby worked and fasted in the shadows. As a member of that lobby, I joined other members of Pax, a Catholic peace group, in going from bishop to bishop, from cardinal to cardinal, with a draft of a peace statement.

It was at that time, in the fall of 1965, that a group of nineteen women from five countries embarked on a ten-day fast in Rome's Cenacle Convent just before the peace issue was introduced. The fast was organized by Lanza del Vasto of the Community of the Ark in France. He had lobbied and fasted for peace at earlier sessions of the Council, and his wife, Chanterelle, was one of the fasters. Dorothy Day was also among the fasters. The communal fast was not a protest, but a way of "entreating the Lord to inspire the Council Fathers with the evangelical solution for which the world is waiting." The group statement adverted to the Sermon on the Mount as "not only a way to personal perfection

221

but also a power capable of transforming institutions and giving a new meaning to history."

These women were particularly moved by the appeal in the Message to Women cited above: "Reconcile men with life and above all, we entreat you, watch carefully over the future of our race. Hold back the hand of man who, in a moment of madness, might attempt to destroy human civilization."

A decade later, when Pope Paul opened the Holy Year of Reconciliation, he reiterated the call to women to take on the burdens of peacemaking and reconciliation. But Catholic women who wish to contribute actively to peacemaking and reconciliation, and to offer alternatives to the philosophies and thought systems that support violence and warfare, are forced to an inescapable but realistic conclusion. If society at large treated them in the same manner as the ecclesiastical society of the Catholic Church, their effectiveness in saving the peace of the world would be minimal. The Vatican is a bastion of maleness. (When the American humorist Will Rogers toured the Vatican and viewed its treasures, he was asked for his reaction. It came in a laconic comment, "It lacks the woman's touch.")

Vatican City, the one-hundred-and-eight-acre state within the confines of Rome, is not Mount Athos, the Orthodox monastery where all females (even female animals) are excluded. However, women are allowed to enter Vatican City only by the service entrance. Religious Sisters are noticeably present in the charity storerooms, in the charity clinic and in various housekeeping and service tasks. When, however, a woman was named as a member of a diplomatic mission to the Holy See, she was refused accreditation simply because of her sex. Despite protests by Catholic women's groups, the 1968 ban on the presence of Dr. Elizabeth Muller as member of the mission from the Federal Republic of Germany was never lifted. No explanation was offered by the Vatican, though one cleric pointed out that Dr. Muller would be called upon to attend evening meetings with high personages of the Vatican. This break with tradition was somehow unacceptable. Do we see here the age-old stereotype of the woman as temptress, as source of evil, as somehow defiling and polluting, as, in fact, Eve?

The Muller case attracted world attention to the anachronism of a woman-free Vatican. Publicity had its effect. Within five years a woman was accepted as representative of her country to the Holy See. When Bernadette Olowo presented her credentials from the government of Uganda, she was quietly accepted. She is the first woman to be listed as a diplomatic representative in the Annuario Pontificio—no small breakthrough in a church still covertly nourished by subterranean springs from the old "misbegotten male" tradition.

St. Thomas Aquinas in his day echoed St. Augustine, who had simply echoed the defective biology of Aristotle in calling women a "misbegotten or castrated male." To St. Thomas, woman was made exclusively for procreation and "she was not fitted to help man except in generation, because another man would have proved a more effective help in anything else." A deep undercurrent of fear of woman flows through the thinking of many early Church Fathers, surfacing in such famous attacks as that of Tertullian. "You are the devil's gateway . . . you are the first deserter of the divine law." St. Jerome, outside of his admiration for learned virgins and ascetic widows, fulminated against women as sensual objects who are the downfall of man.

The Vatican, as a mini-state and as the central body of the Catholic Church, mirrors the negative stereotype of woman to which the whole Christian community is heir. Yet, from the Vatican comes the call for women to become "the creators of reconciliation in families and in society."

Certainly, peace is the over-arching need of our nuclear age and if Catholic women are called to be reconcilers and peacemakers, let us accept the call with deadly, perhaps we should say, living seriousness. We should address ourselves to a great lack, a yawning chasm, in church teaching, namely a unified teaching on peace.

Just war theology, which has dominated Christian thinking since the fifth century, is a totally male construct. Like much theology, it makes use of abstractions. In this case, the abstractions are several conditions which a war must meet to make it a just war and thus "justify" the killing of human beings. These conditions are found nowhere in the Gospels, nor do they appear in the teaching of the Fathers of the infant Christian Church. We know that during the first four centuries Christians were noted for their refusal to form a part of a killing army. The simple "non decet" of St. Marcellus describes the attitude of a soldier in the Roman army who realized the chasm between Christianity and soldiery. "It is not fitting," Marcellus said, as he set aside the uniform and weapons of the Roman army. Like many other Christian conscientious objectors, Marcellus died by the sword for laying down his sword.

The change in thinking regarding participation in the military came about during the Constantinian period of the Roman Empire. St. Augustine of Hippo searched for a way to enroll Christians in the defense of an empire which had ceased its persecution of Christians and now was menaced from without by the marauders from the north. The Roman Empire provided the sinews of order and social peace which allowed for the growth of such green shoots of fresh thinking and lifestyle as Christianity.

St. Augustine never deviated from the gospel nonviolence of the early Christians with regard to personal conduct. A Christian put upon by an unjust attacker must prefer death to slaying the attacker. However, Augustine found a rationale for Christians to kill in war in the work of the good pagan, Cicero. In the treatise "On Duties," Cicero outlined the ethics of the "just war," stating that "no war is just unless it is entered upon after an official demand for satisfaction has been submitted or warning has been given and a formal declaration made."

Augustine built on Cicero and erected a just war theology that was clarified by Thomas Aquinas who reiterated the concept of killing for the defense of the commonweal. Meanwhile, one could not have recourse to the sword as a private person, nor should clerics be soldiers because "it is unbecoming for them to slay or shed blood and it is more fitting that they should be ready to shed their own blood for Christ, so as to imitate, indeed, what they portray in their ministry." Theologians in time rounded out the criteria for the just war to seven: a formal declaration, a just cause, right intention, last resort, right and proportionate means, and a reasonable expectation that the good achieved would outweigh the evil perpetrated.

Every criterion of the so-called just war must be met if the war is to be considered a just war.

Certainly, the fidelity of theologians to the just war criteria indicates how and why they have merited the description "merchants of abstraction." Many such theologians were scholar-priests or professor-priests who were not subject to conscription, and, therefore, were far removed from the concrete necessities of waging war.

Women, I am convinced, tend to think in more concrete categories than men. Whether such a difference is innate or springs from life experience (including care of children) and culture, is not the question here. The differences are there, and they are important for the future of the world.

Women, who have seen their world destroyed by the war games of men over the centuries, know that only when the war is over and the corpses piled high, is there a decision made as to which side was justified and which side was unjustified.

That the Church is veering from the just war criteria became clear when Pope John XXIII, in his epochal *Pacem in Terris,* never referred to them. He did say something revolutionary, something which brings us back to gospel nonviolence, when he announced, "The same moral law which governs the lives of individuals also governs political communities."

In this sentence, the chasm between personal, Christian morality and the morality of the obedient citizen in war—a chasm that had been opened by the Augustinian acceptance of Roman ethics—began to be healed.

The "just war" tradition, in effect, displaced the Christian imperative of love from its centrality in Christian life. It permitted Christians to perpetrate, as citizen-soldiers, acts that would have been abhorrent to them as individuals. This is moral schizophrenia.

It is much easier for women to comprehend this since they have, for the most part, been on the sidelines of wars, picking up the broken bodies and the debris of their homes and lives. As Mahatma Gandhi pointed out, family life consists of the working out of the force of love in the reconciliation of differences.

"Little quarrels of millions of families in their daily lives," he wrote, "disappear before the exercise of this force. History is really a record of every interruption of the even working of the force of love. And, what is true of families and communities is true of nations. There is no reason to believe that there is one law for families and another for nations."

Kropotkin, and many others, agree with Gandhi that history has been written to emphasize the role of power, competition, violence and war. Women know that there is another history, written from the bottom rather than from the top, and that is where most of their history is hidden.

It is in their hidden history that women have found ways to reconciliation in family and community disputes—disputes that were bitter and even murderous. It is their concrete experiences in keeping their own families alive that may keep the human family from extinction. But Catholic women will make a minimal contribution, even after the generous call of Pope Paul VI, unless they can play a role hitherto denied them, that of participating with men in developing the theology of a church which includes one-sixth of the world's people. Women's concrete approach to life and the living of the gospel might help develop what the world and the Church desperately need, a *theology of peace.*

The quality of nurturing, generally attributed to women, the quality that has preserved life and peace in families and communities over the centuries, must now be applied to the human race. Catholic women, in responding to the papal plea that they be reconcilers in society, can initiate their contribution to a theology of peace not from the standpoint of dogmatic or moral theology, which has spawned so many abstract legalisms, but from what has been called ascetical theology, the highest counsels given by Jesus.

In the Gospel we learn from the mouth of Jesus how His followers are expected to treat their opponents.

"You have heard that it was said, 'Love your friends and hate your enemies.' But I say to you: Love your enemies and pray for those who mistreat you so that you will become sons of your Father in Heaven."

In the same sermon, Jesus reiterates, "Blessed are the peacemakers for they shall be called the children of God." The Sermon on the Mount gives the basis for gospel nonviolence in the "contradictions," where Jesus tells His followers to reject contemporary morality (contemporary to Jesus as it is to us) in refraining from an angry response, in letting go one's cloak to the one who would snatch one's coat, in going two miles with one who would force the first mile, as well as in loving the enemy. Those who base their nonviolence on these teachings of Jesus are often called "Sermon on the Mount" pacifists.

In my work for Catholic Relief Services, I saw how millions of lives had been destroyed in Europe by allied forces, as well as by axis forces.

It occurred to me that mercy, which is only love in response to need, is not only interrupted but reversed by war. Christians, who are called upon to love their opponents (and to perform for them the works of mercy—of feeding them when hungry and giving drink to them when thirsty) in wartime, go further than not feeding them or not giving them to drink. In war, and particularly in modern war, the works of mercy are obscenely reversed. Food to the enemy is blockaded so that noncombatant civilians will starve (since soldiers have first call on food supplies). A great exploit in World War II was the destruction in a bombing raid of one of the largest reservoirs in Europe. The aim was to cut off the supply of drinking water to the enemy community and was justified as a means of destroying the will to fight. The less active of the enemy population would, of course, be the worst sufferers, children, the ill, the aged, the blind.

How perilous a course it seems for Christians to take part in a war when we must reverse every work of mercy that we are called upon to perform for the neighbor in need. In the parable of the Last Judgment, we learn that whenever we meet the need of another, we are meeting Christ. He is always the "least of the brethren." The "least of the brethren" during wartime would be the person who is declared our enemy. There is an element of surprise in the Last Judgment parable when the question is posed, "When did we see thee hungry . . . thirsty?" Could it be that the surprise that might await the Christian would be to find that the enemy who starved to death, who was obliterated with his city, napalmed with his village, cremated alive with countless noncombatants, is an accusing Christ? The works of mercy, as the opposite of the works of war, are the truest works of peace. A theology of peace must consider the Last Judgment as well as the Sermon on the Mount.

The Catholic theology of peace has a third dimension—a dimension beyond the peace witness of the historic "peace churches" and of traditional "Sermon on the Mount" pacifism, namely that of the Eucharistic Feast. Catholics, by this meal, enter a holy communion through the central act of Catholic worship. They become one with Jesus and with each other.

At the Eucharistic meal (the meal of thanksgiving) we eat the bread that Jesus left us saying, "The bread that I will give is My flesh for the life of the world." This is the bread that was left as a legacy to all His followers on the day before He died the death of the "suffering servant." To the end, He loved His enemies and asked forgiveness for those who tortured and legally executed Him. By His innocent suffering, Jesus reconciled people to God and to each other, and He gave those to come the same task of reconciliation and the same nonviolent means, loving acceptance of self-suffering.

The Eucharistic Community would be expected to be the reconciling community of humanity. Women peacemakers may help it to assume the reconciling witness which will only begin to grow strong as we unlearn the "just war" application to human conflict.

Women as witnesses for peace will be plumbing the depths of the implications of the Sermon on the Mount, of the Last Judgment parable, of the Eucharistic meal, and of the sense of being a community of the Resurrection. The message of loving the enemy, whoever and however lethal he or she may seem, is still as scandalous a message as it was when first pronounced by Jesus. It is surely the work of the "new creature" of the Gospel. For those who are mired in material concerns, it is total madness. It only comes clear when the power and grace of God are recognized as, in the end, irresistible forces in the human economy; when the Christian, by countering hatred with love, allows the grace of God to operate within him or her and within the adversary—the adversary being given the chance to see love in action rather than resistance in kind.

Women as witnesses for peace will only be fulfilling the role of witness that Jesus gave them in a society that did not recognize that a woman could be a witness. Jesus broke in a revolutionary way with the tradition of that society by making a woman the first witness of His messiahship. He first announced unequivocally the fact that He was the promised Messiah to the Samaritan woman at the well, certainly an unlikely witness. She belonged to a heretic sect, the Samaritans, and she was living a far from exemplary life. Starting with the concrete, the need for water, Jesus opened up to her the reality of living water. When she stated her belief that a Messiah would come into the world Jesus said simply, "I am He who is speaking with thee."

As Rachel Conrad Wahlberg points out in *Jesus According to Woman*, "the Samaritan woman's response to Jesus is a sense of mission resulting in action." And the people's response to her preaching is action. They not only come to hear Jesus, but "many believed."

Another example is Jesus' entrusting the greatest news, after the Incarnation, in the entire history of the human race, the Resurrection, to women. On the first day of the week, after the crucifixion, Jesus met Mary Magdalene and the other Mary, as they were running to tell the disciples the message of the angel about the Risen Lord. Jesus Himself commissioned them to "Go and tell my brethren to go to Galilee and there they will see me." This is Mark's account. In John's account, Jesus asks Mary Magdalene not to touch Him for He has not yet ascended to His Father, and then gives the message: "But go to my brethren and say to them: I ascend to my Father and to your Father, to my God and to your God."

One of the suggestions to the Universal Church during the Holy Year was that a theology of women should be developed. The proposal came from the Rev. Jean Galot, who stated in *Civiltà Catolica,* a Jesuit review, published in Rome: "People ought to be speaking about the necessity of a theology of women if theology wants to be faithful to its goal of studying the divine plan of salvation in its human realization." But theologizing by male theologians, with women serving as the passive "objects," is exactly what is not needed.

Many of us would counter that more to the point would be the urgent need of theology by women, with its authors admitted to every level of church gathering, up to synods and councils. After all, Jesus clearly opened the scriptures to His women followers, and chided Martha when she wanted Mary to stop absorbing His message and attend to household tasks.

It is of interest that during this Holy Year of Reconciliation and International Women's Year, a woman is one of the nominees for the Nobel Peace Prize, namely, Mother Teresa of Calcutta. To her, Jesus is not an abstract concept. He is before her in the concrete, in the man or woman covered with maggots and dying in the gutter. Whether or not the Nobel Peace Prize is awarded to her, her nomination is evidence that the works of mercy are being recognized as works of peace, reconciling person to person. Here is where the task of the peacemaker lies—in constant works of peace, and in refusing, and teaching refusal, of their opposite, the works of war.

Man-made theology and man-made weapons threaten the future of the human family; they have, indeed, brought humanity to an obvious dead end. Jesus who entrusted the good news that He was the redeemer of humankind to a woman, and who entrusted women with the news of His Resurrection, may yet use women to be witnesses to His message of peace. Will any church structure oppose such a witness?

SEPTEMBER 1976

❊ Bread for the Hungry

DOROTHY DAY

EDS. NOTE: *This talk was delivered at the Eucharistic Congress in Philadelphia on August 6, 1976. Dorothy Day was among those invited to respond to a paper entitled "Women and the Eucharist." Meanwhile, in the Cathedral two miles away, a Mass was being said for the armed forces; this in spite of numerous protests over the insensitivity displayed in scheduling such a Mass for Hiroshima Day. Several Catholic Workers were among those who vigiled and leafleted outside the Cathedral. As it turned out, this was Dorothy's last public address. Days later she suffered a heart attack, and retired from public speaking.*

I SUPPOSE I AM asked to contribute my thoughts on this subject because I am associated, in the minds of those who know the Catholic Worker, with bread lines, with hungry men and women, and all the destitute in our big cities where we have Catholic Worker Houses.

Long before our work started—I mean the work of publishing a paper, *The Catholic Worker,* and trying to literally do as Jesus said, "feed the hungry," I attended a Eucharistic celebration on the Lower East Side of New York. On Corpus Christi Day every year the Italians had processions on the Lower East Side. Streets were decorated as for a festa, altars were set up every few blocks. Benediction was given after holding up the Blessed Sacrament to the people. Instead of banners, colorful bedspreads of every color—red, cerise, blue, green, purple and gold—hung from the windows of the crowded tenements. The streets teemed with people; pushcarts sold delicacies—there was an abundance of food for body and soul.

The Catholic Worker daily soup line is also a celebration (of a kind). Our store-fronts are homelike places, banners and pictures abound: St. Joseph, and Our Lady of Guadalupe, Protectress of Cesar Chavez and the Farm Workers (who, though the harvesters of food, do not earn enough to feed their families adequately).

Two blocks away from St. Joseph House is the Municipal Lodging House where about a thousand men, three times a day, are fed. Many of those same men come to us in their hungers, which bread alone (or even the best meal) does not satisfy. They come to us for human warmth—to satisfy another kind of hunger.

I think we all share in Sister Angelita's expressed wish that, by what we say in this session, all of us here will grow in "their faith in, love for, and commitment to Jesus in the Eucharist, according to the purposes of this Congress."

But I would like to stress my own experience again. My conversion began many years ago, at a time when the material world around me began to speak in my heart of the love of God. There is a beautiful passage in St. Augustine, whose *Confessions* I read at this time. "What is it I love when I love Thee?" it begins, and goes on to list all the material beauty and enjoyment to be found in the life of the senses. The sea, which surrounded us—rather, it was a bay leading out to sea—provided food, fish and shellfish in abundance, even the sea weeds, which a Japanese friend told me were part of the food of her people. Our garden grew vegetables; the fields berries, the trees fruits. Everything spoke to me of a Creator who satisfied all our hungers.

It was also the physical aspect of the Church that attracted me. Bread and wine, water (all water is made holy since Christ was baptized in the Jordan), incense, the sound of waves and wind, all nature cried out to me.

My love and gratitude to the Church have grown through the years. She was my mother and nourished me, and taught me.

She taught me the crowning love of the life of the Spirit. But she also taught me that "before we bring our gifts of service, of gratitude, to the altar—if our brother has anything against us, we must hesitate to approach the altar to receive the Eucharist."

"Unless you do penance, you shall all perish." Penance comes before the Eucharist. Otherwise, we partake of the Sacrament unworthily.

And here we are on August 6, the day the first atomic bomb was dropped which ended the Second World War. There had been holocausts before—massacres, after the First World War, of the Armenians, all but forgotten now, and the holocaust of the Jews, God's chosen people. When He came to earth as Man, He chose them. And He told us, "All men are brothers," and that it was His will that all men be saved. Japanese, Jews, Armenians.

It is a fearful thought, that unless we do penance, we will perish.

Our Creator gave us life, and the Eucharist to sustain our life.

But we have given the world instruments of *death* of inconceivable magnitude.

Today, we are celebrating—how strange to use such a word—a Mass for the military, the "armed forces." No one in charge of the Eucharistic Congress had remembered what *August 6* means in the minds of all who are dedicated to the work of *peace.*

Why not a Mass for the military on some other day? Antoine St. Exupery, a flyer in World War II and the author of *Wind, Sand and Stars,* tells of the feeling men at war have for each other—the sense of being united in a common cause, "a readiness to give all, *to lay down one's life."* Such expressions are used in all sincerity.

And who does not love bands, and the discipline of marching men, and the banners!

I myself had grandparents who fought in the Civil War—on opposite sides, however, and animosities remained between families in my childhood. My two brothers were in the First World War and one in World War II, and my grandson was in our most recent war, when he was in the jungles in Vietnam, in the small bands who went out "to search and destroy."

Women, who were born to nourish, to bring forth life, not to destroy it, must do more than thank God we have survived it.

I plead, in this short paper, that we will regard that military Mass, and all our Masses today, as an act of penance, begging God to forgive us. I am gratified for the opportunity given me at this congress to express myself in this way. I thank God for the freedom of Holy Mother Church.

I must not forget Ammon Hennacy, who died in 1970, one of the old editors of *The Catholic Worker* who, since Hiroshima and Nagasaki, fasted from all food, solid or liquid, allowing himself only water, giving a day of this penance for every year since the bombs were dropped.

If he were with us today, he would be fasting over thirty days. The last years of his life he fasted, carrying a picket sign all day in the hot sun, in front of some Federal building, in whatever city he happened to be living. He died in Salt Lake City after a heart attack, which occurred during another picketing, protesting the execution of two young men in Utah. Ammon reverenced life.

Today, some of the young pacifists giving out leaflets here are fasting, as a personal act of penance for the sin of our country, which we love.

JANUARY 1977

 # Maryhouse I

MEG BRODHEAD

ON CHRISTMAS WE celebrate the coming of the Source of the message Maryhouse seeks to express and to radiate vitally to the world. In daily life we often fall short of realizing the fruits of this endeavor; but even I could appreciate the joy of our Christmas festivities here. On Christmas Eve we sang carols by candlelight with readings from Isaiah and Luke. As we breathed deeply, filled with the words and their sound in music, a spirit came in us, lifted us as we lifted our voices. We had midnight Mass at St. Joseph House, and gave thanks, and danced and ate fruitcake after. The day itself was busy with laying a feast for some sixty people. The bustle of a great house, throwing aside its routine chores and bedecking itself in holiday, lent the occasion its special energy. The house beat with gaiety, as it often does not; food and gifts were plenty, as often they are not. Holidays still radiate their festive glow when the threads of workaday life are picked up again. They illuminate and sustain the pace of all days.

So it was with good cheer that about twelve of us from Maryhouse and St. Joseph went caroling after dinner. It was raining as we began. After a couple of stops we decided to go to the Municipal Men's Shelter, "the Muni," a block away on Third Street. Many of us had never been there. We went up the front stairs, singing to the indifferent men standing about. The guards at the front desk smiled confusedly; several men, gathered intently at the other side of the room, looked at the noise we were making and turned back. One fellow joined us, as though to sing, and gestured obscenely at the policeman on duty. The guard grabbed him away.

Lee and Cliff went among the men, some of whom they knew, giving out Christmas cookies. We walked into the "Big Room," lined with benches and men in all attitudes of languor, illness, drunkenness. They are called Big Roomers, because this is where they live. Someone turned off the television. Some averted their eyes; some slept on; some sat up to hear us. I was almost breathless from the brittle anguish of the place. We sang on, there was nothing else to do, we sang to fill the blankness of which the room reeked. We were not on a lark any longer. Our presence became fiercely in earnest. We must have sung fifteen songs before we exchanged thanks and Christmas greetings and left.

The rain had turned to snow. At the corner we were met by the man who had tried to join us inside. His voice had a whiskey roughness. He had pneumonia, he said, and asked to stand in the middle of us. He cursed and asked for a light. He cursed at us again and I touched his arm. He jerked it away and looked into my face. "And don't give me any of that sympathy. Silent Night . . . ," he intoned hoarsely. He mimicked us perfectly. It was a parody of exactly what I was afraid we had sounded like.

We walked away from him then. At the Women's Shelter around the corner the men with us had to stay in the anteroom, for the occupants' protection. The mood here was more dispirited than desperate—a slightly less brutal kind of barrenness, perhaps because there were fewer women in the television room than there had been men, even though a guard announced over the loudspeaker that they were all to report to hear us.

Our stay with the women was shorter. By then I had lost sight of what we were doing, our motive, what we thought we were giving. All I knew was I liked to sing, so I put the rest away when we trundled up the stairs of the Palace Hotel, one of the many flophouses into which the city pays 1,100 men every night. Even Christmas night. The dismay of the deskmen there echoed that at the Muni. We had to sing to the men through a metal grille, which the desk operates to ensure that no one sneaks up to a bed without paying. There, too, was the big, crowded television room. We sang over the sound. The men got really interested when the gate was opened for someone and we handed cookies through.

Whoever reached the tins first grabbed as many as he could. In face of the disarray thus caused, the guards suggested we exit. When the cookies were gone we took a request for "Joy to the World." It was our last carol of the evening.

I have thought hard on this Christmas night. What redeemed us from the facile puppetry the cursing man charged us with? What gave the singing meaning beyond the jingles of a rather motley crew in holiday humor?

We sang, "Ransom captive Israel/That mourns in lonely exile here." An eternal cry is always the cry of the world now. Where shows more clearly the exile of the world, the captivity of its people, than here, now, on the Bowery? When Father Jack Egan talked to us several weeks ago, he spoke of the necessity of finding the cracks in technological society, the areas within and around us where systematized, normalized inhumanness does not absolutely overwhelm and constrict us. I would understand this image differently. In the Bowery, we live in such a crack in society. It is cracked wide open, its people are cracked, riven with demon poverty, demon ego, demon alcohol, demon despair. Ignorant oppression and banal personal frailty break lives, and there are sharp edges here. People are gashed in the spirit, the city is ripped with violence, men and women are estranged from themselves and their fellows. Oh! we sang for ourselves.

We witnessed that night the disavowal of dignity, of the image of God, of personhood. This is the source of all the fractures in ourselves and in the world we make. It is this negation, refusal, which is the source of despair. We sang of the night of our Savior's birth. Of course, it was black as hell when He was born: He comes in the night of the soul. And we are each of us called out of that depth, out of exile, to fulfill and make whole the person within. In *The Sickness Unto Death*, Søren Kierkegaard writes, "To have a self, to be a self, is the greatest concession made to man, but at the same time, it is eternity's demand upon him." Only from that growth of soul comes the recognition that we are in union in this gift, this responsibility; and from this recognition springs the charity which makes us one, which reconciles and heals the world, fills the cracks with hope. Charity is sharing another's burdens, not because that is His law, but because it is the empowering vision Christ gave. If we are in union as persons, we are united in our joy and sorrow. This vision is alienated from no one, it embraces all men and women as neighbors, as persons; and so by its nature, this charity among persons is the action which frees us from our refusals, our failure: the future which binds us apart, a fragmented people.

I write this. I do not live it. We sang, "Let ev'ry heart prepare Him room." Preparing room in the heart for Him, for neighbor and enemy, needs emptying it of all the junk that the "fat, relentless ego" (Iris Murdoch's phrase) hoards there. Mine, I know, is still full, and weary of that weight, and weary of the stone of despair which is the secretest nut of every selfishness. So that my patience is thin; my generosity and understanding are starveling things in this House of Hospitality. The little clutter in other people's hearts angers me. You know what I mean. What might we do for each other, we who are yet pining in sin and error, how may we open our hearts to charity? We might confess to one another that we share darkness. Despair shared is in that measure vanquished. It might be the first burden we share together, as brothers and sisters.

That we take on in a small degree the bedeviled lives of the men and women here on the Bowery pardons our Christmas caroling of mockery. The more deeply we share pain, the more deeply we can draw into embrace human experience and human beings.

I honestly do not know that this life can be healed. But it can be shared, it can be treasured, and so we may survive within the significant whole of our shared lives and condition. We look for meaning in the dreariest, most difficult of our struggles and tasks. We look to the joy. We turn from the revelation of Christmas to the human city with hope.

MARCH–APRIL 1977

❊ A Recipe for Catholic Worker Soup

Make Too Much, Invite Too Many

ONE OF THE by-products of involvement with the Catholic Worker movement is a deeper enjoyment of soup. It would not be reckless to say that the soup line at noon has introduced many hungry people to a culinary experience that would make Julia Child, the Galloping Gourmet, the kitchen staffs of Luchow's and Le Pavillon all hang their heads in shame. There is no secret receipt for Catholic Worker Soup; the unstructured and arbitrary methods by which it is produced have at times resulted in disappointments, but are more often striking examples of the poetry engendered when the undisciplined imagination confronts kitchen hardware and barren icebox.

The hardware problem is easy; a large pot, a long spoon, and a sharp knife. That elegantly simple trinity, if your goal is good, honest soup, is all you need.

Some things to be kept in mind:

1. In the early days of the Catholic Worker, Peter Maurin and Dorothy Day thought that it would be a good idea to keep a soup pot simmering at all times. This could be continually replenished by whatever vegetables the people of the house could acquire. It was a brilliant idea for a symbol of communal sharing, certainly. But, even more certainly, it was responsible for delicious soup. The longer soup simmers, obviously, the better it tastes, and the vegetables and flavors that do not become compatible, even complementary, after four hours' companionship in a boiling pot are rare.

2. Far too many modern problems (our fascination with violence, our racism, our waste of resources, our fragmentation as a people) are grounded in unnecessary fears. One minor but definitely unnecessary fear is the fear of making too much soup. Soup that has been reheated after forty-eight hours in the refrigerator tastes much better than the soup you made this morning, and serves as an excellent theme for even better soup. I like to think that in the soup I had at noon today, there may have been a few dim atoms of the soup served on the day our house here opened. Good soup is one more way we can preserve the treasures of the past, and demonstrate that tradition is never a dead thing, but always a fresh and enriching perspective on the present. Good soup has, in common with great art, and the Gospel itself, the characteristic of eternal freshness and beauty.

3. The phrase "too much garlic" is meaningless.

4. So is the phrase "too many onions."

5. The idea may be unorthodox, but sometimes, by concentration on visual aesthetics, to the exclusion of the more vulgar urgings of the palate, one can stumble into higher realms of soup-making and soup-eating pleasure. About a month ago, I emptied an annoying can of catsup (it had wasted space in our icebox for too long and its moment had come) into what had previously been an uninteresting liquid of drab, brown appearance. I stirred in the catsup hesitantly, watching deep red clouds from the bottom of the soup kettle merge gently with the brown. Soon the pot was simmering again, this time with a wine-dark surface. It smelled wonderful, but tasted strangely sweet. Onion salt, gradually added, brought the taste of the soup from sweet to rich. More space in the icebox. Better looking soup. Better tasting soup (the men in the house nearly all came back for seconds) and a proud and happy soupmaker. All of this as a result of inclusion rather than exclusion.

A person of longer association with the Catholic Worker could make other suggestions, and in the interests of space conservation this should be cut short. It wouldn't hurt to remember that soup is best as a shared food; that all food becomes better when shared. This is what the miracle of loaves and fishes teaches us. This is what the child's story "Nail Broth" celebrates. Most people on the North American continent have at this moment, in their refrigerators, ingredients which, when added to a quart or so of boiling water, could delight and enrich them. Especially if they used too much of everything, and invited too many to eat with them. The reason that such an idea is preposterous to us is our own unnecessary fear.

We should pray that our fears be left behind in the ashes of this Lent, in the ashes of our false, limited, dying selves, and that we may all feast together, without fear, in the new kingdom which Easter announces.

 # Unashamed Moralists in the Personalist Tradition

ROBERT COLES

EDS. NOTE: *This article appeared in a special May issue of* The Catholic Worker *commemorating the centenary of the birth of Peter Maurin.*

ALL THROUGH HIS LONG poem *Paterson,* William Carlos Williams struggles to expose the banalities, the crudities, the outright evils of modern capitalist industrialism, while at the same time clearly indicating that for him Stalin's bureaucratic totalitarianism was certainly no desirable alternative. Nor was he willing to abandon skepticism when considering the socialist bureaucracies that have their own way of becoming callous, if not mean. He was an anarchist of sorts, a libertarian who worried about the poor, worked with them every day as a physician, and wanted better things for them—not with the condescension of *noblesse oblige,* but out of an awareness that the suffering and exploitation of others turns out to be everyone's source of shame and sorrow, or, as he knew some would put it, a continuing cross to bear. He was especially suspicious of the demands abstractions can make on people—the distortions, the all-too-convenient denial of life's ambiguities, ironies, inconsistencies, and contradictions, in the interest of someone's ideological formulations ("No ideas but in things"). He was a restless man, intensely spiritual in his own way, yet utterly practical and preoccupied with the concrete, the here-and-now. And he was obsessed with words—their opportunities, their possibilities, their frustrating, demanding presence.

When, in college, my mother would put before me Peter Maurin's warnings, urgings, moral statements, outcries, laments, all gleaned from her reading of *The Catholic Worker,* I would think of Dr. Williams, whom I was lucky enough to know. Unalike in many respects, yet they struggled in similar ways to affirm their particular idiosyncratic selves—and each of them wholeheartedly committed that "self" to the needs of others, while all the while spelling out in words, thousands of them, what the nature of such a commitment ought to be. They were, that is, unashamed moralists, peculiar ones at that—in the non-pejorative sense of that adjective. I believe them both spiritually kin of the personalist tradition.

Personalism as a manner of regarding the world, and our place in it, was not meant to be yet another "belief" or "system" that claimed the allegiance of various (claimed) numbers of men and women here and there, now and then. In his book *Personalism* (1950) Emmanuel Mounier makes it quite clear that he is not afraid to set down ideas, to render generalizations—but that personalism "introduces into the heart of its constructions a principle of unpredictability which excludes any desire for a definitive system." Beware the pedant—or writer of an essay on what personalism is, and is not. Still, one tries to approach the mental and spiritual world Mounier and others chose to portray—its values, ideals, purposes; and does so, perhaps, most successfully through the examples certain lives offer.

Personalism affirms the importance of each human being in God's (or the world's) scheme of things; and, thereby, denies the authority of anyone (an entrepreneur, an official of the state, and yes, an intellectual) to take anyone else for granted. Personalism is not interested in the psychology of "adjustment," does not bow below the imperatives of the "practical." Personalism makes a strong case for transcendence— "the surpassing of the self," which Mounier pointedly insists "must not be confused with the breaking-out of the vital impulses." So much for hedonism, enlightened self-interest, and, too, Marxist materialism. "To accept suffering and death," Mounier tells us, "in order not to betray human values—this or any other heroic sacrifice is the supreme act of the person." In Gabriel Marcel's words, those of a Christian existentialist, "I am more than my life."

One thinks of Simone Weil, blazing with passionate self-sacrifice; or Edith Stein, walking into the gas chambers of Auschwitz; of a worn-out, tired, increasingly ailing Dr. Williams, persisting in those house calls to the poor and working people of New Jersey's industrial slums; and, not least, of Peter Maurin's stubborn, exhausting, itinerant search for a place, a purpose, a community of listeners. The point of such a search, with its varying degrees of self-sacrifice, is not easy to spell out.

"Personalists," Mounier insists, "cannot willingly surrender the person to anything unpersonal, and most of them seek in one way or another to personalize these values." Christian personalism, of course, reminds us of God, *the* Person, and of Christ, *the* Person become incarnate. By the impersonal, Mounier had in mind not only capitalist ideology, or Soviet totalitarianism, but the welfare-state insofar as it, too, treats people *en masse* and, often enough, with arrogance, condescension, and a peculiar bullying masked as "compassion."

I suppose Mounier and Marcel and others like them can be dismissed as anarchists, as cranks, as impractical, as utterly "irrelevant" in their concerns of the day-to-day lives of ordinary, often rather hard-pressed men and women and children. Yet, the yearnings of "plain people" are not unlike those Mounier refers to; are not unlike those the poem *Paterson* tries to evoke; are not unlike those Peter Maurin tried again and again to speak of. There is in personalism a direct assault on the resignation that accompanies so much of twentieth-century Marxism and Freudianism: "Teaching that is materialistic or deterministic," Mounier pointed out, "whether implicitly or openly, cannot consistently exhort to action or to the guidance of action. If whatever happens in the world is regulated in advance by irresistible processes, what remains for us to do?—except to wait upon events and regulate our feelings so as to suffer as little as possible?" In contrast, Maurin exhorted his fellow human beings to think, to work, to take action; to live in altogether new and redemptive (he believed) ways. And Dr. Williams thought, as he once put it in a letter, that "every day I can change the course of history—a single life helped to grow, bud, flower." And a migrant farm worker, perhaps impatient with his observer's protestations of commiseration, insisted rather strenuously: "Each day I thank God for giving me this life. It's a hard life, and a lot of the time I wonder why I wasn't born with more luck. But I was born. That's a gift! I hope that when I die I'll be able to say to myself that the world is different, because of me—different because of the crops I harvested, and the family I've been a part of, and the children who have had to keep listening to me, even when they've not wanted to."

He is, besides being a migrant worker, a "lay minister of the Gospel." He is also a tough union organizer. He is both of this world and of another—a secular political activist and a spiritual man who knows the difference between his "impulses" and "needs" and "desires" and a larger order of things, a realm that does not belong to anyone, to any "system" or nation-state, to any of various "powers and principalities." There is an edgy side to personalism—don't fence me in. One feels that side, that balance of the worldly and the spiritual, in Peter Maurin's writings, in the Catholic Worker tradition, in the "stand" taken by many individuals—the physician-poet, Dr. Williams, a migrant farm worker, and one knows for sure, thousands upon thousands of particular human beings who want a chance to affirm their distinctive humanity, while at the same time holding out their hands to others in affection and support.

❊ Franz Jagerstatter: A Pilgrimage for Peace

MICHAEL HARANK

AUGUST 9 IS generally remembered as the day the U.S. government dropped an atomic bomb on the Japanese city of Nagasaki. One bomb, the most scientifically sophisticated and most destructive weapon ever developed by the human species, killed an estimated 34,000 people.

Two years before the Nagasaki bombing, on August 9, 1943, one of the most primitive weapons developed by the human species was used to take the life of a man named Franz Jagerstatter. A Catholic Austrian peasant, father of three daughters, Franz Jagerstatter was beheaded on that day in Berlin for refusing to serve in the Nazi armed forces. His decision not to serve was inspired and sustained by an extraordinary and abiding faith in God. This faith enabled him, alone among the people of his village, to resist the logical and persuasive political, religious and personal arguments for serving the ignominious ideals of the Third Reich. He was truly one of those rare persons in recent history worthy of the Kierkegaardian title, "knight of faith."

The full life story of this martyr-peacemaker can be found in a book, *In Solitary Witness, The Life and Death of Franz Jagerstatter,* written by Gordon Zahn, the American scholar and peacemaker.

While on a visit to Europe last autumn, I made a personal pilgrimage to the village of St. Radegund, Austria. It was in this farming village, located north of Salzburg, where Franz lived as a tiller of the soil, a devoted husband and father, sexton of the village church, outspoken critic of Nazi ideas and social programs, a man of prayer and friend to the poor. In 1946, his ashes were transported from Brandenburg, Germany to St. Radegund, Austria and ceremoniously buried beside the west wall of the fourteenth-century church he served so faithfully. Before I share the story of my sojourn in St. Radegund, I must briefly relate how Jagerstatter's witness touched my life in a profound and enduring way.

In the Autumn season of 1971, I returned unexpectedly to my family's home in central Arizona. Prior to my return, I lived in eastern Massachusetts where I had just finished high school and was preparing to enter college in the fall. However, my plans were disrupted during the summer when I learned that my oldest brother had decided to oppose the Vietnam war by refusing induction into the armed forces. After some serious thought, I cancelled my plans to attend Holy Cross College and determined to stay in Arizona to be with my brother and ascertain the reasons for his decision.

From September until his imprisonment in December, my brother and I discussed a variety of ideas, personal experiences and religious questions (he had just left the seminary after five years) which had helped him form his conscience and led to his decision to resist the draft. During these long and sometimes difficult discussions I learned, for the first time, about ideas such as Christian nonviolence, pacifism, resistance, and anarchism. My brother always explored these bold ideas in terms of the lives of certain people throughout history. Among the most prominent were: St. Maximillian (patron saint of draft resisters), St. Francis of Assisi, Henry David Thoreau, Leo Tolstoy, Mahatma Gandhi, Peter Maurin, Daniel and Philip Berrigan, Thomas Merton, and finally Franz Jagerstatter.

Somehow, most of these persons and the ideas associated with them had escaped mention during my twelve years of education, nine of which took place in Catholic schools. Of course, these few and provocative ideas, discovered in the context of my brother's resistance, affected my mind like a fire set to a bale of dry hay. However, this experience was not without its pain; not physical pain, but the anguish which came from watching my handcuffed brother taken away to a federal prison and learning about my country's involvement in the destruction of the Vietnamese people and their land.

Sometime during this often strained period of time, my brother narrated to me the story of Franz Jagerstatter's witness against the Nazi regime. I remember his telling me that while he was encouraged and comforted by the support of some family members and friends, Franz had done it all alone. After hearing and reading of Jagerstatter's story, I could only draw some personally meaningful parallels. While the consequences for similar acts of resistance and the level of public support were radically different, my brother, like Franz, encountered formidable opposition and misunderstanding from family and friends. Most of the opposition stemmed from a completely docile belief in the country's inability to make a grave error. Other arguments were rooted in a paralyzing and crusading form of anticommunism. Both Jagerstatter and my brother were Roman Catholic laymen who faced opposition and indifference from the clergy and from other members of the Mystical Body who zealously embraced the just war weapon of the sword and dismissed the gospel weapon of love revealed in the Sermon on the Mount as "unrealistic." They both experienced the cruel realities of prison life, among the most difficult being separation from their families and close friends. Yet they both maintained with unshakable faith the belief that every Christian has a duty to use the gift of freedom in a way that contributes to the creation of a more just, peaceful and loving society, where, as Peter Maurin was fond of saying, "it would be easier for people to be good."

The story of Jagerstatter's heroic witness enabled my brother and me, as Catholic conscientious objectors, to feel a sense of historical and spiritual community which reached beyond the boundaries of family, culture, and nation. Most importantly, the story served to ease the harsh burden of spiritual isolation which comes from thinking you stand alone and powerless before what St. Paul called the powers and principalities of this world. My special purpose for the journey to St. Radegund was to thank God for the gift of Jagerstatter's life and the special graces which I received from his act of ultimate love. I also wanted to offer a prayer for peace in a world permanently scarred by the wounds of war, hunger, economic oppression, and the madness of the spiraling arms race.

On October 16, a cloudy and overcast morning, I boarded a bus in Salzburg for the hour-long ride to Tarsdorf, the village neighboring St. Radegund. The young woman seated next to me introduced herself and asked where I was from and where I was going with my bright orange backpack. I told her I was from the United States and on my way to St. Radegund to honor a man named Franz Jagerstatter. To my surprise, she informed me that her father was raised in St. Radegund and knew of Franz while he lived there. Gabrielle honored the memory of Franz as a man of great courage and moral integrity, even a national hero. However, she could not fully understand her father's opinion of the martyr. She said he believed that Franz was a good and decent man who was "carried away" by his religious beliefs.

I was not surprised to hear the opinion of Franz expressed by Gabrielle's father. One of the most interesting points which Dr. Zahn's social biography revealed was the reaction of the village residents to Jagerstatter's act of resistance. In Dr. Zahn's interviews with a substantial number of villagers, they confirmed the opinion held by Gabrielle's father. Apart from the Jagerstatter family, Dr. Zahn discovered that "the rest of the village saw Jagerstatter's refusal to serve in the army as a thoroughly tragic and ultimately senseless act of religious fanaticism, born of a sadly disordered mind."

Upon reaching the village of Tarsdorf I thanked Gabrielle for sharing her story with me and said goodbye. I crossed the narrow street and headed west for the seven-kilometer walk to St. Radegund. With the pack on my back and my face set toward the sun, I walked slowly along the shoulder of the hilly country road. About half way to the village a car pulled over and a thoughtful man offered me a ride. I declined as I wanted to walk the road which Jagerstatter used on his final departure from the village in February 1943.

It wasn't too long before I arrived at the village border identified by a sign with St. Radegund printed in block letters. As I continued to walk down the main road I immediately recognized the onion-shaped steeple of the church. I turned the corner and the small white church with its brightly flowered cemetery came into full view. Overcome by a feeling of humility, I walked inside the church gate, located Jagerstatter's grave, removed my pack, placed some flowers there and knelt to pray amidst the afternoon silence of the Salzach valley.

On the wall of the church, just above the grave, hung a large, wooden crucifix, weathered by time and almost entirely engulfed by the verdant ivy that climbs the walls. Red rose bushes stood on each side of the grave, while delicate white edelweiss flowers bloomed on the grass-covered mound of earth. Inscribed on the headstone which rested below the crucifix was the name of Franz Jagerstatter, followed by his birth and death dates and below that a quote from Scripture which, translated, reads, "For anyone who wants to save his life will lose it; but anyone who loses his life for my sake will find it."

Tired from the walk to the village, I walked up the road to the Hofbauer Gasthaus, an interesting combination of restaurant, hotel, and barn for the cows. Just inside the door, I was greeted by the curious face of Mr. Hofbauer. In halting German I tried to explain the reason for my visit and my intention to stay overnight. He nodded his head and took me into the restaurant. A few minutes later I was served a delicious meal of soup and bratwurst.

After I finished eating Mr. Hofbauer led me to the second floor. There, at the top of the stairs, stood a small elderly woman who was introduced to me as Mrs. Jagerstatter, Franz's widow. Evidently, Mr. Hofbauer had gone upstairs and without my knowledge informed her of my presence. She greeted me warmly with a gentle handshake.

It had not occurred to me that I would have the opportunity to meet Mrs. Jagerstatter but I had brought a letter in German to leave for her, explaining the reasons for my visit, my admiration for her husband's courage, and the moral strength her husband's witness gave to many Catholic conscientious objectors in the United States. Now I reached into my shirt pocket and gave Mrs. Jagerstatter the letter. She explained, through a young woman who translated for me, that she didn't have her glasses with her and would have to read the letter at home. She thanked me, adding that she hoped to see me after Mass on the following day.

Morning arrived the next day with the shrill sound of a rooster calling in the sun. Before long the church bell rang throughout the village, announcing the Eucharistic celebration. In the next fifteen minutes, families dressed in their best suits and dresses streamed into the church and filled the ancient wooden pews. This was the church which Franz once served as the parish sexton. He would have been pleased with the condition of the church and the beautiful white baskets of flowers that stood on each side of the altar. In the back of the church, where the choir loft is located, are two small stained glass windows donated to the church as a memorial to Jagerstatter. One of these windows bears the Latin words, "Mary, Queen of Peace, Pray for Us."

After an intensely devotional liturgy, the families gathered outside in the cemetery to pray at the graves. The Jagerstatter family gathered at Franz's grave. As I walked over to the grave, Mrs. Jagerstatter greeted me and introduced me to her daughters Rosalie and Marie. In his prison letters to his wife, Franz always wrote a message to the children, counseling them to pray regularly and help their mother with the household and farm chores. Now they are mothers themselves with families and farms of their own to care for. Also present were two of Mrs. Jagerstatter's grandchildren whom she introduced with grandmotherly pride. The two little ones, around the age of five or six, extended their little hands to greet me. Mrs. Jagerstatter explained to them that I had come all the way from the United States to visit the grave of their grandfather. With the introductions and greetings finished, the family and I knelt to pray.

Mrs. Jagerstatter then pointed to a bronze plaque which hung on the church wall located to the left of the crucifix. This plaque, she explained, was donated by an American in Missoula, Montana. The plaque consists of a long inscription beginning with the words, "Thank God for men like Jagerstatter. He knew in his heart that all men are brothers."

After introducing me to the priest who had said Mass, Mrs. Jagerstatter, her daughters and grandchildren, expressed their gratitude for my visit and we said goodbye to one another. I promised them that as a future teacher I would always have my students read of her husband's story with the hope that they would be inspired by his example to live a moral and religious life dedicated to building a more just society through the Christian means of love and nonviolence.

Late in the afternoon, I returned to the Gasthaus and prepared for my departure. A young woman there offered me a ride to the bus station in Tarsdorf along with a brown bag of fruit and vegetables. Before I left the village, I walked down the hill to the church and offered a final prayer for peace in the world. As I stood next to Jagerstatter's grave, I looked over the vast and colorful Salzach valley. The setting sun broke through a space in the thick, grey clouds and cast golden rays of light across the landscape.

Thomas Merton once wrote that "the real question raised by the Jagerstatter story is not merely that of the individual Catholic's right to conscientious objection but the question of the Church's own mission of protest and prophecy in the gravest spiritual crisis man has ever known."

❀ Property and Poverty

EILEEN EGAN

As NEW REGIMES are installed in countries around the world, some wedded to Marxist doctrines, some to socialism of a less doctrinaire type, and some to an acceptance of varying degrees of the capitalist ethos, Catholic citizens find a certain security in stating "The church and the faithful can live under many systems."

The key word is "under." People who are followers of Jesus have had to live "under" regimes not of their own choosing from Jesus' time to our own. An assumption that flows from the willingness to adapt to various political systems is that Christians can accept, and accommodate to, a variety of economic systems. This assumption is false because underlying it is the belief that Jesus did not bring to His followers a distinctive way of life involving specific teachings on what we now call economics.

The most visible and immediate impact of the teaching of Jesus on His followers in Jerusalem was on their attitude to property and to poverty. They began to share their goods with one another so that their life took on the shape of real community. Those who were so poor that they could not share anything became the common responsibility of the community and their needs were met by the deacons. To the deacons, seven of whom were commissioned for the work, the donations of the Christian community were entrusted. The deacons then administered the goods in accordance with the needs of the members of the community. The first Christian martyr, Stephen, came from among these seven ministers to the poor.

The clear duty to share one's goods with the needy did not end with the needs of one's immediate neighborhood. As Christian communities formed across the face of the ancient world, something wild and strange occurred: they began sharing with each other and meeting each other's needs across all barriers of tribe and race. In that period, and in many societies to this day, help is given on the basis of kinship, familial or tribal. The extended family system, whereby the needs of the weakest and most helpless members are met through a pooling of resources, has been the social security system of most of the world since the beginning of time. It follows that the extended family, sometimes extending as far as the tribe, does not plan for help to those outside the kinship circle.

Paul, who first brought the message of Jesus to the people of Macedonia, went back to them a third time and pleaded for help for the Christians of Jerusalem who had fallen on evil times. Though poor themselves the Macedonian Christians insisted on giving even more than Paul had hoped to meet the needs of their faraway brothers and sisters. All barriers of kinship, of tribe, had been transcended by the message of the Universal Brother, Jesus. The sharing of the Eucharist, in which each communicant became one with Jesus, and with every other communicant, was so deep a reality that it was transferred to daily living.

When Paul appealed to the Christians of Corinth for funds for Jerusalem, he asked that the Corinthians give of their abundance so that the want of the Jerusalem community be met and that an equality be established between the "haves" and the "have-nots." He quoted from the Hebrew scriptures to illustrate his point: *He that had much had nothing over; and he that had little had no want.*

This came from Exodus and referred to the manna, the bread from heaven, that the Lord provided to the children of Israel in the desert. In the morning, wafers appeared on the ground, white, like coriander seed, and tasting like flour and honey. The hungry Israelites were ordered to pick up enough of the manna for one day only.

Yet the desert wanderers, when they saw the wondrous wafers, cried to one another, "Manhu?" "What is this?" When they realized how good the miraculous bread was, they did not all obey the command to gather up no more than what they needed for one day. But the greedy ones who stocked up for the future (and it is understandable that they did so, being close to famine in the open desert) learned a practical lesson. What they gathered over and above their needs "became full of worms and it putrified." Only for the Sabbath, when the manna did not appear in the morning (nor the quails for the evening meal) did the food remain sweet and edible for more than one day.

Paul was giving a many-layered lesson to the Corinthians. One aspect linked their giving with the Eucharist, since the manna that came down from heaven, actual, material food, is the foreshadowing, the type, of the spiritual food, the "bread from heaven" which Jesus provided for His followers. In the spiritual bread of the Eucharist Jesus gave Himself, becoming poor that His followers might become rich in the life of the spirit. Another aspect is a clear lesson on the Christian doctrine of property. What the Christians save over and above their needs, while others die from lack of necessities, can become full of worms and putrefaction—at least in the salvation sense. This message is echoed in the letter of James to the Christian community of his time. James warns the rich, and especially those who have defrauded workers of their just wages, "Weep and wail over the miseries that are coming upon you. Your riches have rotted away and your clothes have been eaten by moths."

Thus, the irreducible core of the Christian doctrine of property is that one's surplus belongs to those who lack necessities.

The crucial question, then, becomes: On what basis does one decide what is surplus in one's life and possessions?

This brings us to the basic question of Christian poverty. From the beginning, Christians have been exhorted to honor poverty, to preach poverty, to embrace it in their personal lives. Almost no Christian teaching has been so feared, misunderstood, distorted, or thrust aside as the teaching on poverty. One terrible block to an understanding is the confusion of poverty with misery: How to preach poverty to people living on the streets in Calcutta or in hovels in Bogota? The misery of daily hunger, degradation, and homelessness has nothing to do with the poverty of the Christian. Another block is the teaching that "poor in spirit" means simply not to be attached to one's possessions, in which case no limit is put on the possessions one might amass. Another block to a right understanding of poverty is the possibility of different applications of it to people with different responsibilities to the community. The "poverty of the teacher" is a special poverty that may call for a person, in a vowed or lay capacity, to dedicate him- or herself to a cause and depend on the operation of Providence for its survival—as well as personal survival. Such a free choice of voluntary poverty is a direct road to freedom in serving people and serving a cause. The poverty of religious orders is of this kind. But even this poverty has nothing in common with misery.

If poverty is what one needs to live a truly human life, then the same scale of life cannot be applied to all. The "poverty of the teacher" (in the sense of the prophet or teacher of the gospel, of course) is not the poverty of the householder. The householder has responsibilities to a family and to the community that cannot morally be thrust on anyone else. In his first letter to Timothy, Paul asserts that "If someone does not take care of his relatives, especially the members of his own family, he has denied the faith and is worse than an unbeliever."

Poverty, then, in the Christian sense, is having what one needs for a truly human life with the emphasis on simplicity of life so that there will be something left over for those who are in need. Such a broad concept allows for many things—education and some leisure, as well as adequate clothing, food, and shelter—but it also excludes many things that Christians of our day may allow themselves. Let each reader list the ostentatious and costly things that we know in our hearts are surplus to our lives but which we justify as necessities.

That the early Christians made practical application of Christian doctrines of property and poverty became clear at the time of the break-up of the Roman Empire when Christian communities had been implanted over the face of the ancient world. During the upheaval that accompanied the break-up, needy Christians of many racial strains, including Jews, Greeks, and Romans, coming from all social strata, from slaves to members of aristocratic houses, wandered about, driven and persecuted. The infant churches acted as communities of refuge for the stranger at the gates. Our word "parish" comes from *para oiko,* meaning "around the house," and refers to the faithful and the strangers who gathered about the house of God. A bishop of Nyssa in Asia Minor described the dislocation of the times. He was St. Gregory, and he gave a description of the situation that engulfed his society toward the end of the fourth century that applied to many societies after World War II.

"These days," said Gregory, "have brought us naked and homeless in plenty; a host of captives is at everyone's door; strangers and fugitives are not lacking and, on every side, begging and out-stretched hands are there to see. Their home is the open air; their lodgings are the arcades, the streets and deserted corners of the markets; they lurk in holes like owls and birds of the night. Their clothing is tattered rags; their means of living, the feeling of the compassionate."

Gregory told his people the reason for putting their resources at the service of the stranger and for extending hospitality to dispossessed people, who were bound to them by no ties of blood or tribe: "Clasp the afflicted man as if he were gold. Take the sufferer to your arms as if he were your own health. Do not despise men in their abjection; do not think of them as no account. Reflect on what they are, and you will understand their dignity. They have taken upon themselves the very person of the Savior."

The early Christians, then, did not strip themselves of everything, nor merely earn sufficient for their immediate needs. They gathered surplus possessions in order to be able to accept the stranger who appeared at their door and to make it possible to send funds across seas and borders to hungry people they would never see. Their simple springboard of action was that to meet another's need is to meet Christ himself.

There are many in the Christian community who might think that the simple example of St. Paul, taken from the Exodus experience, "He that had much had nothing over; and he that had little had no want," can say little to us today. We live in a world where surplus is seen not as what we set aside for the needy, but as the means of investment which will bring riches through no effort of our own. Yet, the unchanged teaching still comes to the Christian community. In the encyclical letter of 1967, "The Development of Peoples," Pope Paul asserted, "No one is justified in keeping for his exclusive use what he does not need when others lack necessities."

How can the Christian of today's world of multinational corporations, of incentives to invest our money so that it will breed through interest while we sleep, resist the accepted economic ethos of our day? After all, in modern life, there is no reason to stop the spiral of our possessions; in fact, there is every reason to help them spiral ever and ever upward, until the possession of riches proclaims their possessor a success. Insofar as capitalism is concerned with the increase of wealth, it has at heart an ethical void. The early thinkers of capitalism pointed out that if each served his own best interests in production and money-making, an "invisible hand" would guide the ensemble so that the best interests of all would be served. It was, therefore, not necessary to inject such moral concerns as the "common good" since the "common good" took care of itself. Regrettably, it did not, and greed was unleashed on the world in a way not possible in any earlier period of history. The "visible hand" of government has stepped in, along with labor unions, to heal or prevent the worst effects of the unleashing of greed as a commendable social virtue.

The Christian may seem to be left with the option of accepting a doctrine of property that sets no limits to acquisitiveness or of joining movements to abolish whatever is left of capitalism in favor of new structures. Neither the old system of capitalism, which did not take its start in a church which forbade interest, nor new structures, which propose to correct the evils of the old, have answers that fully satisfy the Christian, who sees an intimate relation between the "new creature" of the Gospels and any new system which will meet the human and spiritual needs of any society. Crucial to any movement for change in which the Christian could be engaged is the recognition that there is not only a clear gospel perspective on property and poverty but a gospel imperative. This imperative is actuated by how we view our neighbor; if we see a person, whether homeless or diseased, disfigured or humiliated, enemy or friend, near or far away, as having taken upon him- or herself "the very person of the Savior," then we can accept for our own lives the simplicity of Christian poverty and we can make our property available for the works of mercy.

❊ The Faces of Community

HENRI J. M. NOUWEN

THERE IS LITTLE DOUBT that in our competitive world much emphasis is placed on those aspects of our personality which make us stand out. The thousands of advertisements that bombard us every day inform us of the outstanding quality of their products. The sports reporters who speak to us in daily papers and through radio and television call our attention to the outstanding performances of their heroes, and when we go to a play, a movie, or a circus to be entertained, we quickly focus on the outstanding activities of the artists. This emphasis on what is "outstanding" is so pervasive that we are hardly aware of how much it influences our emotions, passions, and feelings. But when we stop for a moment and reflect on the way we perceive ourselves and our neighbors, we soon discover how much of our energy is invested in comparing ourselves with others and wondering how we are special and where we stand out. Maybe during the first six years of our lives we are still able simply to enjoy life as it comes to us and to respond spontaneously to our surroundings. As soon as we go to school, however, we begin to ask the fatal question: "Am I doing better or am I doing worse than my classmates?" From then on we find ourselves struggling for grades, prizes, and other special rewards for our accomplishments.

In this context, it is not surprising that our sense of self, our self-esteem, begins to depend increasingly on those aspects of our life in which we are different from others. We wonder if we are more or less smart, fast, handsome, or practical than others, and our vocabulary quickly becomes full of comparative terms. The more we allow this way of thinking to dominate our lives, the more we become victims of the grade-givers in our society and succumb to the illusion that we are the difference we make.

It is not hard to see that this emphasis on the "outstanding" prevents us from forming community. Concerned with maintaining our differences, we live in constant fear that someone might take them from us and so undermine our sense of well-being. And so we start clinging anxiously to what we have: our possessions, which set us apart from others; our skills and techniques, by which we can do what others cannot do; our insights, by which we can impress people; and even our spiritual experiences, which give us a sense of being special. Learning then becomes a battlefield in which people try to get for themselves that which allows them to stand out and make a difference.

The Gospel radically criticizes this way of living and thinking. The great news of the Gospel is that self-identification based on outstanding differences makes us competitive and violent people who hold on compulsively to our distinctions and defend them at all costs. Jesus Christ reveals to us that our real identity is not to be found on the edges of our existence where we can brag about our specialties, but in the center where we can recognize our basic human sameness and discover each other as brothers and sisters, children of the same God. This is not a theoretical statement made by Christ, but a reality made visible in the life of Christ Himself. The great mystery of revelation is, indeed, that Jesus Christ did not cling to His equality with God but emptied Himself and became as we are. He revealed Himself not in being different from us but in being one with us, in sharing our joys and pains and dying a human death. This is very hard for us to understand fully, but we need to keep trying to stay close to this most profound mystery of God's love. God showed His love for us not by taking away our pains and frustrations and erasing our difficulties, but by becoming part of our condition and living as we do. What is central here is that by accepting the human condition God in no way became less than God but, on the contrary, revealed to us what His being God for us really means. He revealed to us that it belongs to the essence of His nature that He does not keep distant, but enters with us into the human struggle.

Based on this understanding of God as a God with us, the Apostle Paul could say to the Philippians: "There must be no competition among you, no conceit; but everybody is to be self-effacing. Always consider the other person to be better than yourself, so that nobody thinks of his own interests first but everybody thinks of other people's interests instead. In your minds you must be the same as Christ Jesus" (Phil 2:3–5).

To live the Christian life, therefore, requires a radical conversion. It requires us to look for our identity not where we are different or outstanding but where we are the same. This is far from easy because it requires us to give up many cherished illusions and to face directly our real human condition. It seems realistic to say that we have such deep fears and are filled with so many doubts and insecurities that facing our own broken human condition is beyond our own strength. However, it is also realistic to say that the love of God made visible in Jesus Christ can open for us the road to a new identity based not on our differences but on the full recognition of our human sameness. It is the experience of the unconditional love of God that allows us to recognize our common human brokenness and our common need for healing. When we are possessed by fear, we cannot be self-effacing or consider the other person as better than ourselves. That would be mental suicide. But when we are liberated from fear by God's unlimited love then we can give up our illusions and live out our human sameness with great freedom.

One of the most remarkable aspects of the lives of the saints is that the closer they came to a full understanding of God, the closer they came to being human. The more they experienced God's love in their life, the more they became aware of their own sinfulness and brokenness, and stressed that they were no different from others. This has nothing to do with masochism, self-flagellation or false humility, but it is an expression of the knowledge that in the full recognition of the broken human condition our true identity finds its anchor place.

All this makes it clear that living according to the Gospel, living with the mind of Christ, leads to community. Whereas a life based on our differences makes us strangers to each other, a life based on our common human brokenness and our common need for healing brings us closer to each other and so encourages community. Community starts becoming visible as soon as we perceive ourselves as fellow travelers, as people on the same road. It seems important to stress here that community is not so much something we create after we have given up our defensiveness and competitiveness. Rather, it becomes a reality when we relate to each other according to our true identity. Secondly, it is important not to limit too soon our concept of community. One tends to think immediately of people living together in one house or forming some kind of life together. But a classroom can be a community. People coming together for worship can form community. People writing to each other can be in community. Teachers, health care workers, and people in different professions can all form community. It all depends on the way we come to each other. Human beings are created for each other, are alive to give and share. As this truth becomes the basis of action, and as the paralyzing fears and isolating divisions begin to dissolve, community again becomes visible, revealing itself as natural, obvious, and self-evident.

It is in community that people begin to discover each other's uniqueness. Community is the place where talents can be discovered and made fruitful. Here we touch the great paradox of sameness and uniqueness. When we are willing to give up our outstanding differences and come to each other in mutual vulnerability, aware of our basic human sameness, then we create a space in which individual talents can manifest themselves not as divisive qualities but as uniting gifts. On the common ground of shared brokenness, our gifts can reveal themselves as gifts for each other. The most remarkable aspect of Christian community is that it does not encourage uniformity and suppress individual gifts. On the contrary, it creates the milieu in which, through great attentiveness to each other, hidden talents are brought to the foreground and made available for the up-building of communal life. Precisely when we have discovered that our sense of self does not depend on our differences and that our self-esteem is based on a love much deeper than the praise which can be acquired by unusual performances, we can see our own unique talents as gifts for others. And then we realize that the sharing of our gifts does not diminish our own value as persons but enhances it. In community, the unique talents of the individual members become like the little stones which form a great mosaic. The fact that the little piece of gold is part of a brilliant mural makes it that much more important since it is now an essential part of a greater picture. When this becomes clear, then our dominant attitude toward each other's gifts becomes gratitude. With increasing clarity we see the beauty in each other and call it forth so that it may become a part of our total life together. With increasing confidence we expect God's love to become visible in new ways through those who dare to meet on the common ground of their humanity.

So sameness and uniqueness can both be affirmed in community. We need to recognize the illusion that we are the difference we make and come together on the basis of our sameness. Indeed, we must have the desire to live out this sameness to the fullest. We have to experience our humanity to the core, our brokenness as well as our need for God's healing grace. But above all, we must realize that it is right in the center of this sameness that we will discover the gifts we have to share and the talents we can offer each other.

MARCH–APRIL 1978

❈ Reflections on the Marketplace

JUANITA NELSON

UNTIL EIGHT YEARS ago I was merely a consumer of food. Since then I have also become a producer of food. Taking on this second role has made a world of difference in my perception of the value of a pound of green beans. I was never a voracious consumer, but I naturally wanted to come by whatever I did consume at rock bottom prices. Food was something to be had as cheaply as possible, so as to leave the bulk of one's income for the good things of life like books, travel, entertainment, telephones. We do not, after all, live by bread alone (though we cannot live at all without it).

Just as I was never the biggest consumer, we are hardly agribusiness producers. Wally and I have a macro-garden in western Massachusetts which we estimate, by the pacing method, to be three-quarters of an acre. The primary purpose of the plot is to provide our own food as the basic and most easily accomplished step to becoming as self-sufficient as we can manage, disentangled to that extent from getting our living from a system built on injustice. (A big mouthful of a reason for having a garden, and sometimes I'm ready to eat those words.)

It is amazing how much one can grow in a small space. Even from a quarter (estimated) acre in Ojo Caliente, New Mexico (where we set out on this new venture, this added approach to our concept of nonviolent direct action), the earth yielded such bounty that we were unable to unload it all on friends and neighbors. As fate would have it, it was during that year of our first garden that farmers' markets were started in Santa Fe, Los Alamos, and Taos. We raked in two hundred and fifty dollars. Though it probably cost us that much to make those 120-mile round-trips to Santa Fe, it felt good to be earning from the work of our unskilled hands. That was how we backed into the notion that we could make what cash we'd need from a mini-mini truck garden. I'd had to concede that we would most likely not be able to avoid cash altogether, and providing wholesome food seemed about as honest a way to make a living as any—more honest than most.

When a garden plot gets beyond the forty-by-sixty-foot scale it hardly comes under the heading of pure recreation. It's a job—a demanding one. But there is the satisfaction—out there hoeing under the punishing sun, picking off Japanese beetles whose only interest seems to be recreating themselves, despairing over tenacious weeds, rejoicing in the aromatic abundance of raspberries—there is a satisfaction in knowing that you're taking care of one little bit of the earth's surface, that the sometimes back-breaking work is essential, because neither you nor I can live without somebody doing it.

We sometimes seem prostrate before our food supply. But the satisfaction continues through long hours of canning and shelling beans and sorting squash and onions for storage. There is even a barely repressed smugness as those long hours of sweat over a wood fire turn into colorful shelves of winter stores.

Ah, but the good feeling begins to fade when it comes to exchanging the joint efforts of the earth's gifts and our labor in a market economy, and that's the only one we have access to. Here and there one can find a more direct barter. But how many gallons of gas do most of us grow in our backyards, how many hospital beds, how many hoes and shovels? The farmers' markets that have sprouted here in New England like alfalfa seeds in a sunny window promise a partial alternative: lovely organic vegetables direct from producer to consumer, without the intervention of brokers and teamsters and supermarkets. But there are, alas, some roadblocks on that direct route.

The first is a simple resistance to selling food. Somehow it seems that food, of all things, should be a gift. There is confusion especially with friends, whom I like to send home with armfuls of just-picked carrots, lettuce, and peas. But they, knowing we depend on our garden for cash, try to insist on paying. This is especially awkward when I want to get rid of stuff that will otherwise end up on the compost heap—I am reluctant to offer for fear of having money pressed upon me for my garbage, as it were. It's like having friends over for dinner and being offered payment because one runs a restaurant. I carry over something of the same feeling about selling food, even to strangers at the market. But I shake my finger in my face and remind myself that I have performed a service for which I should be able to claim a share in the production and services of others, that if people don't grow their own food they have to put energy into it some way or other.

That settled, there looms ahead that more bothersome roadblock on the direct route from me to you. I can charge, I should charge, but how much? How much is a pound of green beans worth? (In that question I could wrestle with the whole problem of justice, morality, and economic theory.) I have said that I have a different sense of their value than when I viewed those same beans in a plastic bag in the grocery or at the open-air market in Philadelphia. Now, I see them from single bean seed to bushel basket. And there is no way that I know of to figure exactly the time and labor involved in getting those beans from one state to the other. Even if I could do that, how do I determine an even swap of my time and labor for the time and labor put into something that I need or want?

The garden is visible for only a few months, but it is a year-round labor: ordering the seed, planning the garden, preparing the soil, planting, thinning, weeding, de-bugging, mulching, putting the garden to bed. But I need not take account of all that; the cataloging of each step could take a page. It is enough that I feel in my bones the work that has gone into those beans since yesterday, when we spent hours stooping or on our knees to pick. Darkness found us still washing and picking vegetables by flashlight. Up, then, on Saturday morning before dawn, still chilly even in summer, and often raining, to harvest those items most perishable, fit all into the truck and hustle to market to set up before eight. (Those Saturday mornings are colder and wetter as the year wears on.)

No, I do not know how much that pound of beans should bring. By the time I get to market it seems worth at least a couple of dollars. (Strange that the equation should go in that direction; why not a couple of dollars' worth a pound of beans? Or a pound of beans worth a pair of mittens?) That's what I feel. But what I do is accept the mimeographed sheet from the market master with price ranges for each commodity for that week. The range is wide and prices fluctuate insanely from week to week, depending on supply and demand and, I suspect, more than a little manipulation. I despise that list. It has nothing to do with what has gone into production, with any reality that I can deal with. It has to do with conglomerates that can afford to dump because their profit is somewhere else, and with brokers who never see a bean, let alone weed any. Yet I, not knowing the value of a pound of beans, let that list dictate to me. Usually, I take the middle of the range, but often, for fear of asking too much, the lower end.

On the other hand, I do not wish to be exploited. I am unwilling to subsidize people with cheap food so that they might have more to spend on books, travel, entertainment, telephone calls, to say nothing of stereos, new cars, dishwashers. Such a line of reflection can lead to all sorts of probing. So, I am glad to note that it's time for the market to open and that, thrusting theory aside, I must straightforwardly and forthwith deal with economic reality. I scribble forty-five cents on a triangular piece of cardboard and stick it into my basket, relieved to be done with the business and reasonably content with my decision—until I chance to cast an eye to my right.

My neighbor is selling his beans for twenty-five cents a pound! A moment later I feel ashamed. He is simply not so mercenary as I am— perhaps he is basing his price on what he needs, and his needs are less than mine. Then I realize that the truth is that my neighbor's price has to do neither with cutthroat tactics nor simple living. He has a full time job, does not depend on his produce. He has brought the surplus from a lovingly tended garden because he enjoys the carnival. Perhaps he will earn enough to pay for his seed, but it doesn't matter.

Still, his price will cut into my sales. I am sure he has not thought of that and I would be embarrassed to bring it to his attention. How do you tell someone he ought to charge more? Maybe, to tell the truth, he should be charging even less, or giving his beans away since he doesn't need the money.

Oh-ho. The vendor across the way is charging sixty-nine cents for her beans. Outlandish! She'll give the market a bad name, people will stop coming because they'll think the market is a rip-off. She remains quite serene, though she must have heard the loud complaint intended for her ears. She is, obviously, convinced that her beans are worth sixty-nine cents. I am sure they are—even so she'll hardly earn a minimum wage—and I admire her for not being intimidated by dirty looks. She told me she had once plowed under a field of tomatoes because the price dipped too low.

Two approaches to the price of beans: easy-going benevolence and hard-nosed cost-plus accounting. And me, trying to chart a course between the shoals and about to go aground.

I am tempted just then to propose a pricing policy for the market, if it's no more than to huddle each Saturday morning and decide on common prices for the day. We would avoid the great gaps and bad feelings. For me it would be easier. As it is I feel guilty for undercutting my sixty-nine-cents neighbor, greedy for charging more than my twenty-five-cents neighbor. But price fixing? That would put us in the same boat, if not the same league, as the huge conglomerates with their under-the-table deals to the detriment of the consumer and our great "free enterprise" system.

There appear to be only two approaches to exchanging that pound of beans that seem anywhere near principled. The first is to calculate the time and materials expended. But I have concluded that's impossible for us. The other is to try to determine just how much I need to live on, and charge accordingly. More the "from each according to one's ability, to each according to one's need" method. Trouble is that I can see only one side—my own needs and abilities—unless we all do it together. It would be all right for me to take only what I need if it didn't involve the likelihood of working twelve hours a day to satisfy minimum requirements from exchange with people who might not have to work at all. Maybe it would be best to give the food away and make the cash in some other fashion.

But there is a third alternative. How about simply putting the vegetables out with a container on the table and a sign inviting people to deposit what they think they should pay or what they can afford? Transfer the responsibility for price setting from me to them.

Which brings me back to myself as consumer. On the other side of that counter, I wonder how much I'd toss into the bowl for a pound of string beans?

JULY–AUGUST 1978

❊ Long Days, Dark Nights in a County Jail

ROBERT ELLSBERG

EDS. NOTE: *Sixteen miles from downtown Denver, in a desolate area known as Rocky Flats, an unusual factory produced plutonium "triggers"—the equivalent of the Nagasaki bomb—for every American thermonuclear weapon. Beginning in the summer of 1978 until its final closing in 1991, nonviolent protestors maintained a constant presence at the plant. A number of members of the Catholic Worker community were among those arrested there for sitting on railroad tracks, blocking the trains that regularly delivered and received the deadly radioactive cargo. Robert Ellsberg was arrested there on May 12, 1978 and spent sixteen days in the Jefferson County Jail, during which time he fasted and was held in solitary confinement.*

THE TOWN OF Golden is host to the Jefferson County Jail. And over the main street, a picture of a smiling cowboy welcomes travelers to the town "Where the West is Still Alive," welcomes even this scruffy band of desperados as the sheriff escorts us to safekeeping.

The jail is an old one—dark and overcrowded, a home for over 199 prisoners who are locked up twenty-four hours a day in small, unlit cells. Some have spent three months here in virtual twilight, never seeing the light of day or breathing fresh air. Like most jails, it is designed in a colorless "neutral" style. Every reminder of life is white-washed, every reminder of a world outside is erased or covered over with bars. Every detail not simply left to economy reflects the coordinated effort to remind the inmates that this is not life, this is jail.

The only official decoration consists of several large, plastic-coated signs listing jail regulations, meal times, phone calls, visiting hours. It is an impressive sign with plenty of words, and reading it over through the bars must substitute for magazines until visiting day (15 minutes on Wednesdays). Three books a week are permitted, one six-inch pencil (with eraser), no newspapers, one toothbrush, magazines (of suitable quality), one jigsaw puzzle (no more than 500 pieces). But after many conscientious readings of this sign (and especially the part about privileges: one shower a week, one phone call a week, *unlimited* phone calls to attorneys permitted), I would learn from an officer that "some of this stuff is pretty out of date."

There are forms to fill out, uniforms to be issued, and I am the first among our group to be called: "Ellsberg, body only!" There are sliding doors on our cells that roll with no warning but a deafening clatter. When a prisoner is wanted they yell his name and "Body Only" meaning, leave your bedding and toothbrush and jigsaw puzzle behind because you'll be coming back. But this is the first time I've been summoned in such a fashion, and I like the sound of it; they have to admit they've got no more of me under lock and key than my "body only." I plan to keep it that way.

And now you are searched: Open your mouth, lift your tongue, guard's fingers through your hair, lift your arms, dance in the air, hands on the wall, one foot at a time, lift your soles . . . I comply passively to this point.

Now, bend over and spread your buttocks. And suddenly procedure grinds to a halt.

"What did you say?"

"I'm afraid I said no. That is one thing I will not do for you." I seem to be speaking a foreign tongue.

"But you *have* to do it."

I do not *have* to do anything, I answer, explaining that I have thus far given my cooperation to their procedure but I will not voluntarily submit to this assault on my dignity. I add that I don't intend to offer any resistance but I feel obligated to insist on my humanity, regardless of what is felt to be "necessary."

As I deliver this speech, standing naked and feeling foolish at my seriousness, an eye to the hard tile floor and wondering how badly I'm going to emerge from this altercation, I'm aware of a sudden reserve of confidence that I try desperately to project to my voice.

Another large guard has arrived to investigate the delay. I am told, "Thousands of people go through here and they all have to go through with this—if my own father were in here he'd have to do the same."

No doubt. They insist that "whether I like it or not," I will be searched, and how do I think it makes them feel to have to do this, anyway? What I think is that this whole procedure helps to transform me, in their eyes, from the status of person to prisoner. Instead, I am insisting on my personal freedom—that is, my ability under all circumstances to say yes or no—and that by the same measure I hope to return that capacity to my jailers. They listen thoughtfully, then leave me in the bathroom, prepared for their imminent return, I am sure, accompanied by reinforcements. But instead, the door opens only for a hand to toss me my new uniform.

As I dress quickly, brimming with satisfaction at the ease of this apparent "victory," a voice emanates from behind the toilet, apparently a prisoner forgotten in the confusion over my buttocks: "I hope you've at least got some dope up there, buddy!"

They walk me down another hall. Nothing is said of our little misunderstanding. A steel door swings open. "Mr. Ellsberg, would you mind waiting in here for a few moments, thank you." And I find myself in a soundproof, empty room.

Dinner is served silently. And later it is removed, untouched. I stay in that room for ten hours, while my friends are transferred to another jail.

*

Cell #3 is lined with bodies from floor to ceiling. There are twelve short, metal bunks fixed to the walls in double tiers. But there are sixteen people in this cell, so four of us must lay our thin mats on the concrete floor, leaving no room for movement without tripping over someone else. The last to arrive, I must take my own place in the least desirable spot, beside the toilet.

At 9:30 the lights go off and a hundred voices stretch themselves across the echoing jail like coyotes baying in the moonlight. One man never stops at all, calling to his wife in a strange delirium and carrying on the most realistic—one-sided—conversation until his cellmates demand that he be removed to the "cooler."

"I'm right here Betty. Tell them to let you in. Oh I'm so glad to see you, Betty. Wait, Betty, I swear I haven't had a drink—don't cry darling. Beeeetttyyy!" He is convincing enough to have me wondering whether he could possibly have his wife in here.

"Aw, he's just a screwball," says Cherokee. I guess so.

"Hey man, Betty's in here with us, cell #3. She says she ain't going with no drunk."

The Chicano youth beside me, three weeks in jail so far, awaiting an appearance in court, spends the afternoon carving a bar of soap with his fingernails. Out of margarine he saves from lunch he can fashion a crude but effective lamp. It gives off a smoky light and stinks up the place until someone complains. "What's the matter—you 'fraid of the dark?"

Someone else says he knows how to make a bomb out of an ordinary bar of soap but he's not telling how.

Chico is writing on the wall the names of all the women he knows, but be careful, Tony warns, not to write your own name on a jail wall or otherwise you'll be back. Tony's twenty-four and has been back already six or seven times—this time, shoplifting—so he should know.

"That's a crock," says Curtis, a crusty old curmudgeon who spent the first drunken night swinging his fists at the bars and challenging the guards to take him on "man for man." And he was once a prizefighter (when he was not also sheriff of this county, a United States Senator, a prospector in Alaska, and an Air Force pilot). He says, "They got me here this time on the frame-up charge of 'harassing my wife.' "

"I'll give you my old lady's address for when you get out and you can go harass her for awhile." That's Zulu, "main man" for cell #4 where they are putting the black prisoners. He calls to me, "Hey Rocky Flats, how you doin' today? I'm with you, man!" He's been here three months, longest of the misdemeanors. And he instigated one bit of mischief this afternoon.

Meals arrive under the bars on metal trays with a plastic spoon that they count on the way out and a tin cup of coffee. Suddenly out of cell #4 there's an explosion of clattering trays and cups flying through the bars and into the halls that brings the duty officers running to the trouble.

"Who's throwing trays!"

"Nobody thrown no trays, man."

That night, no meal for cell #4. But someone must have gotten the message. Prisoners go two weeks without a phone call or a shower and trays are going to fly.

*

The guards are generally "decent"—they seem harried and over-worked and I have no quarrel with them as individuals. But the great question and tragedy of our age is not a matter of personal decency but the degree to which obedience to authority and "conventional morality" implicate so many of us in a process and a system that may some day be judged criminal, if not also suicidal. I am more impressed by the decency of the prisoners who must overcome such conditions to perform a courtesy or kindness that would be taken for granted on the outside. And the surprising thing is that there is such a rich community of mutual aid and cooperation. I prefer their "decency."

I must make it clear that I will not allow these walls and bars to define the limits of my freedom and trust in human dignity. I have chosen to non-cooperate with my imprisonment in certain critical respects. I am continuing the fast I began with my arrest. When so much else is taken away, this remains my way of communicating several things. First of all, the life and death seriousness of what we are saying. Secondly, I am withholding critical consent from my imprisonment, refusing to relinquish the scope of personal freedom that is responsible for my being here, and that, I feel, when exercised by sufficient numbers, will be the decisive factor in the prospects for human survival. My body is given for a purpose and I am trying to convert each beat of my heart into an urgent prayer for peace and a gift of hope in my brothers and sisters who have replaced us on the tracks, who are, at this moment, buying time for humanity with their bodies. Nothing of good occurs unless individuals take responsibility for making it possible and are willing to pay the cost personally.

*

My Bible is left me and I spend the evening sitting against the bars, straining for enough light to read the Psalms. "O my God, keep me from those who rise against me. They lie in wait for my life, not for my sin, O Lord. Swords are at their lips, for who, they think, will hear us? O my strength, I will wait on Thee, for God is my stronghold." How little I understood the Psalms until I was a prisoner.

*

Day six

"Ellsberg, body only!" It is visiting day, and I had begun to think no one would come. Although you can't be in the same room with your visitors, you still have to be frisked. I shuffle down the hall; they've taken the laces from my shoes.

The visiting room consists of a row of telephone booths that look into another room through small plastic windows. You have to shout through a dense metal grate below the window, the phones having been recently removed, and keep your ear close to hear the dim sounds from the other side. The sound of a dozen voices seems to get lost in the wall, like the dull roar of the ocean in a shell, one conversation overlapping with a dozen others, becoming one sustained, reverberating outburst: "Baby I love you what'd the lawyer say I miss you Chico fine Mama don't cry honey love you too baby Cherokee and me we run this place I'll be ok Mama I can't stand it no more man you know I do Johnny," over and over. And every conversation ends the same way: "OK, guys, time's up."

*

Day seven

Little sleep, both from noise and the growing pain in my groin that makes me walk with a limp and every shifting position a steady throb. From 4:30 A.M. (which is when they wake us) to nearly ten, I'm asking and waiting for the nurse (no doctor on duty). The nurse is sort of a middle-aged hipster who stands apart from other jail personnel both by his mod style—paisley shirts, flared trousers, shag trim—and his seemingly resolute indifference toward those he "services." Twice a day he dispenses aspirin, and on his morning rounds I stop him and tell him about my troubles.

"Groin swollen?" No. "Happened before?" No. "Drinking water?" Yes. "Name?" Yes, I have a name. "What is it?" Ellsberg. "Hmmm." Interview complete, he turns on his heel and proceeds with his job. "Aspirin in this cell?" Even in his speech he has discovered a way of reducing human contact to a minimum.

*

I am called out, body only, frisked and guided to the examining room. The nurse sits me down. On the basis of our interview he has decided I don't have enough symptoms to justify a complete examination, but he has decided to take a blood sample.

"How much are they paying you to be out here?" he asks. An odd question. "You heard me—what do you get for being out here?" When I say I'm here on my own time he tells me I've got a "pretty weird idea of a vacation."

"Listen Ellsberg, when you've worked in a place like this as long as I have and listened to enough belly-aches from guys saying, 'Oh, I'm in pain,' and you put 'em in solitary and in a couple of days they're saying 'I'm fine, get me out of here'—well, you'd be pretty cynical too."

He rubs alcohol on my arm. " 'Cause buddy, this place isn't for human beings—it's made for animals. These people, you don't know 'em like I do." He reaches toward my head with an alarming gesture. "They'll pull your wife's hair, they'll rape your daughter! When you have kids you'll realize that this kind have to be locked away to protect decent people." I feel the needle in my arm. "I'm not saying you're necessarily the same as the rest—we'll see this afternoon when the tests come back."

I ask him whether this job is worth the price he's paying—he's in prison, too, as well as the guards, and he seems to be working on an ulcer. "Maybe it's not worth it—the only satisfaction I get in this lousy job is when I come up with some symptoms." I hope I can accommodate him. "This examination's over—send in the next one." He slams the door shut behind me.

And so in jail there are no sick or well, but only guilty and innocent.

*

Yesterday lots of people thanked me for my "strength." They don't know me. I have so little strength or faith. I am racked with doubts, self-recrimination, insecurity. I feel at a crossroads, afraid to trust myself to the light. I know in each of us we carry the personal equivalent of Rocky Flats. And we are stumbling, stumbling.

In one of my favorite Hasidic tales, it is the night of the Passover. A peasant is rushing to finish his work in the fields so he can attend to the holy service. But alas, the sun drops and it is darkness when no travel is permitted. Next day the rabbi spots him and asks where he's been. "Oh Rabbi, it was terrible—I was stuck in my fields after dark and had to spend the night there." "Well," says the rabbi, "I suppose you at least recited your prayers." "That's the worst of it, Rabbi. I couldn't remember a single prayer." "Then how did you spend the holy evening?" asks the rabbi. And the peasant answers, "I could only recite the alphabet and pray that God would rearrange the letters."

We are the same. We are in a dark age, the light has dried up, and we are so few, and we seem utterly helpless, ineffective, and lost. We are not saints; we are painfully aware of our total unsuitability for the urgent task in which, by some mysterious grace, we have been invited to participate. And so what can we do? What can anybody do? There is nothing to do but try to remember some of the letters of the alphabet and to recite them in faith, and trust that a greater wisdom than our own will somehow put them back together. We have to be modest, we must have a sense of humor. Because there is no intelligible way to explain any of this.

*

Day eight

At 4:30 the lights go on and the crazy, clanging ritual begins again. At least in my case, however, fortune has taken another turn. I was transferred yesterday to solitary on account of my fasting. So far as change in lifestyle, let's say I am not entirely upwardly mobile. I am now reduced to a cell six-by-eight-feet with a double set of bars, no sink, light, bed or toilet (a hole in the concrete floor suffices for my humble needs)—talk about "simple living." The pain in my groin seems to have disappeared (thought so: another malingerer!). The procedure is that I will be put in the hole for thirty days and then transferred to a hospital.

Yesterday I was called into a room with the Lieutenant and a Sergeant. We had a very decent conversation—almost like a consultation between fellow professionals.

"Robert," says the Lieutenant (no longer just Ellsberg—I am Mr. Ellsberg or Robert, and I'll wager I'm promoted to corporal if I stay here long enough), "are you aware of just how many services we provide here? We have guidance counselors, social workers, a medical staff, family assistance programs, human resources workers—things you never would have dreamed of ten years ago—and it's getting better all the time." How come I've been here a week and I haven't seen all these guys? Well, I never asked, did I? And that's just the beauty of it. You see, the philosophy they go by is to respond to the "individual needs of the particular inmate." You don't treat everybody the same, lik : in the old days. The program has to be geared to the unique demands of every person. Which means you may never see any of this, but knock and the door shall be opened!

I remain incredulous. After spending a week trying to get a lousy clean towel, I can't believe it would occur to the average prisoner to ask if a "human resource" worker might be available to sit down and rap for a couple of hours.

The Sergeant has a liberal attitude and concedes that jails solve no problems, but are only an emergency treatment of symptoms. Neither denies that most inmates gain nothing from this experience that will serve them any good, are just as likely to commit further and more serious crimes in the future, that jails hold only a small portion of those convicted, who represent, in turn, a small portion of those apprehended, who represent a smaller portion of crimes committed, and that in this selecting process it is the poor who are left. Where does that leave us? As Anatole France said, "The law in its majestic equality forbids rich and poor alike to beg, to steal bread, to sleep under bridges."

In this country you steal a car and you go to jail; steal an election and you go to the White House; steal a million and it's called a good investment. If it's law and order you're concerned with, how can you spend billions on prisons and a pittance on the social development needed to prevent crime? Prisons are only one aspect of a society that has no coherent notion of what human life is for—so, obviously, all attempts at "correction" and "rehabilitation" fall flat because they fall short of correcting a system that is based on the respectability of theft. They are considering crime only as an individual problem and not,

correctly, as a social problem, susceptible, in the end, to social correction. Society is too big—the velocity of life is too fast, too impersonal.
You have to be a "professional" just to cope. And the system pushes
those who can't make it (those whom it is more profitable for the system
to ignore than to usefully employ) out to the margins where they are
absorbed in ghettos, welfare, drugs, and (at least a quarter of a million
of them) in jail.

"You need more than average compassion to take a job like this,"
says the Sergeant. "It just wouldn't be worth the money alone. But on
the other hand, you also have to be a professional, because you see so
much suffering and human misery that if you didn't keep detached
you would be overwhelmed, you couldn't function." (I restrain myself
from asking how much of this overwhelming suffering he figures is a
direct consequence of his "functioning.")

I share my experiences at the Catholic Worker, and life on the Bowery
where you practically step over bodies on your way to work. If we did
as we are told in the story of the Good Samaritan, it's true, there
would be no end to it. But the answer doesn't seem to me to be more
professionalism. My experience with social workers so often is that they
do not serve, they service. They lose respect for the people they are
trying to help, partly because of the one-sided nature of their relationship. There's no sharing going on, so what is meant as a gift is really
a kind of theft. They realize how few people they can help and begin
to feel guilt, which turns to resentment for the people who are making
them "feel bad." I know myself that I couldn't expose myself to such
brokenness for the sake of professionalism, even idealism, much less
as a nine-to-five job. Only true compassion makes it possible, which is
not sentimental feelings, but active faith; not a virtue, but a gift of grace.

I explain my fast—not a "hunger strike," I insist. They tell me I have
their complete respect, to which the Sergeant adds, "Robert, I consider
you to be a bright leaf in a whirlwind."

Since then everybody's been acting much nicer. The change was
immediate. I got myself a shower, new clothes and bedding, and a ten-
minute phone call(!), before moving to my new accommodations. Best
of all was simply the respectful tone of our conversation and the beginning of some kind of mutual understanding.

I don't want to be totally naive and ignore the fact that they probably
don't recognize me as an "average criminal"—perhaps in their eyes I
am practically "one of them."

And yet, and yet . . . It confirms my belief that by remaining faithful
to one's principles, by sticking to the truth in spite of personal consequences, one makes it possible for the most miraculous changes to
occur. My statement that noncooperation—the refusal to be a prisoner—is really a precondition for dialogue is confirmed. And when we
put ourselves in God's hands, trusting not in our own wisdom, but

making ourselves most vulnerable, then we open ourselves to enjoy the full grace of God's protection.

The way of nonviolence is a humbling, a reduction of our selves in action to the point where the Truth speaks through us, an obscurity so small that the wind and the dust could bury us.

I feel better today. Plants can live almost forever on light and water (as Simone Weil says, a tree is actually rooted in the sky). There is so little light here. What is the spiritual equivalent of chlorophyll that allows us to receive love and transform it into the material of life?

*

Solitary is quieter. No radio, no conversations into the night. It is a punishment cell for prisoners who "endanger themselves or others." My cell is darker than before, but it is off the main hall where the light burns twenty-four hours a day. The prisoners call it the cooler. My mat covers half the floor. As before, I have no sheets or pillow. It is a strange kind of solitude that allows no privacy. No toilet here—a drain in the floor flushes from outside the cell—and no sink. There is a tap outside the bars, and, with a plastic cup, I can reach through the bars and draw water.

I am taken from my cell once a day to be weighed, and I enjoy this excursion. A certain Officer Rollins, a young man and quite thin himself, always takes me to the scale. I don't see him record my weight yet he always remembers what it was the day before. Today, the tenth day, I was down about fifteen pounds and he seemed troubled and concerned for me. He lingered before putting me back into my cell. I thank him and for a moment I think we might have a conversation. Perhaps tomorrow.

No space, no time. Only a mechanical rhythm indicated by noise, the shifting of faces, and the delivery of non-meals that sit on my bars until I ask to have them removed. And one day a note: "Rocky Flats—Hang on, my man. Signed, your friendly neighborhood Zulu."

*

The kitchen is across the hall and I make friends with the chef (head of "food management"), a friendly, corpulent man in a white uniform. Not a guard and not a prisoner.

"Well, sonny, I guess you're fasting."

That's right, nothing personal, of course.

" 'Course, not," he laughs. He is a Christian and likes to stop and chat between the bars or even squat down and "share some Scripture."

"The way I see it," he says one day, "jail is nothing but a warehouse." An apt definition when you consider that warehouses are for things, and when you take a thing out, it's the same as when you put it in. But put a person into a warehouse and see if they're the same when you retrieve them in a month or a lifetime. Are they better or worse?

One day it's the story of Jonah, the serious-browed prophet who rebelled against God's order to warn the people of Nineveh of the destruction that would follow their sin. Jonah wants the people of Nineveh to get what is coming to them. But after being delivered to his assignment by an unusual vehicle, Jonah reluctantly delivers the warning and has to watch as the people make a miraculous conversion. They fast and put on ashes and sackcloth and pray for forgiveness. And God is merciful. Yes, even the most hell-bent of societies can be spared the logical consequences of its actions and be changed.

And in this cage we are like Jonah, carried against our will, our narrow understanding, our meager faith, to God's will for us, buried somehow in the belly of an absurd and lonely paradox. We will feel dry land.

*

I lie on my back, I wait, I check off the passing days on my wall, I write letters to the outside which I hide in my shoe. The steel door beyond my bars provides extra security to myself and the prison population that I am "endangering." At 4:30 each morning, a trusty begins polishing the floor outside my cell with an electric contraption that sends sparks through my nerves. This morning he slams the outer door shut to cover the space behind.

With the door closed I am in total, silent darkness. It takes approximately thirty seconds before the sensation of being buried alive has me shaking the bars and crying for help. This time the door opens.

There's a metal window in the door and I don't panic so long as they leave that part open, as the Corporal did one morning. "Gotta close this, Ellsberg—people coming through." (Don't want "people" to think we're running a jail here, do we?)

The people seem to be a group of school girls. One of them peers curiously into my darkened cave. Her eyes fix on something living: "Look, there's a person in there." I feel more eyes. "Where? I can't see anything." Like the dumb animal I am, I simply stare, silently, into the giggling faces. "See, there he is."

I seem to be on the outside looking in. "Who are you?" I ask myself. "Who wants to know?" comes the shadowy reply.

*

On appeal, the courts have upheld the conditions for our release—a promise not to return to the tracks. We are likened to a compulsive wife-beater—surely the court must issue restraints to make sure he doesn't go right back and beat her again! And while a dozen of us dangerous "wife-beaters"—worse, criminal trespassers—sit safely behind bars, only a few miles off scientists and technicians work behind sealed doors, fashioning their plutonium "devices." With due respect, those bombs render the court's decision irrelevant, "moot." Those bombs annul the Constitution and all the other documents on which our laws are written. All our rights—not only to due process and freedom of speech, but our right to sing, to look at the sky, our right to give birth to happy, healthy children—all, all subject to unilateral annulment. We are living under suspended sentence of death. And the courtroom exists in another world. It deals in bits of law, precedents, and rulings, and meanwhile lives slip through like sand. Because the reality of the arms race constitutes a crime so vast that the court is incompetent to handle it. Words are incompetent. It shatters our concepts, a crime so total that it doesn't distinguish between guilty and innocent, victim and aggressor. A crime that will take judge, witnesses, jury, as well as court-room, jails, and Jefferson County itself with it. A crime for which some are guilty, all are responsible.

*

Day fourteen

Nurse drops in for a chat. "When are you going to start eating, Ells-berg?"

When I'm free.

"I'll just bet you will, and that's why I have no respect for you. You're on this great hunger strike; but watch, the minute you're free you're gonna stuff your face. You know what you are? You're nothing but an agitator"—he spits the word—"an outside agitator; and you're lower than all the rest of these guys, 'cause you think you're above the law, don't you?"

Do I look like I'm above the law?

"You broke the law, Ellsberg—I mean, you broke the law! Listen, I don't know about you but personally I don't want my children growing up speaking Russian!"

This continues interminably. I try to keep pace but it tires me, my ears are aching, and it is a relief when a ringing phone calls him away. Such complete contempt would seem almost ridiculous if it weren't also frightening. Such blinding feeling that causes many people to describe a peace march as an act of violence. And they are telling the truth. Because violence, for them, is what strikes at their fears and we have not found a way of speaking the truth without challenging the deepest and most vulnerable fears and myths. Unless we can uproot those fears, or somehow defuse them, if we allow ourselves the slightest luxury of pride or judgment, good citizens like this will conscientiously and unhesitatingly (as they did at Kent State) shoot us down in "self-defense."

Merton was right. Fear is the root of war.

*

It is late—the radio has been off for hours. I'm thirsty and stand to stretch my cup between the bars. I'm laying my cup under the tap. Then it's gone, it becomes a yellow wall, the ceiling . . . Strange sounds from under water . . . No, I am under water . . . I am lying on my back, but I'm not in bed. Then, suddenly . . . the world comes into focus, a little too quickly; someone turns the volume back to normal, and the present returns with a painful thud.

I feel both parched and nauseated. I must call for help. "Guard, please, guard!" The bars slide back, someone pulls me to my feet and leads me toward the bathroom.

"Do you want some vitamins?" It is Officer Rollins. Every part of my body is speaking, telling me I have reached the limit, this—I—simply cannot go on. All the fears I have been neatly suppressing suddenly break like the ocean over my head. What am I doing, what have I done to myself? I know at this moment that I will take anything they offer—food, juice. I've lost the will to say no. But all I can say is, "Yes, I would like some vitamins."

My limbs are shivering with an electrical charge. I can't open my hands. I imagine that I've gone into shock and will die right there on the toilet seat. My face is hot, then cold and clammy, and then slowly I seem to come to for a second time. The pain has left my arms, my pulse has returned to normal. My head clears, and I wash my face as if nothing has happened, slightly embarrassed for all the fuss, deeply ashamed at the fears I had denied. I return to my cell, worrying how to renege on my request for vitamins. But wonder of wonders, they're not offered.

Officer Rollins looks at the floor, embarrassed. It seems the Sergeant says I'll have to check with the nurse in the morning if I want those vitamins. We chat for a few moments. He's trying to tell if I'm really all right and I reassure him.

"You know," he says, "I want to tell you I admire your strength. You shout now if you need anything."

And then I'm alone as before.

I don't sleep much that night. Of course, I have only fainted; but it feels as if I have looked death in the face. How easily I can be broken! Each of us must face that point of humiliation, loneliness and utter darkness. But what joy that knows we have touched the bottom, and now every step leads toward the light! Suddenly I feel prepared to face what might happen. I know simultaneously that it will not be by my own strength, because I have seen the limit of that. From this moment we know, whether we rise or fall, it is purely by grace. Our course is set. The consequences are not in our hands.

My lungs are filled with the sweetness of life.

*

The fifteenth night

Tomorrow morning is my arraignment. The judge will want a plea. But I don't want a wall of legal technicalities to stand between the two of us. Neither "guilty" nor "innocent" describes my attitude as well as "content," but I don't think he'll accept that. Doesn't a plea give recognition to the court's jurisdiction over our conscience? Best not to contest the charges and simply make a statement. That will be taken for a guilty plea and I will be sentenced directly. The judge could then send me back to jail or he might impose a fine which I wouldn't pay. He might even enter a plea of not guilty which would return me to my cell until trial in a month or two. I must remember that the court's decision will reflect political as well as legal considerations. He sets me free or he keeps me here. His decision will be made before I enter the courtroom. Since my arrest, another dozen people have been apprehended on the tracks. Perhaps he'll want to set an example. What's the difference? It's beyond my control now. All that's left for us is to shape our attitude and be at peace. I prepare some notes for court.

The bars roll back. They want to put a drunk in my cell so they move me across the hall to the visiting room. There it's dark and quiet. I am drunk with thoughts of home and loving faces and I cannot sleep, missing them so.

*

Day sixteen

Breakfast comes and goes, as usual, before I wake. But in the dark I have no sense of time. Now I have no water, and not even a drain in the floor. I'm feeling weak and sick—probably exhaustion. Through the window I catch sight of a guard.

"What do you want?" he asks. Some water and use of a bathroom. "Five minutes," he tells me, and then he's gone.

Five minutes later the door opens. "OK, Ellsberg, you're going to court." How soon? "Right now."

I'm dry as dust and totally unprepared for this short notice. But a group of handcuffed prisoners is already lining up and waiting—evidently for me—to go. They frisk me over and while the duty officer signs some forms I drop down on my heels to conserve my waning energy.

"Get up, Ellsberg!" I stare up blankly at the towering guard. "I said stand up!" I look at the Corporal, whose eyes tell me not to worry. I push myself up the wall as I feel the steel bracelet clip onto my wrist.

Things are moving slowly, so I squat down again, not trying to be defiant, only wondering where I'm going to get the strength to walk the hundred yards to court.

"Ellsberg, are you gonna stand up, or what?"

"Are you going to carry me, or what?" I snap in kind.

After sixteen days my nerves are already frayed. Get a hold on yourself. Only a few more yards, not far, take it slowly. O my strength, I will wait on You, for God is my stronghold. Of whom shall I be afraid?

An officer helps me to my feet. "You gonna make it?" I suppose so. "You've done a good job, Bob. God bless you."

*

The Jefferson County Jail is only a smaller version of a jail in which I and all the world are hostages. Between that jail and this smaller one, is, in my opinion, one continuous crime, from which I wish to withdraw my consent and my participation. The final word, if our children are to see a future, must not be judgment, punishment, and retribution. The ethical precepts of mercy, forgiveness, and understanding have become a practical imperative.

Personally, I have hope. Because I believe there must be, somewhere deep inside of us, buried under the encrustation of a hundred repressive institutions, perhaps encoded in our very DNA molecules, a memory of the unity of life, and an urge to rediscover it. And I am happy in this jail, because I know that on the outside there are people who share my hope and are willing to pay the price to make it real.

*

Then we're marching silently, down the hall, past the bars, locks, the guns, into the warm, clean air, blue sky, the trees, tears and laughter, the spinning seasons, even more precious than we left them.

———————————————————————————— JUNE 1979

❊ Maryhouse II

MEG BRODHEAD

I HAD SEEN HER before. Thin, young, extremely nervous. She'd come to the house seeking shelter last summer, never could quite find the words to tell us how she'd wound up this creek, and outstayed what we deigned to call her "welcome."

When she showed up at the door last night, just as I was closing the house (how does a house close? closing its eyes for the night? closure of possibilities?) I met her at the threshold. Perhaps I was heading her off at the pass. It is so much simpler to say no before someone has really made her presence felt in the household. And I knew I "must" say no, since a few days earlier we had decided that the hospitable limits of our house were utterly strained and would rend if one more person came to live with us. In making that decision we did not quite come to the language of over-extended resources. In reply she talked about this uncivilized city, and I nodded in profound agreement and pointed to the door. She sighed and went to wash her face and said to me as she left, "If you wanted to discourage me, you have." I sighed and went to make a phone call to someone who, I knew, had a bed for the night.

Well, I was on the phone for five minutes when it was brought to my attention that this fragile, precious young woman was standing outside our door weeping. I groaned and went down and kind of leaned out the door impatiently at her, sizing the two of us up. I grabbed her sleeve and dragged her in the door. I gave her half a box of cookies and told her she could sleep on the half-couch we keep in our auditorium. This morning I looked for her, to remind her that it was only for one night, but she had already gone.

So, I would say, the practice of hospitality is a two-way street, by which I mean that it is the essential spirit, the only spirit in which we are able to meet and know one another. Thank God, thank God people make demands, demand that attention be paid. Even the quietest soul makes the "clear crystalline cry" that Yeats knew God hears; our prayer is that we be His instruments. Sometimes, we remember here that it's not for nothing that Christ had to command us to love our neighbor. When the question is posed to Him in the Gospel (in our selfishness!), "Who is my neighbor?," He stands that affrontery on its head, or on its proper footing: rather, To whom will you be neighbor? Will you dare to recognize your brother, your sister?

Well we won't, not on our life, not without a great deal of help. We pray for drops of water on the heart of stone. I remember a woman who came in off the street, and she hadn't slept anywhere for a couple of days. All I had to give her was a luke-warm cup of watery tea. Before she drank it she praised the Lord most unabashedly for His mercy and goodness. All I could do was flush with shame, and I wanted to bow to her, because this woman was offering hospitality much more earnestly than I.

It's not a one-shot-at-a-time performance; like pacifism, hospitality is a way of life. A house of hospitality is a house of peace, *fiat*. It is a way of life I would heartily recommend to everyone. There is no better way to learn how fascinating is every individual, how miraculous our ability to communicate at all, how sinful the violence done to so many by the modern priorities. Beyond these insights our greatest joy, if only we had the brains to know it, is in the service of the Lord and His people.

Oh, there's such a thing as the Catholic Worker Blues; the sadness, the weariness, the sense of futility run very deep at times. The romance of living on the front lines wears thin. If the sadness worms its way into you, it's not romantic or dramatic—it's spiritual catastrophe. I do not mean to discount these things. Then, too, one of our great modern problems is busyness, being busy every moment, and hospitality, in whatever form, can get distorted into more of the same. Still, you do what you can, and sometimes you don't. But it's a lousy feeling when, in the midst of it all, somebody we just couldn't help strides out the door and flings over her shoulder, "And you call yourselves *Catholics!*" You'd like to laugh or roll your eyes, but that's a direct, stinging challenge, one you cannot withstand alone. It's a challenge made to the whole Church, and with God's help it will fall upon the Church's heart of stone.

I certainly hope more Christians become involved in the work of active hospitality. I'm concerned that the houses we have now will start to feel like a necessary evil, tending the people left to choke on the dust of the mobile generation, but not exactly heralding the new society. If houses of hospitality are allowed to become agencies on referral lists—if it becomes our "job" to take care of the poor—we will be forced into the embarrassing, sickening position of merely supporting the status quo. The tragedy of homelessness is going to get much worse, I think. What we've got in New York City is thousands of abandoned buildings, thousands of ex-mental patients pouring into the city, lower-priced hotels closing or renovating with an eye to higher income brackets, stricter welfare regulations than ever. The poor are getting squeezed of their lifeblood, as the rich move back in to spur the "urban renaissance." We understand that this is the trend in every major city in the country. For a while we were turning away ten people a day. It is very, very difficult to live hospitably when every other word out of your mouth is in the negative.

So, in the Lower East Side of this uncivilized city, flustered and assaulted by its vicissitudes, sometimes anxious and uncharitable, sometimes surprised by the Lord and His hidden prophets, we struggle to make a liveable life here at the Catholic Worker. We celebrated our birthday, May Day, in high style. When the occasion demands it, we're a happy-go-lucky crew. We ate and sang between mouthfuls until midnight in our spacious auditorium at Maryhouse. We'll make parties at the drop of a hat; say it's your birthday, even three times a year if you're clever about it, and we'll have ice cream; find an old cake mix tucked away in one of the thousand cupboards in this house and use it up before it gets any older; win some money at a local bingo game and buy soda and cookies for EVERYBODY. It's not a health food paradise, but these simple signs of gaiety mark the newness of each day and, who knows, may even precurse the eternal banquet.

Well. Summer is coming, slow but sure, like herself. We pray and hope for peace.

MARCH–APRIL 1980

36 East First

MARK HORST

I WAS SITTING at lunch recently with a woman who had volunteered her services on the soup line. As our conversation progressed, I learned that this woman was a reporter eager to write about the Catholic Worker and the tasks that make for life here. I asked her what she thought of the place and she responded with enthusiasm. "It's incredible!" she said. I agreed that it was, in fact, an incredible place.

The luncheon visitor found the work here incredible because it was unlike anything she had ever imagined. Here was a place, as she described it, where service, sharing, and self-denial seemed common place, a community from which greed and enmity, struggle and strife seemed all but banished. In her eyes, the community took on heroic proportions. Many of us saw the same things when we first came here. I was certainly dazzled by the novelty of the place. It's almost inevitable, because the Worker really is a different kind of place.

But, after mopping the floor, washing dishes, and doing the countless other tasks that keep a house running, day by day; after the newness dulls and the stimulation of novelty has faded a bit, you learn just how ordinary a place this is. The trouble with that initial amazement—the experience of utter novelty—is that it can keep people from the deeper recognition of God's work. When the work itself is so strikingly different it becomes the focus of attention. Our visitor was filled with an admiration often directed toward heroes. She was drawn to our work in admiration, but she was at the same time kept at an enormous distance from it. Now, it's been my experience, that God is revealed not so much by looking at the work but in looking along with it. I mean that the work becomes a way of seeing and understanding God's love.

I think that's why, to return to the lunch table, a fellow worker objected to the reporter's incredulity, saying, "There's nothing incredible about this place. It's all very ordinary." He noticed the implications of her enthusiasm, how it put a great distance between our work and her life. He wanted her to see that the Catholic Worker is not something so far removed from the possible. It is ordinary, as plain as daffodils, and until you see that, you can't see what is truly incredible in it.

I have another story. This one is about someone who seemed intent on capturing the incredible and the dramatic in order to show it off.

Early one morning, the other day, as I was reading in our second floor office, the telephone rang. A man, representing one of the local television stations, wanted permission to film our soup line. He was very polite, yet he asked for permission with the air of one whose very question is a gift. As if he wanted to say, "You know, I don't ask just anyone this question."

Now I'm not exactly accustomed to reporters, and I admit, even though I'd rather not, that the self-assured, intensely energetic qualities of many journalists often excite me into thinking that something very significant is at stake. I was inclined to agree with the man on the phone that he was, in fact, doing me an enormous favor by asking to film our soup line.

But, at the same time, I remembered the television shows that claim to report news; how they manage to work murders, muggings, and wars into a light-hearted routine designed to compete with *M.A.S.H.*; how entertainingly horrid a murder looks through the tube of a television; how satisfyingly tragic the faces of the bereaved appear; how thin the truth looks on that glass plate.

So, in an excited way, the way one would feel turning down an invitation from a glamorous star, I told the gentleman that our soup line was a private affair. I pointed out that it is not only a soup line but a fragile haven of peace which might be disturbed by photographic intrusion. I explained that many of our visitors have relatives or friends in the area and wish to remain anonymous. Finally, I informed him that our house is not for show but for hospitality; it is a home rather than an institution.

The camera crew arrived shortly thereafter and began shooting pictures of the poor waiting for soup. A few of us preparing for the soup line interrupted the busy crew and reminded them that we had denied them permission to film. They reminded us that the sidewalk was public domain. The earlier request had apparently been an insignificant formality. I responded by opening the door and letting the long line of men and women into the kitchen. The people streamed in, the camera hummed, and the reporter's face reddened a bit as she saw her story disappearing into the house. But her eyes glittered with the righteous fire of a crusader and, after a few moments, she burst out with impassioned certitude, "Don't you see we're on the same side? You want to help these men and we do, too." I hadn't really considered the possibility that the reporter wanted to help the poor. So I asked her, "How do you want to help them?" She replied, "We want to expose their wretched condition. We want to bring their plight before the eyes of New York City and show off the good work you are doing."

That evening, I'm told, though I didn't see it, the reporter reported to the eyes and ears of New York the plight of the poor. Their wretched condition was exposed. I think the reporter meant well. She seemed to admire the work being done. Perhaps she even found it incredible. The next day the soup line was a bit more crowded.

In the midst of the controversy that morning on the soup line, someone said to the reporter and her film crew, "We think the best way to help the poor is to share what we have with them." Shortly after that they left. The reporter was rather perturbed and a little confused by our lack of cooperation. I, too, was shaken by our encounter and could not help wondering at how easy it was to gain admirers, and how difficult it was to find people willing to involve their lives with the poor.

The poor, and the services devoted to them, are the latest media rage. No news service is complete without a feature article on them. But as long as the poor are incredible in a dramatic way they will be uninteresting when the drama fades.

The unceasing quest for novelty often blinds us to anything truly novel. We get so used to looking at things from the outside, from the dramatic exterior, that we risk never understanding them from the inside. It happens at the Catholic Worker when people admire the uniqueness of the community without seeing the ordinary. It happens in New York City when people view the poor as a social problem instead of as brothers and sisters. It happens wherever people seek glamour and excitement instead of transforming their own lives into instruments of wonder. When I spoke of the Worker as an incredible place I was referring to something beyond the cloak of novelty. I was amazed not because we do amazing things but because God does. That's hard to see looking in from outside.

Some of us were sitting around the dinner table last night having just finished off some delicious zucchini casserole. Tom asked a member of our community, who likes to be called by his full name, Mister Harold Henry Gay, if he had seen the St. Patrick's Day parade. Harold replied that he didn't need to see any parade because he was a part of the parade of life. That's just my point. We discover the truly incredible from the inside; by going beyond the drama until the everyday becomes dramatic. Then we can understand what G.K. Chesterton meant when he said the world will never starve for want of wonders but only for want of wonder.

❊ Romero: The Fate of the Seed

JANE SAMMON

ON MARCH 24, 1980, Oscar Romero, the Archbishop of El Salvador, was assassinated while saying Mass. That night, when we heard the news, Marj Humphrey and I recalled our time in Latin America. Our sorrow is tempered by a moment of grace spent in El Salvador in the presence of this courageous servant of the Church.

March 10, 1979. A sultry day in San Miguel. Only ten in the morning and already perspiration dripped freely even from a people accustomed to sub-tropical heat.

The bus ride down from the capital proved a pleasant mix of fiesta and pilgrimage. The documents from the Latin American bishops' meeting in Puebla would be symbolically deposited in San Miguel at the feet of the Virgin of Peace, Patroness of El Salvador. The faithful would come by the bus loads to San Miguel to watch and to pray—hungry for something much more than symbols and ceremonies.

There was an acute sense of celebration in this cathedral town. Perhaps the joy of the occasion could momentarily vanquish the images of the uniformed gun-carriers—reminders of the perpetual state of siege in El Salvador. Eerie to be in that country, with lush green terrain, reminiscent of Ireland. Hauntingly beautiful El Salvador; desperately impoverished El Salvador.

We walked toward the Cathedral with a mixture of anticipation and curiosity. At this point in our travels we were well aware that the Church in Latin America was persecuted, and even within its own ranks all would not share the vision of Puebla.

Upon our arrival not a single seat was left. The dense crowd fanned itself languidly. We remained standing at the back of the church, crowded together with the poor—workers and peasants—bodies wearied from years of oppression. How long had they journeyed to San Miguel? What were their expectations of the Virgin of Peace?

We stood very close to an open side altar where we would witness a spectacle peculiar to North American eyes. In the midst of this vast congregation, the priests and bishops of El Salvador donned themselves in the ancient robes of the Church. Among some of these celebrants

276

there was a jubilant quality accompanied by laughter and the exchange of pleasantries. For others, it was as if a burdensome task had been given them; as if robing in vestments of lead while nervously eyeing the multitudes before them.

A strange anxiety built up within me transforming this scene into Greek tragedy, for even at this moment of homage I felt the tension in this Cathedral could be cut with a knife—or killed with a gun. I had to shake myself free of this thought, to return to the atmosphere of joy and solemnity. Without my realizing it, the procession had begun and the white-clad line passed slowly by, curving left and up toward the front of the Cathedral. The dim murmuring in the church crescendoed into thunderous applause. We knew, intuitively, that Archbishop Romero was passing with the other celebrants. I strained to catch a glimpse of him—an unassuming figure humbly acknowledging the tumultuous adulation. I recalled him in another context—a crowded meeting room at Puebla, when believers and non-believers alike rose to their feet in tribute to his courage. As the Mass began, I spotted a man from our bus in the back of the Church hawking pictures of the Archbishop—people from all sides of the immediate area were digging into pockets and purses, a few coins in exchange for a precious memento.

The Mass was now more than half over; the Kiss of Peace was about to be offered. This scene, more than any other, remains firmly rooted in my memory. The dreadful reality of the divided Church was pathetically played out in this gesture of a Peace that surpasses all human understanding. Upon the altar in San Miguel the Bishops of El Salvador greeted each other in robot-like rotation. Finally, the Archbishop approached Arturo Rivera, the one bishop known to have been his most faithful supporter. With tender poignancy they fell, as if exhausted, into each others arms, a mutual embrace of fidelity and affection.

The organ struck a recessional chord; the Puebla Documents had been deposited; this time the excitement of the crowd burst into uncontrollable frenzy. I felt myself unwillingly swept out the doors and onto the top step of the Cathedral. A large group of passersby mobbed the entrance, swelling the ranks of those pouring out of the Church. For a moment I was afraid; the press of the crowd crushed me from all sides. I felt a sandal slip from my foot. "*Viva Monseñor Romero!*" cried a lone voice. "*Que viva!*" replied the chorus. Other shouts of solidarity pelted the motionless air of San Miguel. The Archbishop emerged from the darkened interior into the brightness of the early afternoon. I wondered if he would be crushed by this kaleidoscopic mob. Hands, seemingly detached from bodies, thrust forward to touch him, pat him, to assure him. With remarkable serenity the shepherd walked amidst his flock, offering back their Kiss of Peace. In a few moments I could see him no more—he seemed to have been swallowed up, consumed by this passionate sea of humanity.

We were back on the bus, journeying toward the capital. As we neared the city, the droning of military helicopters precipitated a reflection on the meaning of peace in El Salvador. When we finally arrived in San Salvador, my reverie was shattered by a different kind of frenzy—a woman, out of breath from running, unable to conceal her fear, paused long enough to warn us: "Get off the streets, the Guardia are shooting the people." The morning scene in sunny San Miguel flashed quickly through my mind—the humble shepherd among his flock.

I see him still, March 24, 1980, and recall the words of the psalmist: "The just man is an everlasting remembrance."

———————————————————————— JANUARY 1978–NOVEMBER 1980

❁ **On Pilgrimage**

DOROTHY DAY

EDS. NOTE: *The following are excerpts from Dorothy's final columns.*

I REJOICE TO SEE the young people thinking of the Works of Mercy as a truly revolutionary, but nonviolent program. The spiritual and corporal certainly go together, and often involve suffering. To oppose the nuclear buildup has led to the imprisonment this last month of two of our workers, Robert Ellsberg and Brian Terrell, in Rocky Flats, Colorado— and solitary confinement is suffering indeed, and added to that, a hunger strike is certainly dying to self.

Meanwhile, I am confined in another way by weakness and age, but can truly pray with fervor for those on active duty, and sternly suppress my envy at the activities of our young and valiant workers.

*

45th Anniversary dinner on May 1st at Maryhouse! The party was a great success. All the dining-room tables were set up in the auditorium. Folks from St. Joseph House, many from the farm at Tivoli, and old friends came.

It is so good to be eating downstairs again regularly at night. Good, too, to have men and women, so young and strong, helping us. They

hold each other up when tense moments occur. Women fight as well
as men!

The dining room at Maryhouse is pleasant as a sitting room too, with
its red, calico curtains, women sewing or playing solitaire, and one
woman reading Scripture.

*

Went to the Friday night meeting—Fr. George Anderson, S.J., prison
chaplain, spoke. I recall prisons I have been in. Ugly, in some ways, but
rewarding in others. A deepening understanding of the poor.

Frank, with the help of Lee LeCuyer, has finished making out the
annual report on our finances. He says we gave out more than we took
in this past year. Our voluntary poverty enriches us daily. In friendships, too.

*

When the young complain, I remember my mother used to say, "But
you have youth!" I still complain, and, as I write this, I remember Hans
Tunnesen, our seaman cook at the farm, who used to say, after his
game of cards after supper, and wanting to go to bed—"Shall we go to
the chapel and 'complain'?" meaning "say compline," our evening
prayer.

June 1978

A BRIGHT, SUNNY, cold morning. Last night I saw a film about Harlem
on television, showing some of the beautiful architecture there, like
ours here on Third Street. The sun is creeping down the buildings
across the street. Elaborate carvings on the frames around the windows,
different on each floor. I sit in my window often, looking at them and
watching neighbors on the street. On First Street, opposite St. Joseph
House, there is an abandoned corner tenement building from which
the carvings of angels and flowers have been carefully removed.

*

I read my morning Psalms in the Anglican prayer book and hymnal
which Ann Perkins gave me—it is so much easier to find one's way
around in. The words "ordinary time" in our own prayer book put me
in a state of confusion and irritation. To me, no times are "ordinary."

*

"Happy the people the Lord has chosen for His own." The Jews are
indeed God's chosen, and *God does not change.* I read a long interview
with Chaim Potok. My heart warms to him. His books are all beautiful,

bringing to my mind the high esteem in which Jewish men hold their wives, mothers of their households.

To have lived through the era of Father Coughlin is indeed to have seen something of the persecution of God's chosen. Msgr. Edward Lodge Curran, the Brooklyn anti-Semite, wanted to buy *The Catholic Worker* for $2,000. Naturally, we refused. To Fr. Coughlin's credit, he did, with the contributions of his immense following, build a great number of rural churches in the deep South, which I came across on my speaking trips around the country. But his talk of international Jewish bankers stirred up a wave of anti-Semitism.

*

Read some of *The Golden Notebooks* by Doris Lessing. She seems to make a religion of sex. Sex is, of course, fundamental, but religion transfigures it. Dostoevsky's "Love in practice is a harsh and dreadful thing compared to love in dreams," is a half-truth. Or rather, love is a cross—transfiguration a necessity.

*

The house is cold this morning. Sometimes the water is hot enough for an immediate hot drink, but nothing works this morning. St. Therese of Lisieux said there was nothing she suffered so much as *cold,* and since then Carmelite convents have been heated in winter.

*

There has been much discussion about closing the farm at Tivoli. The three houses there make squatters a problem. John Filliger, our farmer since the 1936 seamen's strike, and George Collins, our saintly hermit and pot washer since he came from jail after World War II, have been with us for many years. We must pray to St. Therese—"All things work for good to those who love God." Reading old diaries, I find the same unrest as the last year I was at the farm. Our human condition—our discontent. "Now is the winter of our discontent."

*

Fr. John J. Hugo used to remind us that "He who says he has done enough has already perished . . ." and "You love God as much as the one you love the least." I recall his words often. He has been a great influence on the lives of our Catholic Workers.

October–November 1978

WOKE UP THIS morning with these lines haunting me: "Joyous I lay waste the day." "Let all those that seek Thee be glad in Thee, and let such as love Thy salvation, say always, the Lord be praised."

This afternoon I listened to "Tosca" on the radio.

*

Beautiful cards are sent in with donations. One came from an Eskimo Cooperative in Canada. I have been keeping the card as a book mark in my Bible. "The world will be saved by beauty," as Dostoevsky wrote.

*

We had hard, baked potatoes for supper, and cabbage overspiced. I'm in favor of becoming a vegetarian only if the vegetables are cooked right. (What a hard job cooking is here! But the human warmth in the dining room covers up a multitude of sins.)

Another food grievance: onions chopped up in a fruit salad, plus spices and herbs! A sacrilege—to treat foods in this way. Food should be treated with respect, since Our Lord left Himself to us in the guise of food. His disciples knew Him in the breaking of the bread.

*

I woke up this morning with a tune running through my head—"He has the whole world in His Hands. He has the whole wide world in His Hands." So why worry? Why lament? "Rejoice," the psalmist writes, "and again I say, rejoice."

February 1979

THE LITTLE GINKGO tree, that was brought to me from Avon, Ohio some years ago by Dorothy Gauchat's son, David, is growing and budding in a gallon can in the office. A sign of hope, of perseverance. Across the street, a lone tree, now covered with green leaves, reaches to the third floor of the apartment house.

*

My godchild, Jean Kennedy, came to hear Frank Sheed speak at our Friday night meeting. She brought a beautiful afghan that is hanging over my rocking chair, and also a delicious fruit salad. I ate it all! How sensual I am. A glutton. Was it St. Catherine of Siena or St. Angela Foligno who wanted to tie a baked chicken around her neck and run through the streets, shouting, "I am a glutton!"

May 1979

I WOKE AT SEVEN this morning, thinking of the thousands converging on Washington, D.C. to protest nuclear weapons and nuclear energy. A carload left from here last evening.

My job is prayer—sometimes I feel it is like a prayer-wheel, mechanical.

"His strength is as the strength of ten, because his heart is pure." Pure in this case means single-minded. Our Catholic Worker family has this single-mindedness. "It all goes together." Our program.

My mind goes back to the first time I met Peter Maurin and he began "indoctrinating" me with his simple program: 1) round-table discussions for clarification of thought; 2) houses of hospitality where the works of mercy, corporal and spiritual, can be practiced and taught; 3) farming communes, which will lead to decentralization of our capitalist economy.

We have tried to stick to Peter's program, but sometimes I got myself involved in labor conflicts such as strikes in industry, and Peter would say sadly, "Strikes don't strike me."

And as to "organizing," he would point out that *self*-organization is the beginning of a healthy society. "Be what you want the other fellow to be," was one of his slogans. He liked slogans, because in a few simple words they "made a point."

June 1979

WOKE UP REMEMBERING that we go to press soon with our minuscule (compared to the *New York Times*) eight-page paper, and I think my usual wandering thoughts of what I could write about myself, as a woman born in 1897, a woman of long life, of varied experiences.

*

"Whose face is on this coin?" Jesus asked. "Render to Caesar the things that are Caesar's, and to God the things that are God's." "The less you have of Caesar's, the less you have to render to Caesar." The New Testament and the words of Jesus—the Sermon on the Mount—the foundation of our work—voluntary poverty and manual labor. "Sowing and reaping." "Sow sparingly and you will reap sparingly."

*

Bright and sunny. I slept hard until eight a.m. Woke to symphonies and a pleasant sense of a good day yesterday, a celebration of Catholic Worker beginnings. There are beautiful flowers (an iris and two roses) on my television set, and a plastic swan, given to me by one of the women in the house, which reminds me of Wagner's "Lohengrin."

June 1980

PROGRAM ON TELEVISION on the "right" to suicide—"Rational Suicide"! When a son of a friend of ours took his own life years ago, I asked the

Spanish priest at Our Lady of Guadalupe Church on 14th St., "Did he die in mortal sin?" I was remembering Kirilov in *The Possessed* by Dostoevsky. The priest said, "There is no time with God, and all the prayers and Masses said for him after his death will have given him that moment of turning to God in penitence."

*

Watched a documentary on China on television—one of the oldest civilizations—sixth century B.C.—now open for the first time in twenty-five years. Many years ago, having read, in *Time* magazine, news about Mao Tse-Tung and the Chinese Revolution, my enthusiasm caused me to announce that, for a Friday meeting at Chrystie Street for which we had no speaker, I'd talk about China. Chinese from all over the city, Columbia University, and Chinatown, came to hear me, much to my embarrassment.

July–August 1980

THE MORNING GLORIES are up to the third floor of Maryhouse. I can see them grow each day!

*

We made pilgrimages when we lived on Mott Street—one to the Mother Cabrini shrine way up on the West Side. We started at midnight from Mott Street and got to 115th Street at 6:00 a.m. Many of the Italian women walked barefoot or in stocking feet. Those were the days when we had to fast from midnight until after Communion. No stopping for a cup of coffee along the way!

*

I used to fill my prayer books (my Little Office of the Blessed Virgin Mary and a thirty-day prayer to the Blessed Mother) with the names of those I prayed for, "of all who bothered me," someone in our family said. Once, Jane O'Connell erased all the names.

A TV program exploring the galaxies made me think of the astronauts who walked on the moon, and my getting a recognition from the Pope with one of them. We were chosen to receive Communion from Pope Paul VI in St. Peter's in Rome.

*

I walked a little in the hall today, getting my "sealegs" under me—a family saying. My mother's forebears in Marlboro and Poughkeepsie were whalers.

*

Took a little tour around Maryhouse. It is much bigger than I remembered it!

*

My sister Della used to quote, "Had I foreseen what was to befall me, I would have rued the day." I do miss traveling as I used to—to all our houses, by bus. You feel you are really seeing the country, as you speed along the highway, over plain and mountain.

*

My sister-in-law, Tessa's sister, Tina de Aragon, is in St. Rose's Home. She will still be close to us all there, where so many of our Catholic Workers—at least eight—are employed part or full-time. It is a home for cancer patients, started by Nathaniel Hawthorne's daughter Rose in her own apartment, when she took in a neighbor who was dying. Like so many small projects, it grew miraculously (there are now homes in several other cities), and it seems to be a place where people are cared for and helped to die with dignity and love. I was reading Rose Hawthorne's book about their beginnings, *Sorrow Built a Bridge*, when I met Peter Maurin. And now Tina is there. We continually are reminded of Tina at every Mass we have in Maryhouse, because the beautiful statue of the Madonna, which she carved for us out of *lignum vitae*, faces us from behind the altar.

October–November 1980

(Dorothy Day died at the age of 83 in her room at Maryhouse on November 29, 1980.)

DECEMBER 1980

❃ Dorothy Day: Illuminating Dark Times

PAT JORDAN

I FIRST MET Dorothy in the change of seasons. It was in 1968. She was sitting in the empty house on First Street, awaiting a delivery for the contractor. (Renovations of the "new house" were far from complete, and encountering the usual delays.) All Worker activities were still being carried out at 175 Chrystie Street, and Dorothy, while in New York, lived in one of the Worker's rented apartments on Kenmare Street. (The new First Street house was to seem a palace.)

Dorothy was seventy at that time, but her energy, wit, and insight were clearly unimpaired. Over the next twelve years there would be an interplay between these powers and a growing intimation of finality, between her uncanny strength and remarkable charm, and sheer human entropy. This dialectic fluctuated like the very change of seasons in Fall: bounteously full of light, warmth and bursts of energy, yet graphically, irrevocably slouching to the final dropping of the leaves one cold November evening.

One of my first impressions of Dorothy was that she couldn't sit still. She had nervous, active hands (hands of a formerly chronic smoker), hands used to work and enhanced by it. I shall never forget seeing her at work at her typewriter. Intense concentration. Intense silence. Then bang! Her hands swooped down, her fingers like lightning cracking out a sentence, perhaps a whole paragraph. Slam, the carriage, slam again. Then stop. Perfect concentration, as deep as silence. Then, crack again.

Those twelve years were ones of endless travel for Dorothy. As she said, she wanted to wear out, not rust out. She hit every continent except South America, and crossed this country a half-dozen times. Movement was a source of thought and action for her. It was the basis of her freedom, and also her gift to those of us who stayed at home. For her returns and her stories renewed us all. We awaited her comings and would escape to her room to talk for hours. Often entrapped when we could "stay but a minute," we were regaled with events and people, taught lessons in literature, instructed on the season and locale of a particular flower, introduced to a figure in radical history, given a book, an article, a story to cover.

Dorothy thought of trips in terms of space and peanut butter sandwiches. She once wrote Kathleen and me, while we were in the midst of a long bus journey, "Over the years I found those bus trips not just hardships—they were certainly that during WWII days—but times in the desert—alone, on my way, tired from speaking, incapable of anything, but still resting in the hands of the Lord—being renewed, in a way. Rest your eyes from reading, too. Look into the distances, and wait for the Lord."

But all was not waiting. While preparing to attend the funeral of Jenny Moore in the fall of 1973 at the National Cathedral, she instructed me to bring along one peanut butter sandwich apiece—"Washington is a one-peanut-butter-sandwich trip." Distances were quickly gauged in this measure. That trip to Washington proved to be a perilous intimation. The bus broke down in Maryland, and Dorothy's heart, anticipating the crowds and pressing at the Cathedral, went into a flutter. We had to rush out of the bus to escape the smoke that filled it, and Dorothy gasped for breath on the side of the highway. She gradually recovered, some semblance of color returning to her face. Another Greyhound eventually picked us up, and we arrived in Washington, but late.

Every public appearance from that time on took a toll on Dorothy. Any speech might cause her weeks of anxiety; writing an appeal was going through the wringer. I think this was so because of her elemental shyness and her almost Victorian modesty. (As Dorothy said, writing about oneself was like going to confession.) Once when some of us went to hear Joan Baez in concert at the Fillmore East, Dorothy was approached during the intermission and invited backstage to meet the singer. Dorothy blushed and told the intermediary that no, she could not come; she wouldn't think of putting Joan Baez through a meeting when the young woman must be exhausted from her beautiful singing. (Years later they did meet and correspond.) Even Dorothy's laughter, which could punctuate her conversations and talks like a refrain, was tempered in modesty. It was young and enchanting, rather like the giggle of a young girl than the deep laughter of the accomplished. There was in her speeches, as Peguy wrote of Bernard Lazure's, "a sort of goodness perfectly awake and perfectly aware and incredibly deep with an eternal strength, with an eternal gentleness."

Looking at back issues of the paper during the late sixties and early seventies, I am struck with Dorothy's consistency. There is always something in her writings about the struggle of the farm workers under Cesar Chavez, about the primacy of the spiritual, about prisoners like Martin Sostre and the Berrigans. She repeatedly contrasts the works of mercy with those of war, counsels that to do the works of mercy and resist war we must repair to the spiritual weapons and a disciplined spiritual life. She had learned, sorrowfully, that in the painful imprisonments of many young Workers during the Vietnam period, ill-grounded in the spiritual realm, came the utter collapse of their selves in prison. (She realized she bore a responsibility for this, and, in general the Worker must be faulted for its failure to support those who "did their time alone.")

Yet, Dorothy did try to instruct the young. When several of us ill-advisedly published a lead article condoning violence to preserve a particular revolution (an inconsistency later shrewdly lamented by Gordon Zahn in a *Commonweal* article on the Catholic Left's flirting with violence), she did not dogmatize. She merely wrote in her own "On. Pilgrimage": "These are hard questions, indeed. I feel that these young men have grown in honesty and seriousness. They have begun to see what serious study lies ahead (for those who wish to fashion a nonviolent revolution)." Later Dorothy would write me, on one of her terse, newsy postcards: "Not enough praying around here, so keep us in your prayers.

X and X are so pessimistic about nonviolence. They have all the Panther literature and hunger for violence. I am sad. D.D."

When these burdens and the bedlam of the house and farm would overwhelm her, Dorothy would weep, weep over the hardness of her own heart, weep and wonder whether the whole thing was worth it. When she got too highhanded at First St. Dorothy would flee remorsefully to Tivoli. She wrote from there, in the Fall of 1972: "I am unnerved. I found myself weeping with weakness. Please don't let yourself get into this state." And in the paper: "I am here at Tivoli, where I am remaining now, not only because of a cold affecting my throat which is hard to shake off, but also to escape some of the demands of visitors, telephone, hospitality, problems, overcrowding, noise, etc., which make up our life at First St." At those times Dorothy was "burdened with an eternal responsibility" (Peguy). Yet once, finding her in such a state ("unhinged," as Dorothy herself would put it), Kathleen and I spontaneously offered her sympathy. Instantly Dorothy pulled herself up through her tears, "Don't pity me," she stated: quietly, firmly, with a stunning transcendence.

There were some particularly virulent attacks on Dorothy and the Worker at this period, from a man who probably idealized it too much. Should this man be outside the house, and thrust one of his printed "exposes" at Dorothy when she was returning from Mass or a trip, she would get inside and nearly collapse. She took to heart what he wrote, and prayed for him. But she also felt a sincere gratitude toward him; as she said, he wasn't as hard on us as he might have been.

While she was speaking and traveling widely these years (and, with her seventy-fifth birthday, was accorded a certain world-wide acclaim), Dorothy could be terribly self-deprecating. She would repeatedly quote the prayer of St. Ephraim and criticize herself for her sloth. "We at the Catholic Worker," she would say, "merely muddle through." On the other hand, her spiritual advice was as poignant as ever, and she was preparing for other battles.

Stanley Vishnewski once replied when asked on a television interview to describe Dorothy's approach to prayer: "Dorothy, like the Pope, is in favor of prayer!" The Catholic Worker "positions" likewise state that the Worker is trying to live by the teachings of the Gospel, whether explicit or implied, in every aspect of life and society. Dorothy had the most remarkable, organic sense of the Gospels I have ever encountered. They permeated her. Indeed, she intuited them and somehow lived in them as a "rule of life." "I once had a chance to visit the Holy Land," she told Kathleen and me. "It was a choice between the Holy Land and visiting Danilo Dolci. So I went and visited Dolci, at the bottom there with the poor." When faced with a political question, as in the tax case of 1972, she responded from the Gospels. When presented with a personal quandary, she would respond from the same dayspring.

Yet, unlike most of us, Dorothy never spoke with platitudes. In these matters, what she said always rang true. "My gift," she said more than once, with no trace of self-pride, but with the honesty of having been chosen a vehicle of grace, "has been to be able to speak of these things others can't."

To me, Dorothy's life was of a piece. She was imbued with a most real sense of sacramentality, whether in offering to do the dishes and sweep the floor in later years on Staten Island, or planting radishes on Tamar's birthday, even if it meant asking Doris Nielsen to dig through the March snow. She put the elements together. "There was a man," she wrote in May 1974, "who each year on the feast of the Incarnation, went out and knelt down and kissed the earth because Christ had taken on our humanity. Our food, our drink, our furniture, the houses we inhabit, the coffin which we are buried in (once a tree), all come from good earth, made holy by Christ putting on our human flesh." She introduced us to Edmund Wilson's remarkable articles on the imagery of *Dr. Zhivago*, filled with references to the Resurrection. And she constantly repeated Julian of Norwich's wisdom when we would be overcome by tragedy or the apocalyptic: "The worst has already happened and been repaired." Her advice to the violence of the houses: "Pray and endure." To loss of friendship and betrayal there was St. Paul's "Nothing can separate us from the love of Christ." And to our own seeking of a vocation, Dostoevsky's "Beauty will save the world."

But I must touch on two events which symbolize Dorothy during my years at the Catholic Worker: the tax case of 1972 and the efforts to establish Maryhouse, 1973–75.

In January, 1972, the Worker received notice from the Internal Revenue Service that it was being assessed nearly $300,000 in fines and penalties for unpaid income tax during the previous six years. There was nothing to do but fight the case. (The Catholic Worker pays no wages, and all the money goes for the service of the poor and the publication of the paper.) But as in all of life's important perils, the crux was how. Over the next six months, with the expert advice of John Coster, our lawyer, and Ruth Collins, our faithful real estate advisor, and in countless discussions with the members of the CW household, Dorothy came to a sound and clarified position. As she wrote in the May, 1972, *Catholic Worker:* "It is not only that we must follow our conscience in opposing the government in war. We believe that the government has no right to legislate as to who can or who are to perform the works of mercy."

The case, of course, had its complications, and this is not the time to write of them. But for a while it looked as if everything would be confiscated, the work completely stopped. "I beg the prayers of all our readers, whether or not they are sympathetic to us. I'm sure that many will think me a fool, indeed, for jeopardizing the work on behalf of this principle." The daily press eventually picked up the story, and with a number of well-publicized editorials in several influential papers declaring the government to be senseless and obscurantist, both the IRS and the Justice Department, which were bringing the case, wanted to back out. In a meeting at John Coster's office on June 26th that year, Dorothy and a number from St. Joseph House met with William Hunter, an Assistant Attorney General. Dorothy was as bright and sharp as a winter's morning. She wrote later of the meeting: "I think Mr. Hunter shared with us the conviction that you could not kill an idea, and that we would continue to express ourselves and try to live the Catholic Worker positions as best we could no matter what steps were taken against us by the government. To resist and to survive.

"Yes, we would survive, I thought to myself, even if the paper were eventually suppressed and we had to turn to leafleting." Pray and endure; she had said it again. If the government closed the house and farm, the young people could find part-time jobs. We'd rent apartments, take people in, begin all over again. There was no stopping this work, no stopping her.

On several occasions she looked Mr. Hunter straight in the eye. "The point of the matter is this," she said (a code that, whenever she used it, caused one to drop everything, and listen): "We are paying for war if we pay the tax. It is so important for us to hold to our stand even if you [the government] lower the level [boom]. We have an absolute faith that we will keep going even if we lose everything. Our principle is what we are living for."

The government backed out of the case the following month, acknowledging the religious principles and charitable work of the Catholic Worker. But Dorothy pointed out that the battle was not over, and that the fray would likely be renewed, that the calm was but an interlude.

Buber has written, "To be old is a glorious thing when one has not unlearned what it means to begin." That Dorothy bore fruit even in her old age is most evident perhaps in the establishment of Maryhouse. As soon as the tax case was resolved, she was directing that we must begin looking for apartments on the block for homeless women. By May, 1973, she wrote, "We are daily tormented by the need for a women's shelter." This need, and Anne Fraser's articles on the matter in *The Catholic Worker*, brought a remarkable response. In the next issue Dorothy wrote that she was making "a resolution on my part to start work at once to find a home for them. A letter from a Trappist abbot containing a down payment for a house confirmed my decision." Soon, she and Ruth Collins were out pounding the sidewalks of the Lower East Side. And with the July 1973 issue, in the midst of a discussion on prayer, she disclosed that on St. Benedict's Day two wonderful things had happened—a location had been found for the women's house in the former Third Street Music School settlement house, and a small group of contemplative Maryknoll sisters had moved into the neighbor-hood.

The renovations and delays to order and license Maryhouse far out-stripped anyone's anticipations. Mother Teresa visited and was appalled that the building could not be immediately occupied. A year and a half later Dorothy was still writing. "Weeks pass and the Building Department of the gigantic City of New York has not found time to put an O.K. on the plans. Patience, patience. I often reflect that the word itself means suffering." The house was finally opened, almost surreptitiously, in 1975.

Dorothy spent the winter of 1974–75 at the beach house on Staten Island. She threatened to write her "true autobiography" there, and no doubt we shall now have revelations from others about her life that for tact she had never written for publication. " 'Least said, sooner mended,' my mother used to say." She wrote us in August: "My winter's rest has done me much good. People treat me as though I had returned from the grave!!!"

In my perception, the next years of decline proved a grace for the Catholic Worker. Into the vacuum of her waning leadership stepped a variety of dedicated people. She had anticipated as much when she had written in May 1973: "I may be held responsible for what goes in the paper, but I am a member of an unincorporated association of the Catholic Worker, made up of a very active group of young people. Whatever happened to me, I could count on them to carry on Peter's program. They would be a group amongst whom always the one would be looked to as leader who works the hardest at 'being what you would have the other fellow be,' who takes responsibility and perseveres, does not grow weary, rejoices in tribulations, who knows how 'when there is no love to put love and so find love' (St. John of the Cross)—and so the work would go on."

She told Kathleen and me in 1975: "I think of the Catholic Worker as just beginning." And she spoke of her conviction that her own voca-tion to the Catholic Worker was an absolute necessity for herself. She looked us in the eye, that truthful, pure, deep-piercing gaze, and said that following her prayer at the Shrine of the Immaculate Conception in 1932 and her meeting with Peter Maurin: "I just knew. I never doubted it once." The Catholic Worker community was "an absolute necessity" for her because it was the place, and perhaps the only place, where her particular gifts could bloom. Hannah Arendt has written that such a community, a community of the oppressed and the poor, the pariahs, "can breed a kindliness and sheer goodness of which human beings are scarcely capable. Frequently, it is also the source of a vitality, a joy in the simple fact of being alive, rather suggesting that life comes fully into its own among those who are, in worldly terms, the insulted and injured." In her bond with those who came and would come,

Dorothy wrote before Maryhouse opened: "They stay until they die, and then, too, we find that spot of earth they still need, and bury them. How tiny a plot of earth does a woman need!"

Even in the darkest of times, Hannah Arendt has written, "we have the right to expect some illumination." This comes less from theories and concepts than from the light engendered by some men and women who "in their lives and their works, will kindle under almost all circumstances and shed over the time span that was given them on earth" a light in dark times. Several weeks after Dorothy's death, our five-year-old daughter Hannah had a rather remarkable dream. In it she saw Dorothy contained in a box. Then, the dream proceeded, "She broke out, just like Jesus."

Now the dialectic is finished, the leaf-seed has fallen into the ground. "Such friendships the Lord has sent us in this life," she wrote us one time at parting. "God is good. We can't thank Him enough. Thank you. Thank you, Lord, for everything, but friendships especially. We are not alone."

DECEMBER 1980

❈ A Measure of Light

DANIEL BERRIGAN

I THINK OF Dorothy Day first of all as a teacher. This was the service she did me and many others. As seminarians and young priests, first in our seed beds, then set loose in the world, we were little more than lapsarian sprouts: ignorant, eager, and innocent beyond belief. That world of the fifties was mobilized for yet another war; we went toward the bristling phalanx as though its horrid instruments were designed to plow fields instead of mutilate limbs. Alas, know it or not, the main business of that world was the forging of swords; plowshares, where they turned the earth at all, were part of something called a "war effort," a horrid euphemism. They were, in fact, in service to the Sons of the Sword, readying the earth for its sowing of dragons' teeth and its harvest of the armed and arrogant.

Even this moral grotesquerie was not all. The world was seizing on the biblical image for its own uses, turning it on its head. Plowshares were not only secondary to the main enterprise; they were being deliberately converted to uses of death, broken, melted down, beaten into swords. A world of at least relative right order was flipping its mind.

Dorothy was born in a different world; from the point of view of metaphor and methods, almost a different planet. It was a world unconvulsed with world wide war. She was to live on and die in a world in which two universal wars set the swords whirling in an ever wider and bloodier arc. With more to follow.

The great wars wrought yet another horror, less palpably deadly, spiritually more so. They ravaged the wisdom of the heart, uprooted it, burned it like a debris. Up in smoke went a vision which formerly, if it had not prevailed, at least here and there turned lives around. Thou shall not kill. Love your enemies. Walk a further mile. By 1945 the words, declared irrelevant (which, indeed, they were), passé, apolitical, visionary, not for real, judgmental, harsh, sabbatarian but hardly hebdomadal, etcetera, etcetera—they all but vanished on the wind. The Mount of the Sermon, and the Sermon itself, had been, so to speak, nuked out of existence.

It was this loss of ours, this immeasurable tragedy, this lost wholeness, which the teaching of Dorothy restored, healed in measure.

It is important to me to remember that she, too, for many years, was bereft of the sacred hegemony; she tasted our endemic illness, whose modern name is alienation, anxiety, dread, sense of being askew, off center, in a void. She was a modern being—all but incurably so. No matter that the world of her youth (and of ours, too) came on strong, a new jargon, new credentials and claims: "a new sensibility," "the unity of technique and self-understanding." It was all a great lie. The modern world was a void. She was born in it, grew to adulthood breathing its fetid air. Then she was lifted out of the pit, by an act of God.

How closely in this she resembled Thomas Merton, whose gifts in so many respects dovetailed with her own; especially, it occurs to me, that gift of speaking the truth in a tone, nuance, coloration which penetrates, conveys hope.

To be ill is no vocation; to be healed is a glory beyond measure. Dorothy's wisdom, in the Pauline sense, was her passage from the illness named sin, to grace. This was the story she had to tell; implicitly, as in her monthly column in *The Catholic Worker*, "On Pilgrimage": explicitly also, as in her autobiography. She simply recounted her life; where she had come from (a child of a family, an elderly woman on a night-long Greyhound bus)—in a deeper sense, where she had been led; with wry wit, concretely, personally, drawing her ethic from long travail, from the taste of death which anointed her tongue at birth, a bitter aloe, and lingered on in age; a warning.

She had gained a wisdom which her early life had impelled her to ignore or despise; grace brought it passionately to the fore, until it transfigured her face. Let me not call that wisdom something so jejune as "How to live," as though life's secret lay in the pages of a mechanic's handbook, the darling and dream of Americans. And yet her wisdom played tantalizingly along the line of that "life." Not a "how to" (nor an interior sense of, symbols of, esteem for, celebration of, the price of—life itself.

It was a complex rhythm, and her elegant and eloquent hands played all its stops and starts.

There was a tragic undertone, too. She was drawn out of hedonism and moral bewilderment, merely to join America on a better footing. Her conversion does not read: religious at last, safe at last, selfish at last. If it was granted her at long last, to taste life, to taste the Author of life on her tongue; and if that taste cleansed her of the ashes and aloes of death, she understood that her momentous gift had changed nothing of the world around her. She was to live on in America, where life was cheap as dirt, and death fitted the scene like a greased glove. As did religion, commonly understood and practiced.

She entered a church that, by and large, for reasons too complex to dwell on here, had made its peace with war. It was a church which needed her almost as desperately, one is tempted to say, as she longed for the faith. How were the humiliation and moral splendor of Christ, the cry of desolation, the transfigured world of Easter, to be manifest in such a world, short of resistance against mass murder? Her question went to the heart of things; the writing, the jailing, the, so-to-speak, detoxifying of academics, the spurning (but always gently) of camp followers and the curious, and much more of task and sorrow and burden—and then her death; these raised the question, again and again.

She could offer, she would say, only the glimmering of an answer, or a measure of light on the question. And that was enough. If even one, or a few, would live their lives in the eye of consequence, would take the punishment and heat, would live as though death had no dominion—ah, then what might not be expected?

Hers was the struggle the ancient Easter hymn recounts: *Mors et vita duello conflizere mirando.* (Life and death are locked in mortal struggle.) The words and music might have been the swan song of her ascension, as they had been the overture of her surrender to Christ, her characteristic and crowning chord.

It was never a struggle whose outcome was in question, a gnostic struggle of titanic equals. The hymn ends, as her life among us ends, with a cry for liberation which is the very evangel of liberation achieved: *Tu nobis Victor Rex miserere,* (Lord, victorious One, be merciful to us).

PART VII

The Journey Continues
1981 —

❊ Justice and Charity

THE AIM OF THE Catholic Worker movement is to realize in the individual and in society the expressed and implied teachings of Christ. We see the Sermon on the Mount and the call to solidarity with the poor at the heart of these teachings. Therefore, we must look at the world to see whether we already have a social order that reflects the justice and charity of Christ.

When we examine the society in which we live, we find that it is not in accord with justice and charity:

—The maldistribution of wealth is widespread; the fact that there are hungry and homeless people in the midst of plenty is unjust. Rich and poor suffer increasingly from isolation, madness, and growing individual violence, side by side with a governmental emphasis on implements of war instead of on human well-being.

—The rapid rise of technology, without a fitting development of morality, emphasizes progress based on profit rather than human needs. The triumvirate of military, business, and scientific priorities overwhelms the political process. "Democracy" is reduced to a choice between "brand names" in products and politicians. Bureaucratic structures make accountability, and therefore political change, close to impossible. As a result there is no forum in which to express, effectively, different views of the events shaping our life. The individual suffers as much from these transformations as does the whole social order.

—On a scale unknown to previous generations, the poor throughout the world are systematically robbed of the goods necessary to life. Though we realize the United States is not the sole perpetrator of such immoral conduct, we are North Americans and must first acknowledge our own country's culpability. We deplore U.S. imperialism in its various expressions. Multinational corporations, economic "aid," military intervention, and so forth, have led to the disintegration of communities and the destruction of indigenous cultures—blatant violations of justice and charity.

—The proliferation of nuclear power and weapons stands as a clear sign of the direction of our age. Both are a denial of the very right of people to life and, implicitly, a denial of God. There is a direct economic and moral connection between the arms race and destitution. In the words of Vatican II, "The arms race is an utterly treacherous trap for humanity, and one which injures the poor to an intolerable degree."

To achieve a just society we advocate a complete rejection of the present system and a nonviolent revolution to establish a social order in accord with Christian truth.

The Catholic Worker envisages a social order based on St. Thomas Aquinas' doctrine of the common good, in which the freedom and dignity of the person are fostered, and the good of each person is bound to the good of the whole in the service of God. A person's primary responsibility is to this common good, and not to a political entity.

—The Catholic Worker advocates a society that is decentralized—a society in direct contrast to the present bigness of the state, mass production in industry, in education, in health-care, and agriculture. Specifically, we look forward to a life closer to the land and are encouraged by efforts toward family farms, land trusts (rural and urban), hand-crafting, and appropriate technology that fosters a respect for human dignity and the environment. In towns and cities, too, decentralization can be promoted through worker ownership and management of small factories, through food, housing, and other kinds of cooperatives.

—We advocate a personalism in which we take on ourselves the responsibility for changing conditions, to the extent each of us is able. Houses of hospitality have been opened to feed the hungry, clothe the naked, and shelter the homeless. We strive to do this as a family, for hospitality is more than supplying food: it is opening ourselves to others. We see community as a potent remedy to the isolation and spiritual destitution prevalent today. We should not look to the impersonal welfare of the state to provide solutions or to do what we, as Christians, should be doing.

—The Catholic Worker sees voluntary poverty as an implication of Jesus' teaching on the unity of justice and charity. Through voluntary poverty we ask for the grace to abandon ourselves to the will of God, and we cast our lot in solidarity with those whose destitution is not a choice, but a condition of their oppression. We cannot participate in their struggles for justice if we do not recognize that we have both responsibilities and limits in our use of goods. "No one is justified in keeping for their exclusive use what they do not need, when others lack necessities" (Paul VI).

—We believe that the revolution to be pursued in ourselves and in society must be nonviolent and cannot be imposed from above. We condemn all war and the nuclear arms race; and we see oppression in any form as blasphemy against God, Who created all people in His image. When we fight tyranny and injustice, we must do so with the spiritual weapons of prayer and fasting and by noncooperation. Refusal to pay taxes, refusal to register for conscription, nonviolent strikes and boycotts and withdrawal from the system are all methods that can be employed in this struggle for justice.

We see this as an era filled with anxiety and confusion. In response, we, as a lay movement, seek our strength and direction in the beauty of regular prayer and liturgy, in studying and applying the traditions of Scripture and the teachings of the Church to the modern condition. We believe that success, as the world determines it, is not a fit criterion for judgment. We must be prepared and ready to face seeming failure. The most important thing is that we adhere to these beliefs, which transcend time, and for which we will be asked a personal accounting, not as to whether they succeeded (though we should hope that they do), but as to whether we remained true to them.

——————————————————————————————— JANUARY–FEBRUARY 1982

❁ In Search of God in Rikers Island

PETER RAPHAEL

RIKERS ISLAND is the largest penal institution in the United States. Located only six miles northeast of Times Square, New York City, it houses some 7,000 women, men, and teenagers in six different prison complexes. On an island less than a mile and a half square, most of these 7,000 are poor, approximately 6,600 are male, 60% are black, and 30% Spanish-speaking, at least half of whom understand no English. Many of the male prisoners are illiterate. Newspaper and magazine reporting are generally negative and tend to emphasize crime, violence, and recidivism. Here we present a view that contrasts with the usual.

—A man was sitting, motionless. "What's the use of praying? Where is God? I've been here six whole years! I've lost everything. They admit I'm a victim of circumstances, accused of homicide. The guy who could have told exactly what happened never showed up. Now I'm fifty-five and my life is not worth a damn. So why should I pray?"

—"You may not believe it, but some people are really glad to be here. You can get used to anything. You can get high in here. You can fight. Whatever. But I changed in prison. I was really bad outside: I did everything. My friend was stabbed in here and died. Now I'm searching for God and I hope to make it."

—"Can I ever be forgiven if I've killed somebody?"

—"I'm sixty-nine! I've had nine bullets pumped into me. I was tough all my life. Here, I have no more personal glory. But, I've found God. It took me sixty-nine years!"

—"God took away everything that was ever meaningful to me. Now, I have nothing left except Him."

—"Why so damn many religions and preachers? I'm not interested in any of them. Why am I here? They never helped me before. I'm here to rot and die in jail, that's why!"

To go to Rikers Island four times a week for a few hours may seem useless. Routine sometimes neutralizes our impressions, blurs the buildings, wipes out the realities with which we live. Prisons are really not meant to shine like castles. There is something here that seems camouflaged, something like the end of a tunnel that no one knows is there. The endless rooms and underground passageways are many times empty, often frightening, with almost cave-like proportions as they stretch eerily out of sight, unknown to the world above.

However, the public has a strange interest in this mysterious world of the prison. The media are forever pursuing prison tales as much to discover the hidden truths as to provide the reader or viewer with the sensational: overcrowded cells, human behavior while in confinement, mounting tensions and their motivations. The reader or viewer in search of statistics and documentation on this incredible melting pot of some six to seven thousand prisoners moving in and out of here day in and day out should look to the more competent reporter or producer, for I am neither a sociologist nor administrator. I am merely a priest, who, in the past two years, has come to devote some twenty hours a week to the growth of the Gospel among the men who live within the prison walls of Rikers Island.

To be here with the Gospel, to listen and to learn, to see and to feel with these men is to understand again the whole history of humanity throughout the ages; it is to recognize Jonas or Job or the Psalmist in an earthshaking atmosphere, the emotional and spiritual struggle of people in search of God as they waver between hope and despair.

It is because I share this condition of humankind that I wish to communicate this extraordinary experience in writing. It is also because a prison, being a jungle of aggression and frustration, may deceive you into thinking that in here all is risk or snare, that the pressures of this life lead only to stress and to a daily need for therapeutic care. But it is mostly to share some of the marvels of the ministry, the privilege of sharing the Church with these men who speak out and question ceaselessly as they share their faith or their potential of faith with us that I write.

I am a Catholic chaplain for some 3,500 incarcerated men at Rikers Island and share my ministry with Sister Simone of the Little Sisters of the Gospel, whose community works mostly with the families of these prisoners. There are several other chaplains from a variety of denominations. During the time which I spend among the prisoners each week, I see them individually and then collectively at such gatherings as the Sunday Liturgy, weekly biblical discussion groups, or during a retreat day which occurs once every three months in each of the three buildings we serve.

It is a blessing during those days of retreat to spend the entire day—from nine to five—with our "parishioners," to have lunch with them, to witness a community being born! Thanks to concerned prison authorities the daily routine of prison life changes for those hours. Life takes on new meaning. At the end of each retreat, we realize that our lives have been enriched as we have searched for Christ in His joys and in His sufferings. Amidst the silence, laughter, and sometimes tears, these men begin to see their lives as an earthly pilgrimage in pursuit of Christ's promised new life.

It would be easy to conclude that these "days of recollection" are merely a means of escaping the daily monotony behind bars at the price of playing a "game of faith." Prisoners who can, read seven times more during incarceration than they do outside; many of them spend those readings hours in the company of their Bible. That some may enjoy this one-day break from the harsh realities of prison life or from the fantasies they occasionally entertain in their cells is perfectly normal. But when they discover with one another that their goals can be worked out in a context of Christ's truth and compassion, each according to his own personal experience, this becomes one of the deepest joys in the life of this small church.

The experience is overwhelming for us all. The "nothingness" of prison life allows the Word to become Flesh in a way that is often impossible in the average parish. There are no masks, no defenses, no excuses, only the simple cry heard down through the centuries and now echoed by a handful of God's children jailed at Rikers Island, New York City: "Be it done according to Your word." Then at the end of the day, to stand around the altar, to share the bread and wine as Body and Blood of Jesus Christ becomes the symbol of how our lives, too, can be changed. The Mass, well prepared, sung, prayed as we never prayed otherwise, is a moment that none of us forgets too soon.

This is not a monastery, of course, but a prison where violence and tragedy stalk the unwary, where the strong can take advantage of the weak, where the unending jets from nearby LaGuardia Airport continually shatter the few moments of silence that are possible. In these circumstances we are made forcefully conscious of St. John of the Cross' simple statement: "It is during life's darkest moments that God's light shines the brightest."

It is at Rikers Island that Virgil Georghui's daily reminder is brought home over and over again:

> The police seek in every human being a murderer;
> The wise man and philosopher seek in every murderer a
>   human being;
> We Christians seek God in every person, even in murderers!
> And each of us will find what he seeks;
> The police will find their murderer;
> The philosophers will find their human being;
> And we, we shall find God in every person!

❧ The Integrity of Work

GEOFFREY GNEUHS

SOME OF US at the Catholic Worker have outside jobs to pay monthly expenses for small apartments we keep near our two houses. Dan works as an orderly at St. Rose's Cancer Home a couple of days a week; Jane cooks there. Marj is an ambulance attendant; David works as a bicycle messenger, and, since February, I have worked at a restaurant in Greenwich Village—receiving deliveries, running errands and doing whatever needs to be cleaned, fixed, or painted. I guess the job description would be "handy-person."

The other day my "handiness" was called into question. I was painting a ceiling in one of the dining rooms. The walls were already white. The wood beamed ceiling was to be painted brown. I wasn't consulted on the aesthetics of the project; I was simply told by the manager to paint the ceiling—"that's what Archie wants." And so I began working, careful not to splatter brown paint on the beams or the white walls—only the plywood surface was to be brown.

A few hours later, the owner, Archie, came in. Archie, I'll admit, seems to have inexhaustible energy, and often, without condescension, takes on any number of the manual tasks—from dishwashing to sweeping to painting. He asked, "You've done the other side, haven't you Geoff?" "Not yet," I said, "I'm trying to be careful so as not to splatter." "Well," he responded with a smile, "I hate to say it, Geoff, but you're slow." And I, with a smile, said, "I'd rather, at the end of the day, Archie, that you say I'm slow, but a very neat painter." "Well, paint faster and be sloppy," concluded Archie. Off I went, not satisfied, but then, Archie's the boss, it's his restaurant, and I need the job. Jobs today are hard to come by, nearly ten million are now unemployed, and we're told that 50 percent of young blacks are without jobs.

What is involved in that incident are some important aspects about the idea of work. On the one hand, work can be and often is "just a job." Many people go through their jobs each day, nine to five, in sheer boredom and drudgery. Thus, a major portion of their life is meaningless. In a religious vein, distorted as it is, some mistakenly believe work is a burden and curse of our human condition, and some others, also claiming scriptural authority, have propounded over the centuries the view that one's material success is a gauge of one's righteousness before God. How the capitalists have seized upon that: God and Mammon working hand in hand.

On the other hand, from the personalist perspective, work is art, and as such involves the whole person, that is, one's reason (intellect) and emotions; in other words, imagination. Personalists believe that each individual is created in the image and likeness of God, and thus, the ability to imagine is the expression of our personhood, of our humanity. And the more we imagine through work/art the more we become "person."

With this view in mind, I obviously felt I understood "work" somewhat differently from Archie. I, with reason and emotion, imagined the task at hand and said to myself, "paint carefully—in the long run the painted ceiling will be pleasing," and that which is pleasing is the good. I was looking at it and enjoying it as work/art; Archie saw it as a job to be done in order to busy me with other jobs. Thus, for me, for the rest of the day, the personal dimension was discarded, and the painting in a small way became pressure and drudgery. And I was frustrated; no longer was I responsible.

This story illustrates a kind of depersonalization, a separation of the person from the work. On a larger scale, and in many instances, far more severe situations of this fragmentation have been happening for centuries, but we have accelerated in the nineteenth and twentieth centuries to such a degree that individuals and societies have more or less given up trying to rethink and imagine the other way.

Eric Gill (1882–1940) was a twentieth-century man, an artist, a worker, a scholar, a laborer. His craft was stone carving, sculpting, and lettering. Donald Attwater described Gill as possessing "integrality and completeness: he was a whole man, and every aspect of himself, his works and his beliefs, was integrated and interdependent, fusing into one shining personality." It is not surprising then that Peter Maurin considered Eric Gill "one of the best" and quoted and referred to him in his essays more than any other individual.

Gill was not romantic or sentimental. In fact, after capitalists, his most caustic remarks were for romantics and sentimentalists yearning for a return to a past "ideal" age. He lived in our century, and critically observed the current ideas permeating civilization. He condemned those systems—economic and social—which encouraged the depersonalization of the human being. For him "commercialism" is a system based solely on the motive of profit. It is materialism which puts "things" above "persons." It is inherent in what is known as communism, just as much as in capitalism. In both systems, work has become a commodity. It is no longer art expressing the person—free and responsible.

In his book *Art,* Gill sets forth his analysis of the present, so as to give some hope for the future. He describes work in this way: "The word 'work' we commonly reserve for those occupations by means of which we get food, clothing, and shelter, the necessities of life. It is clear, therefore, that work is a good thing, for the very good reason that that which enables us to live must be good. We must assume that to live is good, and that, therefore, to work is good."

What has happened over the centuries is that wage earners have become instruments, used like machines, to be used and exploited for profit. In other words, the worker becomes object, no longer truly the subject using means to acquire the necessities of life. In fact, today, when it is no longer profitable even to use the worker as a machine, the individual is actually replaced by a machine—a robot! In Japan, robots do some of the work in automobile factories. In the United States, some high-technology plants and arms factories are using robots.

This is the trend. Do we want it? What are we doing to ourselves as persons, and as a society? This is the question which faces us, and the industrialist, the corporate executive, and the collectivist. What is the meaning and purpose of work? President Reagan reads the want ads and says that there are plenty of jobs available. Where? for whom? and for what? What if you are not trained in high technology, for instance? And if the jobs are to be found in California or the Southwest, how does that benefit a young person unemployed in Harlem? These realities, these facts, are not considered by those who hold economic and political power. To "save" labor usually means to do away with labor, and, thus, increase unemployment. Mass production tends to take away the laborer's freedom and responsibility for the product being made. Enough studies have shown, for example, that the fault with malfunctioning automobiles is not always due to their defective parts, but often to lack of "craftsmanship," that is, lack of interest and involvement of the worker in the thing being made.

Gill believed that work is, by its nature, pleasure and enjoyment. Art is that which is pleasing to the intellect and the senses; therefore, work is art. Under the present systems, Gill pointed out that "personal business is ruled out between maker and user, between the maker and the work." Art, itself, has become specialized and understood as the "fine arts," supported and encouraged by patrons, by the rich, the elite. At one time, art was the communal labor of the common people; for instance, building a cathedral for practical use as a place of prayer, socializing, celebrating. Now, expensive churches are built to be gawked at, not really used, and often they are kept locked!

For Eric Gill, the worker/artist is "a collaborator with God creating." So, of course, those things which are needed and useful are supposed to be beautiful. Why should they be anything else? Why should beauty be divorced from usefulness? And, yet, that is now generally the case. The worker/artist uses both the mind and the will. To use less than that is to use less of the person. The person, the activity, and the thing produced become separated; and the purpose and usefulness of the thing being done fades away. That is the division of labor.

It is helpful to remember, however, that most of our inventions have been made not by specialists or scientists, but by workers who were scholars, not in the pompous, decreed way of today's academic scene, but in the sense that they thought about what they were doing and used tools that were helpful. Galileo even made his own telescopes in order to observe the heavens and make discoveries. Other inventions, like the steam engine, the telephone, and even the airplane, were not invented by professional scientists, but by workers thinking and feeling. Eric Gill, the sculptor, expressed it in this manner: "I think and then I draw my think." So it was with those other workers/inventors/artisans.

Last fall Pope John Paul II issued an encyclical "On Human Work." Unfortunately, it is written in a rather cumbersome style. But it could be read as a supplement to Gill's far more lucid and invigorating book. John Paul reiterates the personalist theme of the priority of labor—that is, the thing done, and the one doing it—over capital, money. He criticizes the materialism and consumerism of both capitalist and communist ideologies, but hedges in confronting the deeper systematic structures which affect both ideologies.

Of course, both Eric Gill and Pope John Paul are in the tradition of Catholic social teaching, which holds that the goods of creation are for all. Private property is a right, and the Catholic Worker holds to this, too, but it is secondary to basic human needs, food, clothing, and shelter. The right to property should be enjoyed by all. Today, ownership is concentrated in the hands of a few—whether in the United States or in the Soviet Union. The worker needs tools and a workshop, the farmer needs land. Factory workers should be able to exercise more responsibility in their work place, through worker ownership and self-management. In the United States, despite our theory of free enterprise, fewer and fewer people enjoy that ideal. For instance, it is virtually impossible now for a person or family, for the majority in America, to buy a home. Interest rates make this prohibitive. Yet, a generation ago, this was a possible dream for many, and a good dream at that. In our neighborhood here on the Lower East Side, a number of small shops, and long-time owners and workers are being pushed out due to excessive rents, and corporate speculators.

It is time to realize the true dignity of work/art and to reassert those principles in our economic and political life. The worker needs to be responsible, using intellect and will, "collaborating with God creating." As such, the worker is a person in the image and likeness of God. Work becomes personal; the worker is a maker, an artist. Barriers are broken and bonds are made. Buyers and sellers engage in an exchange of things which are needed and useful; not to the exclusion of any, but for the inclusion of all. That then is the common weal.

It is in this sense that Gill wanted to reintegrate "bed and board, the small farm and the workshop, the home and the school, earth and heaven." That was holiness for him: "Holiness is the name for that quality in things by which we judge them good. Its full meaning escapes definition in words. It is a spiritual thing; it must be apprehended by the spirit. And I am not speaking of holiness as a moral quality. Holiness is not a moral quality at all. It is above and beyond prudence. It is loveliness itself. It is the loveliness of the spirit."

MAY 1985

❄ How I Met Dorothy Day

ADE BETHUNE

IN THE Spring of 1933, while Dorothy Day was sitting at a typewriter in her brother's apartment over a vacant storefront on East 15th Street, pounding out copy for a brave new paper she wanted to call *The Catholic Worker*, I was in art school, dreaming of color and light in stained glass. I did not know that Dorothy Day even existed; nor did social issues interest me in the least. I was nineteen. My interests were totally in the arts and crafts.

In May, at the same time as Dorothy was selling her little penny paper at Union Square, I was at the drawing board in my family's apartment on East 91st Street, industriously figuring out a design for a competition that Boston's great stained glass man, Charles J. Connick, was promoting, after giving a series of three lectures on the craft to the students of the National Academy of Design.

Lee Krasner, who was later to marry Jackson Pollock, both becoming famous twentieth-century painters, was then a fellow student. But Lee was not interested in the glass competition. I really was. It meant everything to me. More than anything else, I wanted to make a real stained glass window. I wanted it so badly that I had even tried to apply oil colors to a piece of glass, but they were neither transparent nor brilliant. Edam cheese from Holland came wrapped in red cellophane. I saved the cellophane and glued two layers of it to my window pane for a truly bright red. A scrap of yellow cellophane was also lovingly rescued from a garbage can on the street, and glued to my fake window. Oh, but being able to do the real thing! Not a phony, but real! How great that would be!

The winner of Mr. Connick's competition was to be invited to the workshops in Boston to learn how to execute the winning design, with his or her own hands, in real glass. Nobody in the world could have been happier than I when, in late May or June, the prizes were announced and, yes, I had won the glass prize.

That summer I went to Boston, lived at the YWCA and spent every available minute at the Connick Studios where the workers apprenticed me to the mysteries of cutting glass and melting solder. On Saturdays and Sundays, I haunted the Boston Museum of Fine Arts and roamed the streets, getting the feeling of people, houses, churches and public buildings in a city quite different from the New York City to which my family had immigrated five years earlier.

In September, I took the bus back to New York, my head spinning with luminous jewel colors and the determination to become a "stained glass man."

Every Wednesday evening, a group of five school friends met for supper. Gertrude and Agnes McLoughlin were Canadians, from Niagara Falls, Ontario. One sister studied music at Julliard; the other was an aspiring graphic artist, together with Ann Weaver of Selma, Alabama, Lalah Durham of South Carolina, and I, originally from Belgium and just now returned from "The Hub."

Agnes and Gertrude were Catholic, as was I. They could hardly wait to tell me a new thing they had heard of, called the Catholic Worker. It was a storefront on East Fifteenth Street. Two women were publishing a paper, offering hospitality, and sleeping on the floor. I went for the idea of hospitality and decided at once to find out what the Catholic Worker was all about.

But my interest was not that great. I procrastinated. Finally, the day came; I took the Third Avenue "El" and found my way over to 436 East Fifteenth Street, almost at Avenue A. There, indeed, was a little basement storefront in the shadow of the outdoor steps leading up to the tenements above. In the window was a sign with the words, "The Catholic Worker," next to a small statue of St. Joseph.

Timidly I opened the door, entered, and stood tongue-tied. Several people were sitting on chairs along the walls. Fortunately, a short, plump young woman with dark hair appeared from the back room, told me she was Dorothy Weston, a graduate of Manhattanville College, and engaged me in conversation. In fact, she had to do all the talking. I was so shy, I could barely produce a word. Maybe she introduced me to Peter Maurin. I don't remember. If she did, he was probably reading a book and neither of us said anything. Peter had no use for small talk.

Dorothy Weston must have given me the tour of the place. Behind the front room, there was a small "middle" space with bundles of clothes, a typewriter on a wobbly table, some cartons of correspondence, and back issues of *The Catholic Worker*. That middle space, in turn, opened onto the kitchen at the rear.

A table covered with oilcloth reigned in the middle of the kitchen, surrounded by odds and ends of secondhand chairs. I could see the sun pouring through two big windows in the far wall facing south. There was a yard beyond, with a tree of heaven and other lusty weeds, a little the worse for the winter. On the left was a kitchen range and, next to it, a wall sink with a splash back. In the far left corner, a bathtub was covered with a wood lid that could be used for kitchen work when the tub was not needed for bathing. On the other side was a small water closet with a toilet of dubious vintage and a tiny window stuck shut from successive coats of paint.

On the stove, a pot of hot coffee was steaming next to a large kettle of soup. The food, the sunshine, the make-do simplicity, all appealed to my instincts. But I had no words to express anything. Dorothy Weston finally got rid of me by pressing three or four copies of *The Catholic Worker* into my hands and suggesting I take them home, read them, and then come back to help. The paper was then an eight-page tabloid. The latest issue, just off the press, was Volume 1, No. 7, December 15, 1933.

Riding uptown on the "El" I started to devour *The Catholic Worker*. Obviously, it was not Communist, but Catholic. I understood the articles about hospitality. But strikes were a mystery to me. As I was later to hear Peter Maurin repeat many times: "Strike news doesn't strike me."

Still, what impressed me was the paper's lack of telling pictures. Communist publications, such as *The Masses*, were illustrated with bold, black and white prints. Although I had never read these magazines, I had seen them in the hands of fellow art students and had been impressed with their virile and stunning design.

Immediately I knew what I wanted to do. Without reading further (I was never a good reader), I got home and started at once making a black and white picture on a theme that I thought would be appropriate: Joseph and Mary being thrown out of the inn in Bethlehem by an irate innkeeper.

The Gospel of Luke says nothing about an innkeeper. It merely states that Mary wrapped her firstborn Son in swaddling clothes and laid Him in a manger (implying a stable) "because there was no place for them at the inn." I certainly was not a Scripture scholar. On the basis of popular notions, probably elaborated in the mystery plays of the Middle Ages, a fat innkeeper found his way into my drawing and raised a menacing fist. At least, let us say that he illustrated the idea of "lack of hospitality."

For a Christmas card the year before, I had cut a linoleum block showing a tearful Mary carrying her Child into exile in a cold and strange land. I redid this design as a brush drawing. Again, its essential theme was "lack of hospitality."

Having, I thought, exhausted all that could be done on the subject, I decided to search for suitable themes in the Catechism, where I chanced upon a list of "the fourteen works of mercy." At the top of the list was "harboring the homeless." Great! Here was "hospitality" herself!

Without further delay, I launched into a series of circular designs. Number one showed a forlorn young woman being greeted at the door by an older one. Others in the series would include "feeding the hungry," "clothing the naked," "visiting the sick," and so forth.

To round out my first offering to *The Catholic Worker,* I made a black and white version of a design of Saint Joseph the Worker which I was really yearning to make into stained glass. Joseph, wearing an apron, stands at his carpenter's bench, carving a piece of wood. He is surrounded by tools of his trade.

With pounding heart, I mailed my hard-worked drawings to the *Catholic Worker* editors, and prayed that they would not reject my earnest, if youthful, offering.

And in due time, a postcard came saying that the drawings had been gratefully received and would be used.

Gathering old clothes was my next aim. By February, I had managed to fill two shopping bags, so I boarded the Third Avenue "El" again to deliver them to East 15th Street. When I arrived, I stood bashfully inside the door hoping that cheerful Dorothy Weston would appear once more to rescue me from an intimidating situation.

Instead, a tall, bony older woman with straight, graying hair strode the full length of the room toward me. I nearly panicked. A flash went through my mind: "What business does this woman have taking over? Who is she anyway?"

But she looked at me with compassion and said: "Are these your things? I am terribly sorry, we have no more room. But we will try to find another place for you."

There was humor in the situation, but I was speechless. At last I managed to stammer: "I'm, I'm the girl who sent pictures. Here are some clothes also."

"Oh, you are?" the tall woman replied. Taking the bag of clothes with an air of command, she dropped them off in the middle room, sat me down on a pile of newspapers, took a Missal (a book containing the prayers and readings of the Mass for every day of the year) from the typewriter table, and came to sit on the pile of newspapers next to mine. I still had no idea who she was. But she spoke with authority.

"The March issue is at the printer's," she continued. "The next issue is April. Now let's see." She flipped through pages of the Missal. "In April we have the feast of Saint Catherine of Siena. She was the twenty-first child of a dyer and, rather than going to church to say prayers, she had to cook for her father's workmen. So she made the kitchen her temple. Catherine also visited a prisoner, who was to be executed, and helped him to repent."

Could I make pictures of these great stories? Yes, I could. "Then, there is also John Bosco. He will be canonized this year and his day will come in April. He made a home for street boys. He taught them trades so they could earn an honest living by the work of their hands."

A great program opened up before me. In the lives of two actual holy people of the fourteenth and nineteenth centuries, this energetic woman had sketched a lifetime plan for me. Catherine and John alone illustrated "feeding the hungry," "visiting the prisoner," "counseling the doubtful," "converting the sinner," "giving a home to the homeless," and "instructing the ignorant"—six of the fourteen works of mercy! I went home full of enthusiasm, guessing that the woman sitting next to me on the pile of newspapers had to be the "other" editor, Dorothy Day.

Dorothy was thirty-seven at the time, in the prime of her life. Her hair was only beginning to turn grey. She was a newspaper woman and smoked like a chimney. She also had a little girl of six. She loved children's drawings, plants, animals, sunshine, babies, old people, the poor, the suffering. And she found spiritual sustenance in the feasts of the Liturgical Year, the Gospels, and the lives of the saints.

Naturally, I wanted to imitate such a total character, though I never had enough courage to take up smoking. Besides, smoking was expensive. As yet, I had no livelihood. I cooked for my family and also earned a dollar now and then by giving a private French lesson. But even spending a nickel on the fare to travel the subway or the "El" was an expense that had to be weighed carefully. You also needed a second nickel for the return trip home. This was the depth of the Depression. My dream of a job in a stained glass firm was just that, a dream. No churches were being built. No new stained glass workers could be hired. I understood that and had to accept it.

What came as an unexpected salvation in my young life was the Catholic Worker. The influence of Dorothy and Peter (Dorothy was to quit smoking totally before long) opened up my whole life.

Little did Dorothy know the future struggles and problems that would, in time, turn her hair snow white, but that she would continue into four-score years to meet with constant faith. I will ever be grateful to her for directing my youthful efforts toward the liturgy, the common prayer of the people.

The March 1934 issue included all four of the pictures I had sent in. In the April issue, Dorothy printed two pictures of St. Catherine of Siena and one of St. John Bosco, all three accompanied by a little story she wrote. For the May 1934 issue, I continued the "Works of Mercy" series with No. 3, "visiting the sick." Peter Maurin's essay, "Big Shots and Little Shots," intrigued me and I tried my hand at illustrating it. On page 8, Dorothy printed a picture of "The Garden of the Heart," together with a short article I had written.

The June issue was decorated with an attempt to devise an "Our Lady of Labor," also a "Repentant Peter at the Cock Crow" and Works of Mercy No. 4, "feeding the hungry." This latter, as well as No. 2 in the April issue, were mounted crooked so that the table tilted. I was distressed, but it was my own fault for making circular designs. How could the printer guess which was the top? I was learning about publishing.

The July-August issue had only four pages. On page three appeared a picture of St. Vincent de Paul protecting three little orphans from icy blasts. His feast was July 19 and I was beginning to get the hang of doing the saints' pictures a month or two in advance of their day, so that they could be printed in time. St. Vincent's picture served as a starting point for a short essay by Dorothy on Frederick Ozanam.

I also experimented with texts from Scripture. "Ask and you will receive" illustrated a brief essay of mine, obviously influenced by the Catholic Worker and Peter's teaching. For the September issue, I illustrated the parable of "The Unjust Judge." The young volunteers at the Worker teased me, saying that the unjust judge looked just like Peter. I was grieved; that was farthest from my mind. But the boys were right; I loved and admired Peter, yet something of his features had somehow found their way into the "bad guy's" face! Artists reflect what they see, not always appropriately.

How do you depict evil? For September 29 I had also produced an athletic Michael the Archangel in a T-shirt, boxing a bloated "evil spirit," who grabbed a poor little person in his claws. The evil one looked prophetically like Jabba the Hut from "The Return of the Jedi." I remember one of the Catholic Worker boys, riding uptown on the subway with me, asked me over the din: "What nationality was St. Michael? Was he Italian?" It was hard explaining about pure spirits, both good and bad, in the lurching subway car.

October came and I had the picture of St. Francis of Assisi all ready for the deadline; also St. Crispin hard at work, mending shoes. For the November issue, I worked on St. Elizabeth of Hungary, taking care of the sick.

To dress up the December issue, I produced a three-column Christmas design in the form of a cross. Dorothy liked it so well that she put it at the center top of the front page. Nor did she hesitate to reprint some of my earlier pictures. They were becoming a part of the paper, somewhat as were Peter's "Easy Essays," and Dorothy's "Day by Day" column.

I tried to get friends to contribute pictures, too. My stained glass teacher, Charles J. Connick, sent in a two-column picture of St. Martin of Tours for his feast, November 11, and Bill Cladek had two pictures of construction workers in the January 1935 issue. Later, Carl Paulson and other friends made pictures, and Father Edward Catich was to contribute many illustrations.

Dorothy also suggested the story of St. Francis de Sales taking care of his valet as the latter returned drunk from a day off. Dorothy had to come face to face with some alcoholics and took comfort from the example of St. Francis de Sales. She also loved the picture of "Christ and the Little Children"; she said one of the children looked like her own daughter, Tamar. "The Garbage Cans" and "The Workers in the Vineyard" were among her other favorites.

In the March 1935 issue, Dorothy reprinted my first St. Joseph, now a year old, in one-column size on the front page. I had also worked full steam for that issue, having produced both St. Benedict and St. John of God (hawking the paper in Union Square) and a complete set of fourteen pictures forming a double spread for the Way of the Cross. The paper had grown to twelve pages, the circulation to 65,000.

It was time to work on the paper's somewhat uninspiring masthead. At opposite ends of the title, two small cuts depicted the half figure of a black worker holding a man on the left, and on the right, a white worker shouldering a pick. In the first few issues, both workers had been white. An astute reader having pointed out that the interracial justice advocated by the editors was not expressed by the masthead, one of the pictures was replaced by a cut of a black worker. Had Dorothy obtained the two workers from odds and ends of leftover cuts in an old case at her printer's? I never found out. At any rate, I proposed to surprise her.

The two workers at opposite ends of the page looked as though they were not on speaking terms, I thought. Somehow or other they must come together and shake hands in solidarity. I added the figure of Christ stretching His arms over their shoulders.

Without training in lettering, I bravely rushed in where angels fear to tread and, after great struggle, produced abstract, undecorated sans serif letters in the art-deco style of the period. I thought these letters were free of Victorian frippery, expressed a clear vision of the future, and would last for the ages!

To celebrate its second birthday, in May 1935, *The Catholic Worker* had a new masthead of its own. Below it on page one was a black and white rendition of "Christ Chasing the Money Lenders from the Temple." This time, the office wags said Dorothy had been the inspiration for the figure of Christ. Well, I admit it, it was vaguely true.

Before you knew it, fifty years had slipped by. First Peter, then Dorothy had been called to the Father of us all. I, too, was now turning seventy. It was pointed out that *The Catholic Worker* masthead had become "sexist." A new one was needed.

I thought long and hard to offer Dorothy's spirit a new surprise, exactly half a century after the first. I thought of her love of little children, of the land, of feeding people. The result? Our new masthead. A woman, mother and agricultural worker, replaces the old male worker with the shovel. With this and minor changes, we present a new masthead, to quote Peter, "with the philosophy of the old, a philosophy so old that it looks like new."

MAY 1985

 ## "I Was a Stranger . . ."

JENNIE GILRAIN

EDS. NOTE: *During Lent, Jennie spent several nights sleeping in Manhattan's three central train and bus stations, and one night in the New York City shelter system for women. Her intention was to experience, first-hand, something of the suffering facing the homeless women who come to our door.*

I WOULD LIKE TO make this article into a prayer.

Sunday, March 17, Grand Central Station: First, I pray for Joa, a thirty-two-year-old man from Portugal, union construction worker, father of an eight-year-old boy whose $7,000 operation left Joa in debt. Joa came to New York because there was no work in Portugal. Construction is slow in the winter time, even in New York, but he has a job starting in mid-April. Meanwhile, he is without money and without a place to live. He chooses Grand Central Station over the city's Men's Shelter because, in his experience, it is safer.

My prayer is one of thanksgiving. I thank God for Joa's generosity. He gave me his baloney sandwich and half-pint of milk from the midnight food runs of the Coalition for the Homeless, which gave out hundreds of bagged meals that night to the homeless people who filled the station. He shared his orange and showed me a safe place to sleep, where the police would be least likely to find me (although they did find me and escorted me out onto the streets at 1:30 a.m.). He asked me very few questions, yet shared his life with me. My prayer doubles as one of supplication. I ask that Joa be able to secure his job in April, that he can afford a place to live, and eventually be reunited with his wife and son.

Monday, March 18, Penn Station: Second, I pray for Mike, the policeman in Penn Station. At 3:30 in the morning, when I had just laid my head down to sleep, I was awakened by the reverberating sound and feeling of his club against my bench. "What train are you waiting for?" he asked. "I'm not waiting for a train. I would just like to stay here for the night," I answered. He said that the city had shelters for that, but they were closed now. I said that I would just like to stay for the next couple of hours until morning. He looked as if to say, "I'll overlook you this time, but don't let it happen again," and walked away. I thanked him.

Later, when I walked to get a cup of coffee trying to stay awake to avoid the club, I ran into him again. He asked me, "Why don't you have a place? You shouldn't be homeless. You're young and healthy. What happened? Do you want to talk about it?" I was embarrassed and touched by his sincerity. I assured him that this was a temporary situation, that I would be all right, and thanked him for his concern. Fifteen minutes later, I watched him bang on the bench of an old woman, force her to gather her bags and move on. My prayer is one of thanksgiving for Mike's concern for my youth and health, and a prayer of hope that the same concern for another woman's age and tired brokenness might be born in him.

Tuesday, March 19, Port Authority Bus Terminal: Third, I want to pray for Marion, a seventy-eight-year-old woman, born and raised in Manhattan, now on Social Security and living in Port Authority. Make no mistake about it, Marion has all her wits about her; amazing, considering the amount of sleep she gets in a night, two hours at most. Together, Marion and I were herded, with hundreds of other homeless people, out of Port Authority at 2:30 a.m. by five policemen with two dogs. Together we sat in a pizza shop until it closed and a coffee shop until we had to return to the station at 3:30 to use the bathroom. Together we were politely moved from side to side by the maintenance crew who had to mop the floors, and rudely awakened by the echoing clubs and barking dogs of policemen.

Marion likes ballet, Broadway, and all sports. When I invited her, if she was ever downtown, to come to Maryhouse, she scoffed. "Oh no, those places depress me. If I'm going to go out, I want to go someplace that will cheer me up, like a Broadway play or the ballet." Marion keeps her ID strapped in a pouch underneath her clothes to protect it from thieves. In case she dies, she wants them to know who she is. At one point, I stupidly asked her, "Marion, don't you have a place to stay?" She kept walking and answered, "Now don't you worry about me. I have everything I need." At the coffee shop she bought an egg sandwich and offered me half. "Everything she needs" is a Social Security check that is enough to afford food, but not enough to afford a room. I pray that someone will adopt this spunky, wise, old woman as their grandmother. I thank God for her company that night. In a station full of anger and fear, Marion took me under her wing.

Saturday, March 30, Women's Shelter. Fourth, I pray for Betsy, a thirty-five-year-old mother burned out of her Harlem apartment a week before I met her. Her three-year-old was sent to the hospital, she to the women's shelter. She called the hospital to locate her son. The hospital told her that he was in the orphanage. She called the orphanage. The orphanage said that he was in the hospital. Betsy's case worker is trying her best to resolve the situation, along with the many other cases on her desk. Meanwhile, Betsy is alone, not able to see or talk to her son.

Together, Betsy and I were processed at 350 Lafayette Street in Manhattan, and referred to Flushing, Queens. We waited until 1:00 a.m. for the van to come. Together with eight others we rode in the van to 26th Street where two got off, then arrived at the Flushing shelter to discover they only had three beds available for eight of us. So, back to central processing in Manhattan. Together, at 2:30 a.m., we received a referral to Greenpoint shelter in Brooklyn. With five others we rode the van again to 26th Street—two more got off, then we arrived at Greenpoint at 3:30 a.m., where they had enough beds for us five remaining. We were told that we must take a shower before going to bed, and three of us waited in line for one working shower, finally to bed at 4:00 a.m., wake-up call at 6:30. Betsy burst into tears several times during the night, in despair over the loss of her son, in frustration and helplessness. I thank God for Betsy's trust in me, for the bond I felt with her through the night. I pray that she is reunited with her son and someday is able to create a safe home for him with her.

St. John of the Cross said, "The purest suffering produces the purest understanding." As I listened to the reading of St. Mark's Passion on Palm Sunday, the day after my night in the Women's Shelter, I heard it in a way I had never heard it before. I saw Betsy, Marion, and Joa beaten by the Romans, stripped, crowned with thorns, and nailed to the cross. I saw Jesus in Grand Central Station, Penn Station, Port Authority, and the Women's Shelter, sharing His food and company, awakened by clubs and dogs, herded like cattle and bused to another borough. The justice of His promises seemed so much more necessary: "Blessed are you poor, for the Kingdom of God shall be yours" (Luke 6:20). The basis of His judgment of me made more sense: "For I was hungry and you gave me food, I was thirsty and you gave me drink. I was a stranger and you invited me in, naked and you clothed me" (Matt 25:35–36). My part seemed without question, necessary, and somehow easier: feed the hungry, clothe the naked, shelter the homeless. Easier, because the hungry and homeless were no longer a large and frightening mass. My friends Marion, Joa, and Betsy are hungry and homeless. Jesus is hungry and homeless.

The irony of my experience at the stations was that, in their vulnerability, Marion and Joa invited me, a stranger, into their homes and comforted me. In their poverty, they gave me food and drink. Why is it so often difficult for me to do the same? In my fear, I have created too many walls of protection. My closeness to Marion, Joa, and Betsy dissolved my fears. I was healed. If each of us was able to make human contact with one homeless person, to allow the walls of fear to dissolve and ourselves to be touched, then a reciprocal healing might take place. If we could open ourselves to receiving that person, rather than giving at arms' length with averted eyes, through the safe distance of established institutions, then the Kingdom of God might be born in us, between us, among us.

JANUARY–FEBRUARY 1987

❊ Confessions of a Latter-Day Luddite

KATHARINE TEMPLE

"LATTER-DAY LUDDITES," that's how Lawrence O'Neill, president of Riverside Research Institute (RRI), dismisses those who question the military-related work he oversees. Combined with a reference to "pseudo-intellectual, pseudo-moral clutter," this phrase makes it clear that he believes the groups who demonstrate outside his building to be a mob of ridiculous, negative, irresponsible, irrational ne'er-do-wells. To call someone a Luddite seems a worse slur than to call the person an anarchist.

It takes some doing to rescue the Luddites from what E. P. Thompson (in *The Making of the English Working Class*) calls "the enormous condescension of posterity," and, at best, they have been put into a sub-plot in Charlotte Bronte's *Shirley*. The Oxford dictionary describes them as members of a "band of mechanics (1811–16) who raised riots for destruction of machinery." Little does it hint that they were a grassroots, egalitarian movement whose influence was well-nigh revolutionary throughout Northern England. The Industrial Revolution was just getting going under the influence of the new inventions in the wool industry. These, plus the disastrous Napoleonic wars, brought about massive unemployment and even more general discontent. In response to the dislocations, popular movements sprang up, and the most popular of them all was the Luddites. Groups of men, after all demands for redress or for new organization remained unheard, attacked the actual machinery—the shearing frames and looms—that epitomized everything that was wrong. The Luddites outraged the status quo because they struck at such a central nerve and were so widely supported in towns and villages that they were hard to track down. Eventually they were suppressed only with a large and brutal expeditionary force.

Ned Ludd and his followers saw the danger in the new means of production and wanted to preserve their traditional rights that were being stripped away, and it's never been shown that they were wrong. Nor was their rebellion merely a blind lashing out, for they were also "announcing [an] alternative political economy, albeit in a confused midnight encounter" (E.P. Thompson). What we now have, in a society that breeds nuclear weaponry, are the full fruits of what they intuited at the seedling stage. In the matter of the vigils at RRI, the Luddite accusation can hardly come from a horror of violence, so much as from a disdain for anyone who dares to desire limits to technological progress. Not that Mr. O'Neill would see it this way, but the charge could be taken as a compliment—whether or not it is fully deserved.

Maybe we should take up the gauntlet and find even more ways to be latter-day Luddites, to recapture their insight, verve, and courage, in a less inflammatory way. Joseph Weizenbaum, who knows "the state of the technological art" probably all too well in the Department of Electrical Engineering and Computer Science at M.I.T., has made one suggestion:

> I think the Luddites have been grievously misrepresented in what outrageously little history is taught in the American schools. Their actions closely parallel those of our people who pound sledge-hammers on the hulls of submarines and missiles. These are actions of last resort, all other attempts

to appeal to reason having failed. I think we need a period of detoxification with respect to our science and technology. They have become toxic to our spirit. We need a moratorium on progress. If such thoughts are Luddite, then I am a Luddite, too.

Official reactions to Plowshares Actions (which inflict only symbolic damage) including prison sentences up to eighteen years, for instance, while not as extreme as in nineteenth-century England, when machine beating was made a capital crime, betray a nervousness not all that far removed. Joseph Weizenbaum also supports the Star Wars refusal campaign, where scientists pledge not to solicit or accept financial support for specific research. Another campaign in direct opposition to unlimited development, it is also not pleasing to the government, but is harder to prosecute.

Then there is tax resistance. This route may not seem as dramatic as smashing the looms that spell unemployment; still, it does strike, nonviolently, at the life-line sustaining the corporate-military mechanism. (Certainly, the State takes it seriously. Consider the lengths they go to collect meager amounts from people who openly withhold money to protest military spending.) Refusing to pay the piper may be the most direct and non-confused way to say "No!" to the forces that enslave.

Most of us don't stop to think how many ways tax resistance can be practiced. At one end of the spectrum is the public and outright refusal to pay, a stance that limits employment possibilities and risks heavy fines or jail. At the other end is the decision, equally fraught with hardship, to live below the taxable limit. In between lie other, less extreme options, such as a partial withholding, working within a lower tax bracket, avoidance of the telephone tax collected for military debts, exchanges of labor without money transactions, rationing (or even giving up!) highly taxed goods, etc. Given that more than half the federal budget goes to military expenses and hardware, every tax avoided through pure means is a moral and political statement of the highest order.

These decisions are not to be taken lightly, for the consequences can bear a heavy price. Any wise builder, we are told, will "first sit down and count the cost whether he has enough to complete it" (Luke 14:28). Presumably, it is not the best idea to act only in confused, midnight encounters, or to make costly gestures frivolously.

At the same time, if we dismiss tax refusal out of hand, just as when the Luddites have been dismissed, the concern is not always about violence, or the cost, but the futility. Isn't it all doomed to failure? The die is cast, so that neither demonstrations nor symbolic action, nor direct refusals will make the slightest difference. This is what stops us from even the smallest actions. The assessment of failure, though, is always a later one, and we shouldn't give in to historical determinism.

"Our only criterion of judgment should not be whether a man's actions are justified in the light of subsequent evolution" (E.P. Thompson). Furthermore, as Christians, we must hold to belief in the economy of good, that no good action, no matter how seemingly inconsequential, is lost in God's plan.

DECEMBER 1988

❊ Thomas Merton and the Catholic Worker

Waking from a Dream of Separateness

JIM FOREST

ON MARCH 18, 1958, while on an editorial errand in Louisville, Kentucky, Thomas Merton stood still at the corner of Fourth and Walnut Streets. No one paid any attention to him—his name was well known but not his face.

Those moments pausing at the busy downtown intersection proved to be a crossroad in his life. Until that day, he saw his life in isolation from others. His tendency toward condescension and sarcasm had been little changed by his conversion to Christianity, his entrance into the Catholic Church, or his becoming a Trappist monk. He had been attracted to a monastic environment in part because he saw the monastery as a place of radical, even God-blessed apartness where one could walk out on the world and slam the door.

The following day he wrote in his journal about what had happened in Louisville. "[I] suddenly realized that I loved all the people and that none of these were, or could be, totally alien to me. As if waking from a dream—the dream of my separateness, of my 'special' vocation to be different." Later, preparing parts of his journal for publication, he explored at length the event in Louisville, the significance of which had continued to unfold and deepen:

The whole illusion of a separate holy existence is a dream. The sense of liberation from an illusory difference was such a relief and such a joy that I almost laughed out loud. It is a glorious destiny to be a member of the human race, though it is a race dedicated to many absurdities and one which makes terrible mistakes: yet for all that, God Himself gloried in becoming a member of the human race. A member of the human race! I suddenly saw the secret beauty of their hearts, the depths of their hearts where neither sin nor desire nor self-knowledge can reach, the core of their reality, the person that each one is in God's eyes. If only they could see themselves as they really are. If only we could see each other that way all the time. There would be no more war, no more hatred, no more cruelty, no more greed.

Merton concluded these pages—I have left much out—with the observation: "I have no program for this seeing. It is only given. But the gate of heaven is everywhere."

*

How did Dorothy Day and Thomas Merton start corresponding? In February 1959, Dorothy was reading Merton's autobiography, *The Seven Storey Mountain*. She was not altogether happy with the last part of the book. She felt that Merton had "plunged himself so deeply into religion that his view of the world and its problems is superficial and scornful." Dorothy decided to write to Merton. She also started sending him copies of *The Catholic Worker*. He responded on July 9, 1959. He wrote:

I am deeply touched by your witness for peace [referring to the arrest and imprisonment of Dorothy and other Catholic Workers who had refused to take shelter during civil defense drills]. You are right in going at it along the lines of Satyagraha [Gandhi's term for nonviolent action; literally, it means the power that comes from living in truth]. I see no other way, though, of course, the angles of the problem are not all clear. You people are the only ones left awake, or among the few that still have an eye open.

Rereading Merton's letters to Dorothy, I am occasionally reminded of what he had recorded about the event at Fourth and Walnut. The link is most vivid in a letter Merton sent Dorothy about his visit on February 3, 1960, with the Little Sisters of the Poor in Louisville.

I realized that it is in these beautiful, beat, wrecked, almost helpless old people that Christ lives and works most. And in the hurt people who are bitter and say they have lost their faith. We (society at large) have lost our sense of values and our vision. We despise everything that Christ loves, everything marked with His compassion. We love fatness, health, bursting smiles, the radiance of satisfied bodies, all properly fed and rested and sated and washed and sexually relieved. Anything else is a horror and a scandal to us. How sad. (Letter to Dorothy Day. August 17, 1960.)

What was important about the link Merton made with the Catholic Worker movement was not that he suddenly saw for the first time that the Christian commitment had radical social consequences. Rather, he realized that people in the Catholic Worker movement were trying to live a vocation that had much in common with the monastic life and gave even more striking witness to the presence of God in each person. He valued Dorothy and the Catholic Worker for daring to connect love and justice and for taking an active stand against war—something practically no other Catholic institution, certainly no monastery, was willing to do.

It was in the pages of *The Catholic Worker* that Merton first made public the new turn in his thinking. He sent Dorothy a carbon copy of "The Root of War is Fear," a chapter that would be appearing in *New Seeds of Contemplation*, asking if she wanted to publish it. He wrote some further paragraphs especially for *The Catholic Worker*. They remain impressive nearly thirty years later.

> The task is to work for the total abolition of war. Unless we set ourselves immediately to this task, both as individuals and in our political and religious groups, we tend by our very passivity and fatalism to cooperate with the destructive forces that are leading inexorably to war. First of all, there is much to be learned. Peace is to be preached, nonviolence is to be explained as a practical method, and not left to be mocked as an outlet for crackpots who want to make a show of themselves. Prayer and sacrifice must be used as the most effective spiritual weapons in the war against war, and like all weapons, they must be used with deliberation: not just with a vague aspiration for peace and security, but against violence and war. (*CW*, October 1961.)

There is not space to trace the development of Merton's correspondence with Dorothy and others close to the Catholic Worker, or to review the twenty or so articles, reviews, and letters by Merton that were published in *The Catholic Worker*. Instead let me summarize a few of the main emphases.

The more Merton became engaged with groups involved in protest, the more he became aware of how hard it was for those involved in protest to grow in patience and compassion. It can be intensely frustrating to try to change the way people think. Without compassion, the protester tends to become more and more centered in anger and may easily become an obstacle to changing the attitudes of others. The majority of people, Merton noted, crave undisturbed security and are threatened by agitation even when it protests something—militarism, nuclear weapons, social injustice—which really threatens their security.

> [People] do not feel threatened by the bomb but they feel terribly threatened by some student carrying a placard. We have to have a deep patient compassion for the fears of men, for the fears and irrational mania of those who hate or condemn us. (Letter to Jim Forest, January 5, 1952)

Where compassion is absent, actions that are superficially nonviolent tend to mask deep hostility, contempt, and the desire to defeat and humiliate an opponent. "One of the problematic questions about nonviolence," Merton wrote, "is the inevitable involvement of hidden aggressions and provocations."

> [We] have to consider the fact that, in its provocative aspect, nonviolence may tend to harden opposition and confirm people in their righteous blindness. It may even in some cases separate men out and drive them in the other direction, away from us and away from peace. This, of course, may be (as it was with the prophets) part of God's plan. A clear separation of antagonists. [But we must] always direct our action toward opening people's eyes to the truth, and if they are blinded, we must try to be sure we did nothing specifically to blind them. Yet there is that danger: the danger one observes subtly in tight groups like families and monastic communities, where the martyr for the right sometimes thrives on making his persecutors terribly and visibly wrong. He can drive them in desperation to be wrong, to seek refuge in the wrong, to seek refuge in violence. We have got to be aware of the awful sharpness of truth when it is used as a weapon, and since it can be the deadliest weapon, we must take care that we don't kill more than falsehood with it. In fact, we must be careful how we "use" truth, for we are ideally the instruments of truth and not the other way around. (Letter to Jim Forest, February 6, 1962.)

Merton often sensed that the peace movement (though not the Catholic Worker) was excessively political, tending to identify too much with particular political groups and ideologies. Ideally its action should communicate liberating possibilities to others no matter how locked in they were to violent structures. "It seems to me," he wrote, "that the basic problem is not political, it is apolitical and human."

> One of the important things to do is to keep cutting deliberately through political lines and barriers and emphasizing the fact that these are largely fabrications and that there is another dimension, a genuine reality, totally opposed to the fictions of politics; the human dimension which politics pretends to arrogate entirely [to itself]. This is the necessary first step along the long way of purifying, humanizing, and somehow illuminating politics. Is this possible? At least we must try. (Letter to Jim Forest, December 8, 1962.)

Not to be confused with disinterest in achieving results, detachment means knowing that no good action is wasted even if the immediate consequences are altogether different than what one hoped to achieve.

> Do not depend on the hope of results. When you are doing an apostolic work [such as work for peace], you may have to face the fact that your work will be apparently worthless and even achieve no result at all, if not

perhaps results opposite to what you expect. As you get used to this idea, you start more and more to concentrate not on the results but on the value, the rightness, the truth of the work itself. And there, too, a great deal has to be gone through, as gradually you struggle less for an idea and more and more for specific people. The range tends to narrow down, but it gets much more real. In the end, it is the reality of personal relationships that saves everything.

The big results are not in your hands or mine, but they suddenly happen, and we can share in them; but there is no point in building our lives on this personal satisfaction, which may be denied to us and which after all is not that important. The great thing, after all, is to live, not to pour out your life in the service of a myth: and we turn the best things into myths. If you can get free from the domination of causes and just serve Christ's truth, you will be able to do more and will be less crushed by the inevitable disappointments.

The real hope is not in something we think we can do, but in God, Who is making something good out of it in some way we cannot see. If we can do His will, we will be helping in the process. But we will not necessarily know all about it beforehand. (Letter to Jim Forest, February 22, 1966.)

Despite his personal commitment to nonviolence and membership in pacifist groups, Merton never condemned those who resorted to violence in self-defense. He accepted the possibility that just wars could occur and never insisted that a Christian must be a conscientious objector to all wars. But, as he wrote to Dorothy in 1962, the issue of the just war

is pure theory . . . in practice all the wars that are [happening] . . . are shot through and through with evil, falsity, injustice, and sin, so much so that one can only with difficulty extricate the truths that may be found here and there in the "causes" for which the fighting is going on. So in practice I am with you. (Letter to Dorothy Day, June 16, 1962.)

What he found valid in the just war tradition was its insistence that evil must be actively opposed and it was this that drew him to Gandhi, to Dorothy, and to membership in the Fellowship of Reconciliation, a movement committed to active nonviolent struggle for social justice.

One of the most striking of Merton's insights had to do with human unity.

He spoke of this deep sense of God's presence everywhere and in everyone in a talk given to his brother monks when he was moving into a hermitage at the Abbey of Gethsemani:

Life is this simple: We are living in a world that is absolutely transparent and God is shining through it all the time. God manifests Himself everywhere, in everything—in people and in things and in nature and in events. It becomes very obvious that He is everywhere and in everything and we cannot be without Him. You cannot be without God. It's impossible. It's simply impossible. The only thing is that we don't see it. What is it that makes the world opaque? It is care.

In the talk he gave in Calcutta a few weeks before he died, Merton said:

> The deepest level of communication is communion. It is wordless. It is beyond words, and it is beyond speech, and it is beyond concept. Not that we discover a new unity. We discover an older unity. My dear brothers, we are already one. But we imagine that we are not. What we have to recover is our original unity. What we have to be is what we are.

It was precisely this unity that he experienced at Fourth and Walnut in Louisville when God woke him from his dream of separateness.

(Thomas Merton's letters, including those cited here, are collected in The Hidden Ground of Love: The Letters of Thomas Merton, *William H. Shannon, ed. [New York: Farrar Straus Giroux,* 1985]. *Eds. note.)*

SEPTEMBER 1989

❈ God Is Slow to Anger and Rich in Mercy

ANN CLUNE

DEAR JIM,
You asked me to write something for our newsletter about abortion, but it has become very hard for me. I used to find it easier to discuss and I don't really understand what has happened to make me so reluctant. Maybe it is that much of what is written by both sides is so strident and judgmental. Maybe it is that we know so many good people on opposite sides of the issue and have learned that it is dangerous to presuppose understanding by "our friends," that makes writing it out for our newsletter a "chore" rather than an "opportunity." Whatever the reason, I think that putting my thoughts in the form of a letter to you, in whose love I feel secure, might make the task easier. Our friends can then read these words as they are meant to be, a sharing of years of prayer and reflection, and perhaps not feel preached at but rather

invited to know how I understand the moral issues involved, and to reflect for themselves on what a loving God asks of them.

Do you remember years ago, when we worked in that city hospital in the Bronx, interviewing patients, checking their medical charts for diagnoses to write on the bills, and the first few abortion cases I was assigned to handle, how upset I got? I cried when I read the medical chart of one patient and read of aborted twins delivered still alive and set aside to die. I felt so outraged that I went back to my supervisor in tears and told him outright that I could not interview any abortion patients with any kind of sympathy and understanding and refused to handle any more such cases. So I was given mostly maternity cases from then on.

But the poverty we saw around us and the desperate need I met in some of these women, many of whom couldn't speak English, led us both to realize that society was certainly as much to blame as desperate women were in the evil of abortion.

And when I lost our first baby in miscarriage—a baby I had so very much wanted—and had to go to a hospital for a D and C, I got yet another perspective on the whole question. I was heartbroken over my loss and awoke from the general anesthesia in a bed in a recovery area crying and also shaking with chills (a common reaction to the anesthesia) and a very cold nurse glanced over at me and harshly asked, "What are you crying about? You got what you wanted, didn't you?"

Of course, she thought I was in for an elective abortion, since my doctor had just added me to his waiting line for afternoon abortions.

Even though I was personally anguished over the horror of people deliberately choosing what I had so unwillingly suffered, I knew that there could be no room, in a Christian response to this evil, for so callous and judgmental an attitude. If I were a woman who had chosen an abortion out of a sense of despair and desperation, and regretted it and cried over it, shouldn't a Christian response be one of forgiveness and guidance? I knew then that I could never fight legalized abortion by being judgmental and harsh.

How, then, could we respond to this societal evil? We didn't know where to begin, but prayer and shared reading of the Bible and other thought-provoking literature eventually led us to the conclusion that in order to say "No" to abortion we were duty bound to offer a real alternative—some concrete help.

So, after a couple of years of struggling to find a way, we ended up here in Binghamton offering emergency shelter to women in crises. From very early on some of the best help we were able to give was a safe place to live to await the birth of a baby and a safe place with experienced help to come home to with a new baby.

Of course, there have been times when that was not enough. There have been times when guests have left us to have an abortion, hoping to put an end to the anguish they didn't feel strong enough to face—and leaving me feeling depressed and as if a failure.

You know, all too well, of one young friend with one child already who, finding herself pregnant again, was pressured to have an abortion. Her father threatened to write her totally out of his life—no more money or sympathy, ever, if she didn't abort this child, because he said he'd be embarrassed to have two illegitimate grandchildren. Her welfare case worker told her there was no way she could handle a second child and she should hurry up and have an abortion before it was too late. And, of course, there was her former counselor, a psychologist she had learned to trust in another city. She called her long distance for help, and was told by this psychologist not to worry about it, it wasn't a real baby yet: "At this stage it just looks like a duck. Go have an abortion." The father of the unborn was just a kid himself and couldn't see any way out.

And the person who had been the most supportive of her with her first child, the first child's paternal grandmother, let her know that there was no way she would feel the same about this baby—it wasn't her son's—but she was willing to keep her grandchild overnight so the mother could go and have an abortion.

Of course, we were helping her as much as we could. I spent hours and hours listening to her, talking to her, and helping her care for her child—but how could I compete with that kind of pressure? She knew how I felt about abortion—she had even expressed a strong opposition to it herself—and she couldn't even bring herself to tell us the truth about her decision.

The afternoon she left to have her abortion I had an awful sinking feeling she might be about to do it, but I couldn't bring myself to confront her and bring it out in the open.

When she returned pale and crying that evening with her story of having a miscarriage, I was devastated. She nearly had a nervous breakdown over it. She began talking to the protesters she'd met outside the clinic and insisted on telling me in great detail all the horrors she learned from them about abortion—yet she couldn't bring herself to admit to me that she'd chosen to have one, and I couldn't figure any way, short of calling her a liar, of letting her know I already knew. So I prayed constantly and listened endlessly, and became more and more depressed. Her initial reaction was to try to join the protesters wholeheartedly—but their strong fundamentalist religious fervor had her so up and down over the next year or so that she finally gave up on them and began to listen to other people's harsh criticism of them and to echo it herself.

I'm retelling you a story you know too well, because it highlights several of the worst elements of the problem.

If abortion were not legal, then authority figures could not push it as the solution to the problem of an inconvenient or a very troubling pregnancy. But if we are strident and condemning of the desperate women who are often very scared and unhappy already, we may do them more harm than good in the long run, and we are unlikely to change the heart of society which is at the root of the whole problem.

Many good people see the drive to outlaw abortion as a drive to re-establish dominance over women who have suffered too long under an oppressive attitude that keeps them as objects to be used by powerful men and society. But I see legalized abortion as a societal "cop-out." If society offers women the "solution" of abortion it doesn't have to bother to offer any concrete help with the problems poor women face.

By offering legalized abortion, society betrays its lack of commitment to the value of life. The problem is how to persuade society to become committed to life.

We have to somehow mirror the love of God in our actions—not condoning selfishness and hedonism, but always merciful and ready to forgive and guide home. We must invite people to trust God and to choose life. Abortion is wrong. You know I believe that. Once conceived, the whole person is present—the growth and change are only that, growth and change. Is a newborn baby any more different from a four-month fetus than it is from a mature adult? Life is a continuum.

Abortion is the killing of another human being, which I know to be wrong. As a radical Christian pacifist I can condemn the act of abortion as consistently and forthrightly as I condemn acts of war. But can I employ the same tactics to try to turn the country aside from abortion as I employ in trying to turn it away from militarism? That is my dilemma.

Since all too many of those involved in acts of civil disobedience to try to stop abortion are at the same time very militaristic and authoritarian, it is very hard to become involved in such activities without being identified with them.

And it seems to me that these acts of civil disobedience are perceived by most people, especially the women seeking abortions, to be personally condemning and threatening, more so than similar actions at weapons plants are, for instance—which gives them a character of violence we want at all costs to avoid.

But to do nothing to stop this social evil is also wrong. And so I guess we have to continue trying to do what we can. Praying; offering concrete help when and where we can; counseling, grieving and feeling like failures at times; and, yes, writing very difficult-to-write articles for our newsletter.

So I hope this letter somehow fills a need. Thank you for asking me to share it.

Love,

ANN

(Ann and her husband Jim live and work at Zacchaeus House in Binghamton, New York. Eds. note.)

MARCH–APRIL 1991

❧ Lena Rizzo

MICHAEL HARANK

EARLIER ON THE morning of the day I received Jeannette's letter, telling me of Lena's death, I had noticed on my way to work in downtown Oakland a rather large woman sitting with all her bagged belongings at the entrance to the BART station on 14TH Street and Broadway. Somehow, the sight of her brought me back to an image of Lena camped out near the entrance of the subway on 14th Street at Union Square in New York City. She was anchored amidst a roaring sea of shoppers, taxi cabs, cheap clothing stores, delis, drug addicts and pushers, business men and women—the flotsam and jetsam of the East Side. These were the people who helped Lena survive on the streets while she camped in the spring, summer, and autumn seasons. She counted on them for a hot cup of coffee or a sandwich, or maybe even a kind word.

Some folks of means spend the harsh New York winters amidst the tropical breezes of Florida. Not Lena. When the mercury began to fall in the late autumn, she, too, would gradually and somewhat reluctantly make her way down to Maryhouse. She knew when it was time to make her winter trek and settle into the warm foyer of the main entrance surrounded by her earthly belongings stuffed in bags. Like the loaves and fishes, these bags would miraculously multiply in the coming months. It was one miracle the Catholic Workers could have lived without.

There, outside the large auditorium adjacent to the offices where she could always sniff out Jeannette's presence, and down the hall from the chapel, Lena encamped herself on a long, wooden church bench. There she sewed her quilt-patch clothes, greeted some very surprised guests at the front door, and spun her own political theories about why atheists ruled the world. The high walls of that foyer entrance hold a multitude of Lena's stories and homilies in the aging cracked plaster.

My most cherished story of Lena was the memorable meeting between her and Mother Teresa of Calcutta. One day Mother Teresa had stopped by the house to pay a visit to Dorothy Day. Accompanied by her friend and biographer, Eileen Egan, Mother had finished her visit with Dorothy and Eileen asked if I could take her on a brief "tour" of the house. Mother Teresa came out of the chapel after a few minutes of prayer and, finding ourselves in the foyer, I began my "tour" with an introduction to Lena, who was lying on her church bench observing all the activity with great scrutiny.

"Mother Teresa, this is Lena. Lena, this is Mother Teresa." Mother clasped her hands together and gently bowed toward Lena—her white sari bending down with a soft movement of reverence. "Pleased to meet you, Lena," she said softly.

Lena looked inquisitively at this unusually attired nun and asked with her characteristic lisp, "Where are ya from?"

"Calcutta, India," Mother again replied with a bow.

Puzzled, Lena asked, "How did you get here? Did you come on roller skates or toothpicks?"

"No," Mother chuckled, flapped her white sari with both elbows and said, "I flew!" They both laughed. That seemed reasonable to Lena, who was given to some wild flights of imagination.

Impatient with the dragged-out introductory remarks, Lena finally got down to business. Looking Mother directly in the eyes, she said, "Well, now that you are here, do you have a cigarette for me?" It was, as you can imagine, one of Lena's most frequently asked questions of passers-by. Mother Teresa nodded and replied, "I'm sorry, but I do not smoke." Not having any success, Lena went on to the next person with the same, time-worn question. She always found someone around to meet her request.

I hope and pray that St. Peter was ready for Lena's questions when they met in the foyer entrance of the heavenly mansion.

SEPTEMBER 1991

❖ Hospitality Is Mutual Trust and Respect

MICHAEL KIRWAN

IN 1978, I was working as an account clerk at the George Washington University Hospital, in Washington, D.C., and beginning studies at the

University for a graduate degree in sociology. I was living in a university building on F Street, NW. I was very happy and content, and was looking forward to going back to school. I enjoyed my job at the hospital, and had good friends to share my life.

I was out walking one night near the State Department, only a block from my apartment. It was bitterly cold, and as I passed a heating vent at 21st and Virginia Avenue, NW, a man was sitting there. He called out to me and asked for a dollar to buy a bowl of soup. I ignored him and kept on walking. I still remember being very irritated and annoyed that he had disturbed my peace. He kept calling after me. I stopped about a block away and thought to myself, I'll fix him. He doesn't want soup, he just wants a drink; that's what they all want. I'll go up to my apartment and fix him some soup and that'll serve him right. I did this and brought the soup down, set it down, and walked away. I don't remember if he thanked me or not, and I didn't care. I didn't want to know anything about him; I just wanted to be spiteful.

I never saw that man again. I hadn't cared what it made him feel, but I had just helped someone; and actually there wasn't too much to it, and I felt pretty good about it. The next evening, I made more soup and a few sandwiches and some hot tea, and I took the food out to some other men on the heating vent, and I put it down and walked away. I still didn't talk to them. I was still afraid, as well as nervous, and very embarrassed. They thanked me, not knowing what I had brought, but grateful anyhow, it seemed, for the gesture.

I kept doing that night after night, repeating the same menu but gradually bringing down larger and larger containers as more and more people seemed to congregate for the food that I was bringing. One night as I brought down a large gallon-jug of hot split pea soup and set it down on the cement block near the heating vent around which they gathered, a rather rough-looking fellow picked up the jar of soup and, in one motion, broke the jar over my head. The soup ran down my clothes; it was boiling hot, and it burned me, but I was too afraid to feel it. But instead of running away, I asked the man why he had done that. They were probably the first words I had ever spoken to any of them. He told me that I was doing nothing more than bringing food to the dogs. I was treating all of them like pets. I was bringing food, setting it down like I was feeding them out of a pet dish and then just walking away. He said, "Talk to us; visit with us; we don't bite." I told him that I was afraid of him, that I didn't know what to say. But I did tell him that from now on, when I came with food, I would stay and visit if they wanted me to. If not, I would just leave.

What had happened that night was that a first barrier had been broken in my perceptions of who homeless people are. I realized that these men and women on the streets had feelings, just like me; they wanted to be loved and respected and listened to. They cared that someone cared about them, but just giving food and a blanket was not enough.

I continued to go every night without fail after that. I would stay and talk and listen, usually listen. I would begin to fill requests, most very ordinary, for such things as razors, a bar of soap, a bus token. I had always figured that their requests would only be for money, to buy a drink or get a fix. I had always heard and assumed that homeless men and women didn't care how they looked or smelled or acted or what people thought of them. I assumed they didn't want to work, and yet I gave out more bus tokens than anything else. Such little things yet such big assumptions.

Going to the grates at night began to be something I really looked forward to. It wreaked havoc with my personal life. "I have to cook the soup" became the standard excuse before any other outing, seven nights a week.

Everything was fine until, one night, a man asked me if he could come up to the apartment and shower and shave. He had a job he needed to go to in the morning, and he had to clean up. I was stunned. It was fine as long as I could make soup and just bring it down and visit and then go back to my apartment to my "normal" life. No one was the wiser. I would have been mortified to be seen with them; some unkempt and dirty, some a little intoxicated, others suffering from mental and emotional illness. Staying on the grates meant that I could and did deal with these things in a neutral way. But when this man asked to come up, it literally put me on the spot. I told him that I wasn't allowed to have people up who didn't live in the building; what I meant, of course, was that I wasn't allowed to have people like him up, or more honestly, that I didn't want him up. He accepted my excuse, but he kept asking. I could see that I was being tested, not just by him—everyone was looking, listening, and trying to figure out how genuine I was. Many were suspicious that I was working on a sociology term paper and when it was finished, so were they. Others thought I was some sort of do-gooder, or some kind of religious freak; most thought, and still do, that I am a priest, although I never bring religion into it or discuss it unless someone asks.

Finally, after a few days, I said all right, I told him that he could come back with me, take a shower and have a shave, but that he had to leave right away. I can still remember being very nervous, irritated, and afraid. I gave him some clean clothes, of which I had many. He went into the bathroom, and I went into the kitchen to finish the soup dishes. When I came into the living room about a half hour later, I found him asleep in the chair and didn't have the heart to wake him. He looked wonderful; cleaned up and in clean clothes, completely transformed. The next morning I got up and found breakfast on the table, and he was cleaning the apartment. I told him that I had to go to school and to work, but that he could leave when he wished.

It was a tremendous gamble. I had a stereo, books, records, a check book; a few valuable things, at least to me, and I really didn't know him at all. Yet, somehow, he looked so totally different and acted so normal that I trusted him. When I came home that night, he was there. He had never left. He had dinner on the table, the apartment looked immaculate, and he was listening to Richard Wagner on the stereo. He started to tell me about *Lohengrin*. Until that moment, it had never occurred to me that a homeless, unkempt person living on a heating vent could appreciate culture of any kind, let alone Richard Wagner, who was even a bit much for me. It broke barriers of other kinds; that homeless people could be educated, could appreciate the arts and beauty, could cook, want to be clean and live in pleasant surroundings and perhaps even trusted; could be honest, decent human beings.

He stayed for thirty days. He wouldn't leave, because I think he felt I wouldn't let him back in, and I probably wouldn't have. I loved my privacy and the way I lived. But yet I began to feel that there was something right about having him stay there. I just couldn't see forcing another human being out on the streets in the middle of winter, when he took up nothing more than floor space. I also wasn't bothered at all that he wasn't going out to work, the reason for his coming up to the apartment in the first place. I discovered then, and it has been confirmed many times since, that more often than not there has to be a transitional time from the life of the streets to full-time and meaningful employment; there has to be a time to calm down, dry out, come to terms with life, mentally, physically, and emotionally, especially if no structured program is available.

When other people on the streets saw that he was all right, they asked to come up. By the end of that month, I had fifteen people living in my apartment. The University couldn't quite figure out who was letting these people in and where they were going once they got in, because I would give them all a key. It was, in retrospect, perhaps a foolish thing to do, but at the time I thought of them all as nothing more than friends.

People in the apartment respected my need to study and to have quiet time. They would all sleep together in the small living room that I had, next to each other, much as they did on the grates for warmth and security. The apartment became a way station for those who needed to clean up or to make a phone call, or just to rest and to get out of the weather.

One day I was at work and the phone rang. It was my bank. They told me they had a guy there with five of my checks, all signed, and he wanted to cash them. I said "No," and they asked me if they should have him arrested. I again said no, just to give him the checks back and tell him to come home. He was waiting when I got home, and I said to him, "You know you didn't have to do that. Anything in this apartment is yours, if you want it; just ask." I didn't ask him to leave and I didn't make a big deal out of it. I knew he had nowhere else to go. He stayed. He never took anything out of the apartment again, and no one else did either. He became a dear friend, and, as with so many people on the streets, a tragic story. He died a few years ago, after drinking Mennen Skin Bracer one time too many, often a drink of choice on the streets. It's called Green Lizard. It's inexpensive and, because of its high alcohol content, gives one a very quick high. That spring day in my apartment I told him, as I did everyone else, we could only go on like this if we loved and trusted each other. The whole experience was based on that mutual respect, and so it is to this day.

One day a nun called, and said she understood that I was taking homeless people into my apartment. She told me about an eighty-year-old man who was living in a rooming house down the street. The landlady wanted him out because he was dying of cancer, and could no longer take care of himself. She indicated that he would soon be homeless unless I took him in. I told her I had no facility to take care of someone who essentially needed full-time care. But I did take him in, and I got a hospital bed and put it in the little room that I slept in, after moving my bed out. The men were afraid of him, and so was I, none of us having been around anyone who was dying before. I got a visiting nurse to come in every day and be with him while I was at work and school. She was wonderful, and very concerned. The fact that fifteen men were in the front room or somewhere in the apartment didn't seem to bother her at all. She taught me how to change a catheter and bedchucks, how to bathe him in bed, and how to medicate. She could easily have turned us all in. She didn't, though in some ways it really was a crazy situation. How reassuring she was, and how often I've thought of her since.

One Saturday morning, I was in the kitchen and I heard him scream from the bedroom that he was falling out of bed. He had been screaming all night in pain; I went into the bedroom and told him that he wasn't falling out of bed, but I went behind him and pulled him a little further up on the mattress. Just as I did that he lost complete control of his bowels, and everything was dripping down the sides of the bed, diarrhea and urine everywhere. He then took a deep breath and went to sleep. I cleaned him up, changed his sheets, and then went back into the kitchen. I came in a little while later and somehow it dawned on me that he was dead. He must have died when he had taken that deep breath. I wasn't aware of it because I had never seen anyone die before. I was petrified. Here was a man dead in my apartment, and all of these men in the front room. There was no discreet way of getting him to a funeral home. I called my mother. She was very calm, and told me I had to dial 911 for an ambulance. I told the operator that I thought someone had died, and in about three minutes I heard the ambulance, the fire department, the rescue squad, the students who came piling into the apartment, the homicide detectives, and the University officials. It was quite an uproar. I had never been in trouble in my life and I thought for sure I'd be arrested. The University now knew where the homeless people were going, and the jig was up. They told me that I had to get rid of all of these people, and I was violating the lease, but surprisingly they didn't pursue it any further. I buried Al; I didn't ask anyone to leave, and we went on as before. One year passed and we began another.

Another Saturday morning, a few months later, a young man of twenty-four came up to the apartment and asked to shower and shave. He went into the bathroom, and after an hour still had not come out. He had died in the tub of an overdose of drugs and alcohol. He was a very well-to-do young man, and his funeral was at a French-speaking Catholic church in Georgetown. His death brought home to me again that all homeless people are not poor, uneducated, mostly black, as I had thought. Drugs and alcohol pervade, capture, and enslave all racial, economic, and social backgrounds.

This time I knew what to expect. The University told me that I had to leave since I had not cooperated. I told them I could go anywhere since I had a job, a college degree, I was white, and had many resources to call on. I asked them if they would let us stay in one of their abandoned buildings, then held vacant while waiting to be torn down for further University expansion, while I looked for a place. They said no. For the first time in my life, I took a stand. I told them that I wouldn't leave until all of us had a place to go. The University took me to court. The judge was very sympathetic and told me that what I was doing was a good thing, but that I couldn't do it in University housing. He told me, though, that he would give me three months to find another place to live and that we could all stay together.

I found a small real estate ad in *The Washington Post* that read: "Renovator's Delight!" It turned out to be a boarded-up four-room house with no utilities, what was termed a shell, for sale for $22,000. Since I still had my job at the hospital, I could move in. It was quite an experience. It was the first time in my life that I had ever lived in a neighborhood that was poor, in which I was the only white person, in a house that was incredibly dilapidated. The very first night that I moved in, with about fifteen other people, with no lights or heat, and boards still on the windows, the house was broken into. In confronting the guy who was climbing in the kitchen window having pried the boards off, I told him that he needn't have gone to all that trouble; the front door was broken anyway.

We had moved in during September, and by the end of that fall we had forty people living in four rooms. That little house became our first house of hospitality. The homeless men and women who came to the house heard of it by word of mouth. I didn't know most of them, and when I went to work they stayed and were still there when I came home.

Our inner-city neighbors initially didn't know what was going on in our little Llewellyn Scott Catholic Worker House. As I indicated later to them, I was in this neighborhood for the same reason many of them were; it was all I could afford. Some neighbors, as they saw the numbers of people coming in and out of the house, began to question why they had to put up with more problem people. They began to mellow through the intervention of a woman who was a neighbor of ours two doors away, an elderly, black woman. She was very poor and often I would see her in the alley behind the house collecting pieces of wood to heat her stove, which was her sole source of heat. She was in very poor health, but was known in the neighborhood for her kindness and generosity, especially to the children. She taught them to dance; she collected things; gave food and clothing away. Her name was Mary Harris but she was known in the neighborhood as Miss Mary. From the very first, she welcomed us and came over and told us that if there was anything she could do for us, all we had to do was ask. One night our electric power was turned off because I had not been able to pay the bill. Mary came over with a kerosene lamp and told me to keep it as long as I needed it. She said that her electricity had been turned off so many times she had gone out and bought the lamp. I never forgot her generosity and concern; her breaking down the barrier with this neighborhood; her welcoming these homeless men and women even though every act came from her own want. She died a mere five months after we moved into the neighborhood, and I was able to buy her little house. I turned it into a house for women and named it after her. What a lasting tribute. There were nights when upwards of fifty women were in those four rooms, sleeping everywhere.

In 1982, I began to talk about the need to get people out of the city, away from the constant temptations to violence and substance abuse; perhaps a return to a simpler, back-to-basics lifestyle. I saw a little farm advertised in the paper. It was in southern West Virginia, near a little town called Alderson. I was aware of Alderson because it was the location of the federal prison for women, and many of our neighbors had friends and relatives in the prison, 300 miles from Washington. I fell in love with the farm, with its peace and beauty. It was very rustic: indeed, it had outhouses instead of indoor plumbing, and that kind of set the tone for the whole place. I signed to buy the farm for $48,000, to be paid in cash in two weeks. I had no money whatsoever, but the couple I was buying it from didn't know that. I came back to Washington and told my parish, St. Stephen Martyr, that I needed the money. They held a benefit which raised $3000, which was wonderful, but a long way from

$48,000. The next day a woman came to the rectory and offered us the balance.

John Filligar Farm is now home to about eighteen people. Seven are now buried on the farm in our little cemetery. They were people who loved the farm, including a woman who had spent over thirty years on the streets of Washington. Tyra was only at the farm for six months before she died of all the abuse her body had taken on the streets over the long years. But it was the happiest time of her life, as she told me when she lay dying. She had grown up on a dust-bowl farm in the thirties and had never forgotten that experience. In her six months, she taught us all how to farm; another example of a homeless person given a chance to offer herself as gift and example to the rest of us. She loved the land, the animals, and the peace. Our farm for women and children, across the road from our original farm, is named after her.

Now our fields are planted; last year the farm canned 4,000 quarts of produce; our eggs and milk often come to the soup line in Washington at our hospitality house; hospitality is extended day in and day out by men and women from the streets. The farm reflects the needs, wants, aspirations of people caught in an impersonal urban environment out of control, and has given them and us a chance to change direction and rediscover the potential and gifts of each one of us.

Our houses exist in a neighborhood that began as genteel and well-to-do around the turn of the century. After the riots of 1968, the area around 14th and U Streets became a synonym for the worst of Washington, its crime, drugs and violence. Today the old Victorian row houses are being bought up by young professionals attracted by their beauty and grace, their proximity to downtown, and the convenience of the new subway which just opened two weeks ago, one block away.

A woman came from across the street recently while I was unloading the car on a quiet Sunday morning in front of the houses, and she screamed at me that she and other people were moving into the neighborhood and paying $300,000 for a house, and then they had people like us to contend with. She said it wasn't right. No, it isn't, but I don't think we would agree on why not.

It's very difficult, always being made to feel guilty; being made to feel that I'm in the wrong because I give hungry people a meal or floor space so that they won't have to sleep on the streets. What kind of society are we that what we do here is considered so wrong?

Most of all, people need to understand that this house of hospitality is my home; it is a way of life, a continuing commitment, a challenge in faith and love. How often I'm confronted and told that I am operating a shelter, a soup kitchen, charity, or agency. More than anything, people find it impossible to believe that I actually live in the house, as if there were something exotic, romantic, or holy about the prospect.

I really believe, with Franklin Roosevelt, that what we have to fear is fear itself. We must break down fears and prejudices. They feed on themselves; become larger and more complicated. We cannot just listen to or read media accounts of who people are. We must visit and learn in person. We must experience those in prison, in shelters, soup kitchens, in houses of hospitality, those with AIDS, those who are drug addicts and those who are alcoholic or, in some other way, down-and-out on their luck. We must get to know people as people, not as classes or clients, or groups or caseloads, but as individuals. It is not easy; I'm the first to admit it.

I am constantly amazed when I hear the stories of so many of these men and women. I keep waiting to hear something extraordinary, weird, or unique. The stories are difficult, to be sure; some tragic, all sad. But they are all common to the human dilemma, to the human experience. What we don't know can dehumanize us and rob us all of the goodness and spirit and gifts of all the peoples among us.

AUGUST 1992

❈ Adventures in Nonviolence

KARL MEYER

RECENTLY I WENT to a huge air show at Luke Air Force Base just west of Phoenix, Arizona. Advance notice said there would be 200,000 people there to see displays of Air Force planes and the aerial aerobatics of the Blue Angels flying team. I drove out there in my Peace House. It's a unique and colorful truck house that is my home in Phoenix, as well as a traveling center for education about peace and nonviolence.

I walked into the base with thousands of other guests. I spent an hour roaming around in fascination and horror. Thousands of children and their parents were swarming around and through dozens of military airplanes of every variety. There were also displays of other Desert Storm equipment. I was fascinated myself by the massive technical complexity of the planes. It seemed to me that at least one person in Phoenix should witness against this wasteful madness.

I walked back to the Peace House. With luck and shrewd driving choices, I managed to get around a huge traffic jam heading toward the base; I got past all deputy sheriffs who were routing traffic to off-base parking sites. I drove straight onto the concrete flight line where all the planes were displayed. To my own astonishment, I was able to spend the next half hour cruising slowly through the crowds, around all the airplanes. All the while I rang the bell in the bell tower of the Peace House. A television news crew from KTVK Channel 3 interviewed me in the truck, and filmed the Peace House in motion against a background of bombers and fighter planes.

Finally, an Air Force police car pulled up and stopped me. The officers gave me a choice: Either follow them out or they would arrest me. I decided to stay.

They put the cuffs on me and called a towing company to take the Peace House away. To me it was nothing new. I've been arrested dozens of times for protest actions over the last thirty-five years. But the Peace House is only two years old. This was the first time it had ever been arrested.

The Maricopa Sheriff's Deputies were all very courteous. As the paddy wagon passed their command post at the front gate, their supervising officer leaned into the van and told the driver, "He's going to be booked for criminal trespass, and the victim is the U.S. Air Force."

The Deputies had me out on bond within two hours. I was feeling exhilarated, but when I called Knowlton Towing to spring the Peace House I got a disturbing shock. They were asking for a ransom fee of $505, that would increase by $20 a day for storage.

The next morning I called three competitive towing companies listed in the Yellow Pages and asked for a price for a comparable tow. The prices they quoted me were $85, $75, and $51.

Then I called Knowlton Towing and said, "Let's be reasonable. Let's negotiate about this." The owner didn't want to talk or budge an inch. I said I would raise a big stink at the Sheriff's office. He said, "Listen, if you don't want to come out today and pick it up for the price I gave you, you're just wasting my time."

Bright and early Monday morning, I called the Sheriff's office. An officer in the Traffic Division explained the realities to me. All the Sheriff has is a list of approved towing companies to call. A couple of years ago the State Legislature deregulated the towing industry, and the companies can charge whatever they please.

"You mean," I said, "that I was lucky? They could have charged me $1,000 or $1,500, and there's nothing I can do about it?"

I was beginning to pick up a distinct odor of corruption. When a private businessman, acting on behalf of a public agency, can charge six times the prevailing market rate for the work he performs, you feel that there are going to be kickbacks and payoffs for the public employees who steer him business.

I called the editors of two local newspapers that had done feature stories about the Peace House. I told them the facts and asked them to call the Sheriff and ask about my story. They readily agreed. Then I headed straight for the Sheriff's office. I was received promptly by Duane Brady, Administrative Assistant to the Sheriff. He said that all he knows about towing arrangements is that they have a list of approved companies. They are called automatically on a rotating basis, as towing situations arise.

I explained that I would like help in reducing the exorbitant towing fee. I had expected to pay more than competitive rates when my truck was towed at the Sheriff's request, but I felt that I should not pay more than $250, which is twice the competitive rate.

I also told him that through my personal experience I had stumbled upon a serious public policy problem. Under the present system, defenseless citizens could be victimized by greedy towing companies. Also the door is wide open for corruption of law enforcement officers, because towing companies can earn such a big windfall by getting referrals from officers.

The Sheriff needs to establish a standard of rates which approved towing companies can charge, in order to protect those whose vehicles are towed.

On Tuesday, Duane Brady sent a Lieutenant to Knowlton Towing to investigate my claims. He informed me that he had concluded that the towing charge was excessive, but Knowlton Towing was sticking to its position and he was powerless to compel them to revise their charges. However, he could continue to investigate to see whether they should remain on the Sheriff's list of approved towing companies.

On Wednesday morning I went by bus to Knowlton Towing and agreed to pay the charges, which they now calculated at $513.

George Knowlton, the owner, refused to accept my American Express Travelers Checks and insisted on cash money only. We had some angry words about this. It would be necessary for me to walk about a mile to a bank to cash my travelers checks and then return.

When he showed me the order ticket and bill, the basic charge was for a heavy duty tow truck at $150 an hour, for three hours. I had been arrested around 3:00 p.m., and released at 5:10 p.m. The figures now read 3:00 p.m. and 6:00 p.m., but certain parts of the numeral 5 could still be deciphered under the 6, and parts of other illegal numbers under the other digits.

When I called his attention to these alterations, George said that he had blackened the numbers so thoroughly in order that I would be able to see them clearly.

After some more tough and candid words between us, which sort of cleared the air, I went off to the bank to cash my travelers checks.

When I came back, George accompanied me to the Peace House, and I gave it a thorough examination for damage or missing belongings. I invited him to look it over. He asked if I had built it myself. I said that I had. He said that if we had met under other circumstances he might have asked me to work on a bus parked nearby which he intends to convert to a motor home. I showed him a book I have called "Rolling Homes," which is about converted buses and trucks.

After I paid his $513 in cash and signed the receipt for my truck, I laid another $50 on the counter and said "George, I'd like to make a donation of $50 to your company, and this is why: You either need money very badly to keep your business going, or you love money very much. Otherwise, you wouldn't do to me what you did. Now, if I can't transcend my anger, and deal with it, and go on from here . . ." "You'd get yourself into big trouble?" he offered. "No", I said, "I don't really have much anger in me; but what might happen is that I could become real greedy about money myself, and I don't want that to happen. What I want you to do with the $50 is this; the next time you hook up some old lady's car, who can't afford to pay very much, just knock $50 off her bill."

"Thank you," he said.

"George," I said, "it's been very interesting doing business with you." I extended my hand and we shook hands firmly and cordially.

Another adventure in nonviolent action.

The criminal charges against me say that the victim is the U.S. Air Force, but I feel that there were no victims. Everybody gained, and that is why I like nonviolent action. The people of Arizona will gain if the Sheriff reexamines his towing policies and standards. The Air Force police, the Sheriff's deputies, George Knowlton, and I will all gain if we've all seen that there is a way to be strong and assertive, without being violent or exploitative. So, I believe that there was $563 worth of public education all the way around, our tuition in the College of Hard Knocks.

AUGUST 1992

❀ The Anger of God

FELTON DAVIS

FOR THE LAST fifteen years, members of the Atlantic Life Community have gathered in Washington, D.C. at the end of December to commemorate the Massacre of the Holy Innocents. King Herod's order, that all the boys in Bethlehem age two and under be killed, is told in the second chapter of Matthew. As an attempt on the life of Jesus, it failed, because Mary and Joseph escaped with the baby to Egypt until Herod died. As a story, it makes a gruesome beginning for the New Testament. As a Catholic Feast Day, it is hard to dwell on, coming as it does so soon after Christmas.

This past year, the gathering was full of somber reflections about the war against Iraq and the continuing toll on the children of that country. It became clear to us, if it was not clear already, that people in America are still numb to the suffering of others in distant countries and at home. They do not see the bloodshed, do not hear the cries of the vanquished, and as a result, do not call upon their leaders to give up policies and actions of enormous violence.

On December 28, a dozen of us were arrested at the White House. Some climbed the fence and hung banners from the trees on the White House lawn. Some poured blood on the pillars that stand on each side of the long driveway. Some held signs for people to read or passed out leaflets.

In June we go to trial to try to explain our action to a District of Columbia jury. For my own part, I have no lengthy explanation. If I could speak only one uninterrupted sentence to the judge or jury, I would recall the words of Thomas Jefferson: "I tremble for my country when I reflect that God is just."

In court we meet one kind of judgment, and in jail we meet another. I remember a cellblock years ago, twenty-four of us in twelve small cages, the only white face the one I saw in the mirror. It was close to eleven at night, and the guards were getting ready to lock down and turn the television off. A prisoner hurriedly changed the channel to check the news.

"Word up!" he screamed, "there's been an attack! An atomic bomb! They dropped an atomic bomb on Charleston!"

The cellblock was instantly convulsed.

"Charleston?" cried another prisoner. "Charleston, South Carolina? I got an uncle down there! I got an uncle in Charleston!"

"Correction" snapped another prisoner. "You had an uncle in Charleston. That city's gone. You better hope he was out of town tonight."

And then words like "gone" and "leveled" and "off the map" resounded down the cellblock, gaining an almost incantatory character, as the prisoners tried to get a feel for the meaning of the destruction.

"Hey, isn't that what the guy in cell ten was arrested for raising hell about? The protester?"

I knew this was coming.

"Raising hell? He hasn't raised nothin'! Cities blown up, and he laying in his bunk with a book! He ain't no real protester."

"You knew that it would come to this, protester! You knew! And all you had in your hand was a can of spray paint. That ain't right."

"Get over here and look at this, protester!! What do you think's gonna happen now? All the missiles be flyin' in a minute! And all the world up in smoke! You know that!"

"They ain't gonna let one city go without an answer."

"And the radiation be comin' at us right through the walls!"

"I tell you one thing, protester: It looks like we gonna go, one way or another. And face the Man upstairs. And I tell you, the black man will not have to answer for that," he said, pointing at the television and screaming at me. "Do you understand? I don't care what you did, and I don't care what you said, that got you in here. All I'm telling you is, you ain't goin' upstairs with us. The black man did not build that bomb. That's the white man's bomb. That's your bomb. Did you really want to stop it? Did you really care? Well, it's too late now, man. It's over. It's history. Everything is history. Take it up with the Man upstairs! You ain't goin' with us."

"What d'you have to say about that, protestor? Homeboy's put a heavy rap on you."

"That's right. Give him a chance to talk. I was there in court with him, and he had lots to say. What does he have to say now?"

"What I have to say is that you guys are right. I didn't do enough to stop it, and I'm just as guilty as the people who built the bomb, and paid for it, and dropped it, and all the rest. I don't deserve anything better than your judgment and condemnation. This is a more honest and human court, more in touch with basic right and wrong, than all the real courtrooms I've been in so far. And I am guilty. For years I knew it was wrong, and did nothing. I knew the Vietnam War was wrong, and did nothing. I knew all the racism and inequality in our society were wrong, and did nothing. I grew up privileged and comfortable and white, and I'm certainly more of a criminal than any of you."

Well, that's what I could have said. What I actually said was, "Listen, you guys are getting upset over nothing! They didn't blow up Charleston, South Carolina, because that's not the news. That's not real. That's just a movie. If you don't believe me, turn it to Channel 11. See if "The Honeymooners" is on. Don't you think they would interrupt "The Honeymooners" if there was a nuclear war? And don't you think the guards would be talking about it?"

"Man, leave the guards out of this! The guards are only gonna take care of their own stuff. You think they care about us? You think they would let any one of us go if there was a war? No way! They be runnin' out of here to their homes and wives, and leavin' us all to die."

"That won't do any good," said another prisoner. "Where they gonna get to? By tomorrow morning, the whole East Coast will be a parking lot. Check the other stations like he says, before we get locked down."

It was some relief to see Jackie Gleason appear that night, and when the news in fact began on one of the other stations, the announcer explained that people should not be misled by the movie that had just concluded, which was called "Special Bulletin." Correspondents from Charleston were produced, to make lighthearted jokes, and reassure everyone that the city was fine.

For days afterward, the implications of this non-event reverberated through C-Block, and prisoner after prisoner came to my cell to talk and ask questions and straighten it all out. I remember one who came with Bible in hand. Nothing that had been said that night was lost on him, and he was not particularly happy with my response to the scene.

"Listen, Davis," he said, his voice full of urgency. "I think you failed to speak to the issue. It was indeed a heavy rap, about the heaviest one that could be laid on you, and all you had to say was, 'Turn it to Channel 11.' You were afraid of them all, and what they might do to you, and you lost sight of the anger of God. You deflected the situation, and got away with it. But don't you know that even here in the jail, God hears every word you say? And, on the day of judgment, you will have to answer for it. For everything you said, and everything you didn't say. Now listen, no one knows when the hour will come, do they? But the hour will come, and when the anger of the Lord is burning in your face, you are not going to tell God to turn it to Channel 11, are you?"

"Well no, but . . ."

"Of course you are not. Then you will have to speak to the issue. You see what I mean? I'm not saying this to put you down. I'm only saying this because I see you reading your Bible every day, and that's a good thing, but it's not enough. You must come to know the living God, and you must come to know that God is angry, very angry, angry beyond measure."

Eventually, in another jail, on another sentence, to go with my verbal instruction about anger, I received physical instruction, in the form of a beating. I was punched and kicked black and blue, dragged from my bunk and slammed onto the concrete floor. It was not as bad as it sounds, because for most of the beating I was unconscious, and felt nothing. I woke up only as other prisoners took hold of the poor fellow who had flown into a rage, and pushed him over to a corner. The blows I had to feel were few but—I'm firmly convinced of this—necessary. How else is the stupidity of an ordinary American education to be knocked out of a person? Do we expect the enormous frustration and rage of the oppressed to just blow away of its own accord? Is the resentment that seethes in our cities supposed to just evaporate? Are third-world countries supposed to just turn the other cheek in the face of American bombs? No. It cannot be that way. There are more blows to be received. Pray for the patience to receive them. There is more hostility to be absorbed. Pray for the willingness to absorb it. There is more hatred and madness to be purged. Pray for the strength to help our heedless country bring its sickness to the surface, so it can be healed.

Come to the jails of America, you heavy-hearted, burdened, guilty people. Come and share the squalor with the ones you have condemned. Of the children killed by Herod, we know not a single name. Come and learn the name of one or two children today, whose future has been rendered meaningless by a society with no room. Come and listen and perhaps you will hear a foretaste of the anger of God. There is still time.

And even in the anger, there is more to taste than anger. The anger of God is music to the ears of the oppressed. It fills the Psalms with exultation, and drives the symphonies of Beethoven. The meanest strain, when heard another way, becomes a shout of triumph. "All is joy! All is joy! Here's a joyful kiss for all!" (The tenors have to shout, to be heard above the trombones. But the earthly symphony is only a rehearsal of the heavenly symphony, and, in heaven, the trombones will play a little softer.)

"I have a dream, that black and white will go to jail together," said Martin Luther King. Now let us dream that black and white will get out of jail together, that the door will open for both on the same day, and that the freedom will, in fact, be freedom, and a new life for all to live together.

"And you will go out and leap like calves released from the stall" (Malachi 4:2).

_____ DECEMBER 1993

❁ St. Joseph House

DANIEL DUNN

SMILING POLITELY AT abusive behavior is a practice that I have perfected over the years. Being a gentleman, slight of build, it is a skill that has largely kept me clear of the destructive path of bullets, and purchased for me a contingent peace.

So, on the day when Michael pushed his fist through the broken glass and ripped open the window; when he shoved me aside and forced his way into my house; when he grabbed the knife from the kitchen table and held it up to me—I was only mildly surprised. Although, I confess, my limbs were quivering slightly, I stood my ground before Michael and the knife. There were a number of women in the room and I would have been completely disgraced if I allowed any of them to be harmed. (In the South, where I am from, a gentleman never disappoints a lady.) I found the calmness of some of the women in the room to be quite irritating at this point. I even thought I heard the sounds of Kassie going about her cooking. Their lack of fear was deflating my moment of glory. A further irritant was the gross drunkenness of Michael. He was not in a state of mind to appreciate the poetics of my negotiations, nor the sincerity of my voice; besides which, it is my hope to be stabbed by some world leader who is infuriated by the Christ-like grandeur of my theological treatises and aesthetic constructions, rather than the haphazard commotions of a drunk. I was certainly focusing on the knife in his hand when I started day-dreaming about having one of those heroic scars on my face like the one Roger, the kid anarchist, recently acquired. Involuntarily imagining the knife instead plunged into my fragile stomach, I said a quick prayer that my martyrdom might be a painless one.

Intruding upon my muddled moment, Paul, a mere servant of God, entered the scene from stage left. He performed the task for which I am physically ill-equipped, wrestling the knife from the strong man and dragging him from my house. In a pathetic attempt to reclaim the moment, which had already come to pass, I dramatically picked up the knife and hid it beside the coffee machine. My only saving grace, for which I held little esteem, was that I thought I behaved in accordance with the pacifist ideology of my audience. Nevertheless, I polished off the incident by making light of it to the comrades and I called it a day. What I was not prepared for was what would transpire on the next day.

Somewhat annoyed by my own state of mild agitation, I was going about the activities of the morning soup line. About half way through, it happened. I thought I recognized his overcoat in the back of the room and then I was sure. Michael had returned. He was smiling, and it seemed that everyone was smiling. I felt sick. The sight of him penetrated my flesh and bones. The depth of the previous day's events was now felt as real experience, as real pain, as real violation. He appeared to have forgotten everything and his smile felt to me to be the height of cruelty. I had not forgotten; my body would not let me forget, and my pain became rage. I went to him in fear and trembling and told him I wanted to talk to him and I reminded him of what he had just done the day before. As soon as I walked away, I noticed him joking with the people at his table and the rage began again inside me. When Michael came to the back yard, I did what I have not done before, what my methods of mediocre Christianity have not trained me to do: I screamed.

I have always loved the stories of Flannery O'Connor. Her short story, "A Good Man is Hard to Find," tells the tale of an old woman and her family who are murdered for no apparent reason by an escaped convict and his gang. The old woman pleads for her life, making an appeal based on her own good Christian living as well as the good Christian inside the heart of the Misfit. The Misfit replies:

> Jesus was the only one that ever raised the dead, and He shouldn't have done it. He thrown everything off balance. If He did what He said, then it's nothing for you to do but throw away everything and follow Him, and if He didn't, then it's nothing for you to do but enjoy the few minutes you got left the best way you can—by killing somebody or burning down his house or doing some other meanness to him. No pleasure but meanness.

The terror of the moment overwhelms the old woman. She stops pleading her case for her earned mercy, and she awakens to a vision of the Misfit as one of her own beloved children. The Misfit goes on to kill the woman, commenting: "She would of been a good woman, if it had been somebody there to shoot her every minute of her life."

Michael turned the tables on me. His fury broke through the threshold of my polite smiling. His arbitrary raving rendered obsolete my clever condemnations. I am the Misfit and I am the babbling old woman, left staring into the horror or without a case for my own self-defense, my false Christianity left in a shambles. I need somebody to shoot me every minute of my life. I need to put my face in front of every slashing knife or pointed gun I can find. My only hope is in the violent awakening of the undeserved beauty of Christ crucified for love of me. Since for me, the only justification is in this love of Christ, I must throw away everything to be with Him on the Cross, in the violence of love.

❀ Peter Maurin Farm

TOM CORNELL

I SING OF COMPOST: rotting leaves and grass clippings, tea-bags and coffee grounds, egg shells, watermelon and citrus rind, fruit pulp and vegetable scraps, a sprinkling of raw manure for garnish (optional, and only from grass-eaters), melting snow or spring rain to seep through it all, and sunshine. There are as many methods of composting as there are practitioners. Nothing will keep vegetable matter from rotting. Some gardeners cover their heaps with a tarpaulin after they are well established and leave them for a year, using only two-year-old fine, sifted compost. Others dig in as soon as decomposition is far enough along to make the bottom level dark and homogenous, and mix that into their garden beds. It's better not to hurry. Premature mixtures will rob the soil of nitrogen.

Ralph and Else compost in a trench. Monica and I pile layers up to three feet. Our son Tommy constructs a bin out of loading pallets. Others use chicken wire to form a circle secured by stakes. Take your choice. Everything works, eventually.

One of the purposes of Peter Maurin Farm is to encourage readers to experiment with what we intend as replicable examples of small-scale agriculture. Why bother if, gardening on a small scale, all you are likely to harvest your first year is some salad? Nothing tastes as good. And, most of all, because it will hook you into the phenomenon of food production. You have read and heard about the world food crisis, how the fertility of the earth's growing surfaces is declining, how new technologies have to be invented each decade to repair the damage done by the new technology of the last and new "miracle crops" developed to stave off mass starvation. You know of the immense investment in machinery needed for traditional farmers to compete in agribusiness, and how so many have been driven out of business by their inability to keep up debt-payments when market conditions sour. There's another way of looking at these realities if you start growing your own food. You will want to learn about soil preparation, tools, weed and pest control, germination and growing time, rotation and companion growing.

Tommy lent us his copy of Eliot Coleman's *The New Organic Grower: A Master's Manual of Tools and Techniques for the Home and Market Gardener.* We are going to have to buy our own copy, and suggest you consider the same. Eliot Coleman was a friend and neighbor of our old friends, Helen and Scott Nearing, in Maine, and he learned a lot from them. Tommy included a note: "When I met him, I mentioned that I am a Catholic Worker interested in small scale agriculture. Eliot Coleman said, 'Oh, Ammon Hennacy, the One Man Revolution. He's one of my heroes!' So there is a philosophical and a personal connection there." Consider Eliot Coleman on pest control:

> What I am proposing is a totally revised way of thinking for the proper understanding of agriculture. We need to develop a biologically oriented thinking that sees our agricultural efforts as participatory rather than antagonistic vis-à-vis the natural world. It isn't a question of whether

pesticides are undesirable or not. The fact is that they are totally superflu-
ous. They were devised to prop up an agro-industrial framework that was
misconceived from the start. When you abandon that framework you can
abandon its superficial thinking pattern. Don't start with industrial theory
and try to naturalize it. Start on another plane entirely. Study the established balances of the natural world in order to learn how to nurture
and enhance those balances for agricultural production. Pay attention
to the existing framework of plant-pest relationships and learn how food
production can be achieved through biological diplomacy rather than
chemical warfare. The potential of such new understanding is as yet
undreamed of.

Even the smallest plot, mindfully cultivated, will give the grower
experiential insight into one of the stark problems facing humanity:
how to feed without starving, impoverishing, enslaving, and poisoning
ourselves. In the end, it's part of what Peter Maurin called cult, culture,
and cultivation. Eliot Coleman admits he has yet to devise a diplomacy
for the potato bug, and Kevin sympathizes, having lost his whole crop
last year to that pest.

Well-water is a problem here. It's full of iron and sulphur. We draw
drinking and cooking water from a spring. The minerals will even
discolor clothing, so we have had to use a commercial laundromat,
until Larry O'Toole solved our problem by installing a system of cisterns,
made from used 55-gallon applejuice containers, bought at $5 each
from a nearby orchard. The system reserves about 200 gallons of rainwa-
ter, gravity-fed into our washing machine. My grandmother did her
laundry in the Colore River, and her children did theirs in the Hudson.
We are not spending much more than they did thanks to Larry.

Despite all last winter's snow, the ground is not as moist as it should
be. We have had days of sunshine so clear, so free of haze that we can
see the Shawangunk and Catskill mountain ranges, and ridges between
with apple orchards in blossom. This week, it has been cool and cloudy
with frequent showers, perfect planting weather. The last frost date just
passed. The first of the tomatoes are in, with many more to go. The
squashes are ready, the cabbage and kohlrabi are hardening. Sweet
peppers and jalapenos and serranos have to wait for warmer earth.

We have flowers, too. Monica's kitchen garden has early and late-
blooming tulips and roses transplanted from our former home in Water-
bury, as well as established climbers and new rose bushes. The red
German garlic and Jerusalem artichoke, planted side by side, are especially thick near the roses, their favorite companion plant. The garlic
is already over a foot tall. We can't keep from chewing the leaves. I slip
some into our salads, along with dandelion greens and chives. Thyme
and oregano are lush, and the sage is coming back; basil and tomatoes
grow and stew together, and everything grows in a pleasant hodge-
podge. All this in an incredibly small space, impossibly crowded, it

might seem. That is a variant of the "French intensive" method. In a small space we can afford the energy to dig deep, a foot or two by hand, removing the larger rocks, mixing in large amounts of well-decomposed compost and sheep manure. This we did in the fall. The mixture mellowed over the winter. In such rich soil roots grow down more than outward, allowing closer planting. That kitchen garden, built on what was clay last summer, with poor drainage, is now so fertile we are tempted to plant stones just to see if they sprout.

The Easter cycle is coming to a close. Next Sunday is Pentecost. *Veni Creator Spiritus.* Pour forth upon compost and field. Renew the face of the earth, and, in us, the fire of Your Divine Love.

AUGUST–SEPTEMBER 1994

❊ Help Thou Our Unbelief

PHILIP BERRIGAN

A YEAR or so ago, in the course of a talk at a university in Maryland, I was questioned by a thoughtful, matronly woman. "How are we to understand the world's mess? What's behind all this war, violence, evil?"

Somehow her question stays with me—perhaps because I gave her only a superficial answer, speaking of economic unrest, neonationalism, and so on.

Now that I'm doing jail time, Holy Mother State offers occasion for more serious attention to her question.

I had asked her to explain her word "mess." She did so with a thoughtful vengeance. "War is the biggest business on earth, the nuclear club expands like a black hole, arms are fervently huckstered everywhere (the U.S. sales alone in 1993 being on the order of $31 billion), some forty-five conventional wars are in progress, famine afflicts the third and fourth worlds, the rich/poor gap grows apace, domestic violence surges, the cancer and AIDS epidemics, contamination of air, soil, and water, ozone depletion, greenhouse effect."

She seemed, to say the least, remarkably familiar with our predicament.

And her anguish!

The woman struck me as someone not content merely to catalog doom and gloom. She was groping for light on matters virtually ignored by Washington, the churches, the media, the universities, experts of every stripe. What underlies and impels and multiplies the terror and death? Must the poor of the world be sacrificed to first-world consumers? How to understand the fatal attraction that holds us captive to the Bomb? Are remedies at hand to prevent destruction of ourselves and our planet?

In jail a year later, I'm driven to return to her question. I opened the Bible to the passage in St. Mark 9, the exorcism of the possessed child.

Descending from the Mount of the Transfiguration, Jesus encounters a father and son. The child is desperately afflicted, wordless and deaf. The father anguishes, and the disciples of Jesus, stalemated, can bring neither relief nor healing.

The reaction of Jesus is curious. Rather than addressing the disciples or the father, He turns to the crowd, "What an unbelieving lot you are!" As though to say, "The boy's plight, deaf and mute as he is, stems from the disbelief of you adults! His affliction mirrors your own—your incapacity to hear or speak the truth. It is you who are deaf and mute, and the child pays for it."

Then, "Bring the child to me."

Identified powerfully and unequivocally, its cover revealed, the demonic spirit asserts a kind of last-ditch power over the child, throwing him brutally to the ground in convulsions. In the past, according to the father's sorrowful account, the same spirit "has often cast him into the water and fire to destroy him," parodying sacramental symbols, turning the signs of water and fire to instruments of death.

In jail, we watch as the nation celebrates the fiftieth anniversary of the allied Normandy invasion. Millions of people perished in the war, thousands were butchered in the week of landings. Yet the vast cemeteries, the rows of crosses stretching surreally to the horizon—these seem powerless to remind (literally re-mind, heal, restore). War never again? All week, the nation, the veterans, the politicians neither hear nor speak a word of peace. The churches unlimber their bells—celebrating what?

A deaf and dumb spirit shadows the land. Our spiritual affliction lies heavy on the children of the world, deaf and dumb before their fate. What war next, and where, and against whom? One thing seems certain, if the past is a measure of the future; war upon war will erupt in a bloody trail.

Jesus addresses the boy's father, and understanding dawns. He has failed to protect his son. "I believe, Lord, help my unbelief!" But the disciples and the crowd mill about uneasily; they have no clue as to the connection the father has drawn so movingly. Jesus assures the man, "All is possible to the one who has faith." And He proceeds to evict the demonic spirit from the child.

What to make of all this?

Something simple, I venture, and unsettling, as is usual with St. Mark.

Which is to say, we Christians are afflicted with "unbelief."

Can we, in any true sense, claim to believe in God, while we hold the world's children hostage with the Bomb? If we believed in God, could we allow the deaths of 40,000 children each day, from hunger and hunger-related diseases? If we believed in God, could the American military slaughter with impunity hundreds of thousands of Iraqis?

If we truly "believed," amazingly constructive events would shortly occur. For a start, the disarming of the nuclear club, a vigorous effort to outlaw war once and for all, a politics in accord with sound ecology, dissolution of corporate capitalism. And, finally, abandoning the lethal divisions of the world into first, second, third, and fourth segments, those bristling frontiers where privilege guards the spoils. And beyond which, the debtors and clients pay up.

One world, finally, one realm of justice, equality, and peace.

How far short of such a vision do we fall! I find shocking the ignorance and ambiguity prevalent among us Christians on the subject of allowable killing.

—We grant to bureaucracies a slack moral code, far in excess of what we allow individuals. (Governments may kill on command; citizens may not.)

—We fail to see that the command "love your enemies" has bearing on our response to the war-making state.

—We seldom consider the moral implications of our work, of livelihoods that imply collusion with the taking of life.

Christians might approve a vague personal adherence to the command "Thou shalt not kill." We might be inclined to hold others to the command, particularly if the prospective victim is young and innocent. But when a government declares war, and surrounds its decree with a barbed enclosure of draconian law, morality falls on its face. How few dare confront the military at the Pentagon or a weapons lab or military base, disarm such places symbolically, and endure the consequent legal wrath?

The nuclear threat is hardly diminished by the demise of the Soviet Union. Nor is the threat ended by the ascendancy of the purported kingdom of light. Consider that lurid light: Ours is the only government in history to launch the Bomb, and we have led the doomsday race for fifty years, threatened unilateral use of tactical nukes some thirty-four times, poisoned the planet with a vast flood of radioactive toxins.

I have asked parents whether it is our duty to protect children from such follies. The response is generally enthusiastic, of course. But when it comes down to practicalities, what one might call the whence and how of resistance, there usually follows a stunned silence.

So I ask it here: Whence? What spiritual discipline prepares us to turn an awful situation around? We know something, at least, after all the years. We know that the turn about requires daily prayer. Bible study, Sacrament—the ancient manna of parched desert travelers.

Another angle. Through such discipline undertaken in community, faith takes on its true face. Which is to say, faith opens its heart to social and political reality. It embraces the Cross, in the old phrase; the Cross planted in the world, in time, in human lives. Faith becomes one with the vocation of all the living; indeed, the very form of that vocation—cruciform. A faith that, in such times as we endure, may well imply suffering, imprisonment, loss of good repute, jobs, comforts—life itself.

And what of the "how," the tactic? Here, too, we are not exactly in the dark. Indeed, the tactics, too, have continuity—they are symbolic, they eschew violence and take the legal heat that is sure to follow. Above all (here spirituality and tactic converge) they are not attached to a measurable outcome.

Two verses from St. John have helped me in this quest for an understanding of faith. "The one who believes that Jesus is the Messiah, has passed from death to life" (5:24). Also, "The one who is marked by love of sisters and brothers, has passed from death to life" (1 John 3:14). Remarkable how faith in the Messiah, and love of others, converge here. To wit: if love of others is excluded by this or that version of faith, the neighbor to whom the Gospel summons us is reduced to a mere object; indifferently viewed, expendable, a blank or blip on a screen.

Let us put this matter of faith as simply as Scripture does. The truly faithful cling to one Law. "The one who loves the neighbor fulfills the Law" (Romans 13:9). This "one law," be it noted, by no means relegates the love of God to second place, or compromises it. The flat statement of St. Paul merely stresses the impossibility of our love of God thriving in a corner—a corner of the heart, or of the world. If there it chooses to dwell, such love can only cower and wither away, out of fear or inanition or both.

St. John and St. Paul, no less than St. Mark, emphasize the primacy of faith. It is as though they were insisting that everything human in our behavior begins there, with faith. Practical and mystical both, world view and view from the heart, one.

AUGUST–SEPTEMBER 1994

❧ To Our Readers—With Gratitude

WE WOULD LIKE to thank all those who have responded to our appeal—as we wrote on many a postcard, our bills are starting to get caught up, and we repaid the money we borrowed. Many of you sent letters as well—it is good to hear what people have to say about our work.

A number of people suggested we save money by cutting down the number of issues we publish a year, or raising the price. There are going to be only seven issues of *The Catholic Worker* this year, and we will see next year on a month to month basis how often we can publish. The paper is only about a third of our expenses, and we are always looking for ways to save money as good stewards should.

As to raising the subscription price, we would rather give the paper away for free. *The Catholic Worker* is meant to be about the clarification of thought, as Peter Maurin had in mind. The price is symbolic, and allows us to meet postal regulations to send the paper out second class—cheaper than first class and faster than the third class rate. We survive on donations, and our hope is that a symbolic price will inspire our readers to feel personally involved in our work, and to support it both materially and spiritually.

Dorothy Day's first editorial, "To Our Readers," intimated that poverty and precarity would be a part of the Catholic Worker, and so it has been for sixty-one years now. "It is not yet known whether it will be a monthly, a fortnightly, or a weekly. It all depends on the funds collected for the printing and distribution. Those who can subscribe, and those who can donate, are asked to do so. The money for the first printing was raised by begging small contributions from friends." She went on to write, "And when we consider our fly-by-night existence, our uncertainty, we remember (with pride at sharing the honor), that the Disciples supped by the seashore and wandered through cornfields picking the ears from the stalks wherewith to make their frugal meals." We hope to continue in this spirit. Please keep writing and please keep us in your prayers.

❦ Index